Loca Motion

Loca Motion

*The Travels of Chicana
and Latina Popular Culture*

Michelle Habell-Pallán

NEW YORK UNIVERSITY PRESS
New York and London

NEW YORK UNIVERSITY PRESS
New York and London
www.nyupress.org

Library of Congress Cataloging-in-Publication Data
Habell-Pallán, Michelle.
Loca motion : the travels of Chicana and Latina popular culture /
Michelle Habell-Pallán.
p. cm.
Includes bibliographical references and index.
ISBN 0–8147–3662–9 (cloth : alk. paper)
ISBN 0–8147–3663–7 (pbk. : alk. paper)
1. American drama—Hispanic American authors—History and criticism.
2. American drama—Mexican American authors—History and criticism.
3. American drama—Women authors—History and criticism.   4. Hispanic
American women—Intellectual life.   5. Mexican American women—Intellectual life.   6. Hispanic Americans in the performing arts.   7. Women in
popular culture—United States.   8. Performing arts—United States.
9. Performance art—United States.   10. Popular culture—United States.
11. Hispanic American theater.   I. Title.
PS153.H56H33   2005
791'.082'0973—dc22   2004023712

New York University Press books are printed on acid-free paper,
and their binding materials are chosen for strength and durability.

Manufactured in the United States of America

c 10 9 8 7 6 5 4 3 2 1
p 10 9 8 7 6 5 4 3 2 1

Contents

Acknowledgments

In a world that offers too few opportunities to share and produce politically progressive knowledge, it has been my great fortune to find a community of dedicated scholars and students who seek social change. My academic career has been an amazing journey, and never in my wildest dreams could I have imagined all the progressive destinations at which I would arrive. A large support network has made it possible for me to create a space for myself.

My work has benefited enormously from the feedback generated by many excellent listeners located at various institutions. At the University of California, Santa Cruz (UCSC), José D. Saldívar was an inspirational dissertation mentor. I thank him for his generous intellectual guidance, unwavering faith in my project, and careful readings of my work. He has helped to make this book a labor of love. Norma Klahn's expertise in Mexican and Latin American cultural production helped me to highlight the transnational in my work. Several scholars at UCSC who took time to listen to my project and who helped make it better deserve recognition: Herman Gray, Angela Y. Davis, Carla Freccero, Susan Gilman, and Roz Spafford. Margo Hendricks was supportive behind the scenes.

The seeds of this book germinated at the University of California, San Diego. I had the good fortune to benefit from the alchemy of three dedicated scholars: Lisa Lowe, whose model of women-of-color feminist scholarship inspired me early on and who later served as an enthusiastic University of California President's Postdoctoral Fellowship mentor; George Mariscal, who introduced me to Chicano cultural studies and directed me to wonderful sources of inquiry; and George Lipsitz, who encouraged my foray into the study of alternative American studies and popular culture. His wise words "It's not *what* you write about, but *how* you write about it" have framed my scholarship. Frances S. Foster was a pillar of support. I thank her for her kindness.

I have also had the good fortune to have academic appointments in departments that supported my work. I especially thank the entire Department of American Ethnic Studies at the University of Washington (UW) for supporting my scholarship, as well as both department chairs, Ana Mari Cauce and Steven Sumida. My colleagues, especially in the Chicano studies unit, have been especially generous in granting me the time to finish this book. Rick Bonus has been a wonderful peer mentor. Special thanks go to Mary Romero, an exceptional mentor and colleague, and Vicki Ruiz, who, at Arizona State University (ASU), welcomed me into the profession.

I would like to thank the institutions and the foundations that financially supported the completion of this manuscript. I appreciate the generous support of the Rockefeller Foundation Humanities Research Fellowship at the Chicano Studies Research Center, University of California, Santa Barbara (UCSB). I am deeply grateful to Carl Gutiérrez-Jones, who provided a productive working environment at UCSB. During the fellowship, I researched the Harry Gamboa, Jr. Papers at the Department of Special Collections and University Archives, Stanford University. I also thank my co-fellows at the Center, Otto Santana, Victor Valles, as well as Carlos Morton, for their insights into my research. Maria Herrera-Sobek, Chela Sandoval, and Francisco Lomelí provided invaluable moral support.

I benefited enormously from a Mellon Foundation Postdoctoral Fellowship for Junior Faculty, administered by the Woodrow Wilson National Fellowship Foundation. Participating in both the Rockefeller Foundation Humanities Research Team "Rockin' Las Americas: The Global Politics of Rock in Latin America," in Bellagio, Italy, and the "Placing Popular Music: Nation, Citizenship, Diaspora" faculty seminar at the University of California's Humanities Research Institute allowed me to fine-tune chapter 5. With the assistance of a Smithsonian Institution Latino Studies Program Postdoctoral Fellowship, I was able to mine Tomás Ybarra-Frausto Research Materials, 1967–1997, the Archives of American Art. The University of California President's Postdoctoral Fellowship permitted me to begin transforming the first draft of this manuscript. A Faculty Grant-in-Aid at ASU and a grant from the Institute for Ethnic Studies in the United States at the University of Washington also supported my writing. Finally, support from Susan Jeffords, divisional dean at the College of Arts and Sciences, helped with the final preparation of the manuscript. At New York University Press, Eric Zinner has supported the book with great rigor and insight, while Emily Park has been of great assistance. Despina Papazoglou Gimbel, Jeralyn Famighetti, and Nicholas Taylor have been ideal editors.

Over the years, a number of mentors have become great colleagues. The wise counsel of feminist scholars such as Angie Chabram-Dernersesian, Rosa Linda Fregoso, and Sonia Saldívar-Hull has helped me expand my work in important ways. I've benefited from their brilliant scholarship and strong convictions. Nancy "Rusty" Barceló has become a great ally. Portions of this manuscript have improved by the close readings of the Women's Writing Group at UW. Yvonne Yarbro-Bejarano does not realize what a long-distance inspiration she has been. For comments in the final hour, I thank Judith Halberstam.

I consider the following to be intellectual traveling companions and thank them for their unending kindness: Maylei Blackwell, who has always been there for me; Sergio de la Mora; Ana Patricia Rodríguez; Marie (Keta) Miranda; Mary Pat Brady; C. Ondine Chavoya; Chris Shin; Deborah Vargas; Margarita Barceló; and Theresa Delgadillo. The Women of Color in Conflict and Collaboration Research Cluster (1992–1996) at the Center for Cultural Studies, UC Santa Cruz, was a great source of strength. I thank all the women involved, including Angela Y. Davis, Jennifer Gonzalez, Charla Ogaz, Luz Calvo, Catrióna Esquibel, and J. Kehaulani Kauanui.

I also thank Claudia Huiza, Christopher Breu, Scott Davis, Felicia Fahey, Ivelisse Rivera-Bonilla, and Phil Rodríguez. At San Diego State University, Kathy B. Jones, Bill Cheek, Aimee Lee Cheek, Dan Johnson, Janice Minor, and Joyce Corpuz sustained me in more ways than one. Other friends and colleagues who have lightened the load of the journey include Steve Shaviro, Jacalyn Harding, Sonnet Retman, Gayatri Gopinath, Chandan Reddy, Shelly Eversley, Raul A. Fernandez, Patrick L. Rivers, Ed Morales, and Adriana Lopez. Thanks to the young women in GAO.

A special note of gratitude to those who have helped me acquire images for this book: Josephine Ramirez (co-curator of *Terreno Peligroso/Danger Zone*), Lina Litonjua, and Concepcion Tadeo. I thank the photographers who granted permission to reprint their photos: Sean Carrillo, Markus Cuff, Juan Garza, Timothy McCleary, Monica Naranjo, Linda Scott, Craig Schwartz, and Jenny Lens (and Rhino Records for helping her develop the proofs). Special thanks to Victor Sedillo for allowing his photo of Concepcion Tadeo to be included in the book.

The artists who graciously agreed to visit my classes and participate in conferences and allowed me to interview them and/or reprint their lyrics deserve special thanks: Luis Alfaro, Alicia Armendariz Velasquez, Teresa Covarrubias, Robert Lopez, Jim Mendiola, Marga Gomez, Monica Palacios, Marisela Norte, Lysa Flores, and Carmen Aguirre. All of them have been extremely generous with their time and materials.

Finally, I need to thank my (extended) families. The love and support of my parents, Robert J. and Eva P. Habell, and my sisters, Kathy Braden and Vikki Habell Jones, has been constant. My grandmother, Pat Madrigal, lit many candles on my behalf. The good wishes of Corinna Fernandez, the Habells, the Cardenas family, the Gellers, the Pallans, the Valadez family, and the Schwinds made life easier. Pamela and Eric Yates provided me with a second home at times. Randy Jr., Kaylin, Julia, Trevor, Simone, Emily, and Isabella showed me how magical life can be. Jaime Cárdenas Jr. has been blessed with an almost endless supply of patience; I hope to never exhaust it. The strength of his love and kindness has carried me to the end of this project. Because of him, I am a better person. And, finally, to the one who has patiently waited, the time is now yours. I dedicate this book to La Vivi, my love.

Last, I proudly state that I am a product of public education. My experience began in public schools in Downey, California. My generation of California students was deeply impoverished by major property tax cuts. Downey was also the first place that I learned firsthand about the harshness of California's anti-Mexican hostility. Later, in graduate school, I benefited from affirmative action policies, the legacy of people who struggled for greater social equality via education. I acknowledge those who struggled before me by striving to keep my end of the bargain.

Introduction

The only hope for a Revolution, lies in getting Elvis Presley to become Che Guevara.   —Phil Ochs via El Vez

In the summer of 1995, El Vez, the "Mexican Elvis," along with his backup singers and band, The Lovely El Vettes and the Memphis Mariachis, served as the master of ceremony for the first show ever of its kind to take place at the Mark Taper Forum: *Diva L.A.: A Salute to L.A.'s Latinas in the Tanda Style.*[1] Directed by Diane Rodríguez and Luis Alfaro, the codirectors of the Mark Taper Forum's Latino Theater Initiative, the show brought a variety of Latina artists to an enthusiastic audience. The *tanda* was a long overdue public acknowledgment of local Latina talent.[2] The likes of Marisela Norte, Diane Rodríguez, Rita Moreno, Hilos de Plata/Silver Threads (a Mexican folk dance group whose members range in age from sixty-six to eighty-eight years), and others graced the stage designed by the well-known Chicana artist Patssi Valdez. The night was remarkable because the directors not only acknowledged the Latino performance past by invoking and translating into English the *tanda* form, so popular with Spanish-speaking audiences before World War II, but also honored the present by centering women artists on stage, while recognizing an approaching future of Latino performance by including María Fatal, a popular Los Angeles-based rock en español band.

This performance, and others like it, lies at the core of this book. It is the lens through which an examination of contemporary transnational social dynamics comes into focus. Using Chicano/a and Latino/a popular culture (spoken word, performance art, comedy, theater, and music), in the following pages I argue that the role played by this work in the construction of new cultural forms and identities is considerable. The increasing circulation and reception of Chicano/Latino popular culture within and beyond the hemisphere, in places like Vancouver, British Colombia, Mexico City, London, and Berlin, demonstrate a growing appeal that cannot be overlooked.[3] Moreover, an analysis of Chicana/Latina popular performance culture is crucial to understanding the impact of globalization on contemporary national and local culture and constitutes "part of an emerging paradigm of local histories" within Latinos studies, "whose raison d'être is to deal with global (epistemic) designs."[4] It addresses some of the most compelling social questions of our historical moment, those regarding shifting conceptions of national culture, citizenship, sexuality, and identity. This book is a study of themes across genre. As one reads it, it becomes clear that an analysis of ethnicity/race or nation cannot be fully achieved without an account of power relations structured by gender, sexuality, and desire. This analysis advances, in important ways, the theoretical foundations built by Chicana and women-of-color feminist theorists, whose pioneering work on theories of intersectionality is very much engaged with this scholarship.

The particular Chicano/a and Latino/a performance texts selected for this study are important because they construct transnational imaginaries within the Americas that are shaped by a particular historical moment, politics, and humor. In addition, the talented artists discussed have produced their work with an artistic sensibility animated by the creative and critical energies fueled by punk D.I.Y. (Do-It-Yourself) aesthetics. Punk aesthetics and its counterpart, hip-hop, emerged, in part, as a response to the crushing privatization of neoliberal economic policies. The strain of punk aesthetics illustrated in this book can be seen as a direct response to the neoconservative queer bashing and anti-immigrant hostility that the artists discussed in these pages have faced in their everyday lives. The interdisciplinary frame of this study allows for an exploration of the ways in which Chicana and Latina diasporic performances and resignifications of the subject-citizen and noncitizen reproduce or alter national identities. Each of the artists included is U.S.-born (except for those in the Canadian Latino Theater Group), and much of their work illustrates the differences and negotiations that exist between U.S.-born Chicanos and Latinos and recent immigrants from Mexico and Central America.

This analysis of popular performance culture serves as a launching point to examine the way that the themes, iconography, and sounds of Chicana/o and Latina/o cultural practices resonate in both the northern and the southern reaches of the hemisphere within the framework of a critical transnationalism. This critical transnationalism considers what

Angie Chabram-Derneresian calls "geopolitical and linguistic complexities" within "Las Américas," complexities "that arise from making strategic connections with others in the Americas."[5] This conceptual framework calls for a nuanced understanding of the cultural effects of late-twentieth-century neoliberal economic restructuring on the continents of North, Central, and South America.[6]

More specifically, narratives found in Chicana/Latina popular performance culture in the 1980s and 1990s register a demographic and political shift that provides the conditions for the current explosion of U.S.-Mexican-Canadian border culture, as well as the cultural conditions leading up to the passage of the North American Free Trade Agreement (NAFTA) in 1994. This Agreement engendered a "transnational imaginary" that strengthened the preexisting ties of Mexican immigrants to the United States and Canada, as well as U.S. Latinos' cultural ties to Latin America.

In the following pages, the reader is introduced to the lives and work of a number of highly talented and creative artists: Luis Alfaro, recipient of a MacArthur genius award and a performance artist, playwright, director, and Director of New Play Development at the Mark Taper Forum; Marisela Norte, the poet laureate of Boyle Heights and the East L.A. ambassador of culture, best known for her spoken-word CD *NORTE/word*; Marga Gomez, a popular performance artist and the daughter of a Puerto Rican father and a Cuban mother, best known for her solo performance piece entitled *A Line around the Block*; El Vez, an incredible Chicano Elvis Presley translator; Jim Mendiola, a film director whose 1996 D.I.Y. film, *Pretty Vacant,* which was inspired indirectly by the punk pioneers Alicia Armendariz Velasquez and Teresa Covarrubias, earned him a Rockefeller Foundation Intercultural Media award; and the Vancouver Latino Theatre Group, a theater company formed by the playwright and actress Carmen Aguirre, whose innovative work focuses on the experiences of Latinos and Latinas in Canada.

The work of these artists, and others like them, offers a rich and largely untapped reservoir of material from which to understand the complex dynamics of race, class, gender, and sexuality. These artists, and the work they produce, are part of a long history of Latino theater and performance in the United States that took a dramatic turn in the 1980s as it moved away from the dominant forms of cultural nationalism that had, until then, dominated the work of Latino artists. In examining this performance history, we can see these artists confronting the ideas of the

Latino artists who came before them, as well as their own Latino communities. At the same time, their struggle with the expectations and notions of the dominant U.S. culture is revealed. The performance criticism that emerges from their powerful work is one that taps "mainstream" popular culture while simultaneously intervening and disrupting the status quo. In other words, these artists are quite innovatively reshaping the master's tools to dismantle the master's house. What results is nothing less than a highly sophisticated, and completely underexplored, rethinking of identity politics from which the larger discussions of American studies, Chicano and Latino studies, and gender studies can benefit greatly.

Travel and humor are two themes that play an important part in the pages that follow. Images of travel, crossing, and destination abound throughout the narratives of the artists examined in this book as they invent critical travelogues of local and distant destinations. I use the trope of travel cautiously here, making sure not to assume its transparency, recognizing Caren Kaplan's reservation that metaphors of travel are gendered.[7] In the context of this study, however, the artists' use of travel imagery functions as "guerrilla metaphor," working toward the "destabilization of a single view of history" and place.[8] The artists suggest that marginalized Western subjects employ travel as a metaphor and social practices as a critical tool; these artists remind us about the polyvalence of the word "travel." Travel is a variation of travail, which means to work extremely hard. In fact, these artists' representations of travel activate a series of associations linked to the obsolete meanings of the word, such as to harass, to torment, to torture, to trouble, to labor, to toil. The etymological root of "travel" is the old French *travaillier* and suggests the Spanish word *trabajar,* to work. In the United States and Canada, the Latino diaspora travels to labor, to toil for industries that depend on these workers to maintain profitability, and endures various forms of harassment and torment simply to make a living. This book examines how artists document the contemporary conditions of the Latino diaspora through what I've called a critical travelogue. Equally important is the labor their work performs as it travels throughout the "floating borderlands" to audiences within and beyond the United States.[9]

Although acknowledging that their point of origin is important, these artists are much more focused on a politics of destination. They are inventing alternative routes, trying to get to places they've never been. Through their rides, trips, tours, they are making global moves to construct alternative worlds. They are getting their word out using alternative circuits and media, creating alternative forms of travel. Deploying the metaphor of travel as toil, these artists mark the class and gendered inflections of transportation. Some artists, such as Marisela Norte, even write on the bus.

For some artists, the traveling of their art acts as a stand-in for them, while others actually perform their work around the globe. Throughout all of their works, anecdotes of travel prevail. Often their narratives address the difficulty of travel for particular subjects, as well as a nostalgia and the desire for it.

The work examined throughout this book also reveals a highly significant and original use of humor via bilingual word play as an aesthetic strategy. This humor, which is often utilized to work through moments of crises and to reimagine status quo power relations within and beyond national borders, has not yet been afforded adequate critical attention. The artists in this study have turned to what the scholar Carl Gutiérrez-Jones calls "engaged humor." Gutierrez-Jones argues that "engaged humor" is a long-standing form of Chicana cultural literacy.[10] As the critic Alberto Sandoval-Sanchez so aptly puts it, "they poke fun at cultural icons and institutions, revision traditional values and practices, and perform subjectivities in process as part of claiming agency and empowerment."[11] Contemporary Chicana/o and Latina/o performance and spoken-word artists and musicians continue this tradition and provide interpretive tools for reading hybridity in U.S. culture. Inventing hybrid forms of popular culture that are seriously playful, the artists, with their narrative, help create the conditions for audiences to become cultural critics themselves. The classic Chicano visual icon of two masks, one laughing, one crying, can be seen as an allegory for this critical use of humor.

An analysis of popular culture and cultural politics and the intersection of the two are a major component of this study. Popular culture constitutes a terrain where not only are ethnic and racialized, as well as gender, identity contested, reproduced, and transformed, but also the struggle for and against social equality is engaged. As Stuart Hall contends, "popular culture is one of the sites where this struggle for and against a culture of the powerful is engaged: it is also the stake to be won or lost in that struggle. It is the arena of consent and resistance."[12] Cultural politics as played out in this study presents an entry point for understanding the double stake in popular culture, the double movement of containment and resistance. Discourses produced by the dominant culture in popular cultural production created a conceptual blueprint about Chicanas and Chicanos specifically, and Latinos in general, that continued to be reproduced and contested into the twenty-first century. On the other hand, these artists engage with that same popular culture in ironic ways and invent forms of popular culture that transform those blueprints.

Like Hall, the artists of this study take seriously the stakes of popular culture in everyday life. And, like Hall, this study is interested in the politics of representation within popular culture. This interest goes beyond discussions of what constitutes "good" or "bad" representation of Latinos through popular culture. Instead, this study focuses on ways that Chicanas and Latinas intervene, contest, or reproduce "already" circulating representations of "latinidad."

This book seeks to contribute to an exciting conversation advanced by a surge of scholarship on media culture and latinidad by scholars and critics such as Arlene Dávila, Angharad N. Valdivia, Frances Negrón-Muntaner, and Chon Noriega by examining an alternative popular culture that has not achieved mass or mainstream appeal.[13]

Given that our historical moment is one of shrinking public outlets for the circulation and discussion of alternative and oppositional perspectives, these contemporary artists' reworkings are significant in that they open a discursive space—on the terrain of popular culture—that enables both critique of the status quo and dialogue concerning progressive social transformation. These artists interrogate the reactionary assumption that American national and cultural belonging and identity are (or should be) equated with exclusionary notions of whiteness. And, as we shall see, their engagement with pop culture is subversive to the degree that it has hope for an America that has yet to live up to its democratic possibility. These artists place their cultural production in the service of this ideal.

In addition to constructing individual and collective identities, popular performance culture, as a hybrid form, often articulates social and historical conflicts and allows those who have little access to ways of intervening in the dominant modes of representation (film, television, print) to represent themselves in their own terms. Popular culture in general, and Latino popular culture specifically, is a social and artistic phenomenon through which major cultural and political debates, conflicts, and social expressions about identity, gender, sexuality, community, and nation are staged and performed.

Since cultural politics determine both the meanings of social practices and which groups define these meanings, and because cultural politics involve the struggle over what and whose images of social life will be validated on mainstream television and radio (and what images should remain unseen), it becomes especially important for those who come from traditionally aggrieved groups, and who are determined to transform relations of social inequality, to pay attention to them. As Glenn Jordan and Chris Weedon explain:

> [C]ultural politics are also concerned with subjectivity and identity, since culture plays a central role in constituting our sense of ourselves. The forms of subjectivity that we inhabit play a crucial part in determining whether we accept or contest existing power relations. Moreover, for marginalized and oppressed groups, the construction of new and resistant identities is a key dimension of a wider political struggle to transform society.[14]

Questions of subjectivity and identity also invoke thorny questions of cultural authenticity. Put simply, "identity" can be understood as how one perceives oneself, while "subjectivity" can be seen as how one imagines oneself in relation to others. In her groundbreaking writing on Chicana/o representational practices, *The Bronze Screen: Chicana and Chicano Film Culture*, Rosa Linda Fregoso questions the existence of an "authentic" immutable cultural identity and argues against the production of an ethnic (specifically Chicano) identity built on "a political model of subjectivity grounded in a notion of a fixed self."[15] In this formulation, cultural identity appears as an authentic essence, located in a core subject, whose identity is one of "being," an identity that was the basis for the male-centered subject of Chicano cultural nationalism.

In contrast, Fregoso understands identity as a formation: One becomes a "subject in process" and is never a "fixed self." This understanding allows one to recognize that the production of cultural identity is dynamic and subject to historical, geographical, and political change. Thus, what was once considered to constitute Chicana and Chicano identity is not completely lost in the past but does in some way inform the construction of a future identity, though it does not necessarily determine it. Fregoso's argument assumes that categories of race/ethnicity, gender, sexuality, and nationality are never biologically given—not inborn, immutable characteristics—but are instead shaped by history and are constructed through the stories people tell about them. This assumption allows people (subjects) in their capacity as artists (and as everyday people) to reshape cultural, gendered, and political identity. The artists included in this study have created narratives that reshape Chicana and Latina identity by figuratively "cutting (old) labels out."

I use the term "Chicana/Latina" throughout the book, but with a certain wariness of conflating the two separate terms. Each term emerges from a particular history. However, both terms are useful, if at times contradictory. The conception of "Latinos as a monolithic cultural group, one that shares the same language and geographical space, and that struggles for the same political goal," has been disproved many times over.[16] Yet, the artists identified as Chicana or Latina in this book share a progressive sensibility. For the purposes of this study, the term "Chicana" is never fixed and takes on various meanings in particular contexts. Here, "Latina" is used as an umbrella term that refers to a diverse group of hyphenated identities of Latin American descent living in the United States or Canada (Cuban American, Puerto Rican, Colombian American, Colombian Canadian). "Chicana" is usually specific to the southwest and usually refers to those of Mexican American ancestry and is associated with a history of struggle for civil rights. This study includes the work of Luis Alfaro and Jim Mendiola under the rubric "Chicana," since they both acknowledge the influence of Chicana feminist thought on their cultural production. Of course, this is a somewhat ironic use of categories, because these artists, especially Marisela Norte, as stated earlier, often seek to "cut the label out" of identity categories.

The multiple narratives examined in this book contain protagonists who are subjects in the process of *"becoming."* As they inhabit multiple subject positions both as women who refuse traditional marriage and men who refuse traditional forms of masculinity and as border-crossing laborers, they enact what Fregoso discusses at length as "an alternative formulation of cultural identity."[17] This alternative formulation resists a strictly defined Chicana and Latina identity. The tension these writers thematize as their protagonists resist the pushes and pulls of the Chicano and the dominant cultures fuels their ambivalence about the two, yet their identification with aspects of multiple cultures (Latino, Chicano, Mexican, and African American) allows them to turn to what Fregoso so aptly describes as "the ambivalence of cultural identity into a politics of political identification." That ambivalence leaves room for the construction of something else.

This study's analytical frame is grounded in the currents of border feminist studies, Chicana/o studies, and transnational cultural criticism. I began this project more than ten years ago. As I worked on the long process of writing, an innovative new body of scholarship examining queer performativity emerged. Ground-breaking scholars, including Yvonne Yarbro-Bejarano, Alicia Arrizón, David Román, José E. Muñoz, Juana Alicia Rodriguez, and Alberto Sandoval-Sanchez, who centrally locate their research in queer/performance studies, have begun to bridge these studies to ethnic studies.[18] I, too, share their aspirations. This study modestly attempts to bridge two largely disinterested fields: performance studies and Latino studies. Equally important, it connects recent discussions concerning the categories of race to those dealing with the categories of class, gender, and sexuality that are foregrounded in the writings of recent theorists of popular culture and identity. This study assumes that these key categories are not "natural" or inherently fixed. The study also assumes that, like the category of race, the categories of class, gender, and sexuality are social formations. These various categories are reproduced by discourses and practices—that is, by regimes of representation—that maintain the illusion that they are immutable and have no relation to social context.[19]

Each chapter of the book examines different executions of cultural politics. From chapter 2 on, punk as an aesthetic sensibility runs throughout the chapters. However, for some of the artists, punk sensibility is located less in formal expression than in attitude. This punk sensibility shaped the post-1980s wave of a particular articulation of Chicana and Latina cultural production, one ironic and stylized but still critical of social relations, especially those that marginalized Latinos and Queers.[20]

Chapter 1 provides the popular performance culture context for the body of the book. This chapter discusses the historical context of the Spanish Fantasy Heritage, as well as its formation and modes of distribution. It also examines the ways in which Spanish Borderlands history converged with popular images of the Spanish Fantasy Heritage. The convergence of these two discourses as "set[s] of rhetorical and interpretive strateg[ies]" exemplifies Michael Omi and Howard Winant's conception of the "racial formation" process. This analysis provides a local context for the emergence of "Latin" imaginary and images that most mainstream audiences are familiar with. It is these images that the artists in this book are contesting through their construction of a transnational imaginary, one critical of a fantasy heritage that fixes Latinos in an idyllic nation-based past. The use of historical examples seeks to make clear how and why the current boom in Latino popular culture has not appeared out of nowhere but instead emerges from, yet contradicts, a complex set of social relations. Because this history is not generally well known and is difficult to access, chapter 1 provides the setting for subsequent chapters.

Chapter 2 begins at the U.S.-Mexico border and explores the formation of feminist transnational identities in the context of Los Angeles in the 1980s through the work of the award-winning and self-described listener-supported poet Marisela Norte. My analysis focuses on how Norte's writing projects a transnational imaginary that humanizes the daily trials and triumphs of a transnational female work force caught in the web of economic exploitation and dysfunctional personal relationships. *NORTE/word,* the compact disk recording of spoken-word narratives for which Norte is best known, weaves complex tales about immigrant and other women and girls on the "outside"—women and girls outside the home, outside loving relationships, outside adequate education and health care systems, and outside the mass media. Moreover, *NORTE/word* is at once a subtle and eloquent critique of power relations that attempt to limit the possibilities of Latinas and a loving homage to the city of Los Angeles and the Latinas themselves who keep the city running even as their "stockings lay defeated after hours of crossing and double crossing." Norte's dark humor and her mastery of irony work in combination to create a powerful cultural critique. What emerges from her struggle to represent Chicana experience is a particularly useful form of cultural politics, one that wages its battle on the terrain of popular culture.

Chapter 3 situates the work of the playwright and performance artist Luis Alfaro (a MacArthur "Genius" award recipient) in relation to the histories of Chicano theater and within the Chicana feminist debates of the 1980s and 1990s. Alfaro's critique of continuing racist, sexist, and homophobic cultural practices is illustrated and examined through an analysis of his published plays, live performances, and spoken-word compact disk *Downtown* (all of which re-vision the Spanish Fantasy Heritage). Although Luis Alfaro's texts focus on the urban experience of Los Angeles, his work sketches the heterogeneity of the Latino communities in the border region. By exploring internal hierarchies and conflicts among long-established Chicano families and recently arrived Mexican immigrant families, Alfaro's performances explore the intimate effects of the transnational imaginary as it structures family relations. This chapter's focus on Los Angeles is key, given that historically the city has been one of the most important centers for the production and consumption of Latino performance because of its high concentration of Latino residents and its status as one of the most transnational cities in Las Americas. The chapter also includes an analysis of Alfaro's performance reception outside the United States. Images in Alfaro's performance art work against the grain of a narrow vision of cultural nationalism whose central paradigm of the Chingón/chingada, according to David Román, "inscribes inflexible definitions of masculinity and femininity." Alfaro constructs new visions of masculinity that move beyond structures of traditional male dominance.

Chapter 4 continues the discussion of the Latino community's heterogeneity elaborated in the two previous chapters and addresses issues of Puerto Rican and Cuban American performance. The analysis here focuses on the Puerto Rican and Cuban American Marga Gomez, a former member of the "Chicano comedy" group Culture Clash, and her performance piece entitled *A Line around the Block*. Gomez's piece, which recounts the life of her Cuban immigrant father, a master of ceremonies in New York's "Latin" theater during the 1950s, also alludes to past performers' negotiations of the Spanish Fantasy. In addition, it discusses the influence of Latin American and Spanish-language vaudeville on the contemporary English-speaking Gomez and her representation of how memory reconstructs the transnational flow of popular culture among Cuba, Puerto Rico, New York, and San Francisco. It also explores her collaboration with California-based Chicano comic troupes. In *A Line around the Block*, Gomez intervenes in the dominant discourse that assumes that the term "Latina" is synonymous with the term "heterosexual" as her performance moves back and forth between Latina and lesbian discourses of identity and comedy.

The questions examined in this chapter were provoked by an interview I conducted with Gomez in 1994. This chapter seeks to bring together seemingly disparate narrative forms. Part genealogy, part textual analysis, part ethnography, it situates the work of Gomez in a context of the Latino performance tradition (one that she simultaneously embraces and rejects); examines questions of race, ethnicity, class, gender and sexuality, and nation as articulated by Gomez's cultural production and interview; and opens a space within this study to locate my own role as scholar/ethnographer/cultural critic/fan in examining Latino cultural production, especially around issues of language and hybrid identities. It also allows me to acknowledge my own participation in the discursive construction of new Latina subjects. I take my cue on this subject from the scholars Pat Zavella and Ruth Behar. In the end, like its subject, this chapter is hybrid.

Chapter 5 registers the confluence of cultures now accelerating in the wake of post–World War II global demographic, political, and economic shifts that illustrates that the United States is only one site among many where popular culture, national identity, and gender dynamics were (and are) in the process of being reconfigured by the constant back-and-forth flow of people, culture, and capital across multiple national borders. This chapter focuses on the filmic rendering of this reconfiguration through an analysis of Jimmy Mendiola's award-winning 1996 independent film, *Pretty Vacant,* its representation of a 1990s Chicana feminist punk aesthetic, and its connection to young punk women in East Los Angeles during the 1970s and 1980s. As such, this chapter examines the effect and the reception of the translocal circulation of a musical genre and movement—in this case, British punk (shaped by working-class British and Afro-Caribbean immigrants) and Mexican punk—on the formation of a transnational Chicana subjectivity. These musics, and the film *Pretty Vacant,* imagine and desire cross-cultural relations, what Lisa Lowe characterizes as horizontal affiliations, a process by which marginalized groups recognize shared stakes in the struggle to create counterhegemonic practices and communities, in a national and international context. In addition, the film functions as a visual allegory for the way Chicana feminists and artists, as women of color, at the turn of the century, have turned a critical eye on the public sphere and, in doing so, have envisioned new subjects and subjectivities, as well as mapped out affiliations, with racialized-as-nonwhite women within and across national borders. Ultimately, the film challenges nationalist conceptions (of both the dominant culture and ethnic communities) of gendered identities and completely disrupts the Spanish Fantasy Heritage. The theatricality of *Pretty Vacant* makes it an appropriate subject for a book that is based primarily on performance art.

Chapter 6 examines the Chicano performer El Vez's use of appealing and familiar forms of popular music to make provocative statements about citizenship, immigration, undocumented labor, and sexuality. Here, analysis of lyrics and interviews are key. While El Vez works through and against icons of the Spanish Fantasy, his popularity in Europe points to the ways Chicano and Latino performance resonates across national borders and exceeds in significance as a local and regional art form. It also explores how Chicana feminist thought informs El Vez's brilliant use of humor and sexuality to critique homophobia and sexism. Finally, it considers Robert Lopez, the artist who created and performs El Vez, as a Chicano artist who participated in the development of Los Angeles/Hollywood punk music, which gave rise to artists such as El Vez and informed the spoken word and performance art community.

The epilogue follows Chicana popular performance up to Canada and argues that the transnational circulation of Chicano images and sounds compels scholars to examine more closely their relation to Latino diaspora communities *north* of the U.S. border. Latino Canadian youth culture reinterprets imported images and sounds to construct a counternarrative about North American Latinos living in *Las Américas*. Unexpectedly, yet quite appropriately, it is through Chicano popular culture (for instance, El Vez's lyric "Don't call us Hispanic, 'cause we ain't never been to Spain") that the Latino Theater Group of Vancouver, British Columbia (composed of Canadians with origins in Mexico, Guatemala, and Chile), finds the language and interpretive tools to shape alternative representations of Latino Canadian youth. The Latino Theater Group employs U.S.-based Chicano and Latino popular performance culture to underscore how their own aesthetics and gendered experiences speak to the way that cultural production travels and resonates throughout our hemisphere and succeeds in completely rejecting the Spanish Fantasy Heritage.

Note on Methodology

This study has a modest goal—to put a thus far neglected history of Chicana and Latina alternative culture on the map. In no way do I suggest that the analysis presented here is either comprehensive or definitive. Instead, it is the first step in a recovery process. In addition, the goal is not necessarily detailed accuracy regarding Chicana subculture. In certain sections of the book, the reflections of particular artists shape the narration of this neglected history. Some readers may object to what could be considered the spin of a very few artists, especially in discussion of Chicana punk. Because no institutional archive of Chicano/a punk aesthetic yet exists, I have made an effort to contact those who are considered the main players in this scene. To reconstruct this history, I had to rely on the testimonies of the artists themselves (in addition to the few archival documents I encountered). To forestall criticism that interviews are used to make absolute-truth claims, I acknowledge that each interviewee has a subjective point of view on the scene. As I conducted the interviews, for example, it became clear that the very nature of punk aesthetics was messy and chaotic and that its politics were not always consistent but were always experimental. A small archive is now growing at the University of California, Santa Barbara, and one of the contributions of my book is to bring this material to the fore.

This book suggests that analysis of spoken-word performances, performance art, music, and film is complementary, yet different from the literary analyses that are prevalent in Chicano/Latino studies. Since popular culture is one of the most powerful realms where images of Latino/as are generated and regenerated, there is much to be learned from exploring the strategies of contemporary artists as they use their work to critique cultural representations and expectations. The chapters that follow examine how contemporary Chicano artists have inserted themselves into the national and transnational imagination by launching cultural critiques through popular culture, critiques that privilege the process of *mestizaje* and hybridity. The scholar Alicia Gaspar de Alba notes that until fairly recently, "Chicano/a popular culture did not exist as an academic category of analysis."[21] Her scholarship has helped to open this category of analysis, and my book broadens it by juxtaposing Chicana and Latina popular culture.

Though the artists examined in this book may not reach as massive an audience as pop stars such as Ricky Martin, Selena, or Shakira, analysis of their work is crucial, for it provides us with a map of alternative paths that may lead to alternative futures.

One final note. "The Loco-Motion," the 1962 hit single by Little Eva, inspired this book's title. This 45rpm record my mother (also named Eva) played for her growing daughters was one of the few artifacts she saved from her East Los Angeles teenage years. This book is a tribute to my mother, and to the women and men who navigate the *locura*, the madness of social inequality via their ingenuity. "*Que loca*" ("what a madwoman") is a phrase that can describe the artists in this book. Yet their artistic originality both critiques the limits of social equality and provides models for exploding those limits. So allow yourself to do the loca motion with them in search of better futures.

1

From the Shadows of the Spanish Fantasy Heritage to a Transnational Imaginary

Images flash on the six-by-six-foot screen. The ear-splitting theme from *Black Rain,* the 1980s Orientalist film about a white American cop in pursuit of the Japanese *Yakuza* (Japanese mafia), screeches. The three performers on the stage run in horror to hide from the larger-than-life images of found icons from everyday life in Los Angeles: *Virgen de Guadalupe* candles, Taco Bell® logos, Mission® tortillas, a neon burro-riding *campesino* (peasant), a piñata, fake Mayan ruins, and former California governor Pete Wilson. The juxtaposition of the images—particularly the *campesino*—with the terrified artists is striking. In this powerful performance piece, entitled *Deep in the Crotch of My Latino Psyche,* Luis Alfaro, Monica Palacios, and Albert Antonio Araiza illustrate how they work in the shadow of the enduring popular images that they and other Chicanos and Chicanas negotiate in their everyday lives.[1]

The artists' attempt to run from these images illustrates their desire for their work to be contextualized by more than these one-dimensional images of Mexicanidad/Mexicanness and Mexican Americanness and Latinidad. The work of all of these artists, whether performance or writing, seeks to construct new images of Chicano/a subjects by commenting or signifying on those sometimes hated, sometimes loved, and often worn-out representations. For example, rather than trying to escape the romantic "colorful" pastoral images informed by a mythic California past and articulated by the discourse of the Mission Revival,[2] a reimagining of the Southwest's past passed on the perceived influence of the Spanish Fantasy Heritage. This Fantasy Heritage "evokes the lost world of Spanish aristocrats and their haciendas, Spanish friars and Indian Missions, as well as alluring señoritas and the Anglos who came to possess them."[3]

Publicity photo of Beto Araiza, Monica Palacios, and Luis Alfaro for *Deep in the Crotch of My Latino Psyche.* Photograph by Becky Villaseñor. 1993. (Reprinted with permission from Monica Palacios.)

Absent from this fantasy heritage are Mexicans, without whom California's twentieth-century agribusiness industry would not have flourished. "Anglo Californians used the cultural material of the Spanish colonial past to mask the presences of mostly poor, mixed-race, immigrant Mexicans in their midst."[4] Alfaro and Palacios, as well as the artists Marisela Norte, El Vez (Robert Lopez), and Jim Mendiola, incorporate them, with irony, into their work.

The performance piece just described perfectly captures the main goal of this book: to situate recent performance and writing within the larger context of images, sounds, and performance forms.

This opening chapter traces how scholarly representations of the Spanish Borderlands history shaped mainstream images of Mexican Americans, Mexicans, and Hispanics—images that Chicana and Latina artists negotiate and/or contest in their work—that began to circulate throughout the popular imagination. As we shall see, popular images of Mexicans in the United States link, in complex ways, to a discourse of nation building that began before the transfer, in 1848, of what is now the U.S.

Southwest from Mexico to the United States. This link is important, since, whether or not the artists and audiences are conscious of this legacy, as part of the popular imagination, it shapes the reception of Latino popular culture.

Mission Revival/Spanish Borderlands Context

> The mission literature depicted the history of race relations as a pastoral ritual of obedience and paternalism: "graceful Indians, happy as peasants in an Italian opera, knelt dutifully before the Franciscans to receive the baptism of a superior culture, while in the background the angels tolled from a swallow-guarded campanile, and a choir of friars intoned the Te Deum."
>
> —Mike Davis, *City of Quartz: Excavating the Future in Los Angeles*

Mike Davis's description of mission literature captures the essence of the Spanish Fantasy Heritage. Although the territories that would become Mexico were colonies under the Spanish crown, Spain did not heavily populate the land it called Baja and Alta California. Spain attempted to strengthen its claim to the territories in 1761, when it dispatched friars from Mexico City to establish Catholic missions along the California coast, beginning with San Diego. While the mission culture was one of the most palpable impositions of Spanish social order, it was executed by *criollo* and *mestizo* colonial subjects from Mexico. The cruelty of the friars and the de facto imprisonment of native peoples on their ancestral homelands colonized by Spain are obscured by the Spanish Fantasy Heritage. When Mexico declared its independence from Spain, in 1821, the California territories became part of the newly formed nation. Mission lands were secularized and land grants parceled out to Mexican nationals. In 1848, at the end of the Mexican-American War, the United States annexed more than a third of what was Mexico's territory via the Treaty of Guadalupe-Hidalgo. Overnight, Mexican nationals living in the annexed territories became U.S. citizens. However, most Mexican landowners lost their land to Anglo settlers, despite the treaty's guarantee of equal protection under the law.[5]

The predominant image of Mexico and Mexicans in Los Angeles encapsulated in the phenomenon known as "Mission Revival" was cast more than one hundred years ago. The idea of Mission Revival—closely connected to that of the Spanish Borderlands—was first circulated through romance novels, architecture, real estate lingo, civic boosterism, tourism promotional literature, discussions within legitimate academic circles, and, later, film and television.[6] The process by which things Mexican and images of Mexicanos became obscured or minimized in English-language representations of early California was twofold and occurred simultaneously both in the academic and in the popular realms in the early twentieth century. In the academic world, the historians Herbert Eugene Bolton and, later, John Frances Bannon depicted California as a mythical Spanish landscape.[7] They used testimonials by Californios (individuals of the landed class who called for independence from Spain), collected by the wealthy entrepreneur Hubert Howe Bancroft, to advocate for the study of what they considered the Southwest's—and the United States'—Spanish past. In the popular culture, Helen Hunt Jackson's 1884 popular romance novel *Ramona,* and the public performances it inspired, played a pivotal role in generating a mythic California past.[8] Because of the work of Bolton, Bannon, and Jackson, "a mis-representation of the conquistadores, friars, and rancheros has given rise to a vision of giants."[9] According to the historian Mario Garcia, these misrepresentations helped to construct what the historian Carey McWilliams has called the "Fantasy Heritage" and the scholar Leonard Pitt has termed the "Schizoid Heritage."[10] Both discourses articulate a romantic early California past by exaggerating things Spanish, as opposed to Mexican, as did the Californios themselves. In different ways, each displaced things Mexican and images of *Mexicanos* and Native peoples. Yet, these discourses, often characterized as romantic, quaint, and nonthreatening and often promulgated through tourist and real estate campaigns in the Southwest, operated in opposition to the prevailing Hispanophobia of the period, which cast Spain and Spanish culture as inferior to Britain and British culture.[11]

The Archive

In the late 1800s, Hubert Howe Bancroft began collecting documents pertaining to the early history of California, including commissioned oral interviews with surviving Californios. According to Pitt, Bancroft "willingly offered money for the Californios' memoirs and documents," in search of the Southwest's "true history."[12] However, in her immensely important work on the discursive interventions Californios made in the context of Bancroft's project, Rosaura Sánchez demonstrates that, despite his claims to "truth-seeking," Bancroft commissioned the collection of material from the Californios (the Mexican *criollo* class) in the interest of increasing the profits of his publishing house.[13] Although he paid agents to conduct and transcribe the interviews of the displaced Californios, he refused, for the most part, to compensate the Californios monetarily. Sánchez explains that, "knowing that their manuscripts and dictations had a market value, some Californios were unwilling to provide their time without compensation, but Bancroft was unwilling to provide any reward or wages for their contribution."[14] Despite the profit motive behind the project, and his refusal to consider seriously the Californios' own analysis of their political, economic, and cultural displacement, Bancroft ultimately funded the largest, if fragmented, archival resource on nineteenth-century Californio documents, "including diaries, journals, reports by military and religious officials, regulations, *expedientes,* . . . as well as narratives provided by both men and women of Californio origin for the Bancroft Library but not dictated or written expressly for the historical project."[15] He succeeded in doing so because many did consent to the interviews in the interest of having their lives documented for future generations.

According to Sánchez, Bancroft "held contempt for the opinion of the Californios and held no respect for mestizos whom he thought of as 'a wild, turbulent humanity characterized by ignorance and fanaticism.'"[16] Bancroft also failed to "consider global political and economic relations, as well as the mode of production and class structure of Mexican society" in his understanding of Californio culture.[17] Incredible as it may seem, Bancroft's project, like Charles Lummis's promotion of California real estate on the basis of pastoral images of friendly red-tiled adobes—countered the prevailing Hispanophobia of the period.[18]

In his romantic and sometimes patronizing view, Bancroft tended to conflate the Spanish and Mexican eras into a single "Golden Age."[19] As Sánchez demonstrates, the "nonpropertied classes" and what Bancroft calls the plebeian "humble *ranchero*" are largely absent from the record or are mentioned only in passing. Significantly, the Indians are visible as the "Other" of the Californios, especially in reference to the earlier periods, although acculturated Indians constitute a very small percentage of those interviewed.[20] Bancroft assumed that the contribution of these two groups of early Californians was minimal, despite the fact that the frontier would not have been developed without the often involuntary and exploited labor of Indians; still, their point of view was not considered worthy of publication. In the end, even the interviews of the elite Californio class never reached the public because of their criticism of the ways the U.S. government betrayed them in the process of annexing the Southwest when the United States failed to honor Spanish-Mexican land grants. Sánchez, importantly, was the one of the first to provide an extended textual analysis of the Californio and California *testimonios* (testimonials).[21] She explains that most of the interviews remained in their original hand-written form in the dusty stacks of the Bancroft Library and did not circulate in print culture. According to Sánchez, the fact that "they were never published independently is undoubtedly linked to Bancroft's opinion that the views expressed in the testimonials carried little weight and had even less marketability."[22] Thus, these views, and their often implicit critique of U.S. land acquisition practices, were kept out of public circulation, while Bancroft's views were not only published but also served as the basis for the invention of the Spanish Borderlands Fantasy Heritage.

The Spanish Borderlands: Scholarship

> This book [*The Spanish Borderlands: A Chronicle of Old Florida and the Southwest*] is to tell of the Spanish pathfinders and pioneers in the regions between Florida and California, now belonging to the United States, over which Spain held sway for many centuries. These were the northern outposts of New Spain, maintained chiefly to hold the country against foreign intruders and against the inroads of savage tribes. They were far from the centers of Spanish Colonial civilization, in the West Indies, Central America, Mexico, and Peru.
>
> —Herbert Bolton, *The Spanish Borderlands:*
> *A Chronicle of Old Florida and the Southwest*

This quotation from Bolton's book demonstrates how, from the 1920s on, Herbert Eugene Bolton's and John Francis Bannon's scholarship reproduced the romantic image of California's past in English by repeating the tendency of the Bancroft project to emphasize things seemingly Spanish at the expense of Mexico's history. Their scholarship also continued the inexcusable dehumanization of Native people and naturalized the pilfering of native lands by Spain, Mexico, and the United States. Yet, each saw the necessity for and aggressively advocated a comparative approach to studying the American past, developing in the process the concept of the "Spanish Borderlands."

According to the historian David J. Weber's informative work "John Francis Bannon and the Historiography of the Spanish Borderlands: Retrospect and Prospect," Bolton's name is inextricably linked to the establishment of Spanish Borderlands scholarship in the United States.[23] Bolton first delineated the geographical perimeters of his conception of the borderland space in 1921 (though he had been working on his research since 1917), in his groundbreaking overview *The Spanish Borderlands: A Chronicle of Old Florida and the Southwest.*[24] Bolton's introduction explains that his "book is the first to tell of Spanish pathfinders and pioneers in the regions between Florida and California, now belonging to the United States, over which Spain held sway for centuries."[25] However, Weber is quick to point out what might be considered a conceptual contradiction—that "the United States did not exist during those centuries that 'Spain held sway' over much of North America. . . . [T]he boundaries of the United States as we know them today are not ample enough to contain the historic Spanish Borderlands, which spilled over into what is today northern Mexico."[26]

Bolton's assertion that a study of the area west of the Mississippi before it became part of the United States was necessary to produce a "complete" understanding of the United States' past is compelling. To ignore the space/process that lies beyond artificial borders would be to ignore a key element in the nation's development. Bolton's emphasis on spatiality is key. His recognition of the fluidity of geopolitical and cultural space led him to contest the limited view of the dominant academic discourse about the Southwest, a discourse that sought to exclude the early Spanish history of the territory as an important element in national development. Like more recent postcolonial theorists of the Southwest Borderlands (Américo Paredes, Gloria Anzaldúa, José D. Saldívar, among others), Bolton, in a sense, pointed to the ways in which cultural institutions brought by Spaniards were dispersed throughout the Southwest and had a lasting (though not necessarily positive) impact on the people living in the territory. But, unlike postcolonial theorists, Bolton (and later Bannon) constructed the Spaniards as romantic and heroic. This produced a narrative of beneficent and benign conquest instead of one that recognized the violent displacement and genocide of Native Americans. Bolton's and Bannon's moves to reconstruct the narrative of Spanish contribution offered an alternative view in the larger context of Hispanophobic practices. As Weber explains: "Eager to counter what they saw as an Anglophile explanation of early American history, Bolton and Bannon slighted the negative impact of Spanish colonization on native peoples although they did not completely overlook it."[27]

Bolton's conceptualization of the Spanish Borderlands was rejected first by many of his contemporaries and later by Chicano historians.[28] His innovative connecting of the Spanish Borderlands to the American past argued for the importance of the Southwest and Southeast as sites for the establishment of Catholic missions. Its relevance for study in the twentieth century was denied by scholars who continued to practice Hispanophobia. Many refused to see the connection, the influence, or the ruptures, since many of the Mission structures had crumbled and few people remained to visibly remind them of the influence of that particular past. (The dominant scholarship saw the Spanish culture and people as already tainted; thus, any descendants of the Spanish settlers in the "New World" would have necessarily inherited their racial inferiority).

The Spanish Borderlands school was rejected by Chicano historians/scholars because it emphasized Spanish institutions and culture and did not satisfactorily account for Mexico's rupturing of the Spanish line. Nor did it account for the Mexican American experience, since it iterated Frederick J. Turner's thesis that the frontier ended for the United States in 1893.[29] Bannon's Spanish Borderlands Frontier also displayed the pro-Spanish tendency of the Bolton school. For instance, Bannon explained that his *Mission Frontier in Sonora* told the story of the "advance of civilization into wilderness."[30] According to Weber, the "natives who inhabited the wilderness represented little more than a challenge. Ironically, Bannon took a more sympathetic view of invaded peoples when he wrote about Anglo-American expansion into areas occupied by Spaniards."[31]

Despite continuing resistance from the majority of American historians, Bolton's students worked toward a conception of the extended Spanish Borderlands, one that broadened the "'concept of the Borderlands so as to encompass the north Mexican provinces—Nuevo Santander, Nuevo León, Coahuila, Chihuahua . . . Sinaloa, Sonora, and Baja California.' By this definition Borderlands history spilled out of the arena 'now belonging to the United States,' but [that] was once part of Mexico."[32] These extended coordinates mapping the Borderlands' history coincide with those mapped by the scholar and folklorist Américo Paredes in his analysis of Greater Mexico's influence on the Lower Border Tejas/Mexico culture. Paredes's conception of the Borderlands' relation to Greater Mexico was markedly different from that of previous historians, for he accounted for the people who live in those regions. For Paredes, the term "Greater Mexico" refers to both *México de Adentro* and *México de Afuera,* "the former encompassed by the political borders of the Republic of Mexico, the latter taking in all those other parts of North America where people of Mexican descent have established a presence and have maintained their Mexicanness as a key part of their cultural identity."[33] This conceptualization "situates the Southwest within the larger cultural area of Greater Mexico."[34] Ultimately, Paredes sees a "continuous mutual influence moving in both directions" among groups in *México de Adentro* and *México de Afuera.*[35]

Years after Bolton's initial articulation of the Spanish Borderlands, the historians Howard F. Cline and Donald C. Cutter conceptualized an even larger space. Cline suggested that the "Greater Borderlands included the Central American, Caribbean, and Gulf peripheries, together with the vast area of Aridamérica." Cutter argued that "the Borderlands extends as far as Hawaii, Guam and the Philippine Islands."[36] For the most part, the routes traveled by Latino theater groups at the turn of the century corresponded with Cutter's expansive conceptualization of the Greater Borderlands. For example, the Latino theater historian Nicolás Kanellos explains that Latino theater groups traveled routes that crossed the Greater Borderlands to perform in Guam and the Philippines.[37] Examination of the circulation of Latino theater in terms of the Greater Borderlands is useful because theater was important in the development of a sense of "Hispanicity," to use Kanellos's term, connecting—however tenuously— Latino populations in the Southwest and in the Southeast. This geographical imagining of a *transfrontera* space is consistent with those of more recent theorists of the Greater Borderlands who take into account both areas' territorial conflict and the cultural *mestizaje* that occurs there.

This more expansive conception of the borderlands as a Greater Borderlands *transfrontera* phenomenon laid the groundwork for the construction of the narrative of an inter-American diaspora. The notion of borderlands geography as extending from the Caribbean to the Pacific contributes to the development and understanding of contemporary cultural forms such as literature, music, performance, and film in the context of local and global flows of capital and labor. For example, the writers Gloria Anzaldúa and Cherríe Moraga, the cultural critic José D. Saldívar, and the performance artist Guillermo Gómez-Peña situate the borderlands in an inter-American context by contrasting shared histories of conquest and resistance across the Americas. Their conception of the borderlands contradicts the narrative of a romantic Spanish Borderlands Heritage by analyzing and producing texts that give voice to those who were silenced by the earlier discourse.

Performing the Spanish Fantasy: Cultural Politics and the Mexican Players at Padua Hills

Numerous institutions have been founded in the borderlands to keep the fantasy heritage alive. . . . The Padua Institute, located at the base of the Sierra Madre Mountains near Claremont . . . works hard to keep the fantasy heritage alive. Here, in a beautiful setting, the lady from Des Moines can have lunch, see a Spanish or Mexican folk play, hear Mexican music, and purchase a "Mexican" gift from the Studio Gift Shop. The Padua Institute is dedicated to "keeping alive the romantic life and music of old Mexico and Early California."

—Carey McWilliams, *North from Mexico:*
The Spanish-Speaking People in the United States

[A] young member of the Mexican Players is more than just an employee with a full-time position. He is an actor in the theater; a waiter or a bus boy and an entertainer in the dining room; and an apprentice in the arts of song and dance. These young men and women set up the tables in the dining room before lunch and dinner and then serve the guests. During the meals they leave their duties for a few minutes at a time to dance and sing with the musicians. At night and on matinee days, after clearing the tables, they hurry to the dressing rooms to prepare for their roles the current play.   —Pauline Deuel, *Mexican Serenade: The Story of the*
Mexican Players and the Padua Hills Theatre

You had to smile a lot; that was one of the musts. You had to smile!

—Cristina Martínez, Mexican Player/Paduana,
quoted in Matt García, "'Just Put On That Padua Hills Smile':
The Mexican Players and the Padua Hills Theatre, 1931–1974"

The Mexican Players, a performance group composed mostly of Mexican American youths, was quite popular with Anglo audiences in Southern California from the 1930s to the late 1960s. The group was sponsored by the Padua Institute in Claremont, California, an institute "dedicated to inter-American friendship."[38] The Padua Hills Institute was a place where the "idea of the Spanish Borderlands [and] the view of Lummis, Bancroft, and Bolton and others flourished exuberantly."[39] It also demonstrates, following Weber's lead, that "those writers drew inspiration from popular culture, even as they, in turn, inspired popular culture and gave the romantic view scholarly respectability."[40]

The performances of the Mexican Players between 1931 and 1974 both re-enacted and refigured elements of the Spanish Fantasy Heritage. As such, the establishment of the Padua Hills Institute is an important moment in the development and circulation of images about Mexicans and Mexican Americans in California, and it shows us how representations of Mexican culture and subjects have changed over time. The intention here is neither to judge the individual cultural politics of the Players nor to recount the Padua Institute's history.[41] Rather, what follows highlights how, and in what form, images of Mexican culture and Mexican subjects circulated in public performances, performances through which the codes of the Spanish Fantasy Heritage were revived.

The cultural politics engaged by the Players and their patrons, Bess and Herbert Garner, are compelling. Padua Hills was an early important public site of attempts to re-present the Spanish Fantasy Heritage to white audiences. Although the visibility of *mestizo* bodies onstage at the Institute changed the terms of the Spanish Fantasy Heritage, the Players' own interventions in the reconstitution of Mexican identity were extremely limited and were censored by their patrons.

The image of California's mythic romantic Spanish past, the idea of the nation, and the performance of ethnicity are the common themes that run through the diverse citations just given. The quotations demonstrate that a nineteenth-century discourse constructing early Californio life still circulated and had relevance in the first half of the twentieth century. Of course, the discourse of a Spanish Fantasy Heritage served a different purpose in 1948, when the social critic Carey McWilliams condemned it, than it had in 1888 (just four years after the publication of *Ramona*), when the entrepreneur Bancroft helped invent and circulate a mythic California past for the benefit of his publishing enterprise.[42] McWilliams cites images produced by the discourse of the Spanish Borderlands to juxtapose the predominance of Spanish Fantasy Heritage imagery in Southern California public culture with the (sometimes deliberate and sometimes informal) segregation of Mexican and Mexican American bodies from mainstream public culture. For example, in *North from Mexico: The Spanish-Speaking People of the United States,* after describing popular celebrations of a fictive Spanish/Californio culture in Santa Barbara, Carey McWilliams notes that "so many restaurants, dance halls, swimming pools and theaters exclude persons of Mexican descent."[43]

In the same vein, McWilliams criticizes the Padua Hill Institute because it maintained and circulated this seemingly benign image of a romantic California, one that whitewashed the violence of territorial conquest and the harsh living conditions of most Mexican Americans in California at the time. McWilliams recognized that the Mexican Players' audiences were composed mainly of Anglo tourists such as the "lady from Des Moines," and he was aware of the Institute's stated mission of "inter-American" friendship.[44] However, McWilliams also knew about the recent deportation/repatriation campaigns and other injustices experienced by people of Mexican descent since the U.S. territorial conquest of Mexico and the subsequent signing of the Treaty of Guadalupe-Hidalgo in 1848.[45] He felt that the Institute, by performing the Fantasy Heritage, did more harm than good in furthering Anglo-Mexican friendship, since it obscured the reality of power relations between the two groups. Reenactments of the Fantasy Heritage masked the combination of legal, economic, and social forces that conspired to force Mexican Americans off their land and to deny them political representation. Ultimately, the Mexican Players were required to perform Bancroft's mythic vision of early Californio culture. Even if the Mexican Players wanted to address contemporary events of 1932, such as the deportation and repatriation of Mexican American citizens to Mexico, they could not have done so, since they were never allowed to address "controversial issues" in their performances.[46]

The Padua Hills Institute was a complex site where the struggle over the representation of Mexican culture and identity took place in a pre–civil rights movement context. The Institute functioned to fulfill a multitude of contradictory desires. Located just thirty-five miles from downtown Los Angeles, in Claremont, on what had once been land owned by a Mexican government grantee, the theater was built in 1930 and was part of an adjacent residential community developed explicitly for

A postcard image of the Mexican Players at the Padua Hills Theater. Photograph by Columbia Wholesale Supply. (Courtesy of the Pomona Public Library.)

wealthy whites.[47] The establishment of the Mexican Players first and foremost fulfilled the desire of the wealthy entrepreneur Herbert Garner and his wife, Bess, to rescue their newly built Mission Revival–style theater from closure. According to the historian Matt García, the theater at Padua Hills had been originally built to house a small, locally acclaimed, all-white theater group, the Claremont Community Players.[48] However, economic pressure fueled by the Great Depression rendered many of the actors unable to participate.[49] The absence of the Claremont Community Players left a void that the Garners filled with the invention of a new, lower-paid group called the Mexican Players.

Taking their cue from a long-standing commercial tradition of tapping into popular Spanish Fantasy Heritage and Mission Revival imagery to promote both Southwest tourism and commercial products, the Garners saved their theater by inventing the Mexican Players and offering live re-enactments of the Spanish Fantasy.[50] Reenactments of early California included theatrical performances based on the popular novel *Ramona* (1884), performed by troupes other than the Mexican Players, which, according to the scholar Carl Gutiérrez-Jones, served to provide an almost indelible picturesque rendering of the Southwest.[51]

Performing Mexicanness

[T]he aim of Padua Hills was to give the young women and men work-
ing there the opportunity to express their *Mexicanness*.
—Alicia Arrizón, "Contemporizing Performance:
Mexican California and the Padua Hills Theatre"

Mr. Herbert H. Garner, Chairman of the Board of Trustees of the Padua
Institute, founded the organization because he saw the urgent need for
better relations between the *citizens* of two *neighboring nations*. [Italics
mine.] He deeply believes that prejudice and misunderstanding cannot
exist when people know and admire each other. . . . Diplomacy and intellectual problems are left for government officials; at Padua the "good
neighbor policy" is through the heart.
—Pauline Deuel, *Mexican Serenade:*
The Story of the Mexican Players and the Padua Hills Theatre

The performers who constituted the Mexican Players were largely Mexican American youth who, in addition to acting, did double duty, working
as "cooks, dishwashers, waitresses, waiters, and janitors who staffed the
dining room adjacent to the theater."[52] In spite of their dual roles, however, they were paid only for their service duties. Although it was the
"acts," in terms of both labor and performance, that made the Garners'
theater a success, the exploitation of the labor and talent of young Mexican Americans was not unjust in the Garners' eyes. Nor was the fact that,
even though the Mexican Players could work and perform in the exclu-
sive neighborhood that housed the theater, a neighborhood that explicitly
excluded nonwhites, they could not live there.[53] Although the players
were welcome to maintain the grounds or perform in the theater, they
were unwelcome in the large residential development project of Padua
Hills, once the property of the wealthy Mexican landowner Don Ygnacio
Palomares.[54]

For most members of the Mexican Players, participation in the group
fulfilled a desire to display their talent during a historical moment when
few venues dedicated to representing Mexican culture and experience in
a positive fashion to non-Mexican audiences existed.[55] According to García, Bess Garner recruited young laborers from a "segregated school for
local Mexican students" and approached "parents and children in local
barrios . . . to work at Padua Hills."[56] Space for the Players to transform

the representation of Mexican culture was small: Herbert Garner personally reviewed and approved their performances. Furthermore, the scarcity of avenues for Mexican Americans to perform positive images (as opposed to their mainstream "greaser image") for English-speaking audiences speaks to the unequal social conditions that characterized the cultural climate and artistic performative environment of the era.

That the Players served dinner to the audience between sets tells us much about the Garners' cultural politics. The Garners' decision to commit the Padua Institute to forging better relations between Anglos and Mexicans stood in contrast to the heated public debates and state campaigns, emerging during the Great Depression, that urged Mexican nationals and Mexican Americans living in California to repatriate to Mexico.[57]

During World War II, the Institute also helped to further the goals of U.S. diplomacy; the Padua Institute was viewed as an enactment of the cultural component of President Roosevelt's "Good Neighbor Policy."[58] This policy addressed concerns "about the allegiances of the Latin American nations"[59] and was a diplomatic gesture toward easing "remaining tensions with South American governments in order to maintain hemispheric unity as a bulwark against foreign invasion."[60] By promoting public images in theater and film, images that presented U.S. interest in Latin America and its people as nonthreatening, the United States hoped to demonstrate its trustworthiness to Latin America and to win its loyalty. But what is telling about the Padua Institute's interpretation of friendly relations is that, even though the Good Neighbor Policy was "through the heart," relations were completely unequal. Mexican American youths performed a carefully constructed image of Mexicanness, served the audience dinner, and cleaned up, while (Anglo) American audiences consumed both the images and the food.

The Players continued to contribute to the repertoire of images promoted by the Good Neighbor Policy when they were chosen by Walt Disney to be the only human figures in the animated film *The Three Caballeros* (1945). The scholar Nicolás Kanellos explains that "[during] World War II, Nelson D. Rockefeller's Office for Coordination of Inter-American Affairs asked Walt Disney to make a goodwill tour of Latin America in support of the Good Neighbor policy."[61] The wartime "need to be sensitive to Hispanics" Kanellos explains, provided the context for the production of *The Three Caballeros*, an internationally distributed film that presented Mexican culture in a Hollywood film in terms other than "the bandito, the buffoon, and the dark lady."[62] However, because the Players were limited by the Garners to representing "Mexicanness" in terms of the Spanish Fantasy Heritage, they presented a distorted image and were not able to represent the conditions of their own lives. (What is compelling is how this romantic image still circulates, still has currency, and still influences the public's perception of Latinos. In fact, the film has a double life on home video and can easily be purchased in contemporary department stores.)

McWilliams argued eloquently in 1948 that the Padua Hills Institute maintained "dangerous" and "false" narratives about the Spanish Fantasy Heritage and Mexican culture. Recently, both García and Arrizón have demonstrated that the plays written by the theater's Anglo playwright for the Mexican Players constructed a nonthreatening romantic vision of (early California) Mexico and Mexican/Mexican Americans.[63] They describe how plays with titles such as *Trovador Californiano* (1958–1959), *Noche Poblanas* (1942–1943), and *Como Siempre* (1944–1945) reenacted and maintained the Spanish Fantasy Heritage. This distortion of things Spanish and Mexican typified the programming at the Institute for many years. For example, *Trovador Californiano* romanticizes the annexation of the Southwest to the United States. The play asserts that "Spanish Americans" favored annexation, while the few Mexican men who were opposed were eventually convinced that annexation would save them.[64] Set during 1848, *Trovador Californiano*, a love story, thematized the "American" conquest of California. The storyline focuses on the conversion of a young Mexican soldier, Manuel Dominguez, who is resistant to the rule of the newly imposed government. Manuel asserts that his love for his nation of Mexico is greater than his love for his fiancée when he proclaims, "California will be annexed to the American Union. I will not tolerate that act and I will not accept the new government. Tomorrow, I'm going to Mexico to serve under the Mexican government."[65] Of course, if Manuel leaves, his fiancée will be left to wither, and the rest of the story conspires to keep the young lovers united by preventing Manuel from going to Mexico. At one point, he is imprisoned on suspicion of treason. The play concludes when Manuel is released from prison and all doubts held by the "Spanish American" Californios concerning the status of their land in the new United States are dispelled. In the end, the Californios are grateful for the advances brought by the "yanquis."

What the Institute accomplished, albeit in sometimes simplistic and distorted ways, was to incorporate images of the nation and culture of Mexico and to insert the reality of *mestizo* bodies in the act of performing that had been denied by the Spanish Fantasy Heritage.[66] If the formation of a Spanish Fantasy Heritage displaced the presence of Mexico and *Mexicanos* in California in public imagery, then the Padua Hills Institute recovered images of Mexico but ultimately displaced any explicit reference to the presence of Mexican Americans in the Southwest.

In looking back at the Institute's practice of hiring Mexican *American* citizens to represent *Mexican* citizens, "for better relations between the *citizens* of two neighboring nations," we see that it was not considered odd or unjust to be more concerned about relations with *Mexican* citizens than about those with *Mexican Americans*. We also see that it was considered appropriate for *Mexican American* groundskeepers and domestic workers to preserve the culture of *Mexico* and Spanish California.[67] Although some may have understood the Padua Institute as a place to fight anti-Mexican sentiment, given the Spanish Fantasy Heritage's tendency to mask the violent conquest of Indian and Mexican territory, the repertoire of images available to them was quite limited.

Ultimately, the cultural politics of the Players involved their negotiation with the terms of the Spanish Fantasy Heritage in order to demonstrate the humanity of Americans of Mexican descent. García's article makes it clear that the Paduanas/Paduanos were not duped about their situation at Padua Hills. He criticizes previous investigations of the Players for not acknowledging the Paduanos' agency. García highlights the fact that the Players themselves knew they were performing, even if the audience did not. He explains that, for the players, participation in the group "represented pure drama, and their performances, though they appeared 'natural,' did not portray their lives away from the theater."[68] That the performers referred to themselves not as the Mexican Players but as the Paduanas or Paduanos demonstrates their own intervention in self-representation.[69] Although the Padua Hills theater required the Players to present carefree, happy images of Spanish/Mexican life and forced them to smile, the Players were not happy all the time. Some felt the Garners could and should have been more generous with their pay and upkeep of the theater.[70]

It was only after the farm workers' and the Chicano civil rights movement that English-speaking audiences were exposed to oppositional representations of Chicano identity. Teatro Campesino, one of the best known *teatro* (theater) groups, emerged with the farm workers' struggle. Since Teatro Campesino wanted to promote a grass-roots transformation of the status quo, its primary audience was farm workers, not farm owners. Although performances and plays were produced contemporaneously with the Padua Hills Institute, they presented an image of life in the Southwest very different from that presented by the Players.[71] Teatro Campesino productions, for example, were in Spanish and were attended mostly by Spanish-speaking Latino audiences. According to the scholar Yolanda Broyles-González, this Spanish-language alternative performance legacy informed the teatro produced in the 1960s.[72] Furthermore, the Garners' close control of the Paduanos' representation suggests that the Mexican Players' particular performance of Mexicano identity was manufactured to assuage white Americans' anxiety concerning nationality and citizenship in California.[73] From the Garners' perspective, success in creating friendship between nations—and the success of their theater—depended on maintaining images of Mexican culture that did not threaten the status quo.[74]

These contradictions are presented here not to condemn the Paduanas/Paduanos. Instead, they are brought up to demonstrate that both the distortion of Mexican subjects and the absence of Mexican American subjects have been established through the interpretation of the Southwest's past in Spanish Borderlands scholarship and that they have had ramifications at the level of popular cultural forms, especially in the way Mexicanness was perceived. The Padua Hills Institute's statement of intent—its desire to forge friendly relations between the United States and Mexico—is significant considering that this took place in an intense climate of anti–Mexican/Mexican American sentiment and at a time when a policy was being implemented that would deport and repatriate U.S. citizens of Mexican descent. That this popular representation of Old California coincided with contradictory calls for Depression-era Mexican deportation, as well as attempts by the U.S. Office for Coordination of Inter-American Affairs to create images of friendly inter-American relations during World War II, reveals that even sixty years ago, during a time of social upheaval, Latino images were a site of contradiction and contestation.

Marketability of Conquest

> If Jackson's *Ramona* transformed selected elements of local history and romantic myth (still popular to this day), Lummis was the impresario who promoted the myth as the motif of an entire artificial landscape.
>
> —Mike Davis, *City of Quartz*

Consider the irony of an organization that presented itself as promoting friendship between nations, one conquered by the other, yet presented fantasies of conquest and of mission life for entertainment. What could have happened to the reality of that experience so that by the 1940s the violence of conquest and mission life was palatable and marketable to Anglo audiences? According to the historian Patricia Limerick, the violence of the U.S. conquest of the Southwest, unlike the legacy of slavery, which rightfully came to be seen as a national embarrassment, was largely represented as *adventure*.[75] (The discourse was already circulated by Lummis's writing, which rode on the coattails of *Ramona*'s success and generated the terms for the emergence of the Spanish Borderlands school.) Limerick explains:

> Conquest took another route into the national memory. In the popular imagination the legacy of conquest dissolved into stereotypes of noble savages and noble pioneers struggling quaintly in the wilderness. These adventures seemed to have no bearing on the complex realities of twentieth-century America. In Western paintings, novels, movies, and television shows, those stereotypes were valued precisely because they offered an escape from modern troubles. The subject of slavery was the domain of serious scholars, the occasion for sober national reflection. The subject of conquest was the domain of mass entertainment and the occasion for lighthearted escapism. An element of regret for "what we did to the Indians" had entered the picture, but the dominant feature remained "adventure." Children happily played "cowboys and Indians" but stopped short of "masters and slaves."[76]

In the national imagination, the fact of slavery had become a national disgrace, and the study of it had gained some legitimacy in the academy. However, conquest was never perceived as a national disgrace, and the study of it was not granted importance until recently. The scholars Hector Calderón and José D. Saldívar argue that the "political consequences of emphasizing the Spanish past were quite damaging," because this emphasis ignored the fact that before the United States conquered the Southwest, the Southwest had been Mexican territory after Mexico won its independence from Spain in 1821. The belief in a Spanish past also overlooked the racial and cultural mixtures that transformed the Southwest between 1821 and 1848. Calderón and Saldívar explain:

> It was as if Spain had become the United States without centuries of racial and cultural mixture. Yet this interpretation of the conquest and colonization of Arizona, California, New Mexico, and Texas is still accepted by many Anglo-American critics as the golden age of Hispanic culture in the Southwest and continues to flourish in the present in the popular imagination in literature, mass media images, Hollywood films, and in the celebration of Spanish fiesta days throughout the Southwest.[77]

The Padua Hills Institute story represents a site in public culture where the "subject of conquest was the domain of mass entertainment and the occasion for lighthearted escapism."[78] Examining the history of the Mexican Players illustrates the process of how romantic images of California and *Mexicanos* were transferred from live performance traditions to film, then circulated to national and international audiences through screenings, and, consequentially, inserted into the national imagination.

As mentioned previously, this vision of Mexicans or "Latins" that was made familiar to international audiences when Disney Productions used the Mexican Players as the dancers in their popular Donald Duck film *The Three Caballeros* (1945) was reenacted and transformed by Padua's theatrical contemporaries and, later, by *teatros*. Ultimately, Padua Hills Institute promoted a friendly, nonthreatening image of romantic, colorful, exotic Mexicans who were not makers of their own destiny. This view, these enactments, did not want to address the social reorganization occurring at the time. In *Three Caballeros* especially, Mexico and the rest of Latin America are embodied as beautiful women, not as political actors. Yet, in the midst of the social uncertainty caused by the Great Depression, deportation/repatriation policy, and the threat of impending world war, the Padua Hills Institute was only one site among many where the struggle to define the image of Mexican identity and subjectivity took place.

Spanish-Language Theater: A Place for Controversial Themes

Harmless in many ways, these attempts to prettify the legend contrast most harshly with the actual behavior of the community towards persons of Mexican descent. To the younger generation of Mexicans, the fantasy heritage, and the institutions which keep it alive, are resented as still additional affronts to their dignity and sense of pride.

—Carey McWilliams, *North from Mexico:
The Spanish-Speaking People in the United States*

McWilliams observed, in 1948, that many "young persons of Mexican descent" found that the fantasy heritage did not speak to their experiences of social inequality. At the same time that the Padua Hills Institute was reinventing Mexican identity in terms of the Spanish Fantasy Heritage, *Teatros de Revistas* and *Tandas de Variedades* were being produced in downtown areas throughout the Southwest and in traveling tent theaters, or *carpas*. These *teatros* were redefining Mexican and Mexican American identity in very different and often oppositional terms for audiences likely to be composed of the "young persons of Mexican descent," McWilliams mentions. This alternative performance genealogy touches the contemporary Latino *teatro*, performance art, spoken word, and musical forms used to express cultural critique. However, due to circumstances caused by social upheaval after the 1930s, this multilayered theater genealogy was forgotten, and it remained undocumented for many years. The rise of the Mexican Players came at the very moment when the audience for the once burgeoning Spanish-language theater produced by Latinos was decimated by deportation and reparations scares. Yet, from the turn of the century through the 1930s, Los Angeles, like San Antonio, was home to many thriving professional theater houses. Between 1910 and 1930, Los Angeles was the site of "five permanent houses with Spanish-language programs that changed daily" and the headquarters of many traveling performance groups.[79] But when one-third of the population of Mexican descent living in Los Angeles left the area to avoid forced deportation and repatriation and the effects of the Depression took hold, the professional theaters lost most of their audience. The once profitable professional Spanish-language theater houses (some of which still stand on downtown Los Angeles's Broadway Avenue) were bought by major Hollywood studios and showcased Hollywood premiere films. Many actors who once reigned on the professional stage survived by performing with the traveling *carpa* groups.[80] The *carpas* themselves were able to survive the Depression and World War II by virtue of their low production costs and the resulting inexpensive entrance fees for the audience.

Live Latino theater and performance declined in the 1950s as they were displaced by the popularity of television. Yet, while images of Ricky Ricardo filled America's television sets, the Mexican American performer Ritchie Valens was transforming the sound of early rock 'n' roll. However, in the 1960s, the waning interest in Latino theater came to a screeching halt. Interest in documenting the history of Chicano and Latino theater was sparked by the emergence of Teatro Campesino and the *teatro* movement in general. The United Farm Workers' union, the civil rights movement, and the antiwar movement created social conditions that fostered the emergence of Teatro Campesino. César Chávez, one of the best-known representatives of the United Farm Workers (UFW), strongly supported the young Luis Valdez and Teatro Campesino. Chávez was convinced of the power of performance to present audiences with new images of social relations and to help convey the mission of the farm workers' movement to the people it mattered to the most: Chicano migrant labor. The mission of the Teatro was inherently disruptive: it desired that its laborer audiences question the inevitability of status quo power relations by presenting an image of life in which workers controlled their own destiny. If discussion of labor exploitation was silenced at the Padua Hills Institute, it was the very inspiration of the early Teatro Campesino.

Chávez was right about the powerful place theater held in Mexicano and Chicano culture. What Kanellos discovered in his extensive research on Latino theater history in the United States was that Spanish-language theater "was the most popular and culturally relevant artistic form" in U.S. Latino communities from 1880 to 1930.[81]

According to the historian Lisbeth Haas, theater was a crucial site where "the process of building and defining an ethnic community in the Southwest" took place. The need for inexpensive labor had encouraged immigration from Mexico.[82] In the sense that theater served to unite communities separated by great geographical distances and living in hostile environments, the circulation of Spanish-language theater served a function similar to that of records in Paul Gilroy's notion of a Black Atlantic. Like the "books and records" Gilroy describes, Spanish-language performance forms "have carried inside them oppositional ideas, ideologies, theologies and philosophies."[83] Haas explains the role of theater in Latino communities:

The theater, in short, was an important medium for formulating ideas about national identity and history and bringing them into public discussion. In Mexico and the southwestern United States, plays were often used to tell the national story. . . . Although the national story was often featured on the stage, dramatic offerings were not restricted to the narrow bounds of nationalist exposition. The *teatro de revista* [a form of Mexican vaudeville], for instance, commented on the political life of the nation and brought the sacred, whether of patria or church, into the realm of irony and laughter.[84]

Irony is the key element that distinguished most popular Spanish-language *teatro* performances from Spanish Fantasy Heritage enactments at Padua Hills. Although Padua Hills shared formal elements with *teatro de revista* —live musicians and talented dancers—the content and context, and hence the reception, were completely different. For the purposes of this study, irony is the crucial legacy embraced by the contemporary performers. The cultural politics of the *teatro de revista* contained a counterhistory to that articulated by Spanish Fantasy Heritage celebrations; *teatro* was a site of alternative constructions of nation and citizenship. Haas argues:

Teatro de Revista took up themes characteristic of vaudeville, but it did so "always in terms of appropriation, of Mexicanizing the foreign, of experimentation with one's own." With this new form of theater, vaudeville became a national cultural production as actors appropriated foreign representations of the modern while they experimented with national themes. Brought to the United States during the 1910s, it influenced the content of much Spanish-language urban theater after 1920. *Teatro de revista* maintained the close relationship with the audience that had developed with legitimate theater. . . . The *carpa*, or tent theater, was essentially a version of *teatro de revista* but performed with fewer resources.[85]

The role of the *carpa* (or tent theater) was multiple. First, in the era before television in general, and Spanish-language television in particular, traveling *carpas* entertained Mexican American people. Second, as television functions to provide a common experience, or common culture, *carpas,* as they traveled throughout the Southwest during the early part of the twentieth century, forged a bicultural Mexican American/Mexican experience through performances in Spanish and English. Third, in an era in which the nightly televised newscast had not yet been invented, the *carpas* augmented radio broadcasts and informed people, especially those in working communities, of both local and world events. (As the film *La Carpa* [1992] illustrates, the *carpa* groups often incorporated local incidents in their performance). Fourth, the *carpas* created a place where disenfranchised Mexican Americans could voice their worldview during a historical moment when they were being denied access to mainstream media. "Making do" with the little they had, *carpa* groups invented a *rasquache* form of entertainment that successfully acknowledged the struggles of everyday people.[86] According to Broyles-González, "[p]eriods of *carpa* revival coincide with periods of social upheaval and popular distress."[87]

Performing Subjects: Civil Rights, Decolonization, and the Teatro Campesino

> Generated by the anger and hope of the progressive social movements of the time—such as the civil rights movement, the antiwar movement, the United Farm Workers movement, the Chicano movement, and the women's movement—a widespread theatrical mobilization sought to affirm an alternative social vision that relied on a distinctly Chicana/o aesthetic [that shared a] working-class social experience [and a] cultural heritage of performance forms.
>
> —Yolanda Broyles-González, *El Teatro Campesino: Theater in the Chicano Movement*

> In the beginning the skits were improvisational (actos) which expressed the exploitative living and working conditions of the farmworkers [underscored] the need to unionize against the abuses of agribusiness.
>
> —Yolanda Broyles-González, *El Teatro Campesino: Theater in the Chicano Movement*

> The teatros began to form as the cultural and theatrical arm of campus organizations. During the period of demands for more Chicano students, faculty, and staff on campuses the teatros created actos that reflected those needs.
>
> —Jorge Huerta, *Chicano Theater: Themes and Forms*

Teatro Campesino emerged during a time of great social conflict and transformation. The demands to end racial segregation, the demands for equal
rights, articulated by the civil rights movement, which emerged in the mid-
1950s, intersected national liberation struggles in the so-called third
world (Africa, Asia, the Middle East, and Latin America) and inspired revolutionary fervor in young people all over the globe, including in the
United States. This new global consciousness prompted young working-
class Chicanos (as well as their parents) to question the implications of
their role in the Vietnam War and, eventually, to protest against it.

Chicano nationalism was a response to the cumulative effects of racist
and economic practices against Mexicans and Mexican Americans in the
United States. Chicano working-class youth called for education reforms,
for better working conditions for agricultural workers, for the protection
of farm workers from pesticides, and for economic self-determination.
Though it was an oppositional politics, Chicano nationalism, like most
nationalist projects, privileged a male subject.[88] Though part of a powerful decolonization process, Chicano nationalism concretized itself, reproducing the limitations Frantz Fanon cautioned against in his discussion of
the power and peril of nationalist projects, by requiring a return to a pre-
conquest mythic past, a time before European contact, located in
Aztlán.[89] Yet Chicano nationalism's power was double-edged: In its desire for a time before oppression, it necessarily suppressed the historical
reality of cultural fusion (*mestizaje*).[90] This nationalism reproduced practices of the dominant culture by reinforcing traditional gender roles and
heterosexuality. The theorist Angie Chabram-Dernersesian has demonstrated that during this movement, Chicanas recognized the contradictions inherent in Chicano nationalism and made interventions but that,
until recently, their participation in the Chicano movement was ignored
in the historiography.[91]

Despite its contradictions, Chicano nationalism, for many young people, provided the terms to build an alternative cultural identity, the terms
to resist the hegemonic practices of the dominant culture. Luis Valdez was
intimately connected to the development of Chicano nationalism. After
returning from a life-changing visit to Cuba, in 1964, the young Valdez,
son of migrant workers, put his artistic talent to political use, creating a
new performance form, the *acto,* to meet the demands of decolonization.
Valdez and the emerging Teatro Campesino would drive around the agricultural fields of Central California to perform *actos* for the Mexican
farm workers on the flat bed of their old truck. A hybrid form itself,

shaped by the Mexican performance tradition, the *acto* included migrant workers themselves as performers in short skits to illuminate how unequal power relations might be transformed through collective union organizing.[92] Eventually, Luis Valdez left his post as the cultural ambassador of the United Farm Workers to formally develop Teatro Campesino and to produce theater in which an oppositional Chicano identity could be performed.

Conclusion

The Spanish Fantasy Heritage is still so pervasive that even Teatro Campesino was compelled to engage with it thematically. For example, Teatro Campesino, in its later years, moved away from nationalist iconography and returned to the early Californio days of California for artistic inspiration. It was no accident that the *teatro* thematized Old California/Spanish California history by adapting plays such as David Belasco's *Rose of the Rancho*. Set in California in the 1840s, the original play was written, in 1906, by David Belasco and Richard Tully and was performed very successfully on Broadway. According to Diane Rodríguez, a long-time member of Teatro Campesino and currently the co-director of the Latino Theater Initiative at the Mark Taper Forum in Los Angeles, familiarity with Californio history was integral to the Teatro. She explains: "Californio—it's a major period. And we lived in San Juan Bautista, which was a major Californio town, so were delving into a history." According to Rodríguez, the Teatro began experimenting with performances that thematized the Californio era in the early 1980s: "*Rose of the Rancho* was an old play, and Luis adapted it. It was a melodrama. And it worked great in San Juan Bautista. We had the tourists come." Although *Rose of the Rancho* celebrated Californio conquest, Rodríguez emphasizes that, because the play was performed near the Mission San Juan Bautista, memory of those conquered was always near: "it was an historical site, the Indian cemetery deep with bodies piled on top of each other. So the history was around us constantly. . . . So we were very much into that California history and felt very much a part of it, felt we were continuing the work." Yet Rodríguez recognizes that political and cultural contradictions inherent in the Teatro's contemporary re-enactments of the Spanish Fantasy Heritage such as *Rose of the Rancho* have still yet to be resolved:

Luis Alfaro and Diane Rodriguez in a publicity photo for *Spirits Rising* (1995). Note the allusions to Californiano attire. Photography by Craig Schwartz. (Reprinted with permission.)

And it's so amazing because the whole real estate phenomenon which coincides with the mission revival—"come to California, palm trees, beauty, sun, oranges, real estate, and everybody is Spanish." And they just did away with the Mexicans and just left the architecture and the furniture designs—the mission furniture—that everybody likes. . . . They take the culture, but they'd rather not deal with the people at all. Or they'd rather not deal with the lower class. Much of what is happening goes beyond race and is also based on class.[93]

Although Valdez moved toward the Spanish Fantasy Heritage, he never completely removed his work from the ideals of Chicano nationalism. The cultural theorist Rosa Linda Fregoso explains that the connection between theater and film has always been important in relation to Chicano cultural production. While Luis Valdez was able to break into mainstream film markets with *Zoot Suit,* Fregoso demonstrates how Chicano nationalist ideology is embedded within Valdez's films. Nonetheless, while cinematic representations of the Chicano past were beginning to chip away at the national imagination, a new generation of performers was emerging, performers who had to contend with the new world order of the Reagan-Bush era. This new generation of artists addressed new problems, some brought on by the backlash against progressive gains made in the 1960s and 1970s, in addition to the problems previous generations had encountered. As the social context changed, so did the form and content of Chicana/o art.

This chapter has discussed some of the processes by which representations of Mexican Americans were absent or distorted. It is also important to demonstrate and confirm the importance of producing cultural criticism in popular culture forms. Since popular culture is one of the most powerful realms where images of Latino/as are generated and regenerated, there is much to be learned from exploring the strategies of contemporary artists as they use their work to critique cultural representations and expectations. The chapters that follow examine how contemporary Chicano artists have inserted themselves into the national and transnational imagination by launching cultural critiques through performance and popular culture, critiques that privilege the process of *mestizaje* and hybridity.

2

"No Cultural Icon"

Marisela Norte and Spoken Word—
East L.A. Noir and the U.S./Mexico Border

I am no cultural icon
Not one of the ten most beautiful poets in Los Angeles
I am not your worst enemy
. . . .
I am the one that cut the label out
                              —Marisela Norte, "976-LOCA"

I point black
standing alone
me in drop dead black
and a pelvic tilt
standing strong in my reinforced toes and nude heels
telling no wives tales
lending no cure
arousing the general audience
                    —Marisela Norte, "El Club Sufrimiento 2000"

Late in the fall of 1991, Marisela Norte, the much-loved "East L.A. Ambassador of Culture," who had recently released her spoken-word compact disk, *NORTE/word,* stepped straight out of a Fellini film and entered the Michel De Certeau lecture room in the Humanities Building at
the University of California, San Diego, in black stiletto heels. She carried
a large black binder full of her words, one that contained at least ten years
of her written work. Impressive in her form-fitting black dress, fishnet
stockings, pointy black heels, red lipstick circa early 1950s, and long,
dark hair, Norte brought artistry and a fashion sense that the newly com-
pleted building had yet to experience. As she opened the binder and read,

43

her spoken word narratives captivated the overflow audience of undergraduates, graduate students, and faculty, many of whom were elated to hear a writer thematize a world of underground culture so familiar to them, one virtually absent from mainstream depictions of cultural life in Los Angeles and so removed from the university. Though Norte looked the part of disinterested glamour queen, her words evoked a sense of vulnerability as her narratives fluidly switched from English to Spanish, bringing harsh, livid images of the city, of urban Los Angeles, of immigrant women working, of third-generation Latinas looking for love, of romance and inequality, to the institutional beige lecture room. Her words, delivered in a sweet yet sardonic voice, at once compassionate and brutal, pointed yet vulnerable, deeply personal but still accessible, created an intense intimacy with the audience. Forgetting about the stark furnishings of the room, the audience transformed into characters in her noir narrative, à la East Los Angeles, strolling along with Norte's narrator down those streets of "panaderías [bakeries], taquerías [taco shops], mueblarías [furniture stores], and video palacios [palaces] that beat inside of" her.[1]

Narratives like Norte's "976-LOCA" impressively distill the social dynamics of East Los Angeles social life, often centered around extended family, as they record moments at East Side weddings where defenseless nieces try to run from ubiquitous "Uncle Rudys" who are looking for dance partners for Santana's "Oye Como Va," considered by many a Chicano anthem. Unlike any other writer I had read up to that point, Norte represented a place—Los Angeles County; a community—Mexican American; a moment in time—the 1980s; and a critical sensibility—punk —that I recognized and was shaped by. I understood what her narrator meant when she said, "estoy [I am] destroyed." It was somehow uncomfortable and yet comforting to hear about the intimate details of girl survival in an unforgiving patriarchal world. Norte related these stories of survival with the verbal intonation and appreciation for language play of those who had been raised in East Los Angeles neighborhoods during the second half of the twentieth century. Norte's intonations matched those of my mother, aunts, uncles, and cousins. Yet rarely had I hear such searing stories of failed romance and explicit social critiques at family gatherings. Norte's narratives about dangerous border crossings, the violence of romance, the danger of everyday urban suburban life; about her own longing for places to write near her home in East L.A.; and about Hollywood culture spoke to me as they had to her devoted fans.

But as intriguing as her voice and dark humor was Norte's look: Her postpunk femme fatale fashion paid homage to the glamorous women of the Golden Age of Mexican cinema and of Hollywood's noir B films, but Norte wore this fashion with a postmodern wink, acknowledging that those days were long gone. While the bright yellow, green, and blue hues of hip-hop defined the youth fashion of the late 1980s, Norte's sultry black garments stood out. Though she referenced the music of Mexican *rancheras* and "oldies but goodies," her look was edgy enough to front an East Los Angeles punk band: femme yet at the same time barbed; her appearance matched her words.[2] In her persona of spoken-word artist, she rejected the codes of folkloric iconography invented to satisfy the desires of many non-Latino audiences. Norte's deliberate image did not reproduce the costumed clichés that attempt to mimic and cheapen Aztec flavor.[3] Norte escaped the limits of an official and invented folkloric imagery that emphasize the supposed "quaintness" of Mexican culture.[4] She did this by self-consciously employing, tongue in cheek, the codes of film noir mixed with a punk sensibility to represent what she calls a "Chicana urban experience."[5] Her visual style strategically addressed at least two audiences. It disidentified with Chicano fantasies as elaborated in the first Chicano epic poem, "Yo Soy Jouquín," and the poem's "black-shawled Faithful women," who die alongside their male protectors. It also spoke to non-Latino audiences that often uphold the image of Frida Kahlo as a template for all Chicana artists. If there is any iconic Mexican style that inspired Norte's look, it is the fierce style of the film star Maria Felix, the sharp-witted and sometimes cruel beauty of classic Mexican film.[6] But, like those of other women writers of the moment from East Los Angeles, Norte's words identified primarily with the vulnerable women on the city streets, their broken hearts and stillborn dreams. Unfortunately, the women in Norte's narratives often perish as anonymous victims of violence against women, whose only line of defense at times, as Norte puts it, "is a panty shield."[7]

Though it might be argued that Norte's ultrafeminine appearance unconsciously reproduced stereotypical notions of woman-as-object as defined by the male gaze, Norte's spoken word contradicted this notion: Her words, instead of glorifying the myths of perfect heterosexual romance, smashed it. In fact, her writing has aptly been described as "savagely romantic and savaging romance."[8] This is where film noir sensibility fits in. Norte uses it as a counterpoint to the defenseless-woman-as-object image. But, unlike the noir femme fatale who pays the ultimate price for her transgression of gender norms, Norte's narrators survive, though with little comfort.

Norte's customized femme fatale image possessed an edge that resonated with 1980s indie/alternative self-conjured fashion. In fact, Norte's early readings often occurred at multigenre performances in Hollywood and East L.A. that also included punk bands. If Norte's contemporaries, such as Teresa Covarrubias, Alicia Armendariz Velasquez, and other Chicana innovators of 1970s and 1980s East L.A. and Hollywood punk, expressed their sensibilities through music, Norte used both performance and written word to reach her audience, which included readers of punk 'zines (low-budget, independently produced publications with grass-roots circulation). Norte's early writings were published in alternative and underground journals. In his essay "Poetry/Punk/Production," David James suggests that a correspondence exists between ideological orientation and aesthetic in alternative publications. He explains that, for the most part, "publications that are independently produced and distributed and that negate the conventions of commercial publications almost invariably produce punk ethics."[9] This was certainly the case with Norte, whose "El Club Sufrimiento 2000" appeared in *Rattler*, in 1987. According to James, *Rattler* was part of a group of "periodicals clearly originating from punk subculture and retaining strong references to the music, but whose emphasis is on independent art, either visual or verbal."[10]

Norte's connection to the legacy of the L.A. punk scene is further illustrated by the fact that she allowed Harvey Kubernik to produce her compact disc. Kubernik, who is well versed in the punk genre, released her recording on the New Alliance label, which was "a product of the L.A. punk explosion in the early 1980s."[11] The connection of Norte's writing to the L.A. punk scene continued throughout the 1980s as she shared the stage with such punk luminaries as Exene Cervenka and Joel Lipman. She also performed with Henry Rollins, Lydia Lunch, Dave Alvin, Helena María Viramontes, Michelle T. Clinton, and others in State of the Art and was awarded "Best Overall Peformance."[12]

Though Norte's look was a powerful statement in and of itself, it was her look in combination with her voice, subject matter, and attitude that made her work unique. Norte's spoken word gave voice, literally and metaphorically, to the concerns of working-class women on the east side of Los Angeles. While Norte's words referred to a particular locality, her work represented an entire generation of Chicana writers and intellectuals who were trying to leave in peace, 'dejar en Paz'—to leave behind the pastoral, quaint, and artificial folkloric images of Latinas that tried to contain them and that so often informed mainstream depictions of Latinas.[13]

Fast forward ten years after Norte's reading at UC San Diego. As the fall wind rushed through the giant palm trees that lined the industrial edge of downtown Los Angeles, the bright southern California sun shone down on a sea of faces of a multitude of ages and ethnicities. Gathered around the outdoor stage at the newly built, gorgeously designed Japanese American National Museum, fans came from all parts of the city to the revel in the "The Eastside Revue: 1932–2002: A Musical Homage to Boyle Heights," held in conjunction with the museum's exhibition, "Boyle Heights: The Power of Place." The event celebrated the long history of the mixing of Jewish, Japanese, and Mexican American and African American residents who had lived in the Boyle Heights neighborhood, just east of downtown Los Angeles. The musical event featured Chicano-Japanese fusion, Japanese American poets, a Klezmer-Mexican folk piece, Chicano rhythm and blues, and "Jarocho" punk. The audience was treated to a musical time trip starting with new acts such as Slowrider, the East L.A. 1980s punk band the Brat, and, favorites of the 1960s, Cannibal and the Head Hunters, as well as the legendary Lalo Guerrero, who had been popular since the 1940s.[14]

Eagerly looking forward to the event, especially the East Los Angeles punk segment, I was not prepared for what I would witness. I had been trying to establish, via archival documents, the intersections and confluences of East Los Angeles alternative music, performance art, and spoken word. And here, at this event, the reality of those intersections was being brought to life. The East Los Angeles punk segment brought together cultural innovators who had not shared the stage in recent memory, some for more than twenty years. Ruben (Funkahuatl Ladron de) Guevara, curator and master of ceremonies of the event, invited East L.A.'s Ambassador of Culture, the spoken-word artist Marisela Norte, to participate in the punk segment of the show. Norte had been invited to perform her spoken word and to introduce Las Tres, a Chicana folk/punk group composed of former members of East Los Angeles and Hollywood punk groups. But Guevara surprised the audience and Norte by appointing Norte as the new poet laureate of East Los Angeles. Visibly touched by the new title, Norte quipped that she was reliving her youth by being on stage with Chicana feminist musicians with whom she had shared the stage in the past.[15] Norte enthusiastically introduced the band with a preface that paid tribute to the hundreds of women who must each day navigate the violence, death, and glamour of downtown and East Los Angeles, paying homage to the hundreds of women who never make it from work and the missing daughters who disappear from home. Norte devastatingly juxtaposed the violence of the city to that of the U.S.-Mexican border: "The day after the Academy Awards I saw a photo of a woman's feet inside of a pair of custom-made million-dollar shoes. Outside a trash dumpster in Tijuana, a pair of white sandals remains buried, remains invisible," thereby calling attention to the violence inherent in the absence of representation of these disappearing daughters in the Hollywood media machine.[16] Norte then quoted an original lyric by Teresa Covarrubias from her punk days, "Misogyny" (see chapter 5 for lyrics), and made the point that though this generation of East Los Angeles artists had come full circle since its first days in the 1980s, as performers influenced by the energy and aesthetics of punk, violence against women still remains a pressing issue.

I provide this anecdote to show the interconnections of Chicana music and poetic subculture. I was thrilled that one of my assumptions about the unifying artistic sensibility, punk, of this generation of artists, was demonstrating itself onstage. For the majority of the artists, punk sensibility may be not directly in the formal expression but in its attitude. This sensibility would shape the third wave of Chicana/o cultural sensibility—one ironic and stylized, but still critical of social relations, especially those hostile to Mexican Americans and recent Mexican immigrants.

These artists responded to hostile social contexts: the 1980s Reagan/Bush era of ultraconservative politics, the neoliberal processes of economic privatization, and the growing crisis around AIDS. Punk appealed to many youth, who for myriad reasons (e.g., sexual orientation, class, race/ethnicity) did not fit into the mainstream and were critical of social relations. For many, punk was a first step that led to more nuanced critiques of poverty, racism, homophobia, and sexism. Equally important, punk was founded on a D.I.Y. (Do-It-Yourself) approach to music. The early punk scene was about playing with one's guts and heart, not displaying musical proficiency. Any fan with the urge could participate.

The appeal of punk to rebellious Chicana and Chicano youth makes sense for several reasons. First, the Do-It-Yourself sensibility at the core of punk musical subcultures found resonance with the practice of *rasquache,* a Chicana/o cultural practice of "making do" with limited resources.[17] According to Sean Carrillo:

The one thing that the punk aesthetic shared across all continents—London, New York, L.A., Tokyo, wherever—was something called the DIY aesthetic. . . . And that's what punk was all about. Punk was about, "don't wait for somebody to tell you it's O.K., or to give you the resources or the time or the space or whatever." Just do it yourself in any way and any shape and any form you can do it. DIY has come to symbolize music created outside of the boundaries of large multinational corporations.[18]

In fact, both punk and Chicano aesthetics share a similar spirit of making do with what's at hand, with limited resources, of expressing ideas and emotions that aren't necessarily "marketable" and of cutting and mixing cultural references and sounds to make something new.[19] Like Chicana/o art, punk made space for critiques of social inequality and racism. Mainstream representations of punk represented punk culture as monolithic, yet punk had various and competing strains and was never only one thing. For Chicano artists, deploying punk sensibility and attitude was an early step in a larger engagement with the world at large.

Again, for a particular set of artists, punk sensibility was a rejection of the uncritical folkloric representation of Mexicans that we examined in chapter 1. Their art moved the focus to the urban setting, where mutual influences between musical subcultures (Chicana/o and otherwise) and visual/performance art helped grow the art. I do not want to promote the idea that punk in Los Angeles was without its own messy contradictions around race/ethnicity, class, and sexuality. But at times it was a fluid social space—enough so that young Chicanas gravitated toward the punk subculture as a place where they re-imagined the world they lived in, it was a place where they saw themselves as empowered subjects. Punk was just a stepping-off point for these women; they continued to develop their craft in other musical genres.

Norte's narratives refuse the implied burden of representing an unchanging notion of Chicana identity by constantly interrogating the notion of cultural icon.[20] Perhaps the most powerful evidence of how Norte rejects both the burden and the images her narrators seek to escape is her spoken-word compact disk collection, *NORTE/word*. Written for the spoken-word format, what Norte composes in ink is meant to be vocalized, but not necessarily sung. Its destiny is to be performed live by the writer and listened to in a collective atmosphere as well as heard anonymously in recorded versions circulating via compact discs, cassettes, or the Internet. Ultimately, the reception of the spoken word by the audience completes its meaning.

Yet what makes *NORTE/word* stand out is its format. It was one of the first compact disks released by a Chicana writer. Equally important, Norte's prose narratives and plays contributed to the ever-transforming category of transnational border writing by "explor[ing] the border feminine subject" before the genre was recognized as such.[21] According to the Pulitzer prize–winning writer Victor Valle, "Norte's writing emerged in a decade when Latino writers in Los Angeles made a conscious and semiconscious decision to break away from romantic pastoral tendencies of the first wave of Chicano poetry and instead seek a more urban voice and thematics."[22] The scholar Raul Villa has described these L.A. Latino writers as having a modernist social-geographic aesthetic.[23]

Much is at stake when Norte describes the experiences of Chicanas living in Los Angeles, because these experiences are rarely depicted by the dominant culture with any depth or complexity. Norte's cultural politics —the struggle to acquire, maintain, or resist power—emerge most often as struggles over the supposed superiority or inferiority of a culture, over what is a "central" or "marginal" social group, over official and "forgotten" histories, and over external and internal representations of social relations. Cultural politics in general, and Norte's cultural politics specifically, engage in the struggle over meaning within a context of inequality.[24] For instance, Norte's narrators struggle to define, on their own terms—from an unprivileged perspective—the meanings of particular places like Los Angeles and the U.S.-Mexico border and the function of institutions such as family and marriage and to criticize violence against women.

In the process of describing the contradictions contained in these places, institutions, and practices from the perspective of a working-class Chicana, Norte's narratives contest the meaning and function of these formations. Her narrator's point of view often opposes that of the dominant culture; yet her narratives are more complex than a simple reversal of negative stereotypes. They counter the images of working-class and poor immigrant Latinas put forth by anti-immigrant campaigns, and they refuse to represent Chicana poets in the standard terms of the dominant culture: as earthy goddesses, holders of uncomplicated mythic pasts. Instead, her narratives represent the conflicts and ambivalence that arise around cultural identity and in relation to places, institutions, and practices.[25] In doing so, they open a space, although imaginary, where the possibility of life without hierarchy and exploitation can emerge.

Contexts

Norte's writing emerges in late-twentieth-century Los Angeles, California, the U.S. city that is second only to Mexico City in its population of people of Mexican descent. Her writings and her spoken-word chronicle the daily life of "Nuestra Señora de Los Angeles" [Our Lady of Los Angeles]—a city that from its very establishment in the 1800s has been a cauldron of mixing and clashing cultures, forever shaped by the presence of indigenous communities, Spanish and Mexican colonization, Asian and African American laborers, and U.S. invasion.

Norte's writing, however, documents a great demographic shift in California's population. Her late-twentieth-century East Side emerges from the white population's flight to post–World War II suburban neighborhoods and from the influx of new immigrants from Mexico, Central America, and Asia. Although the official U.S. border begins in San Ysidro, California, Norte's spoken word shows us that culture flows through the border and transforms southern California on its way through. She documents a landscape where fifth-generation U.S.-born Chicanas encounter immigrant seamstresses returning from garment factories, standing on the bus, covered "with red, white, green, black strands of thread."[26]

In addition, Norte accounts for the way Hollywood, with its proximity to East Los Angeles, casts its long entertainment-industry shadow over the cultural life of East Side communities, making it unlike any other Chicano community in the Southwest. Her writing dances to the rhythms of ever-present radio stations competing for Spanish ballad and banda listeners, oldie-but-goodie lovers, and old-school free-stylers, as well as rock and urban hip-hop fans. Her words flicker against the backdrop of 1950s black-and-white television detective series, film noir, and gangster films. In general, the impact and influence of movies on Norte's memory and writing is tremendous.

Norte's performances have been praised as:

> something to behold, her low, sweet voice shifting from English to a passionate, rhythmic Español, her words capturing contemporary moments

as brilliantly as Kodachrome snapshots. . . . "976-LOCA: Call Me," which links phone sex ads to the fetishizing of Frida Kahlo, put[s] mainstream poets to shame by marrying languages and creating a deft mix of styles and concerns.[27]

By the mid-1990s, Norte had captured a crossover, cross-cultural, and cross-generational audience—an accomplishment to which many East L.A. writers aspired. Norte asserts that she does not write for a specific audience but she is thrilled by the way various audiences have received her work. After a local live radio broadcast, she remembers that "All these young girls were calling me, from way out in the projects! They said: 'You make us proud to be Mexican.' Then an old guy called and said: 'I haven't heard anyone mention a ten-cent bus ride in fifteen years! It made me sit down with my wife and remember all kinds of things.'"[28] The young girls were, no doubt, excited by the rare opportunity to hear their world represented by a sympathetic voice. And Norte's reference to childhood memories resonates with more mature listeners.

Born in 1955 and fondly embraced, as an adult, as East L.A.'s cultural ambassador, Marisela Norte began writing because it "enabled me to speak when keeping silent was the only choice."[29] Norte and her brother, Armando, an accomplished visual artist in his own right, grew up and attended public schools in an East Los Angeles suburb during the politically and socially turbulent 1960s and 1970s. Despite the general push at that time for Mexican Americans to become monolingual, Norte's Chihuahuan father's strict enforcement of "Spanish only" at home guaranteed her bilingual fluency; her mother, born in Veracruz, bequeathed Norte her sharp wit. Childhood drives through East Los Angeles on the way to view Hollywood B movies with her father animated her love for the cinematic images that would become so integral to her later writing. In her own words, "we'd get into a car with little gas and coast the dark curves of Little Valley, . . . where he would roll his window down and point at the landscape and tell me 'this belongs to you.'"[30] Norte claims this landscape throughout her writing.

After graduating, in 1973, from George M. Shurr High School, in Montebello, California (an urban suburb east of Los Angeles), Norte embarked on a number of life-transforming visits to Mexico.[31] Upon returning from her first trip, she enrolled in East Los Angeles City College and later transferred to and studied at California State University, Los Angeles, from 1976 to 1978. However, as she states, she "abandoned [her] formal education after an English professor returned a paper I wrote, asking what was I doing in his class and if I was 'illiterate.' . . . I began to write."[32] In fact, it was public transportation that influenced her writing most heavily, especially her "mobile office," the Number 18 bus to downtown. Norte explains:

> As a writer, the bus has been my transportation and my inspiration for the past 30 years. It has become my "mobile office," the space where I write about the daily lives of Angelinos that ride the bus to and from work. My writing circulates as I do through economically marginalized parts of the city in spoken word form. . . . My work is an ethnography of post-industrial Los Angeles culture viewed through a bus window.[33]

Interestingly, in 1997, after many years of writing on the bus, Norte, along with the photographer Willie García, was chosen by the MTA to develop a series of photos and essays to honor Metro System operators; these photos and essays were posted as placards in more than two thousand bus interiors.

Throughout the 1980s, Norte frequented the well-respected Latino Writers Workshop and ASCO's performance collectives to develop her writing (these collectives are described in more detail later). She further honed her craft by performing "at universities, over the radio on KPFK's morning readings, at cultural centers, and at the California Rehabilitation Center for Women at Norco, California."[34] In 1983, she was recognized for her writing by Eastern Michigan University, in Ypsilanti, Michigan, at the National Association of Chicano Studies Conference.

As the self-described "bad girl poet" of ASCO's performance collective, Norte began important collaborations with the writer Maria Elena Gaitan (*La Condición Feminina* play script), the artist Diane Gamboa (whose painting "Mistress" graces the cover of *NORTE/word*), and with the artist Gronk (whose 1995 Hammer Museum painting for the "Four Directions" installation was inspired by *NORTE/word*'s "Baby Sitter Girl"). Norte's recent collaboration, the Ovation-nominated play *Black Butterfly, Jaguar Girl, Piñata Women and Other Superhero Girls Like Me,* was performed at the Kennedy Center in 2000 and combines the writing of Norte, Sandra C. Muñoz, and Alma Cervantes under the direction

In 1982, Sean Carrillo took this photograph of ASCO. From left to right: Gronk, Diane Gamboa, Marisela Norte, and Harry Gamboa. (Reprinted with permission.)

of Luis Alfaro. She has described one of her most recent memoir/performances, *East L.A. Days/Fellini Nights,* as thematizing the "early eighties Chicano urban experience that I was living that you probably wouldn't know, if you picked up certain books, that I was certainly there."[35]

Hija del Propagandista: *East L.A. Noir,* *Transcultural Formations*

During a reading in 2002, Norte claimed the title *"hija del propagandista"* (film projectionist's daughter), since in Mexico her father had been in "the union of projectionists, which they called *propagandistas."* Norte explains that her deep love for the movies was first nurtured by her father's tales about his youthful experiences as a film projectionist in Chihuahua, Mexico.[36] Norte's imagination was at once saturated and stimulated by images emanating from Hollywood B movies, as well as by her father's stories. Growing up only miles from the film-making capital of the world, Norte remembers that "My father used to baby-sit me at the old Center Theater [in East Los Angeles] and spoon-feed me gems like *Blood Feast, The Tingler,* and *Playgirls vs. the Vampires.*"[37] When asked, in 1991, about the place of film in her life, she responded in detail:

> I think the influence shows up in the work, in the writing. It tends to be very dreamlike. I like to think that movies begin as dreams. It's almost as if I'm a witness, a voyeur. . . . I was very much influenced by the black and white bombshells of those B horror films of the 50s and 60s. Those same movies I used to watch on CHILLER [name of a television broadcast] on Saturdays where these drop-dead beautiful women in high heels would be chased by an assortment of monsters and fiends. They wore tight skirts, great shoes and their boyfriends were always handsome scientists, jet pilots or Army boys. At the same time I was watching Mexican movies at the Floral Drive-In where I wanted to look like María Félix, sing like Lola Beltrán and wiggle around in a G-string like Tongolele!
>
> As a child, I went through a heavy gangster/prison film stage. I would refer to my classmates as "lousy screws," roll up my arithmetic home-work into cigarettes and outline the neighborhood kids' bodies in chalk on the sidewalks off of Downey Road. I'd go to Ford Boulevard School with my Brooklyn (and Soto) accent and make sure I lost it by the time I got home.[38]

Norte describes her childhood in 1950s Los Angeles as "a black and white newsreel with a simultaneous commentary in both languages by my mother and father."[39] While trips to the drive-in and movies with her father left a lasting impression on her as much as their drives through East Los Angeles neighborhoods, so did group visits to rehearsals of the Russian Ballet and local county museums with her mother, aunts, and cousins. Norte frames her childhood experience with transcultural images and language—and these shaped her adult writing.

Norte developed her unique narrative style as part of two of the most productive artist collectives in Los Angeles: the Los Angeles Latino Writers Workshop (LLWW) and ASCO. The Los Angeles Latino Writers Workshop continued to expand the space created by the Chicano movement in the late 1960s and 1970s for literary expression produced by Latinos and Latinas. The workshop met regularly and published *ChismeArte* (*chisme* means "gossip" in Spanish). Working double shifts as a writer and "freelance waitress," Norte published "Each Street/Each Story" in an anthology titled *201: Homenaje a La Ciudad de Los Angeles: Latino*

Experience in Literature and Art (a special issue of *ChismeArte* published by the Los Angeles Latino Writers Workshop). She later served on the publication's editorial staff. According to the anthology's introduction, the workshop sessions were initiated by the Pulitzer prize–winning writer Victor Valle and included the noted Chicano writers Ron Arias and Alejandro Morales, Luis Rodríguez, Helena María Viramontes, Naomi Quiñones, Gina Valdez, and Norte. Norte became part of the workshop after responding to a tiny classified ad that the group had placed in a local reader. She recalls that it was a supportive environment for those who attended: "We weren't critical; we were just happy to hear other Chicanos."[40] Valle confirms, "We strove to create that environment in the workshop." He also adds that "we were already familiar with her [Norte's] work, and ASCO's, due to their contributions to *ChismeArte* and involvement with Arte Popular (Carlos Almaraz, John Valadez, Barbara Carrasco, Leo Limón, Frank Romero, Richard Duardo, plus several others,) headquartered in Highland Park. . . . We [Latino Writers Workshop] shared space in a Spring Street loft with Carlos Almaraz."[41]

ASCO, or "nausea" in English, was another artists' forum that played an important role in what critics have called the Chicano cultural renaissance of the 1970s. The Do-It-Yourself impulse and the questioning of the status quo that runs through both Chicano and punk aesthetic currents merged in this group. The founding members, Harry Gamboa, Gronk, Willie Herron, and Patssi Valdez, recognized the importance of the Chicano movement and participated in it but decidedly broke away from the indigenous iconography frequently found in Chicano nationalist aesthetics. Instead, they looked toward urban imagery to comment on sexuality, state violence, and postmodern alienation.[42]

Forging a space betwixt and between Chicano and mainstream art, the group often incorporated members who shared their precarious position within and outside the art world. Juan Garza, who was also involved with ASCO in the early 1980s, remembers the impact of the big screen on the group. Garza recalls:

> when I met Marisela, Gronk, Daniel Villareal, and other ASCO members, I was in awe of their love of movies. We had a lot of things in common, but movie talk always seemed to be a big part of our conversations. In the days when nobody had VCRs, we would get together and have TV parties. We would all go to someone's house and watch *Caged, North by Northwest, Queen of Outer Space,* or some other lost classic.[43]

During her tenure with ASCO, Norte both cowrote and performed, with María Elena Gaitán, a play entitled *La Condición Feminina*. Centering on a conversation between a homegirl from the barrio and a middle-class Chicana Valley girl, the two characters come to realize that they share an inferior position in the hierarchy of patriarchal gender relations. The exhibition "ASCO '83" included another of Norte's plays, *Exito* [Success]. A positive review written by Linda Burnham for *High Performance* of the 1985 video version of *Exito* described the play as "a dialogue with the dead . . . (a)s a crowd of friends hovered about her body, the camera switched to a dialog between a live Norte and a fascinated investigator who wanted desperately to prove she had killed herself for love, which she staunchly denied."[44]

Norte's prose-narratives, performances, plays, and videos—contributed to and benefited from LLWW and ASCO and from the struggle to maintain both intellectual and physical spaces for Chicano/Latino writers and artists. By her own account, Norte remembers the dearth of performance spaces for Chicano/Latinos and writers in general: "there weren't coffee houses on every corner like there are now, or even bookstores. Spoken-word readings weren't as common. Gorky's Cafeteria in downtown L.A. was the meeting place because there was no place else to go."[45]

Along with many other Chicano/Latino writers, Norte continued to write despite another serious lack: major publishing houses' lack of interest in Latino writers. However, Norte's writing caught the tail end of the first publishing wave of small Chicano journals, publications crucial in the distribution of Chicano/Latino writing. "Peeping Tom Tom Girl," which first appeared in *El Tecolote Literario* and was later modified for *NORTE/word,* serves as an excellent introduction to the form and themes of her writing.[46]

Spoken Word as D.I.Y. Aesthetics

On a general level, Norte's body of work thematizes the tensions that many working-class women feel about their lives, specifically the tension generated by the desire for forward movement in the struggle for both economic and social equality and by an immobility that seems, at times, impossible to break. The ribbon that ties these different components of her writing together (to make Norte the consummate storyteller she has become) is her gift of humor and her mastery of irony, which work in combination to create countermeanings. The choice to produce a spoken-word compact disk buttresses the idea that she is "no [folkloric] cultural icon," not only because of her subject matter, but also because of her chosen medium. Utilizing recently available and relatively inexpensive recording technology, Norte has found another way to get her voice heard. In mainstream cultural representations, Latinas are not usually associated with exploiting technology. But Norte's compact disk provides a great example of the empowering aspects of technology to create artistic spaces where disempowered women can un-absent their aesthetics.

As an eloquent writer and a gifted spoken-word artist, Norte struggles to make visible the practices of social inequality in everyday life in Los Angeles by seizing "the most advanced forms of modern technology to present [her] experiences and aspirations to a wider world."[47] What emerges from Norte's struggle to get her work distributed and heard is a particularly useful form of cultural politics, one that wages its battle on the terrain of popular culture in the form of *NORTE/word*.[48]

Marisela Norte's use of advanced forms of audiotechnology to present her experience is not coincidental. Those who have limited access to the production and distribution of the dominant modes of representation, such as commercial film, television, and popular music, find more accessible formats, such as live performance and compact disks, to intervene in discussions about life in the United States and to represent themselves and their concerns, fears, and hopes about and for the future. Because one must see or hear her performance to enjoy the full effect, CD technology favors her work. It is also a medium, when not sponsored by a major record label or other corporation, that allows for total artistic control; Norte is not forced to write what is marketable. Independently produced compact disks are a perfect example of the D.I.Y. aesthetic.

Formats such as spoken-word compact disks are crucial in the construction of new subjects for political identification because they open a space, a countersite, a condition of possibility, where writers like Norte can publicly imagine new ways of constructing racial, ethnic, gendered, and economic identities and where the struggle for social equality can be articulated.[49] As we explore in chapter 5, La Molly, the protagonist of Mediola's *Pretty Vacant*, like Norte, invents alternative modes of representation and distribution for her art.

"Spoken word is instant art, urgent social documentation," enthuses Harvey Kubernik, the most dedicated proponent of the Los Angeles spoken-word movement and producer of *NORTE/word*.[50] There is no official definition for "spoken word" in the Oxford English Dictionary, and therein lies its power. It is a fluid category that resists total codification. What makes spoken word different from printed poetry, for example, is its hybrid form, its cutting and mixing of "nonliterary popular styles" such as "rap music . . . stand-up comedy, evangelical speeches, and television info-mercials."[51] In addition, its use of recording technology corresponds to its primary mode of distribution—the circulation of cassettes, compact disks, and Internet downloads. In some ways, it is anti-genre in its refusal to be contained. Another distinguishing element is that the writer is judged as performer. Although post-1980s spoken word is situated with a tradition of experimental writing, the biggest difference between the two forms is its performative element. Spoken word is the combination of voice, visual aesthetic, and theatricality. Since a key expectation is that spoken word is written to be performed by the writer, one of the main problems for any critic writing about spoken word is that printed text can never represent the paratextual—the voice and image of the writer, as well as the audience's contribution to the performance.

Because spoken-word recordings, unlike printed text, capture the voice and sound of the writer and because spoken word carries the vocal markings of its speaker, comparisons are easily made between spoken-word artists and pop musicians and performers. Since spoken word is as much about the voice as the word, spoken-word artists, like pop musicians, are known for a particular sound and esteemed for their particular delivery.

Importantly, spoken-word recording, unlike traditional print publishing (whose costs limit the numbers of writers published), relies on relatively inexpensive production technology. Because of this, spoken word has been called a more democratic genre. Kubernick argues that spoken word is "instant art; urgent social documentation," and sees it as a place where writers whose form and content don't fit the publishing world's formula can continue to keep their word circulating. Spoken word and the inexpensive production technology available to spoken-word artists has kept the doors open for artists who might not have mainstream market appeal.

Until recently, "spoken word artists rel[ied] on a network of distribution that includes performances in local clubs and coffee-houses, recordings made for independent record labels, and periodicals and books self-published or printed by small, private presses in editions of several hundred copies."[52] As stated, however, new technologies are impacting how young people produce and receive the spoken word. Developments in personal computers and digital recording not only make Do-It-Yourself production much more accessible; they also allow for easy distribution via the Internet though mp3 downloads and file-swapping sites.

The very questions and concerns of distribution and access are what compelled Norte to put her first collection of words on compact disc. Norte found a way out of "being ghettoized in what she calls 'brown paper' Latin-American anthologies ('recycled Mayan gods and burning suns')."[53]

Stylistic Elements and Narrative Techniques

Even though Norte's narratives take issues of race, ethnicity, class, and gender as inextricably intertwined, Norte's cultural production is compelling because her situated experiences as a working-class Chicana enable her to represent broader social problems. For instance, her narratives represent the particular way violence against women is experienced in certain communities but exists as a practice sanctioned by patriarchal culture in general. Class position, however, does have a certain effect on her work. That she rides and writes on the bus—out of necessity, not by choice—impacts the form and content of her writing enormously. Never having owned a car, she has ridden public transportation for the past ten years back and forth to work and to readings.[54] In the liner notes for *NORTE/word,* Norte describes the conditions under which she produces her narratives most of the time: "I write on the bus, the No. 18 bus especially. That's the bus that's taken me from East Los Angeles over the bridge into downtown L.A. for most of my life." For the most part, Norte explains, her narratives are as long "as it takes to get from one bus stop to another."

Norte once attributed her urge to write "to seeing too many things at once and to coffee. . . . Los Angeles is a notebook, a bad film, a post-card, it's *maravillosa*. It's the ink for my pen."[55] The ink for her pen also draws its color from remnants of everyday life—family *chisme* (gossip), *chistes* (jokes), the *brujerías* (witchery), broken relationships with men, strained relationships with women—remnants that straddle the U.S.-Mexico border in some way, as well as the English and Spanish spoken in her home, and finally the people and streets that cross her path as she rides Los Angeles's public bus system. However, the impact of movies in general on Norte's memory and writing has been tremendous.

Not only is Norte's format unique for an East Los Angeles writer, but she is also an innovator in narrative technique. Norte is a wonderful storyteller, or story-insinuator. Her vivid and sometime violent images set up the conditions for the possibility of a story. Norte does not rely on conventional elements of story telling. There are no conventional plot structures, no absolute beginning, middle, or conclusion. There is little dialogue between the characters she invokes. When describing her narrative technique, Norte explains that she tends "to deal first with an image, rather than an experience . . . if you're walking somewhere and you see something . . . that makes a good or bad impression on you, you build your story around that particular incident. . . . It's like the image comes first and everything else falls into place."[56] Part of the reason she likes the openness of spoken-word imagery and form is that it gets away from poetic images of sunsets.[57]

Norte is akin to a cut-and-mix d.j. who samples from the sounds around her (from television, pop songs, and B movies in English and Spanish). She creates new meanings by juxtaposing classic cinematic scenes against East Los Angeles dramas. Norte propels a story with little narrative. She draws vivid images that leave a story behind. She leaves it up to her listeners to connect the dots. Her constructs an aural mise-en-scène with her voice, which is like a camera that freezes the details of scenario.

Norte's narratives use complex irony to call attention to gaps in the logic of the status quo where meaning and countermeanings can be produced and where a new political formation might emerge. Irony, defined in traditional terms, is a rhetorical technique used to hide "what is actually the case, however, not in order to deceive, but to achieve rhetorical or artistic effect."[58] In Norte's work, and in the work of many artists from marginalized communities, the use of irony does not aspire only to achieve a "rhetorical or artistic effect" but strives to make apparent relations of power. Irony and understatement require audiences to read between the lines. In the gap between the lines, a space emerges where the possibility of imagining the future based on economic and gender equality exists. By asking her audience to read between the lines, Norte does not dictate what the future should be but invites them to help imagine it.

The struggle to produce countermeaning takes place most visibly and immediately in the titles of Norte's spoken-word narratives. Titles such as "Peeping Tom Tom Girl," "Act of the Faithless," and "Three Little Words" reverse readers' expectations. Through slight alterations — "Faithless" instead of "Faithful," "Words" instead of "Pigs" — and new combinations, such as "Peeping Tom" with "Tom Girl" instead of "Tom Boy"—these titles subvert standard meanings. These subtle ironic reversals—commentaries in themselves—critique the status quo while provocatively suggesting the content of the narratives.

NORTE/word

Zooming across the geography of the Southwest borderlands, Marisela Norte's 1991 compact disk *NORTE/word* projects a transnational imaginary that humanizes the daily trials and triumphs of a transnational female work force caught in the web of economic exploitation and dysfunctional personal relationships. Envisioned as an "alternative to a book," *NORTE/word* consists of nine tracks of lucid, hypnotic spoken-word narratives.[59] Taken as a whole, *NORTE/word* is structured like a film, composed of a series of fade-in and fade-out vignettes. *NORTE/word,* eloquently bilingual, is about women and girls on the "outside"—women and girls outside the home, outside loving relationships, outside adequate education and health care systems, and outside the mass media. Moreover, *NORTE/word* is at once a subtle and eloquent critique of power relations that attempt to limit the possibilities of Latinas and a loving homage to the city of Los Angeles and the Latinas themselves who keep the city running even as their "stockings lay defeated after hours of crossing and double crossing."[60]

NORTE/word's opening track, "Peeping Tom Tom Girl," a wry meditation on the place of Latina women and girls in the public urban borderland spaces of greater Los Angeles, provides the location, sets the tone for the entire compact disk, and introduces a voluminous cast of characters rarely seen in Hollywood films. The protagonists of *NORTE/word* are many, from a girl in a too-tight pink dress who is forced to listen to her parents fight, to Silent, who can't find child care, a stable man, or a job, to Rosemary, who doesn't know what to do with her future, to a homeless woman who "sleeps in doorways, Hefty bag wardrobe, broken tiara and too much rouge," to finally, the first-person "narratrix" who records the lives of these women.

"Peeping Tom Tom Girl" introduces Norte's listeners to the point of view of her narrators and to the larger issues in Norte's writing. The title itself complicates the meaning of voyeurism. "Peeping Tom," in most cases, describes a man who gets pleasure from watching women without their permission. "Tom Girl," used in place of "Tom Boy," suggests that the narrator is a "femme" female rebel. Norte combines "Peeping Tom" with "Tom Girl" to imply that her narrator watches women, not for voyeuristic pleasure but in an empathic way. Because the narrator identifies with the women, we do not see the women through a man's eyes—they are not viewed as sexual objects, nor does she see them as racial, ethnic, or economic threats. Shifting the perspective from a "Peeping Tom's" to a "Tom Girl's" is just one example of how cultural politics are employed in Norte's work. What Norte's narrators see happening to women on the streets of East and downtown Los Angeles from the bus window are scenes not visible from a room on L.A.'s (wealthy) West Side.

The narrator describes a bus ride to her job, a ride that begins in her East Los Angeles neighborhood and ends at her final destination downtown. Along the way, the narrator travels back and forth in time, peeping at the women and remembering the faces of working-class single women who live on the economic edge of society.

Moving through economically marginalized sections of the East Side and downtown, the narrator in "Peeping Tom Tom Girl" critiques the social practices that force working-class single women to live at the edge of society, on the street, and/or without a job. The character who narrates "Peeping Tom Tom Girl" is no longer the object of another's representation; she claims her own position as subject.[61] She is at once both the Chicana "I" and the "eye" who experiences, witnesses, interprets, constructs, and transcodes images and events as they occur in her everyday life.

Riding the bus through different L.A. neighborhoods, the narrator witnesses the economic stratification of Chicanas and Latinas.[62] For instance, she passes a widow carrying flowers and her counterpart, a homeless woman who "sleeps in doorways, Hefty bag wardrobe, broken tiara and too much rouge." Using the phrase *"nuestra señora de la reina perdida que cayó en Los Angeles"* to describe both the homeless woman and the city's East Side, the narrator ironically twists the meaning of the original Spanish name of Los Angeles: *El Pueblo de Nuestra Señora La Reina de los Angeles de Porciúncula* (The Town of Our Lady the Queen of Angels of Porciúncula) becomes *"nuestra señora de la reina perdida que cayó en Los Angeles"* (Our Lady of the Lost Queen Who Fell in Los Angeles) in order to comment critically on the living conditions of women surviving in the city. This pun on the Spanish name of Los Angeles is characteristic of the linguistic strategies Norte uses to articulate social criticism. She gives new meaning to the name, making it describe more accurately the women's lives. The Spanish Pastoral myth of Los Angeles's limitless abundance is contrasted with the dwindling chances of survival faced by many Latinas in the city.[63] On the same bus ride, the narrator shares a different view of the city with her friend Silent, whose proudly rebellious youth has turned into an unending struggle with kids, diapers, and the welfare office.[64]

The unifying component of the narrative is its theme: single women facing economic hardship in Los Angeles. The sympathetic representation of the women and their living conditions in "Peeping Tom Tom Girl" generally falls to the margins of mainstream cultural expression. The women's representational marginalization is homologous to their economic marginalization within U.S. culture. Furthermore, the traditional model of the Latino patriarchal family delineates strict gender roles in which the ideal Chicana/Mexicana "woman" is constructed to fit two "legitimate" identities: the chaste daughter and the devoted wife. In "traditional" Chicano/Mexicano cultures, La Virgen represents the ideal woman, who is contrasted with the figure of the *Malinche*/Prostitute. Thus, the Virgin Mother–*Malinche*/Prostitute[65] dichotomy—a cultural paradigm—informs the boundaries of possible feminine roles. The women in "Peeping Tom Tom Girl" fall somewhere between the spaces of these predetermined traditional gender roles. They move in public spaces such as the street and institutional offices, rather than in the idealized domestic space associated with traditional middle-class life. Only "the widow" has a legitimate place within the traditional family structure. Even so, she, like the other women represented in the image, live, as Norma Alarcón has written, "unprotected within a cultural order that has required the masculine protection of women to ensure their 'decency,' indeed to ensure that they are 'civilized' in sexual and racial terms."[66] As women, they are also disadvantaged in an economic system that discriminates on the basis of gender. The single women represented here have little or no access to basic necessities, from shelter to child care.

The Chicana/Latina Female Body in the Patriarchal Latino Family

Speaking from their position within the Chicano/Latino community, Marisela Norte's narrators articulate the specific ways in which both Latino and the dominant culture's patriarchal practices converge on the bodies of Chicanas/Latinas.

The Chicano critic Tomás Almaguer writes about the constraints that limit male homosexual identity and behavior in the context of the Latino family. His assertion that "Chicano family life militates against the formation of a [sexual] identity other than heterosexual" also helps to explain the familial constraints that delimit traditional Chicana/Latina sexual identity. Almaguer argues that the structures of the Mexicano/Chicano family limit the emergence of a male homosexual identity. He asserts that traditional Latino family practices prevent "homosexual men from securing unrestricted freedom to stay out late at night, to move out of their family's home before marriage, or to take an apartment with a male lover."[67] Traditional Latino familial constraining practices also circumscribe female heterosexual behavior. The practices that Almaguer claims act as impediments to the emergence of homosexual identities also hinder heterosexual Latinas' attempts to form a sexual identity outside predetermined gender roles.

The Chicano family perpetuates allegiance to patriarchal gender relations by enforcing the Virgin Mother/Prostitute paradigm. However, this paradigm takes on specific nuances in Chicano culture and is articulated as *La Virgen de Guadalupe/La Malinche* dichotomy. The Chicana feminist cultural critic Yvonne Yarbro-Bejarano writes, in "The Female Subject in Chicano Theater: Sexuality, 'Race,' and Class," about how the myth of *La Malinche* influences the gender construction of Chicana women in Chicano theater. She explains that:

> *La Malinche,* as the site of representation of sexuality for a culture, illuminates cultural specificity in the construction of the gender of "woman." *La Malinche*'s presence in the culture is as pervasive as that of her polar opposite, the redeeming virgin/mother, *La Virgen. La Malinche* is the Mexican/Chicano Eve: she too bears the blame for the "fall." During the conquest of Mexico, the noble Aztec woman Malintzin Tenepal acted as Cortez's mistress, translator and tactical advisor. . . . *La Malinche* contributes to the construction of the gender "woman" as object, as other, reserving the active subject role for the masculine gender. Woman is viewed as sexually passive, therefore open at all times to use by men either by seduction or rape. . . . *La Virgen* represents the redemption of her gender though self-abnegations and resignation. She is mother, yet still miraculously intact. The equation of female sexuality with enslavement is translated through *La Virgen* into the cultural values of love/devotion, reinforcing women's subordinate

position of servitude and obedience within a rigidly heterosexual hierarchy. (393)

This construction of "woman" affects the lived reality of Latinas. Daughters who refuse to conform to the submissive gender roles as prescribed by *La Virgen*'s role "run the risk of being labeled *Malinchistas* (traitors)" by the traditional patriarchal Latino family.[68] Their refusal to adhere to these traditional gender roles threatens the power dynamics of the patriarchal family.[69]

Norte's narrators are always in the process of resisting a subordinate, submissive position. In "Peeping Tom Tom Girl," the narrator displays outrage when a friend confesses to her that she desires to perform the role of the "forever *mi'ja*," that is, to give herself to a man who will take care of her financially. *Mi'ja*, a contraction of the Spanish words for "my" (*mi*) and "daughter" (*hija*), is translated as "my daughter." Generally, *mi'ja* is used as a term of endearment, but in the context of "Peeping Tom Tom Girl," Norte ironicizes the term.[70] "Daughter" implies a position of dependency and subordination. Thus, to exist as a forever daughter would imply that a woman would never assume an independent identity; she would remain a dependent object.

In general, cultural expressions of both the dominant culture and the Latino culture tend to represent the patriarchal family in uncritical terms. Mainstream depictions rarely question the dynamics of power within the family. Furthermore, Chicanos/Latinos produce idealized renderings of the patriarchal family.[71] Norte's work is important because she does not romanticize the institution of the family. Norte's narratives construct the patriarchal family and Latina identity within the family as she experiences it. As in classic film noir, Norte represents the patriarchal family as a site where tension, constraint, and domination take place.

In "Shelf Life," not recorded on *NORTE/word,* Norte's female narrator returns to her childhood bedroom. She reflects on her past and realizes that familial constraints on her sexuality were predetermined by patriarchal power. She utilizes sarcasm to critique traditional practices, as when her father barred her in her bedroom "before I was even born / I did all my best slithering into my late twenties / For one more honey / at The Yee-Mee-Lou and The Koma Room."[72]

The image of the barred bedroom serves multiple functions. The barred home speaks to the dangers in the narrator's East Los Angeles Latino neighborhood. Practically speaking, the bars keep intruders out of the home.[73] Although the father did not intend to bar the family inside, the bars also entrap the inhabitants of the home. Barred inside the bedroom, the female body merely becomes another piece of protected property: It is objectified. But the bars serve a symbolic purpose, as well.

The bars represent the social restrictions placed on women. In a larger social context, the line "He put up the bars long before I was ever born" refers to the history of patriarchy and the social practices that restrict the bodies of women born into patriarchal cultures. It is not the father as individual who chooses to oppress his own daughter. Instead, his impulse to protect her is linked to networks of discourse that legitimate ideological bars against women. Catholic discourse, in the form of the Virgin Mother/Prostitute paradigm, prescribes that "legitimate" women be passive unassuming beings. Thus, "true" women should not attempt to move outside the sphere of their roles within the family.

Despite the restrictions placed on the narrator by the family, she subverts them. The bars do not always bar. For, as "slithering" indicates, the narrator manages to escape temporarily from the house undetected into a different type of bar: the bars located in Chinatown.[74] Norte creates a linguistic pun as the narrator literally moves between the bars at home and the Yee-Mee-Loo and Koma Room bars.[75] She finds refuge from family constraints in the bars. Outside the home, the narrator may be able to construct a different identity. Yet, within these public bars, the possibility always exists that she will encounter men who will sexually objectify her.

Transnational Subjects

Norte began publishing narratives that thematized the transnational borderlands in 1982. As a cultural worker based in East Los Angeles, Norte represents a border identity, and the heterotopic spaces it defines, in her spoken-word performances and compact disc and audiocassette releases. That is, like the installation artist Amalia Mesa-Bains, Norte constructs an imaginary space where she can represent "real sites" from a Chicana vantage point. Norte invokes and recontextualizes songs, prayers, one-liners, clichés, icons, and geographical locations, such as "the border" and Los Angeles, ingrained in the local popular imagination and the working conventions of noir. Provoking the audience's memory, Norte's narratives invite the audience into her cultural space, albeit temporarily, and she moves into theirs. Norte demonstrates that she shares an experience of popular culture founded on cultural hybridity that informs an emergent identity for herself and her audience. Though the imagined spaces Norte constructs in her narratives may not be concrete manipulations of physical space, they do function like "countersites." As "countersites," her narratives are a space where an alternative to the representation of Latina, in particular Chicana, identity maintained by U.S. mainstream culture can be imagined and articulated. While Foucault's notion of heterotopias as countersites is useful for describing the space Norte's spoken word constructs, her work problematizes Foucault's theory that heterotopias "are outside of all places, even though it may be possible to indicate their location in reality."[76] Norte's work illustrates that there are no spaces that are completely removed from their location in reality. Instead, even marginalized places are specifically located and immersed in the contradictions of social life.

It is in tying together spatiality with the history of social life that Edward Soja's writings are useful for understanding how the work of Norte represents cultural identity. Pointing to the lack of any discussion of spatiality in C. Wright Mill's mapping of a "sociological imagination" (that is, one in which individuals understand their social experience in relation to others in order to "search for a practical understanding of the world as a means of emancipation versus maintenance of the status quo"),[77] Soja writes, "[t]o be sure, these 'life-stories' have a geography too; they have milieu, immediate locales, provocative emplacements which effect thought and action."[78] The text's narrator—or, as Norte calls her, narratrix—who voices Norte's spoken-word narratives acts as a social critic who recognizes the importance of place and space in the construction of social being or identity.[79] She is always mindful of how social space or geography determines, in part but not completely, the lives lived by women in their communities. Norte's production of critical spoken word helps to construct a critical social space, or a countersite, in which her work makes a twofold critique of the confinements of social space and patriarchal practices.

Norte's narrative entitled "Se habla inglés" [English Is Spoken] exemplifies this twofold critique. "Se habla inglés" debunks myths about Latino/Anglo gender relations, romance, and marriage within the context of both *Mexicano* and U.S. patriarchal culture.[80] In the process of depicting the ways in which Latina women are objectified by both the Latino and the dominant cultures, "Se habla inglés" also depicts the ways in which Mexicanas dream about life in the United States. Norte's Angelina narrator visits Chihuahua, México, on the eve of her cousin's wedding. As the narrator sits with her cousins and aunts at the kitchen table making *"empanadas para los olvidados"* (this pun refers to Luis Buñuel's *Los Olvidados* [The Forgotten], a neorealist film about poverty in 1950s Mexico City) and other sweets for the wedding, her cousins ask her questions about the other side. Her cousins would like to believe the media misrepresentation of a Los Angeles filled with riches and swimming pools.[81]

Moving back and forth across the border through their memories, Norte's narrators often express the ways in which the Latino family objectifies women on the basis of their gender. "Se habla inglés" in particular reveals how the Anglo family objectifies Chicanas/Latinas based in terms of both their gender and ethnicity. The narrative situates the critique by contrasting the women's preparation of the *empanadas* (turnovers) for the cousin's wedding and the narrator's own engagement party, where there were "cold-cuts and Hula punch" and her fiancé's family "crowned" her "Miss Señorita Black Velvet Latina."[82]

Food is used as codes; the significance of the "cold-cuts" and "hula punch" is twofold. The narrator contrasts the *"empanadas"* with the "cold-cuts" to indicate that the boyfriend's working-class family is not Latino. The "cold-cuts" and "punch" convey the narrator's feelings of being put down and pushed out. By highlighting the fact that *"they crowned"* her "Miss Señorita Black Velvet Latina," the text illustrates how the advertising media often stereotype Latinas—Black Velvet Liquor uses seductive images of women of color to market its product—and how those images help determine how non-Latinos perceive Chicanas/Latinas.

After hearing the narrator's story of "real"-life failed romance, the cousins are not satisfied. They still want to know more. They beg the narrator to read in English from an outdated copy of *Cosmopolitan* magazine. As she reads to her cousins, she calls attention to the contradictions between the constructed, idealized *Cosmopolitan* version of romance and the disappointing reality of working-class Latina relationships. Norte's narrator debunks the myth of magazine romance, making fun of the idea of elaborate lovemaking when sex itself must be planned around her family's home life.[83] The final image of the piece demonstrates the ways in which women, along with men, maintain patriarchal practices. By the end of the story, the narrator's cousins assume that the narrator has stepped beyond traditional gender behaviors that mandate that women remain inexperienced.[84] The end of the poem illustrates the theme of constraint that runs throughout women's lives as they push against traditions.

The compact disk NORTE/word covers the geography of the extended borderlands, moving back and forth among Los Angeles, El Paso, and Mexico City, as well as moving across the geography of collective frustration and ecstasy. In addition to showing that different women share common ground in their struggle to survive in the face of economic hardship and gender discrimination, Norte's work illustrates that location in the borderlands shapes Chicana experiences.[85] For example, the urban spaces the narrator rides through in "Peeping Tom Tom Girl" are contrasted with the U.S.-Mexico border-crossing experience in "Act of the Faithless."

She Cleaned Up

Norte's construction of a space within the imaginary where she can represent "real sites," or places, from a Chicana vantage point is an important intervention. As "countersites," her narratives are a space where an alternative to the representation of Chicana and Latina identity maintained by U.S. mainstream culture can be imagined and articulated. The title, "Act of the Faithless," itself scrutinizes the institution of marriage, which ideally functions as an "Act of the Faithful." It also articulates one way in which geopolitical lines drawn between national and economic communities are negotiated by women who live and work across national borders:

> There was the work permit sealed in plastic, like the smile she flashed every morning / to the same uniformed eyes. She cleaned up, decorated her home with . . . souvenirs turistas left behind, Lone Star state of the art back scratchers, all the way from Taiwan.[86]

Considering that Norte herself travels across unfriendly urban terrains to reach her job, it is not surprising that many of Norte's narratives recognize and pay tribute to the lives of the women who must constantly travel across unfriendly terrains such as those of the U.S.-Mexico border to reach their places of employment. Though similar in this respect, Norte's urban experience is significantly different from the woman's border experience: Norte does not have to flash documentation "sealed in plastic" to travel to and from work.

Employed as a domestic worker who crosses the U.S.-Mexico border, the woman in the text, who, we find later, is the narrator's aunt, crosses the borderlands every day to get to her place of employment. For people such as the narrator's aunt who must travel across national borders every day, this borderland space, among other things, is a threatening social space. The aunt can cross the U.S.-Mexico border because she possesses the required documents, "the work permit sealed in plastic . . . she flashed every morning / to the same uniformed eyes." But, for those left without documentation, the national borders are a site of exclusion and many times death.

"Act of the Faithless" represents the ways private spaces are affected by public spaces. Using the past tense, the niece describes what her aunt did on the U.S. side of the border: "She cleaned up," literally and figuratively, by performing her job at the Holiday Inn and by cleaning up after her husband in their home in the Ciudad Juárez; at the same time, the narrator uses the figurative expression "she cleaned up" to make an ironic comment about the goods she collected. With the discarded objects the tourists have left behind at the Holiday Inn, the narrator's aunt practices a form of Chicana *rasquache*. Norte's description of the aunt's home illustrates what Jennifer González describes as "the practice of '*domesticana.*'"[87] In this narrative, the objects the aunt gathers and arranges are not, as González explains, merely a "collection of things" but are rather a symbolic representation of a life lived on the other side of the U.S.-Mexico border. The aunt situates the discarded objects in a new context —her home—in which they signify differently. No longer forgotten objects, the souvenirs become concrete representations of her life—her relation to other people and other places.

The objects the aunt collects, like the "Lone Star state of the art back scratchers all the way from Taiwan," are themselves culturally hybrid, given that they are manufactured in Taiwan and sold to tourists as authentic Texan artifacts. These souvenirs, like the people who are paid to make them, play their part in a late-twentieth-century international tourist economy. These objects, like the aunt, cross national borders according to the demands of the tourist market. The identity the aunt constructs with these objects is determined, in part, by the market, which brings those "Lone Star state of the art back scratchers all the way from Taiwan" to the El Paso/Ciudad Juárez border.

By chronicling the experiences of her aunt, and of many women who must cross the border daily to earn wages, Norte's text critiques the constructions of space that privilege patriarchal practices. Though "uninformed eyes" fail to see the complexity of the aunt's identity, she is more than a "smile" with a work permit. On the Mexican side of the border, she constructs different identities for herself—one of which is that of wife. Juxtaposing the image of the aunt who works as a maid on the U.S. side with the image of her as devoted Mexican wife, Norte demonstrates how this woman must negotiate different systems of patriarchal practice. If on the U.S. side she is seen only as labor for the *turistas,* she also must serve her husband, who leaves his laundry waiting for her. Though she may not be "othered" by her citizen status in Mexico, she is discriminated against because of her gender.

Besides articulating a narrative about a woman's experience on the U.S.-Mexico border, "Act of the Faithless" also critiques the double standard that women are subjected to in traditional Latino culture. As a child, the narrator had romanticized both the marriage of her aunt and uncle and matrimony in general. But the narrative goes on to explain how her aunt and uncle's marriage was anything but ideal. Years later, after his death, the narrator realizes the uncle was a womanizer, and she reflects on his life, wondering if he regretted and appreciated that his wife took care of him, despite his infidelities.[88]

After the narrator realizes the marital situation her aunt had to negotiate, knowing that her aunt was required to prepare food and wash clothes for her unfaithful husband, she takes on a different view of marriage. She recognizes how relations between men and women in traditional patriarchal cultures favor the subordination of women and how patriarchal ideology supports and reproduces that inequality. Despite the fact that her marriage did not correspond to the romanticized images of matrimony found in women's magazines and romance novels, the aunt endures. While watching her aunt clean at the Holiday Inn, the niece listens to the advice she offers. Handing the niece a pair of women's sunglasses she had found in her husband's jacket, the aunt tells her to take care of her eyes because there is "too much you should see." The aunt's advice is double edged; she seems to be both warning her young niece to be aware of possibly harmful situations and giving her hope that there is something worth looking forward to. Leaving unspoken exactly what the aunt herself sees and what the niece "should see," the exchange is interrupted by a lounging Holiday Inn tourist. Displaying a complete lack of cultural respect, the tourist yells for her to come over, calling her "María" and "*Señorita,*" American accent and all. The narrative articulates the anger, humiliation, and defiance the niece and her aunt share, as the aunt quietly swears at the tourist in Spanish.[89]

This concluding segment of "Act of the Faithless" critiques the narrowness of the dominant culture's vision of Latinas. The aunt knows that the tourist with "uninformed eyes" mistakes her for a servant. Though María is not her name, he sees her as he probably sees most Latinas—as part of a homogeneous and indistinguishable group. And though the aunt's defiant gesture of muffled swearing (she cannot swear at him aloud because if she does, she will jeopardize her job) may not be considered radical, it does demonstrate her self-pride and self-knowledge, and her dissatisfaction with the status quo. However, the narrative ends more realistically than idealistically: The tourist remains ignorant of his offensive, racist, and classist actions, demonstrating that there may be too much "to see." Also, the aunt, who is restricted by her own cultural system, fails to tell the niece not to idealize the institution of marriage. It is rather through her acute observations that the narrator arrives at this conclusion. Thus, Norte's narrative does not characterize women as victims but instead critiques the cultural restrictions they constantly negotiate.

Estoy *Destroyed*

Different formations of patriarchy operate in different cultures across the globe and within U.S. contemporary culture. In addition to the critique of patriarchal power relations as figured in representations of the Chicano family, Norte's work offers an analysis of the dominant culture's own legitimation of patriarchal privilege. "Three Little Words," Norte's narrative about childhood summers at the movies, demonstrates the specific ways that patriarchal practices of the dominant culture converge on the bodies of Chicanas and others. To make visible these practices, Norte incorporates samples from mass culture into her narratives. Like rap artists, Norte strategically appropriates "the tools used against [her] to inject [herself] into the venues from which [she has] been excluded."[90] Those "tools" include images found in mass popular culture, such as Mexican and American television, movies, music, magazines, and newspapers. Although mass culture tends to misrepresent women and people of color, Norte self-consciously ironizes, inverts, and subverts popular culture stories by sampling them in a new hybrid reflective of her multiply inflected subjectivity. Her dialogue with mass culture brings to the forefront her situatedness as a gendered subject, citizen, and member of an aggrieved ethnic group.

Using images from mass culture allows Norte to critique sexist practices as they manifest themselves in U.S. popular culture. Her text suggests that these practices constantly work against women's attempt to construct themselves as subjects and to construct their identity outside limited gender roles. "Three Little Words" highlights the objectification of women by defamiliarizing the image of mutilated and dismembered female bodies found in popular movies. Norte's work situates the image of violence against women in a new context in order to combat the ease with which representations of violence against women are consumed, asking the audience instead to question the representations of violence against women.

"Three Little Words" sounds like the title of the well-know children's story "Three Little Pigs." In what follows, however, Norte's narrator describes a story no child should have to see. In "Three Little Words," Norte suggests that popular culture, through horror films, "normalizes" the image of a bloody, dismembered female body. During one horror film she saw as a child, a

> gigantic horse's tongue . . . was extracted from the pink lipped mouth of another buxom blonde, and there is a picture of her laying across a fuzzy white bedspread in a Florida motel room, and there is blood everywhere . . . this is the image that falls under childhood memory, it is not the smell of grandmother's tamales cooking on a wooden stove.[91]

In other words, Norte's text defamiliarizes the representation of violence against women by situating the image in a familial context. Elsewhere the image of the grandmother sleeping through the horror film is at once funny and frightening. Although the audience can never know the cause of the grandmother's slumber, what speaks in this image is the grandmother's inability to protect the cousins from the grotesque images. In "Three Little Words," Norte constructs images that represent Latino childhood in a U.S. urban context. What the narrator remembers are not clichéd images of "grandmother's tamales cooking on a wooden stove." Instead, she remembers the grandmother who took her and her cousins to see the "gigantic horse's tongue, that was extracted from the pink lipped mouth of another buxom blonde." Although mainstream expressions tend to represent childhood in idyllic terms, Norte, like the writers Ana Castillo, Luis Alfaro, and Sandra Cisneros, represents "lived" experiences that have remained unrepresented in mainstream culture. Equally as important, this image of childhood memories expresses the ways in which the articulation of female sexual identity is associated with violence in patriarchal cultures. By shifting the point of view to that of a young Latina, the image also illustrates that it is not the traditional Latino patriarchal culture alone that objectifies women; Norte's text demonstrates that the dominant culture also violently objectifies women.

Norte Noir: Norte American Style

Norte customizes the modernist codes and themes of postwar film noir, whose core consists of "issues lurking behind proletarian literature—city life, the organization of work, social mobility, cross-class desire."[92] As in noir filmic narratives, Norte's critique of domesticity and her rejection of marriage as the only path to self-fulfillment for women and men are the motivating force of her writing. In addition, Norte's postmodern noir sensibility maintains the major urban location but shifts it to East Los Angeles and Latino downtown L.A. Norte's deliberate and unique focus on Mexican and Mexican American women through noir codes highlights the assumptions of binary contrasts of whiteness and blackness in classic Hollywood noir film. In classic American noir cinema, the racial imagination prohibits Mexican or Latina women from embodying the figure of femme fatale. Noir, Norte Americana style, takes off where classic Hollywood noir ends and shifts focus to the Latina whose labor helps to keep the city running.

Though noir sensibility experienced a general resurgence in the popular culture of the 1980s, what makes Norte's version powerful and worthy of analysis is that Norte's femme fatale's rejection of domesticity is not simply the rejection of the traditional homemaker role of wife and mother but the rejection of racialized assumptions around domestic labor and class privilege. It is the rejection of the general public's automatic association of Mexican American, Mexican, and Latina women as domestic workers, the position of maid or nanny as the only role she is worthy of. Numerous Chicana artists have created new figurations of Chicana identity, using the figure of the "maid" in radical ways.[93] Yet the equation of Chicana with domestic labor still persists. Even the internationally known East Los Angeles artist Patssi Valdez recounts the way her high school home economics teacher told her "to pay real good attention since she was going to end up cooking and cleaning in someone's house. . . . I thought she was nuts."[94] Such counseling implies that public education is wasted on these young women since their role has been predetermined. This logic is a catch-22. With limited educational opportunities, Latinas' employment options become very limited. Rarely is the larger social context that keeps these girls in their place represented. This representation has become so engrained in the racial imagination that a high-profile Latina actress like Jennifer Lopez, in her film *Maid in America,* can reproduce this social order, albeit in a fairy-tale representation of domestic workers in the tourism industry, with little or no protest. And though there is a scene in the film in which a Latina housekeeper reveals a wealthy white woman's racialized and classist assumptions that Latina housekeepers cannot speak English, Norte's spoken word sustains critiques of power relations throughout her narratives.

Paula Rabinowitz argues that in classic noir film, the "black maid's domesticity facilitates a white woman's business . . . the maid participates in the maintenance of middle-class white family economic order, helping to support it when there is no man around . . . the black maid, like the detective or the femme fatale, by occupation slides between two worlds."[95] Though Norte's femme fatale narrators slip between worlds, crossing international lines, their independence is not necessarily predicated on another woman of color's domestic labor. In fact, Norte's femme fatale figures are working-class waitresses or office clerks who must ride the bus to work. The domestic help Norte's narrators encounter are family and friends. The murderous trap integral to any noir narrative is one that Norte's narrative is trying to step out of, the trap set by underfunded schools, limited employment options, and violent understandings of romance. Norte's femme fatale is trying to do away with those conditions, with romance's association with violence against women.

It is important to note that Norte's narrator's voice and style always mark her as not-the-maid. Yet, her representation of working-class women is not dismissive; instead, it is empathetic. For instance, as she addresses the conditions of the domestic worker in "Act of the Faithless," Norte creates a critique of the social hierarchy that limits the options of these women.

By intervening in noir codes and putting women of East Los Angeles and the extended borderlands at the center of the narrative, Norte invents a strategy not unlike that imagined by Gwendolyn Brooks and Anne Petry forty years earlier in *Maude Martha* (1953) and *The Street* (1947). These black women writers, through noir codes, focused on "the difficulties black women faced in supporting themselves and their families, analyzing the racial and sexual dynamics of black domestic workers in white women's households."[96] Norte's writing functions similarly for Chicana workers. While the figures of black women function to buttress privileged white women in Hollywood noir, Mexican American women do not register, even in narratives that take place in Los Angeles. By making working- and lower-middle-class Chicanas the center of the action, Norte creates settings parallel to Brooks's and Petry's effort to place black women at the center of action of noir narrative. Just as Books and Petry shifted the urban setting to Chicago's south side and New York's Harlem, Norte writes about Chicana domestic workers located in the tourist industry on the border and in East Los Angeles.

If, as Rabinowitz argues, the Brooks and Petry novels "pushed the discussion beyond analyzing one's own housework as a 'double burden' for the working woman employed outside the home to consider what it meant to maintain two homes—one's own and another's of a different class, race, and neighborhood," then Norte's postmodern noir narrative pushes the debate one step further by demonstrating that border-region domestic workers' double burden intersects with burdens of border crossing and questions of citizenship and nation.[97]

If Brooks's and Petry's writing reveals why "the black femme fatale cannot be visualized in racist America," then Norte's noir reveals how Chicanas and Latinas are frequently visualized as domestic labor, but rarely as the femme fatale.[98]

Exito

Though the codes of noir film narrative are woven throughout Norte's spoken work, Norte's first published play, *Exito* [Success], explicitly follows the noir detective formula. As in classic noir, "the struggle is between two different voices telling the story."[99] *Exito*'s two-person narrative is structured as a tug of war between two voices, those of the dead writer, "La Escritora," and "El Detective," that are vying to explain the death of a woman writer. And, as in classic film noir, Norte's protagonist is a "strong woman in an image producing role," and, like the narrative of *Sunset Strip*, it is framed by the already deceased wisecracking protagonist.[100] El Detective, who is convinced that romance led her to kill herself, questions the dead woman, who insists her death was an accident.

Marisela Norte and Daniel Villarreal in *Exito*. Photograph by Juan Garza. Photo appeared in *Spectacle: A Field Journal From Los Angeles* (1984). (Reprinted with permission.)

Waiting for her stove to heat to the perfect temperature, "I got bored and lit a cigarette . . . and boom." Filled with Norte's sarcastic humor, it is a critique of the underappreciation of living women writers: "no one was the least bit interested . . . but now that I'm dead a couple of hours . . . Interested?"[101] Norte's early experiment with classic noir codes is just one of the ways she launches a critique of the limited options of women of color.

In addition to noir, cult thrillers have influenced Norte's narrative sensibility. The title of Norte's "Peeping Tom Tom Girl" is an allusion to the British cult film Pee*ping Tom*. In glorious Technicolor, *Peeping Tom* depicts a mild-mannered psychopathic killer who films the murders of women with his camera/knife contraption. The film turns on issues of voyeuristic activity; the twist to the story is that the killer has attached a mirror to the camera that faces his victims, who usually happen to be women of the streets, so they watch themselves being killed. What the killer enjoys is not the killing itself but the cinematic viewing of the fear and horror that overcome the women as they watch themselves being killed. Norte's narratives shed light on the fears, horrors, and dangers that everyday women face. Norte's writing functions as a mirror, reflecting the dangers that are difficult to face. Norte's writing shows us what to be afraid of and plays the role of the voyeur, as do her listeners, in order to, as George Lipsitz put so aptly, "face up to what is killing us."[102]

Conclusion

Ultimately, Norte's narratives attempt to make way for new ways of "becoming" a gendered, racialized, and classed subject. In a recent spoken-word narrative called "Untitled," written specifically for the 1995 live performance *Diva L.A.: A Salute to L.A.'s Latinas in the Tanda Style,* Norte's narrator enumerates a series of stereotypical labels used to define Chicanas/Latinas, then turns the list upon its head by boldly (un)defining them.[103] She asserts:

> For the record
> I am not
> Woman Mujer of power poder
> cactus flower eating
> Goddess of whatever?
> No[104]

The narrative then continues to resist the stereotypical labeling of Chicanas/Latinas by telling several stories to represent the diverse experiences of these women. Norte's narrative opens up a space within the imaginary to create new images of Chicanas/Latinas and new ways of being Chicana/Latina.

Although Norte's narratives do not circulate in the mainstream media, the grass-roots nature of their distribution allows them to reach a wide variety of people who do not have easy access to feminist discourse. Producing spoken-word narratives, which are performed and heard at coffee houses, high schools, community centers, performance spaces, and universities, and in the homes of listeners in their CD/cassette form, transforms the social space in which Norte moves and momentarily produces a discourse that unfixes, displaces, and refigures images of Chicanas, Los

Angeles, and the border. Norte's narratives offer not only a new vision of cultural identities, mapped across local and global economies and cultural practices, but also the power and imagination to redefine these "geographies." They change space by making new spaces—in the world and in the imagination—where oppressive social practices based on structures of racism, sexism, and nationalism can be exposed, critiqued, and transformed.

The analysis of Marisela Norte's spoken word helps make clear the role of culture in the struggle to acquire, to maintain, or to resist power. When Norte reconstructs the images of Chicanas, she is struggling for the power to define herself and her own interests, interests that often go against exploitative and unjust formation of places, institutions, and practices. Her narrators are "Revlon revolutionaries," and as a cultural worker Norte hopes to mobilize immobile women by utilizing strategies of humor and irony to pose difficult questions. It is not that critique in and of itself brings change. However, critique opens up a space for imagining a way of life based on social equality, a place where all women have access to health care, education, and safe jobs. In other words, it opens a space where new political projects may be imagined and can emerge—one that might construct a place where no one, especially women and children of color and undocumented workers, will bear the burden of poor health care policies, poor education, and poor living conditions. While the production of spoken word may not be considered a traditional mode of political action, and is only one place of many to engage in cultural politics, Norte's work, as does all cultural production, "plays a constitutive, not merely a reflective role" in the culture of everyday life.[105] In other words, representations of life constructed in forms like literature, popular music, and spoken word do not merely reflect what everyday life is but work to imagine and construct what it could be in the future. Because Norte articulates a multifold critique of the ways patriarchal institutions attempt to impose a cultural and gendered identity upon working-class Latina bodies, she produces a countermeaning about Latina identity and subjectivity, one that constructs women as active subjects ready to critique relations of power instead of as passive, accepting objects.

Unfortunately for the field of performance study, few have critically engaged with the provocative form and context of Norte's writing. Critical engagement with her writing can help readers understand the nature of the transformation that writing, literary studies, and performance studies have undergone at the *fin de siglo.*

3

The Politics of Representation

Queerness and the Transnational Family in Luis Alfaro's Performance

I am an activist who became an artist. . . . I have always felt that art picked me to use my work to create social change.
                    —Luis Alfaro, *Out of the Fringe*

When we tell our stories we are not just entertaining, we are empowering. I can't begin to tell you how many Latinos or queers have come up to me after a show and said, "I had never seen myself on a stage before." This type of work derives its political implication, not because we preach, but because we expose or act as voices for a community that was once invisible. Who do I want to connect to? The people that can hear those stories and see a piece of themselves in them.
                    —Luis Alfaro, personal communication with author, July 1992

The Chicano community is *familia.* . . . There's this very protective thing around it: you can't see it, but it's there. When you break the mold—by being gay and brown and Catholic—it makes people uneasy.   —Luis Alfaro, *Los Angeles Times,* July 21, 1991

Marisela Norte was not the only performer in black garments and red lipstick to transfix the audience in the Michel De Certeau Room that autumn night in 1991 with her downtown glamour. Luis Alfaro, another of the guest performers at the "Speaking Experiences" event that also featured Norte and Chicano Secret Service, electrified the crowd with his stories of life on the edge of downtown Los Angeles, in "the shadow of the Hollywood sign." Alfaro powerfully moved the crowd with his tales of

Luis Alfaro and Marisela Norte at Union Station, San Diego (1992), after a performance at the University of California at San Diego. Photograph by Michelle Habell-Pallán. (Reprinted with permission.)

fall and redemption, his desire for inclusion in the Latino community despite his Queer sexuality. He was one of the first male solo performers to claim a Chicano, Queer, and Catholic subjectivity—using his body as a prop, as a vehicle for expression, Luis performed sections from his solo performance "Pico-Union." Each of Alfaro's poetic gestures—a slap, a shove, a kiss, a flex of his forearm—transported us from the seminar room at the tony La Jolla campus into downtown Los Angeles's bustling immigrant streets, his family's Pico-Union district home, West Hollywood Queer clubs, the bowels of downtown Los Angeles's Federal Building, and his heart. This was six years before Alfaro won a MacArthur "Genius" award for his stunning solo performance art that almost ecclesiastically captured the pathos and hope of downtown L.A. and its Chicana, as well as Central American and Mexican immigrant, residents.

I had actually met Alfaro just a few weeks earlier after his performance of "Pico-Union" at the Los Angeles Theater Center. "Pico-Union" was part of a solo performance event called *True Lies,* which featured Chloe Webb (who played the infamous punk diva Nancy Spungen in Alex Cox's film *Sid and Nancy)* and Rocco Sisto. Mesmerized by Luis's performance,

I did not want it to conclude. It was the first time I had seen any artist capture the spirit of a post-1980s, postpunk, urban Chicana and Chicano experience. It wasn't necessarily Alfaro's Queer take on Chicano culture that drew me in; it was the style in which he represented the intersections of popular culture, spirituality, class, and Chicano life in Los Angeles. Alfaro articulated a critique of racism, a critique of homophobia, a critique of sexism, a critique of forces of impoverishment, with a punk-inflected sense of raw, stripped-down emotion, with a voice very familiar to me, a voice with a rhythm, pace, and lilt that marked him as a child of Los Angeles. What was so moving about Alfaro was his defiance and his hope, his unending search for communion and healing in a "city of hurt, a city of pain."[1]

Flash-forward to the present. Alfaro is one of the best-known and most highly esteemed Chicano solo performers, playwrights, and directors of his generation, as well as one of the most influential person-of-color arts administrators in the nation. He is currently the director of New Play Development for the Mark Taper Forum and Ivy Substation. Granted the prestigious MacArthur Foundation award in 1997, Alfaro has developed his craft at an impressive rate. Equally important, Alfaro has been extremely generous with his influence, constantly promoting and helping to develop the solo performances, plays, and writings of countless artists of color and at-risk youth.

The 1991 event at UCSD was one of the first times that Norte and Alfaro performed together, but it was the beginning of numerous collaborative projects. Norte would eventually co-produce Alfaro's compact disk *Downtown* on New Alliance Records, the label of her own CD. Their most recent collaboration, *Black Butterfly, Jaguar Girl, Piñata Women and Other Superhero Girls Like Me,* received an Ovation nomination and was performed at the Kennedy Center in 2000. This collaboration demonstrates the ways that these artists not only share a similar thematic sensibility but also constitute a community of artists who help and, at times, advance each other's work. Alfaro also helped develop Marga Gomez's piece *A Line Around the Block.* This production is discussed in chapter 4.

Alfaro once wrote,

I believe that alchemy in writing is achieved when we marry passion with craft. I believe that committing a pen to paper to speak truth is a sacred and political act. The most original and creative writers I know are the ones who listen to the unique words, rhythms, and emotions closest to them. A successful literary work of art that bursts on a page is written by a word artist who has an intimate relationship with language and people. I propose that the beginning of the literary journey starts with the memory of self and moves out into the world.[2]

Because Alfaro's career demonstrates so well that successful art making starts with the memory of self and then moves into the world, and because no single book chapter could do justice to his numerous performances, productions, and, writings, the following pages focus on the moment in Alfaro's career just before he became so widely acclaimed. Specifically, the following discussion examines Alfaro's "memory of self" as contained in his 1993 spoken-word compact disk *Downtown*. This compact disk propelled him metaphorically into new worlds and literally into the *Terreno Peligroso/Danger Zone*, a Mexico City/Los Angeles artist exchange. This stage in his career occurred in an era when "multicultural" or "minority" art and cultural production were finally admitted into the institutional arts world, particularly outside Manhattan, as never before. The early 1990s were also a time when multicultural politics was finally being debated seriously within artistic and academic worlds. All of these factors play an important role in the analysis that follows.

Luis Alfaro's innovative artistic vision and brilliant writing and performance art challenges his audiences to think about the process of gendering and racializing identity in the United States, while simultaneously daring them to come together for positive social transformation.

Alfaro's location within two marginalized communities shapes his cultural politics and bleeds into his theatrical representation of the Latino gay male experience. As both a Latino and a gay man living in twenty-first-century Los Angeles, Alfaro creates work that pushes against multiple oppressions that censor discussions about his identity in both communities. Alfaro's struggle for visibility takes place in several arenas.

The intersection of performance and social activism has always been a part of Luis Alfaro's family history. Some time in the late 1950s, as part of a group of farm laborers that would eventually organize as the United Farm Workers Association, the Mexican American woman who would become Alfaro's mother and her sister attended a demonstration in Los Angeles. On the return trip to their home in Delano, California, the two women stopped by a Mexican restaurant located in East Los Angeles. Alfaro's mother met the recently immigrated Mexican man who would become Alfaro's father at that restaurant, where he was employed as a singer. The couple soon married, and Luis was born to them in 1961 at Los Angeles County General Hospital. Alfaro and his two siblings grew up with his family in South Central Los Angeles, and both of his parents remained active community workers throughout his childhood. His parents volunteered for the Catholic Worker, a Catholic left-wing organization, and one of his earliest memories of social activism is of an event that occurred in 1971, when he and his family were cited by authorities as they protested nuclear testing in Nevada. In March 1990, after authorities arrested Alfaro for participating in an "artist chain gang protest regarding censorship issues relating to the National Endowment for the Arts"[3] at the Federal Building in downtown Los Angeles, his family bailed him out of jail.[4]

However supportive of Alfaro and his work his family is now, his family life has not been without tension. As a teenager, Alfaro, estranged from his family, left Wilson High School in El Sereno, just east of Los Angeles, and ran away to live on the streets of the Echo Park district of L.A. Alfaro's life was transformed after he participated in a job program funded by the federal government for at-risk youth. He "was paid $100 every two weeks to attend dance and theatre class at the Inner City Cultural Center."[5] Given this complicated history, it is no shock to find that many of Alfaro's narratives thematize family tensions and attempted reconciliation.

Alfaro, as part of a generation that grew up with punk aesthetics, channeled that sensibility's energy and critique of power relations into heart-wrenching, yet hopeful tales. The simplicity of the solo performance form that he favored, and its sense of risk, have a definite connection to Alfaro's punk sensibility.

Alfaro developed his love for ritual and performance by faithfully attending Catholic mass as a child. The influence of spiritual life and faith are evident in his work. In Alfaro's work, faith is not ironic; it is through trials and tribulations that his immigrant and working-class characters transform their pain. Alfaro's own story is one of fall and redemption. He started out as an usher at the Mark Taper Forum, lost his way through substance abuse, and, twenty-five years and many innovative performances later, became Director of New Play Development for the same venue.

Alfaro's writing came to light in a context that was formed by the struggles of Latina lesbian writers in the 1980s. As his work gained prominence in the 1990s, Alfaro joined artists such as Cherríe Moraga and Guillermo Gomez-Peña in expanding the themes of Chicana and Chicano theater by addressing the social crises and struggles of their historical moment, such as AIDS, the North American Free Trade Agreement, the Gulf War, and the war on terrorism.

During the late 1960s and early 1970s, the Chicano movement organized a political struggle that addressed issues such as the withdrawal of U.S. troops from Vietnam, the United Farm Workers' labor battles against agribusiness, student demands for quality public education, and U.S. restrictive immigration policy.[6] At this time of intense community mobilization, the Chicano theater movement developed "as an arm of the Chicano movement to resist cultural and economic domination."[7] According to Yvonne Yarbro-Bejarano, the initial goals of Chicano oppositional theater "were those of the cultural project of the Movement as a whole: to create an alternative to the dominant mode of production of mainstream theater, to make theater accessible to a working-class Chicano culture, and to create accurate theatrical representations of Chicanos' historical and social experience."[8]

Yarbro-Bejarano writes about the ways that cultural identity and gender have been represented in the Chicano oppositional theater movement and the Chicano movement in general.[9] She demonstrates that critiques of power relations within the structure of the patriarchal family, of the subordination of women's sexuality, and of enforced heterosexuality did not fit into the paradigm of a cultural nationalist struggle, a struggle that symbolized its opposition to Anglo-American culture by using the image of the traditional patriarchal family structure. She explains:

> No homogeneous ideological platform unified the Chicano movement. . . . While some activists, writers, and theater groups called for a materialist analysis of the economic exploitation of Chicanos as a class, the main tendency was that of cultural nationalism. Cultural nationalism located the oppositional relationship between Chicanos and the dominant society in the cultural arena rather than in class identity. Chicano culture as a whole was exalted in opposition to Anglo-American culture, which was perceived as materialistic and impersonal. Such an emphasis was important in creating a sense of cultural pride to counter the years of lived experience in a society permeated with degrading stereotypes of Mexicans. On the other hand, it led to a static view of culture, including the uncritical affirmation of the family and gender roles.[10]

Chicano oppositional theater was a place where Chicano culture was affirmed and a place where "degrading stereotypes of Mexicans" and Chicanos were challenged. But since cultural nationalism assumed a heterosexual male subject, and since groups like Teatro Campesino were informed by cultural nationalism, Chicano oppositional theater also tended to assume a heterosexual male subject.

According to the theater scholar David Román, the representational system that encoded Chicano theater did in fact privilege heterosexual men.[11] Román further explains how the privileging of a heterosexual subject worked hand-in-hand with cultural nationalism to exclude female and queer subjects: "If, on the one hand, cultural nationalism fosters a sense of cultural pride, it also conflates all Chicano experience into a unified Chicano subject."[12]

Because the Chicano movement, like the majority of decolonizing projects, assumed a heterosexual male as the ideal subject, as did Chicano theater, it focused its energies on contesting racist and unfair economic practices of the dominant culture, practices that affected both Chicanos and Chicanas, to the exclusion of critiques of sexist and homophobic practices. Consequently, the struggle to resist and change practices that marginalized Chicano communities economically and culturally took priority over the articulation of critiques of sexual domination, as well as over the discussion of the dynamics of the sexual politics that operated within both the movement and U.S. culture.[13]

However, beginning in the late 1970s, and especially by the 1980s and 1990s, much of the intellectual work produced by heterosexual and lesbian Chicana scholars and writers such as Yvonne Yarbro-Bejarano, Cherríe Moraga, and Elizabeth Martínez openly criticized both nationalist conceptions of identity and asymmetrical gender relations that constituted the organization of the movement, critiques in which feminist and lesbian/gay concerns were clearly articulated.[14] Writers such as Cherríe Moraga and Luis Alfaro use theater to articulate these concerns. Their work demonstrates that Chicano oppositional theater "shift(ed) representation of the subject" from male to both female and Queer perspectives.[15]

Only in relation to these histories of Chicano theater and of gender relation critiques can we understand how the work of Luis Alfaro, playwright and performer, illuminates and critiques continuing racist, sexist, classist, and homophobic practices. The images in Alfaro's performance work against the grain of a cultural nationalism whose central paradigm of "the Chingón/chingada . . . locks women into subordinate roles, inscribes inflexible definitions of masculinity and femininity, and on a larger scale becomes the surveillance test of true nationalism."[16]

To understand better why the theme and form of Alfaro's work differ from those of early Chicano oppositional theater, the conditions from which that theater emerged must be examined.[17] Jorge Huerta explains that it "took a particular cause (the striking farm workers), a special atmosphere (the Civil Rights Movement), and a growing political consciousness (the Chicano Movement) to give rise to a theatrical movement that continues to evolve."[18] Moreover, more recent Chicano/Latino oppositional theater and performance "can be best understood as participating in a longer history of Latino theater practices originating as early as the 1840s."[19]

Despite and against a persistent sexism and homophobia that continues to pervade almost all of Chicano and U.S. culture, Chicana performers use theater as a site to articulate both heterosexual women's and lesbians' experiences.[20] Yarbro-Bejarano explains how "Chicanas working within the Chicano theater movement attempted to counter male domination in their representation as well as in the material conditions of theater production" by establishing a women's caucus called W.I.T. (Women in Teatro).[21] W.I.T. "has provided a much-needed communication network and support basis for Chicanas in theater organizations."[22] Chicanas also formed "all-women teatros."[23] In the early 1980s, newly formed all-Chicana groups "focused on the Chicana subject in relation to sexuality, 'race,' and class."[24]

In contrast to the networks created by Chicanas to support Chicana work, no specific network or *teatro* was formed by or for gay Chicano men to support each others' work. In the absence of such a network, writings by or about Chicano gay men were few. In his analysis of the gay male experience in the 1980s and early 1990s, Tomás Almaguer finds that, unlike "the rich literature on the Chicana/Latina lesbian experience, there is a paucity of writings on Chicano gay men . . . [t]he extant literature consists primarily of semi-autobiographical, literary texts by authors such as John Rechy, Arturo Islas, and Richard Rodríguez."[25]

Almaguer's discussion implicitly attributes the paucity of gay male writings to the larger homophobic practices of the Chicano community. Failing to locate specific representations of Chicano/Latino gay male sexuality, Almaguer turned to the writings of Chicana lesbians who thematize the issue of sexuality to examine the dynamics of family sexual politics and to theorize about gay Chicano identity. However, if Almaguer were to begin his study now, he would find that "in the field of Chicana/o cultural production, gay men have recently begun creating a public voice and presence." Alfaro is part of this wave.[26]

Although Alfaro's work is absent from Almaguer's analysis, it could have been a valuable resource for his project. At the time, Alfaro co-directed VIVA!, "a gay and lesbian arts organization founded in 1988 that serves both as a support network for local Latino/a artists (based in Los Angeles) and a coalition advocating for Latino/a gay, lesbian and AIDS visibility."[27] Alfaro's work was and is one of the few places where gay male sexuality is written about or performed in terms of the family— all the more important considering Almaguer's discussion of the lack of Chicano gay male representation. Alfaro's work, including his short solo performance pieces "Pico-Union" and "Deseo es Memoria,"[28] contributed to a growing body of work that thematizes alternative male sexual identities and discusses "directly the cultural dissonance that Chicano homosexual men confront in reconciling their primary socialization into Chicano family life with the sexual norms of the dominant culture."[29]

Transgressing Chicano

As a young, Los Angeles–based, working-class performance artist, playwright, and social activist in the early 1990s whose work took issue with the ways that gender, class, race, and sexuality converge, Luis Alfaro insisted on claiming and incorporating Chicano culture into his projects. This insistence was a politically necessary transgression given the unquestioned homophobia reproduced in ethnic communities. His performance work also claims and incorporates gay subculture and demonstrates that the gay community is racially and ethnically heterogeneous. Moreover, Alfaro's spoken-word compact disk *Downtown* critiques and reimagines the construction of the traditional Latino/Chicano patriarchal family. He does this both by insisting on the inclusion of gay subjects and by demonstrating the link between his experiences of exclusion and silencing and the comparable (yet different) experiences of Latinas.[30] At the same time, his representation of gay male experience helps to make visible what Angie Chabram-Dernersesian, in her discussion of the construction of Chicano(a) subjects, appropriately names a "new subject for political identity" and identification.[31] His performance also functions as a critique of narrow cultural nationalist ideology, as well as of the dominant culture's racist ideology.

Alfaro's performance pieces help to invent a new Chicano(a) subject whose identity is not necessarily based on the ideology of static Chicano cultural nationalism, which posits an essential Chicano subject (always heterosexual), but instead is based on a subtle understanding of how cultural identity and identification is in constant flux. This new Chicano(a) subject is rooted in Chicano culture, but, unlike cultural nationalists, it is also committed to the politics of antihomophobia and antisexism. He or she resists and changes dominant inscriptions of ethnic identity and dominant structuring of social relations.

Alfaro's cultural work in the early 1990s is compelling because of the way his critique of the status quo circulates in live performance, compact disk, and written forms.[32] By performing in mainstream theaters like the Mark Taper Forum, and in alternative performance spaces like *centros culturales* in California and Texas, or Highways and Self-help Graphics in Los Angeles, as well as performing at Lollapalooza, Alfaro reaches wide audiences, both Latino and non-Latino, as well as gay/lesbian and heterosexual audiences.[33]

Alfaro's bittersweet solo performance pieces that thematize family tensions, sexuality, and Catholicism require minimal props, making it easy for him to travel to these very different performance sites. Depending on the space available, Alfaro strips down or beefs up his performance. His costume consists of a set of inexpensive clothes and some makeup—flannel shirt, black tee shirt, black knee-length shorts, a black chiffon dress, and bright red lipstick. While the tee-shirt-and-shorts ensemble suggests a working-class position, the dress and the lipstick signify, in part, his sexual orientation. Alfaro's cross-dressing also problematizes constructions of gender. He lays bare his gay subjectivity for the audience: He is "out."

In the spirit of Chicano *teatro* produced in the 1960s, Alfaro's production technology is simple. In performance spaces that contain the appropriate technology, Alfaro uses video projections, lighting cues, and audio production to augment his performance, which otherwise unfolds on a bare stage.

Alfaro's richly layered performance is a hybrid of popular songs, prayers, one-liners, clichés, cultural icons, and symbols. He knits these elements together to tell stories that he continually punctuates with well-choreographed, exaggerated, and sometimes violent movements—a slap, a hug, an aching heartbeat, hands fiercely flying at a sewing machine in a downtown sweatshop—which he performs on his body. Like his contemporary Marisela Norte, Alfaro ironicizes, inverts, and subverts popular culture stories and constructs a new *mestizaje* hybrid reflective of his multiply inflected subjectivity. His dialogue with mass culture brings to the forefront his situatedness as a gendered subject, citizen, and member of an aggrieved ethnic community

In his upbeat, witty, and sometimes tragic memory plays, Alfaro invites the audience into his space by playing on their memory through his invocation of shared popular songs, television shows, prayers, and well-known geographical locations. Incorporating these shared elements of popular culture into the representation of his own experiences, Alfaro attempts to demonstrate that his and his audience's experiences are linked. While Alfaro's gay, cultural, and class experiences might be foreign to his audience, he draws out those who do not share his specific experiences by using popular culture, such as the popular song "Downtown" or a visit to Tijuana, as a thread to link them. The audience is invited into his space, and he moves into theirs. In this shared imagined space, Alfaro constructs new meanings and "a structure of feeling" that informs an emergent identity for himself and his audience that is founded on cultural hybridity.

In this new imagined space, it is of no minor significance that Alfaro's movements are affected and exaggerated. For a person who has no place, no presence, no legitimate space, whose presence has been denied, erased, and silenced, taking up space—literally on stage or in an imagined space—is important. It is a form of validation. His exaggerated movements are as important as his intonation in conveying the rich textured and multilayered meanings of his text.

The absence of conditions that once supported large movements for social equality make Alfaro's traveling performances and their sites all the more important. The "special atmosphere" (the civil rights movement) that helped make struggles for equality visible to the larger culture is now relatively absent. There are few places where antiracist, antimisogynist, and antihomophobic discourses are produced and where AIDS awareness is a priority.[34] By helping audiences imagine that they have a stake in the fight against the status quo, Alfaro's work helps to create the conditions necessary for coalition building. Moving his performances across city and state and into various domains or types of sites makes these issues visible to both the local and the larger communities and can perhaps trigger some kind of challenge to racism, misogyny, and homophobia.

In these various settings, Alfaro performs what he describes as "memory plays"—"memory plays" because they are based on his childhood memories of life in the Pico-Union district of Los Angeles during the 1960s, 1970s, and 1980s. In order to connect with his audience, he "plays with" or elicits his audiences' personal memories. In this way, he represents experiences often left unrepresented in mainstream popular culture.[35]

An excellent example of this transcoding occurs in the piece titled "Virgin Mary." This narrative thematizes tensions of family, religion, sexuality, race, and ethnicity. In "Virgin Mary," Alfaro invites the audience into his space by his invocation of shared popular songs (Bloodstones's "Natural High"), television shows (*The Brady Bunch*), and well-known geographical locations (the Tijuana–San Diego border, downtown Los Angeles, California's Central Valley).

Against this backdrop of Catholic imagery and mass popular culture, the multithemed memory play "Virgin Mary" articulates the tensions that a gay Chicano may feel in relation to institutions such as the patriarchal family and the Catholic Church. Like many recent Chicana feminists who invoke the image of the Virgin (in the form of the Mexican *Virgen de Guadalupe*) to represent Chicana power, the narrator invokes the image of the Virgin Mary to launch a searing critique of the family and religion and of the constraints that the two institutions place on the category of sexuality.[36] Alfaro, like Chicana writers before him, "explores the ways families both constrain and empower."[37]

"Virgin Mary" thematizes the intersections of queer, Latino, and cross-cultural experiences and demonstrates the way in which Alfaro successfully articulates the multiplicity of meanings assigned to notions of the family, culture, and religion. The narrative is structured around the appearance of a Virgin Mary doll at three different points in the narrator's life and maps out a geography of the Southwest borderlands. The Virgin's appearance is used to guide the audience through a tour, of sorts, through the class-, gender-, and racially stratified extended borderlands of the U.S. Southwest: the U.S.-Mexican border, the urban Pico-Union district of Los Angeles, the agricultural Central Valley, and suburban Los Angeles. The narrator's liminal position as a queer Chicano allows him to recognize internal tensions within the community, as well as to critique forces that oppress it from outside.[38] Consequently, this is no pleasure tour but instead a critical comment on the social conditions that partially determine the material conditions of the Chicano community. The narrator begins "Virgin Mary" with the remembrance:

> We used to have this Virgin Mary doll and every time you connected her to an outlet, she would turn and bless all sides of the room. We bought her on a trip to Tijuana. One of my dad's drunken surprise Tijuana trips. He'd come home from the racetrack at midnight, wake us up, get us dressed, and we'd hop into the station wagon. My mother drove and my dad lowered the seat and slept in the back with us. My grandmother lived in one of the *colonias* and she hated our 3:00 a.m. visits. But, you see, blood is thicker than water, family is greater than friends, and the Virgin Mary watches over all of us.[39]

The image of the family driving across the geopolitical border speaks to the constant flow of people crossing the border from both sides. Yet their experience, crossing the border to visit in the relative comfort of their station wagon, is markedly different from and cannot be compared to the flow of undocumented workers, struggling to escape poverty and find work in the United States, who cross daily without any comforts and under the threat of violence, rape, and sometimes even death.

However, this particular border-crossing story is less a direct critique of U.S. border violence or the xenophobic ideology that supports it than a critique focused on heterosexual privilege and how it crosses national borders. The narrative turns on one of the most sacred icons of the Catholic community, the Virgin Mary, revealing the image's double-edged quality. Alfaro uses the doll as a sign with multiple layers of meaning. On one level, it is a signifier for Catholicism, the family, and heterosexual privilege. But it also is a signifier for "traveling" border culture. Transported to L.A. from Tijuana, the story becomes an allegory for the way culture travels and how its meaning is transformed in different settings.

The Virgin Mary, along with the *mestiza Virgen de Guadalupe*, is one of the most beloved and visible icons in Chicano and Mexicano religious and national culture. Her significance is multifold and contested. She is the appointed patron saint of the Americas who represents comfort and forgiveness and always signifies self-sacrifice. But, set in the context of the culture of the borderlands, the Virgin Mary doll signifies more. Bought on the Mexican side of the U.S./Mexico border in the city of Tijuana, the Virgin

Mary doll is transported to Los Angeles as the narrator's family crosses the border. The family's trip also invokes the notion of diaspora as articulated by Paul Gilroy. Gilroy asserts that the notion of diaspora "points to a paradigm for thinking cultural processes that encourages us to focus on the transverse, intercultural and trans-national relationships that get overlooked when theorists place the nation state at the core of their concern by default rather than by design."[40]

The image of the family driving across the geographical border also speaks to how culture, in the form of the doll, travels across national borders. The representation of the family crossing to visit a relative and buying the doll refutes the idea that U.S. and Mexican populations and cultures are isolated and homogeneous. The narrative also conjures images of extended family and cultures that stretch across national borders.

In the process of thematizing family allegiance based on blood ties, the narrative also humorously problematizes this type of allegiance. The grandmother, who lives in one of the *colonias* (neighborhoods), does not refuse to allow her son and his family into her home even though "she hated our 3:00 a.m. visits." The narrator explains that she must do so, despite her displeasure, with the ironic commentary that "blood is thicker than water, family is greater than friends, and the Virgin Mary watches over all of us." The narrator repeats this *dicho,* or saying, throughout the piece to illustrate the underside of family structure where the will of the male subject reigns.

But the narrative does not position Mexicanas simply as passive members of the community. The second appearance of the Virgin Mary doll invokes the history of their participation in migration prompted by U.S. labor demands. The narrator remembers that when he was ten, his aunt, "a grape picker from Delano, California," who claimed "that she had dated César Chávez" and that she "knew everyone in Tulare, Visalia, and McFarland counties," "was dying of breast cancer. . . . When she was feeling okay, she would tell me stories about migrant farm workers, the *huelga* movement, and bus trips to Bakersfield." With the hope of making her feel better, he "gave the rotating Virgin doll" to his "Tía Ofelia." Despite his good-willed intention, he ends up making his aunt feel worse when he asks her "quite innocently if he could see her chest" after hearing that "[d]octors at County General took away her tits in hopes of driving away *La Bruja Maldita* (the evil witch) who was slowly eating at her insides."[41] The narrator could never bring himself to visit his aunt after she slaps him and calls him a *"malcriado"* (bad boy). He remembers that he "felt so bad that day even I could feel the *Bruja Maldita* eating away at my heart."[42]

His Tía's cancer is both tragic and ironic, given that one of the demands of the United Farm Workers union was a reduced use of pesticides. After years of exposure to pesticide-doused fields, the aunt succumbs, and she can afford health care only at the county hospital; one of the few places where poor people can get medical assistance, the Los Angeles County–University of Southern California Medical Center is disgracefully understaffed and its employees overworked. As the aunt's illness progresses, the narrator's family and friends become more distressed, and she "slowly started to forget" them. The narrative suggests that culture is linked to memory and vice versa as it laments the loss of memory. Her family tries to help her remember who she is by sending her a "crate of grapes to help her to remember, but nothing worked. . . . The *Bruja Maldita* ate at her bones and she slowly began to slump forward like the G.I. Joe my brother and I melted with burning tamale leaves."[43]

The narrator uses the crate of grapes, another powerful image in the Chicano community, to remind his listeners that this is a critique of the status quo, as well as a tribute to the influential women in his life. In this scene, the grapes are significant because the grandmother understands that for her daughter the grapes signify more than food: They signify culture and personal history. From 1965 to 1970 the United Farm Workers union went on strike. With the image of *La Virgen de Guadalupe* as their symbol of solidarity, farm workers and their supporters boycotted grapes and picketed major supermarkets until the union was recognized as the workers' collective bargaining agent. Thus, the grapes signify the history of labor organizing and community action. The crate of grapes is significant because the grandmother hopes that it will remind her daughter of her past—her hard life of farm work and the struggles of the UFW. The aunt's mother attempts to help her daughter reclaim the strength she once possessed working in the Delano fields. But, almost as if agribusiness had sucked all of her strength, "her cheeks caved in like the plaster *calaveras* (skulls) we would buy at the border, and one day . . . she was gone."[44]

News of the aunt's death travels across the border to family members residing in Mexico, and again the image of the border and extended family surfaces. The scene again evokes the notion of diaspora: "In remembrance of her, phones rang. Food poured in. Little cards with twenty-dollar bills. Hysterical screams from distant relatives on a Mexico-to-L.A. party line. . . . The tears of my relatives were covered by the huge veils they wore to

Immaculate Conception. I had to remember that blood is thicker than water, family is greater than friends, and the Virgin Mary watches over all of us."[45]

The death of his aunt Ofelia prompts distant family to travel from Mexico to Los Angeles. The scene, read in tandem with the previous grape scene, invokes images of the history of the Latino diasporas in which families develop histories of separation and migration prompted by U.S. labor demands.

The scene also problematizes the assumed importance of blood ties. The narrator explains that he "had to sleep on the floor with dark-skinned cousins from *ranchos* in Jalisco and although I hated it, I had to remember that blood is thicker than water." Although color hierarchies exist in Chicano culture, the narrator did not necessarily hate the situation because the cousins were "dark-skinned"; he hated it because they were strangers to him. He resented the fact that he had to give up his bed to people he felt no connection with, but he remembers, of course, the *dicho*.

"Virgin Mary" illustrates that the narrator's relationship to family is not simple. Regional differences explain, in part, why the cousins did not necessarily connect. Life in working-class urban L.A. is quite different from life on a *rancho* in the Mexican state of Jalisco. By focusing on the aunt's life, he is illustrating the quality of life in urban Chicano communities. While the Chicano community in the Central Valley is plagued by unsafe working conditions and inadequate housing, Pico-Union is plagued by drug-related crime, police surveillance, and inequitable urban redevelopment. The narrator explains:

My Tía Ofelia lived across the street with my Tía Tita who lived with my Tío Tony who lived next door to my Tía Romie. Back in those days, everybody on my block was either a Tía or a Tío. They lived in a big beautiful wood-carved two-story house with a balcony overlooking the street below. We were crowded by downtown skyscrapers, packs of roving cholos, the newly built Convention Center on Figueroa, and portable tamale stands, but our families always managed to live together. Because you see, blood is thicker than water, family is greater than friends, and the Virgin Mary watches over all of us. . . .

My Tía lived on the top floor and on the bottom lived the 18th Street gang. There was Smiley, Sleepy, Sadgirl, and a bunch of other homeboys hanging in the front yard playing Bloodstones' "Natural High." Like roaches they split at the sight of a cop car slowly cruising through our neighborhood like tourists on Hollywood Boulevard.[46]

Forced to live in this impoverished area, for better or worse, the families construct a sense of community. No longer separated by the demands of seasonal farm work, the narrator explains, "our families always managed to live together." So, whether he liked it or not, the family, as well as the Virgin, would always be watching him. But, unlike his family, the narrator is somewhat critical of the Virgin's power to protect because, even though she watched over them, she could not stop the neighborhood from turning into a noisy, polluted, overcrowded, and policed zone or help the family move elsewhere.

The image of the grapes reappears in this urban setting, but this time they represent internal social status differences instead of community solidarity. The narrator's "Tía Ofelia" hated *cholos* (gang members), and before she got cancer she would "spit down the seeds from grapes she ate just to annoy them." By spitting down the grape seeds, she demonstrates that she does not respect *cholos* or fear their potential revenge. They like gays and lesbians, are outcast from the community, and are treated as such. Soon after the aunt's death, the Crips, a rival gang, firebomb the 18th Street gang, which lives on the bottom floor of his Tía's apartment.[47] His *cholo* neighbors die in this incident, but his relatives forbid him to attend the funerals of those whom they describe as "*perros desgraciados*" (the translation given in *Men on Men* is "disgraced dogs," but a more meaningful translation is something like "shameless dogs"). The family's attitude toward *cholos* illustrates the internal social hierarchies within the Chicano community. Seen to shame the community, they are disowned, and the family refuses to see the tragedy in their death. The Virgin Mary doll the narrator gave his aunt is also destroyed in the fire except for her head, which his brother uses for "BB gun practice."[48] Trying to deal with their neighbors' violent death, the narrator's brother metaphorically takes shots at the icon, suggesting the brother's doubt about the Virgin's power to protect him or his community.

Thus far, the narrative has taken the most sacred images of the Catholic Chicano community and has disrupted their conventional meanings. However, the final representation of the Virgin Mary completely transgresses all that she normally signifies: a patriarchal family, heterosexuality, and chastity. Eight years later, the narrator tells us, the image of the Virgin Mary doll reappears and is a key figure in the narrator's first love affair. The narrator's encounter with a white boyfriend articulates the complicated intersection of cultures that a gay Latino subject must negotiate. However, non-Queer Latinas/os can recognize traces of their own experiences of negotiating interethnic relationships. Confronting and crossing the multiple boundaries that the categories of ethnicity, sexuality, and class raise, the narrator recounts:

> When I was eighteen, I met this guy with a rotating Virgin Mary doll. He bought it in Mexico, so, of course, I fell in love. His skin was white. He ate broccoli and spoke like actors on a TV series. It was my first love, and like the *Bruja Maldita,* he pounded on my heart. He taught me many things: how to kiss like the French, lick an earlobe, and dance in the dark. He was every *Brady Bunch/Partridge Family* episode rolled into one. He gave me his shirt and I told him about the fields in Delano, picking cherries one summer, and my summer in Mexico. Once my grandmother sent me a crate of grapes. We took off our clothes, smashed them all over our bodies, and ate them off each other.

The fact that the Virgin Mary doll brought the two young male lovers together is outrageous, considering that she is never associated with Queer sexuality but is instead a symbol of the suppression of women's sexuality. By eroticizing the grapes, the narrator speaks to the way that heterosexuality is never questioned or how issues around sexuality have not been addressed the way economic issues have.

The representation of the narrator's love affair challenges notions of the formation of the traditional family. The narrator and his partner construct an alternative union based on an allegiance other than blood. Alfaro's memory play recontextualizes, reinterprets, and assigns new meaning to the name of the family's church, Immaculate Conception, and to the imagery associated with the Virgin Mary.

"Immaculate Conception" is the name of the church that the narrator and his family attend. The phrase also invokes the imagery of the Catholic Holy Family. The Holy Family is considered holy because Mary's child was conceived without physical consummation. The narrator represents his communion as physical, in contrast to the imagery of Immaculate Conception. The two took the grapes, "smashed them all over [their] bodies, and ate them off each other." Again, the new context shifts the meaning of the grapes. The grapes take on an erotic signification as the lovers consume and incorporate them into their bodies.

As the couple consummate their union, they conceive a new type of community. Unlike the Catholic version of Mary's conception, sexuality becomes the tie that binds this new community.

Put in this context, the narrator transforms the meaning of the Catholic communion and Immaculate Conception, yet still maintains a reverence for them. By using Catholic imagery, the narrator endows the encounter with sacredness; it becomes a new kind of Holy Communion. Instead of abandoning Catholic imagery because Catholicism condemns his sexuality, he claims it as his own, refashions elements that are significant to him, and incorporates them into his new community. Understood in this context, and following the path set by Chicana writers who uncover the ways the church "paradoxically . . . offers outlets for sexuality and subjectivity," the lovers' act honors both the grapes and Catholic culture.[49]

Residual elements from this traditional Catholic culture intersect with images from popular culture (e.g., television) to form an emergent community identity based on hybridity for both participants. Popular symbols from both Latino and dominant culture mix and inform formations of a new multicultural family (Latino, Anglo, and gay). The narrative juxtaposes both his family of origin and this new family against the 1970s TV popular culture version of the Holy family—the Brady Bunch.

Blurring these Chicano icons with those from mass popular culture, Alfaro's narrator invokes the image of the 1970s "ideal" family depicted in *The Brady Bunch*. The juxtaposition of the urban neighborhood with that of his Anglo boyfriend illustrates the sharp contrast between the living conditions of an idealized upper-middle-class Anglo family and that of a Latino working-class family and shows the extent of his engagement with the dominant culture. *The Brady Bunch* represents the American dream to which many American families aspire but that they, like the narrator's family, cannot achieve: suburban home, economic stability, trendy clothes, pleasant family dinners, relaxed family relations, and no drunk "surprise trips to Tijuana."[50] But the invocation of this image is also an indictment of the way mass popular culture writes out the interaction that occurs among different communities and also Queer relationships. A *Brady Bunch* episode depicting these alternative interactions was never produced.

As he remembers his brief relationship, this Chicano, Catholic narrator speaks from a position that links his Latino/Chicano identity to his Queer identity and his class position. In this memory play, the narrator does not privilege one subject position over the other. His encounter with the boy who was "every *Brady Bunch/Partridge Family* rolled into one" illustrates how his identities figure into his interethnic/interclass relationship. At the same time, he illustrates how the differences between the two cultures and two classes led to their breakup:

> When he left, the *Bruja Maldita*'s [evil witch's] hand replaced his in my heart, and she pounded on me. And she laughed like Mexican mothers at a clothesline. And I covered my tears with a smile that was like the veils at Immaculate Conception [the neighborhood church]. But my sorrow was so strong that relatives nearby would say, "*Ay?, Mijo,* don't you see? Blood is thicker than water, family is greater than friends, and the Virgin Mary watches over all of us."[51]

The transformative power of this passage lies in the way that it demonstrates that the narrator's family accepts his gay sexuality and empathizes with his pain. The narrator's situation is ideal. Since his biological family never forced him to cut his tie with them, the narrator returns to his family and to his Catholic culture for support. The Virgin Mary, unlike her image in the opening scene, takes on a spiritual significance in this final scene. The first time we are introduced to her, the narrator remembers that "every time you connected her to an outlet, she would turn and bless all sides of the room." The narrator's invocation of the image of the mechanical Virgin Mary doll that literally "goes through the motions" suggests a commentary on how unexamined religious practices can become empty gestures. The narrator parallels the image of the doll automatically repeating the gesture with the repetition of the *dicho* (saying) "blood is thicker than water, family is greater than friends, and the Virgin Mary watches over us all." The tensions between the meanings of the doll and the *dicho* and the narrator's response are never resolved. According to the mythos of Latino culture, the *dicho* is a code to live by. Alfaro's narrator never resolves the tension between accepting the code and completely dismissing it. Instead, he stands in an "in-between" position and disrupts the conventional signification of some of the most powerful icons associated with the Chicano community to produce a counterdiscourse that does not idealize Chicano or mainstream culture. The memory play concludes as the narrator recoups the spiritual significance of the Virgin Mary imagery and family ties. The conclusion suggests that a borderlands subjectivity, such as the narrator's, constantly negotiates between traditional and progressive structures of family relations. Thus, Alfaro's memory play contributes to the invention of a new Chicano subject: one who does not reproduce homophobic and misogynist practices. His work carves out a space for Queer sexuality and empowered women within representations of the traditional family.

Alfaro as Chicana Feminist

What makes Alfaro's CD especially compelling is his feminist understandings of issues relating to Latinas and other women. By dramatizing a less idealized image of the traditional family, Alfaro's memory plays critique patriarchal power relations. He constructs a sympathetic representation of Chicana experience in his piece "Chicana Liberation."

Alfaro's performances insist on including a space for empowered women who both contest and reassert women's position within the structure of the traditional family. Mothers and women are always represented as strong and innovative. "Chicana Liberation" thematizes the particular nuances of a markedly Latino dysfunctional family within a specific Chicano context (larger systems of patriarchal and economic relations produce the dysfunction). "Chicana Liberation" inverts and subverts stereotypical representations of passive women and thematizes Chicana resistance to sexist gender roles, patriarchal violence, and alcoholism. This excerpt illustrates the point:

My mom let my dad have it at the Señorial, no less. Another one of those tacky bars with Lucha Villa on the Jukebox. You can find one on any street corner downtown. We had "El Club Jalisco," "The Señorial," and the "501" on our corner alone. One night we were all sitting around watching TV when my mom got up and shouted that she was "fed up" and we were going to look for my dad. So we all hopped in the orange Monte Carlo and drove less than a block away and parked in the alley—behind Lucy's all-nite taco stand. My mom got off and walked right into the bar. I knew this was trouble. The bars at the corner were reserved for local men and fast women. My mom broke the sacred code. My dad was out, first yanking my mom out the door, twirling her in a sort of violent dance. Then, out of nowhere, my mother broke the sacred code reserved for Latinas across the city; she burst through a pattern established by generations way before our time. Out of nowhere my mother's fist pounded into my father's face. A direct connect to his left jaw. My poor intoxicated father lost his balance and toppled over. My mother calmly walked over to the Monte Carlo, got in, and said, "Let's go sleep at your aunt's in Glendale." This was the beginning of dinners together, AA, Sunday afternoon soccer games, and the women's liberation movement in downtown Los Angeles.[52]

The narrator rearticulates the notion of "women's liberation" by setting it in a Chicana context. The narrative attempts to demonstrate that Chicana liberation encompasses much more than a unidimensional struggle for women's sexual liberation. As a working-class Chicana, his mother must negotiate the dangers of living in an urban center, where after nightfall it is not safe to walk her family down the block, and she must attempt to "liberate" herself from the economic forces that force her to live there in the first place.[53]

"Chicana Liberation" thematizes the struggle for agency of the mother and, consequently, the beginnings of liberation from the effects of alcoholism. "Fed up" with her husband's drinking, the mother is represented as a subject who resists the status quo and attempts to change a situation she dislikes. Disregarding patriarchal ideology—or "sacred codes"—that informs women's supposed proper place, the mother determinedly crosses into a space "reserved for local men and fast women." In doing so, the mother crosses the "imagined" boundaries of her gender role.

In an attempt to put the mother back in her proper place and to reestablish his dominance, the father begins a furious dance of abuse. The husband yanks her out of the bar and twirls her "in a sort of violent dance." Yet, the mother summons her anger and refuses to dance to the tune of resignation: She is no silent partner. She resists the "pattern established by generations way before." She realizes that this behavior, like a dance, is learned and that up until this moment she has been dancing the part of the sacrificing wife. As a dance is choreographed—or constructed—so the pattern of subservience must be rescripted. The mother refuses to continue practicing this particular pattern of relations and reimagines the pattern of abuse. Practicing her new dance, she unleashes her pent-up frustration by pounding her fist into the "father's face."

The mother's action is one that is not prescribed by feminine gender roles, but she performs it anyway. In order for the mother to win this power struggle, and to become an ideal mother in a working-class sense of the term, she has to subvert the Virgin Mary paradigm. At last the cycle is broken as she choreographs "the women's liberation movement in downtown Los Angeles."

Terreno Peligroso/Danger Zone

Alfaro's work reaches wide audiences of Latino and non-Latino, as well as gay/lesbian and heterosexual, audiences. His work has even been translated and performed in Romania.[54] But what makes Luis Alfaro's performance art even more compelling is the way that it travels. Alfaro's first performance in front of an international audience was in Mexico (two years later he appeared in London). In 1995, just a little over a year after the North American Free Trade Agreement (NAFTA) was ratified and the Ejército Zapatista de Liberación Nacional emerged in opposition, Alfaro participated in *Terreno Peligroso/Danger Zone,* the first binational dialogue and performance art exchange between Mexico City and Los Angeles. Binationally curated by Josephine Ramirez, Guillermo Gomez-Pena, and Lorena Wolfer and funded in part by the National Endowment for the Humanities, the Rockefeller Foundation, and the U.S./MEXUS Fund for Culture, the exchange brought together artists from Los Angeles and Mexico. The organizers and participants—Elia Arce, Rubén Martínez, Luis Alfaro, Nao Bustamante, Robert Sifuentes, and Guillermo Gomez-Pena, representing Los Angeles, and Felipe Ehrenberg, Eugenia Vargas, César Martínez, and Eliva Santa María, representing Mexico—held high hopes for the events. The group used NAFTA and post–Proposition 187 California as contexts to activate a dialogue to break stereotypes on both sides of the border and to forge "more profound cultural relations between Chicanos and Mexicanos" and "greater compassion and mutual understanding" (by understanding that because of the new crises and dangers to which the communities are subject, they are both "equally screwed").[55]

Numerous reviews in the Mexican press considered the event groundbreaking.[56] It was one of the first times the Mexican public had an opportunity to discuss the rise in nativist discourse in the United States, which was intensified by NAFTA, and why a majority of Latinos voted for Proposition 187, a proposition that would deny undocumented workers and their children (most of whom are Mexican nationals) access to public schools, health care, and social services.

Luis Alfaro in *Cuerpo Politizado*, performed in Mexico City (1995), as part of *Terreno Peligroso/Danger Zone: A Mexico/U.S. Latino Performance Exchange.* Photography by Monica Naranjo. (Reprinted with permission.)

As Guillermo Gomez-Pena explained, the exchange held the possibility of dispelling the common beliefs that Mexicans held of Chicanos: that "all Chicano artists make barrio murals . . . erect neon altars to Frida Kahlo . . . that they all speak like Edward Olmos in *American Me* . . . and that they all drive low-riders."[57] It would also be the first time a "more fluid and interactive model of Chicana/Latino multi-identity" would be represented to Mexican audiences.[58]

Thrilled to participate in this historic exchange, Alfaro was concerned about how his work would translate once it crossed the border. At what moments in his work would Chicano and Mexicano cultural experiences intersect? What elements of his work would be legible to an audience who might possibly view Spanglish as a "bastardization" of Spanish, instead of as a vital language that reflected the experiences of Latinos in the United States?

In Mexico City, at the X-Teresa performance complex, Alfaro performed "El Juego de Jotería" (a play on the words *lotería*, a Mexican

game, and *joto,* Mexican slang for queer). As a way to overcome translation issues (from Spanglish to Spanish), Alfaro emphasized the visual and
the visceral aspects of his performance. Of course, this was not an issue
when he performed in front of an English-speaking audience in London
as part of the Corpus Delecti performance festival organized by Coco
Fusco.[59] In one of the segments, Alfaro performed on roller skates in a
black slip. As a child, Alfaro was a big fan of roller derby.[60] He skated
around the X-Teresa performance space (located within a historic cathe-
dral in the capital's main plaza), while attempting a conversation with his
invisible father.[61]

At first the audience laughed as the roller-skating Alfaro stumbled,
calling after his father. But as the falls became more frequent, and the calls
to his father more urgent, the audience became concerned that Alfaro was
actually injuring himself. The falls became a metaphor for how Alfaro experienced the rejection by his father, family, and community and for his
desperate need for parental love.

Alfaro's ability to strip down to the raw emotion of a situation is an example of how his work possesses a Chicana punk sensibility, what the pi-
oneer Chicana punk songwriter Teresa Covarrubias calls creating "from
the gut." Not pretty, not nihilistic, but instead critical and, finally, hopeful. In performing the experience of the pain of rejection, Alfaro makes us
see that the son's core struggle is for acceptance and connection. The visceral elements of the performance communicate to the audience, overrid-
ing the need for a literal translation. The audience connects with the image
of a human being who desires appreciation and connection. Alfaro uses
the visual as a strategy to cut through the homophobia, the prejudice.
When the homophobia and the prejudice fall away, straight eyes can see
the pain their intolerance is causing and what its object has to endure.

If, for the first time, Mexican audiences had the extraordinary opportunity to see the multiply inflected identities of young Chicanos sans the
mediation of mass media forms, Alfaro also found the experience profound. He explains:

> My vision of Mexico that was very romantic, and very, based on my rec-
> ollection of Mexico, in line with my father's recollection of Mexico. . . .
> it was *el rancho Mexico,* you know. We didn't have to go to the city too
> much. [*Terreno Peligroso*] was very different from that experience. . . .
> Mexico is actually, politically, very heightened and, before, I had no ac-
> cess to that world.[62]

I did a lot of adventurous things there that I had never done before. I collaborated with a lot of people, which I had never done before. It was really risk taking for me. And I did things that didn't involve language, which was very hard. I'm very used to relying on words, and it was very hard to do a performance there. Most of the week, we were doing performances every day, on the street. My performance where people paid was translated by Felipe Ehrenberg. That was really hard, because it was not the Spanish that I knew. And it was a big ol' dilemma. And it never really quite resolved. How do you do Spanglish in Mexico? I mean, they think you're an idiot first of all, 'cause you're bastardizing the language. What was more successful was stuff about gay culture. I did an audience participatory piece where I had everybody go "Mm Mm Mm." And so they got the swing of it and then I would say, "How many people voted for Zedillo?" "How many people believe that the Zapatistas are wrong?" I purposely asked questions where you could hear one person respond. "How many people think abortion is wrong?" And you hear the single one. And it was very interesting in terms of how they viewed gay culture. And then I asked, "How many people here, how many men have had sex with another man?" And you'd hear a clap. You know, it was really interesting in terms of how willing, how brave they were willing to be, you know. It was very funny. And I had to that all in Spanish, so that was hard.[63]

Terreno Peligroso/Danger Zone became an opportunity for Alfaro to rethink his nostalgia for a Mexico that existed in his father's mind. In chapter 5, we discuss the protagonist of Jim Mendiola's independent punk film *Pretty Vacant*, who similarly negotiates her own father's nostalgia for Mexico and her postmodern experience of the culture.

Conclusion

This very brief historical account of how the subject of Chicano oppositional theater has changed demonstrates why Chicano theater is a place where the struggle against the culture of the powerful is engaged. Additionally, the performative space of new Chicano theater is one of the places where questions of working-class Chicano/Latino genders and sexuality get played out. Luis Alfaro's cultural work powerfully illustrates both of these points.

It is of no minor significance that new Chicano/a subjects and identities are being invented and formed in Alfaro's work. In a context in which Chicanos/Latinos (and other marginalized people) have limited access to dominant spaces of the imaginary, Alfaro's performance is important because it is one the few places where Chicano/a and Latino/a experiences are represented. It is also one of the few places from which critiques of both homophobic and sexist practices of both the Chicano family and of the dominant U.S. culture can be articulated.

In writing about the construction of new ethnicities in Britain, Stuart Hall explains why it is necessary to understand the politics of representation. He convincingly argues that

> how things are represented and the "machineries" and regimes of representation in a culture do play a constitutive and not merely a reflexive, after-the-event role. This gives questions of culture and ideology, and the scenarios of representation—subjectivity, identity, politics—a formative, not merely an expressive place in the construction of social and political life.[64]

In other words, representations constructed in popular culture do not merely reflect what everyday life is but work to construct what it could be in the future. By demonstrating that different marginal groups such as Latinos, women, and queer men stand on common ground in the ongoing struggle against "the culture of the powerful," Alfaro's work helps to create the conditions for future coalitions. As Alfaro's representations construct a new vision of masculinity and queer identity that is firmly situated within and accepted by the family, he contributes to the invention of a Latino culture, a new culture that succeeds in escaping the chains of U.S. and Latino patriarchal dominance. His work carves out a space for Queer sexuality and empowered women within representations of the traditional family—representations that will, it is hoped, play a constitutive role and translate into the culture of everyday life.

Epilogue

Alfaro has been committed to reaching audiences that have often been ignored by mainstream theater productions. It is in the arena of community theater that Alfaro and his collaborators are able to reach underserved audiences with innovative, if not well-funded, productions. In the winter of 1997 Diane Rodríguez and Luis Alfaro, at the time co-directors of the Mark Taper Forum's Latino Theater Initiative, wrote and directed *Los Vecinos: A Play for Neighbors,* which ran from December 4 through December 21, 1997, as part of Cornershop Theater's Boyle Heights residency cycle.[65] The play was significant because it was produced in collaboration with residents from Boyle Heights and incorporated young, nonprofessional actors. It also was one of the first local productions in which Alfaro took part after he won the prestigious MacArthur "Genius" award. Unfortunately, but perhaps predictably, the production was unappreciated by a mainstream *Los Angeles Times* theater critic.

Given Alfaro's new standing in Los Angeles public culture, it is important to note how Alfaro's and Rodríguez's attempt to bridge and postmodernize traditional forms of community theater was received by the mainstream press. The published review itself engaged in cultural politics. The review provides insight into the power mainstream critics hold to perpetuate misreadings of productions that are outside their own scope of expertise. The *Los Angeles Times* critic Laurie Winer focused on the formal elements of the production and decontextualized the play from its own artistic traditions and social context.

The *Los Angeles Times*'s reviewer was disappointed because the play "actually looks like a community production."[66] I, however, was impressed by the allegory's thematic twists and by its innovative use of the limited resources employed by the play's director, writers, and performers. I can only conclude that the reviewer, unlike the appreciative neighborhood audience, missed the play's synergy and artful nuances; she took *Los Vecinos* out of both its artistic and its social context. Winer's review briefly situates the morality play within the long-standing Mexican folk tradition of *pastorela,* or shepherd's play. Although Winer did not mention it, the *pastorela* is a hybrid religious theater that emerged out of sixteenth-century efforts by Spanish friars to evangelize the indigenous populations of Mexico and the American Southwest. Refusing to completely abandon their own spiritual beliefs, the native population superimposed its own spiritual system, language, music, and costume over the Christian allegory, enacted primarily during the Christmas season to teach the native population about the birth of Jesus. Adapting it to their own situation, the native population created a vehicle that had the opposite effect of the Friars' intentions: Instead of submerging native beliefs, the shepherd's play became a vessel to express them. Church officials eventually caught on that the popular *pastorelas,* enacted in the native tongue of indigenous and *mestizo* populations, were not so much about shepherds following the light to Bethlehem as they were about the native population's struggle against the imposition of a foreign religion. Yet, the disempowered populations continued to perform the play in secular contexts as a vehicle to preserve their own beliefs and to expose the consequences of the Conquest from their point of view.

Passed on as an oral tradition for hundreds of years across a large geographical area as a poor people's theater, the *pastorela* existed in as many different versions as there were communities that performed them. Although *pastorelas* were constantly adapted to speak to the pressing concerns of a particular locale and time period, certain elements remained constant: stock characters that represent human virtues and vices and that try to find their way to the "light" as they are caught between an army of angels and devils, and the play's comic spirit.

If one fails to take into account Rodríguez's fifteen years of experience with the ground-breaking and internationally respected Teatro Campesino (Farm Workers' Theater), which performed the play annually, and Alfaro's moving performance pieces about the good and the bad of Los Angeles, one may miss the humorous interventions of the two writers. Rodríguez and Alfaro honored the long tradition of the *pastorela* by channeling local concerns into the shepherd's play, transforming the search for the baby Jesus into a timely allegory of gender relations, community development, and self-realization during a historical moment that supports few venues dedicated to presenting the realities of power relations, human agency, and spirituality from the underdog's perspective.

The crafted quality of the play's writing and directing can be misread as "messy and thrown together" if we do not account for the social theme around which the narrative is structured. The theme of this updated shepherd's play turns on home, displacement, and redemption. Refitted to address the class-stratified Los Angeles of the late 1990s, the play recasts the shepherds as displaced *vecinos* (neighbors)—East Side urban homeowners and apartment dwellers who have suddenly lost their homes and possessions after an earthquake. Since the group of six—Mandona/Bossy (Rosalinda Morales), Fiscón/Stingy (Omar Gomez), Comelón/Glutton (Mario Juárez), Histérico/Hysterical (Pat Nolan), Dudosa/Doubter (Liz Talerer-Falcioni), Vato/Dude (Rodrigo R. Suarez), and Caridad/Charity (Mayte Garjeda)—has been suddenly reduced to homelessness, it adopts the neighborhood homeless person, Desplazado/Displaced (Christopher

Liam Moore), a type found in most urban neighborhood landscapes, and looks to him to help the six survive in their own state of displacement. In the end, the story is about rebuilding a working-class neighborhood, long neglected by city officials (represented as devils), with *los vecinos* (the neighbors) and the homeless asserting their vision as the guiding light.

Unrecognized by Winer's review was the much appreciated gender critique incorporated into *Los Vecinos*. Traditional *pastorelas* symbolize the battle between good and evil using Christian icons San Miguel (Saint Michael) and the scene-stealing Lucifer. However, in this adaptation, that eternal battle is staged between Luzbel (the commanding Armando Duran), who seeks to confuse *los vecinos* by stripping them of their inner power, and the representative of positive forces, Señora Angel (the captivating Maricela Ochoa), who possesses the secret of the light; both masculine and feminine forces share equal time. Señora Angel, a complex figure, is the ultimate in *mestiza* camp: a brown angel in black combat boots and outrageous pink taffeta, her miraculous conch shell linking her to an indigenous past. Luzbel's and Senora Angel's tongue-in-cheek dance of good and evil represents the union of the opposing forces *los vecinos* must comprehend to complete their journey. The romance between Caridad and Vato remakes Caridad (the traditional virginal figure) by having her opt to "think about" getting married instead of accepting Vato's proposal right away (even though his heart speeds faster than his beeper when he thinks about her). She decides to go against the advice of her father because she "wants to go to college." The play's narrative illustrates the scholar Yvonne Yarbro-Bejarano's assertion that, "rather than hindering political movement . . . religion can be marshaled in the service of resistance to oppression and exploitation."[67]

The review also does not adequately address the social conditions from which this production emerged, nor does it mention the imaginative use of inexpensive material to make elaborate and deeply symbolic costumes and props. Since *pastorelas* have always been a poor people's theater, performed wherever space was available, it seems fitting that play was performed at the recently acquired yet shockingly dilapidated former Community Service Organization building on First and Chicago. If anything has a "thrown-together" quality, it was the woefully underfunded community center (which the set designers imaginatively transformed). Granted, the large performance space of the CSO was chilly (despite being filled to capacity with local children and families), but who was to pay for the heating bill when the cover charge was "pay what you can"?

Given that the CSO lacks a stage, much less a professional lighting system, the review's description of "haphazard lighting" missed the creative strategy employed by stagehands whose handheld mobile lights were part of the "make-do" stage aesthetic.

Indeed, the synergy of lighting, music, and staging that was the strength of this production was lost in the review. The importance of light and lighting made itself evident before the beginning of the performance in the unlit lobby. Electric candles lit the way—for my husband and me, as well as for the excited children and families—to the darkened performance space, inviting us to the join the play's journey toward the light. The dark performance space was punctuated only with spotlights until the end of the play, when the characters came full circle and became the light that envelopes the room, lighting the way for us. The props, costumes, and music were comments in themselves. The angels were not your typical winged fare; instead, their sparkling feathers invoked indigenous icons. The writers transformed the shepherds' hooks into survival gear that symbolized each character's individual weaknesses, flaws that would later become weapons for the collective good. Instead of pastoral acoustic guitars, the music had a *rock en español* groove to it.

Given that the play implicated everyone in the audience, I'm not sure why Winer rejected the invitation to temporarily become part of "the neighborhood." I might understand the review's oversights if the play had been conducted in Spanish or was less focused. But the laughing Anglo couple next to me (in their sixties), who seemed to especially enjoy the elaborately staged climatic battle between the armies of angels and devils, demonstrated the cross-cultural legibility and appeal of the production.

4

Translated/Translating Woman

Comedienne/Solo Performer
Marga Gomez, "Sending All Those
Puerto Ricans Back to Mexico," and
the Politics of a Sexualized Location

Even though I don't like to define myself as a lesbian comic, it helps me take the worry out of a situation where I'm traveling hundreds of miles to face people. This way they know where I'm coming from. And it's funny because it's like lesbian is almost a sort of ethnic root. In a way it is a culture unto itself, and the two cultures (lesbian and Latino) . . . a lot of people don't think of Latinos as being queer at all. —Marga Gomez, interview

Increasingly, feminist and other field workers realize that we need to be sensitive to differences between our subjects and ourselves, aware of the possible power relations involved in doing research by, about and for women, and that feminist studies must include a diversity of women's experiences based on race, class, and sexual preference. —Patricia Zavella, "Feminist Insider Dilemmas: Constructing Identity with 'Chicana' Informants"

I don't speak Spanish but I try my best
eso si que es! (S.O.C.K.S.)
—El Vez, The Mexican Elvis, a.k.a. Robert Lopez, in the album *G.I. Ay, Ay! Blues* (1996)

Marga Gomez is one of the most accomplished Latina feminist comediennes and solo performers of her generation. In several television appearances and numerous successful standup comedy and solo performance pieces, she has used the circuits of mass media to disrupt and to reinvent images of Latinas in the national imagination. She has appeared on HBO's national cablecast *Comic Relief 1993* and on Comedy Central, Showtime, and PBS and performed occasionally with the Chicano comedy group Culture Clash in its 1995 self-titled Fox network television program (broadcast in the Southwest). She is featured in Karen William's docucomedy, *Laughing Matters,* and appeared in the Hollywood sci-fi thriller *Sphere.* She was also featured in Culture Clash's live show entitled *Carpa Clash.*[1] In 1994, *American Playhouse* optioned her best-known and highly praised performance piece, *Memory Tricks,* for film production, and her subsequent piece, titled *Marga Gomez Is Pretty, Witty, and*

Marga Gomez as a matador in a 1997 publicity photo. Photography by Linda Sue Scott. (Reprinted with permission from lindasuescott.com.)

Gay, has toured nationally. *A Line around the Block* is a solo performance about her father and the Latino entertainment world of the 1940s and 1950s in which he thrived.[2] *Jaywalker* deals with her hilarious attempts to break into Hollywood film; *The Twelve Days of Cochina* is a dirty take on the traditional Christmas story; and *Marga Gomez's Intimate Details,* a hopeful search for love and romance. *Los Big Names,* a tribute to parents and New York's Spanish-language *teatro* history, opened at the prestigious Kennedy Center in Washington, D.C., in spring 2004.

Before she achieved success, Gomez studied drama and creative writing at Oswego College, in New York, then moved to San Francisco and became a member of the feminist grassroots theater group Lilith. Gomez left that group in the early 1980s and collaborated with the Bay Area Chicana comedienne Monica Palacios.[3] Along with Palacios, Gomez performed as an original member of Culture Clash for about two years. Later, she and Palacios left the group and performed together along the West Coast. As a solo performer, she has performed many standup shows over the past five years and has opened for diverse acts such as Los Lobos, k.d. lang, and others.

Her solo performances, including *Memory Tricks, Marga Gomez Is Pretty, Witty, and Gay,* and *Half-Cuban, Half-Lesbian,* are compelling because they touch upon issues of immigration and assimilation anxiety, as well as racism, misogyny, and homophobia as they occurred in late-twentieth-century America.

The notable scholar Yvonne Yarbro-Bejarano, writing about the importance of the revolutionary Chicana playwright Cherríe Moraga's theater work in bringing the perspectives of lesbians of color to the fore, demonstrates that, within Western drama, "the perspectives of playwrights who are lesbians of color and lesbian-of-color characters are practically non-existent."[4] The same can be said of standup comedy. However, comediennes like Marga Gomez and her contemporaries Monica Palacios and Carmelita Tropicana (Alina Troyano) use the stage in innovative ways, inventing hybrid and experimental genres that present lesbian perspectives through humor. Gomez's humor is similar to how the scholar Alicia Arrizón theorizes Monica Palacios's: It "embodies a critique of homophobia and compulsory heterosexuality."[5] Though adamantly not its primary goal, this humor can work to educate heterosexual audiences about the damaging effects of homophobia upon our collective psyche. It can also educate queer white audiences about the damaging effects of racism on society in general.

The importance of Gomez's work can be seen through a fruitful and friendly comparison to Cherríe Moraga's. While Moraga's profound theater work is situated within the category of serious drama, and her artistic sensibility is not generally shaped by comedy, the two artists' shared commitment to social justice guides the themes of their work. Both cultural workers move through moments of individual and collective trauma in order to heal the hurts of injustice. Both seek to address social injuries caused by homophobia, racism, and class discrimination. But, instead of drama, Gomez uses irony and humor, a bittersweet humor, that comes from acknowledging and "undermin[ing] white supremacist presuppositions," as well as heterosexual norms.[6] Getting Gomez's jokes requires a new type of literacy, a critical reading practice that frames and interprets power dynamics from the perspective of those excluded from mainstream society. I offer this comparison because Gomez's cultural production, like Moraga's, "demonstrates that identity is constructed by relationships of power which may be answered and acted upon."[7]

Gomez's work as a feminist standup comedienne and solo performance artist is remarkable, as is feminist theater in general, for "its commitment to 'centering' women characters, staging their stories, and representing issues of gender and sexuality, [which] makes female viewers, for once, the ideal spectators."[8] And, while it can be argued that the ideal spectator of Gomez's performances is a Latina lesbian, Gomez's critique of racism and class discrimination makes her work appealing to a variety of audiences interested in questions of social justice. According to the theater scholar Alberto Sandoval-Sanchez, Gomez's solo performances, like those of her queer contemporaries, have transformed Latino theater by infusing it with "new dramatic structures, new protagonists, new perspectives, and new ways of articulating, negotiating, and accommodating bilingual and bicultural identities."[9] Gomez brings to the stage the construct of a Latina lesbian comedian, helping to combat the narrow figurings of Latin subjects and almost invisible representations of Latina lesbians. The theorist Judith Butler convincingly argues that the oppression of lesbian subjects is produced by rendering its representation invisible. Butler's theorizing is useful for understanding how the taboo against being a lesbian operates in Latino communities. Butler explains, "Here, oppression works though the production of a domain of unthinkability and unnameability." But the solo performances of Gomez force the Latina lesbian subject "into the thinkable, the imaginable, that grid of cultural intelligibility that regulates the real and the nameable, and forces

Latino audience to confront the possibility of this alternative form of Latina femininity.[10]

For the most part, Latino theater history in the United States consists of disruptions and displacements. What traces remain of its histories are fragmented. However, if one wanted to trace a line of descent from contemporary Latino performance and that produced in the late 1940s and 1950s, one could do so by examining the life experience and the artistic production of Marga Gomez. In fact, Gomez's rewriting of her life story reconstructs not just her family genealogy but a cultural genealogy, as well: Her immigrant family's rise and fall parallels that of the rise and fall of the circulation of Latino live theater.

As the Harlem-born daughter of Latino "showbiz parents," Marga Gomez embodies a link between the older performance legacy and recent expansions of that legacy. Gomez seems to walk in her parents' entertainment footsteps, although they performed in a social context completely different from Marga's. Unlike Latino theater in Los Angeles and the Southwest, the East Coast scene was not disrupted in the 1930s. In Los Angeles, audiences for live performance were disrupted and diminished by the combined effects of the Depression and repatriation/deportation campaigns. But Latino theater in New York survived into the 1940s and 1950s because its audience base continued to grow, augmented by the influx of Puerto Rican, Cuban, and Spanish immigrants.[11] The Southwest theater tradition did not disappear completely, however, since Latino performers who had once performed mostly for Mexican Americans in the Southwest went on to perform on New York stages such as the Teatro Hispano throughout the 1950s and early 1960s, until the popularity of television variety shows in both Spanish and English displaced live performances in general.[12] But before television displaced the live performance tradition, the mixing of Mexican and Mexican American performers on stage with Cuban, Puerto Rican, and other Latino immigrant performers and audiences generated a sense of what the scholar Nicolás Kanellos calls "hispanicity"—the forging of a sense of pan-American Latino identity.[13] According to Gomez, both her parents were key players on the Latino stage during this period. In fact, her father often performed at Teatro Hispano, a place that Kanellos describes as "the most important and longest-running house in the history of Hispanic stage in New York."[14]

Sometime in the late 1940s, both of Gomez's parents—her Puerto Rican mother, Margo Estremera, and her Cuban father, Willy Chevalier—immigrated to New York City to escape poverty, hoping to play leading roles in their own American success stories. They immigrated as performers in a social context shaped by the Good Neighbor Policy, a policy that helped to generate the conditions for the first "things Latin" craze. Since both of her parents never fulfilled their aspirations, partly because of mainstream show business's bias against Latino performers, Gomez characterizes her parents' experience in this country as a failure of the American Dream. However, both parents had their moment of relative prosperity as successful entertainers in the New York Latino theater circuit before televised Spanish-language variety shows became popular.[15] Her mother's story—the subject of *Memory Tricks*—is somewhat different from her father's. Performing as an "exotic dancer" (which in the 1950s meant someone who performed a variety of Middle Eastern and Afro-Cuban dances), Gomez's bilingual mother enjoyed popularity with New York's mainstream audiences as Margo the Exotic, as well as with Latino audiences as Margo Estremera. However, she divorced Gomez's father and married an Italian American man, who insisted that she quit dancing, and she became financially dependent on her second husband.

Gomez explains that the popularity of Spanish-language television was one of the major reasons for her father's fall from popularity. Willy Chevalier, Gomez's father, was a popular comedian, a master of ceremonies, and a producer of live variety shows. In the early 1950s, he enjoyed a large Spanish-speaking audience. But, by the mid-1950s, people who at one time had regularly attended live performances began to stay at home, since telecast shows tended to follow the same format and to feature the same performers (Celia Cruz and Tito Puente, for example) as the live shows Gomez's father had so successfully hosted. Unlike Gomez's mother, Chevalier chose to perform in Spanish. Thus, he never had the appeal to English-speaking audiences that Gomez's mother did as she performed exotic dances in both Latino and Anglo night clubs. Although he temporarily fulfilled the promise of the dream, he was never able to break into the television industry in a significant way, and after a struggle with alcohol and drug addiction, he died as poor as he had been the day he entered the United States.

By renarrativizing her father's difficult life story in *A Line around the Block*, Gomez makes explicit the connection between New York's Latino

Marga Gomez in publicity photos for her 1995 performance piece, *A Line around the Block*. Photograph by Craig Schwartz. (Reprinted with permission.)

performances of the past and those of the present. Marga Gomez, the successful contemporary artist, renarrates her father's complex past, revisiting both his glory days and his descent into alcohol and drug addiction and his return to poverty. Marga's representation of his story coincides with the fragmented record of Latino theater in the United States more generally.

A Line around the Block begins in the 1980s after her father's funeral, jumps back to the late 1950s and early 1960s, to the eve of her father's Teatro Latino opening show, moves forward to the late 1970s, when her father's health and career hit their lowest point, and then returns to the present. The first part of the performance centers around the opening of her divorced father's *teatro* in Harlem in the 1950s. Her dad has just sunk his life savings into the doomed *teatro*, hoping to recapture the hearts and money of the Spanish-speaking working-class audience once so loyal to him. He prays to his home altar for Marga to be happy and asks that God watch over her and "makes my *teatro* a big hit with a line of people waiting to get in the door every week." Marga's mother thinks he is crazy because she knows that nobody "goes to *teatros* anymore. That time is over.

Harlem! He could give you that money, Marga, for when you go to college. But he's going to waste it now!"[16] But the preteen Marga could care less about her college fund at this point. She is ecstatic to help her father with preparations for opening night, especially since her idol—the sultry, glamorous, and popular singer (and undercover lesbian) Irma Pagan—is starring in the show. In grand *variedad* style, Irma Pagan has agreed to be in the show—it was Willy Chevalier who gave her her first break—despite the fact Chevalier can pay her nowhere near what she earns for appearing on Spanish language television's Channel 47. Marga sets up her favorite part of her dad's *variedad* for us—when Irma Pagan sings her rendition of "Pillow Talk"—by framing the relationship between Irma and her dutiful "secretary" as a domestic one. For example, Irma slips when introducing her secretary to Chevalier when she says, "Let me introduce you to Señorita Leonela Albino—my personal secretary—ha, ha, gracias, and she can cook, I mean type." Soon after, Marga, the adult artist, transforms into Irma, the glittery femme fatale, drag and all, and addresses the *teatro*'s imaginary Spanish-speaking audience in English:

> Ladies and gentlemen, I want to ask you a favor. Yes, Irma Pagan, who has everything, two Italian sports cars and mansion in New Jersey just to keep her fabulous clothes. Irma, the star of the most popular television show in the history of UHF, Irma Pagan, who can have any man she wants, if she wanted. She needs a favor from you, and you, and you, Puertorriqueños, Dominicanos, Cubanos, Mexicanos, Ecuatorianos, no matter were you're born. We are all brothers. Because we all share the same native tongue. Our native tongue is powerful . . . share your tongue with me now! Leonela? Leonela eres un León, I can't tame you. Make pillow talk, not war!

This compelling moment in *A Line around the Block* invokes Marga's past, present, and future lives. As an adult performer, she translates into English the atmosphere of the *variedades* for English speakers who, because of language barriers, might otherwise never have known of this tradition. Employing the trope of "native tongue," Gomez invokes the memory of the diasporic, heterogeneous Latino audience that shares the Spanish language, while encoding issues of sexuality. The double meaning of "shared tongue"—in language and communication and in what has been traditionally read as the function of the tongue in lesbian erotics—is expressed humorously as Irma momentarily loses herself in her stream-of-consciousness monologue.[17] It is no coincidence that the performance artist Carmelita Tropicana (Alina Troyano) also comically, yet critically, employs the same double entendre when she states that she is "very good with the tongue."[18]

While invoking earlier days when theater served to bring diverse immigrant populations together, the scene opens a space for the narrative to address Gomez's budding preteen attraction to women, as well as her father's homophobia. Backstage before Irma performs, young Marga thwarts her father's every attempt to keep her away from Irma and "her secretary." Ultimately, when Marga translates and then reenacts/reinvents the character of Irma Pagan (since Irma would have spoken in Spanish, not English), she inserts the taboo figure of the Latina lesbian into Latino performance history and implies that lesbian subjects have long existed "unseen" in the Latino community at large.

In the end, this scene speaks to the present as it casts Marga in the awkward role of translator of the past to her present and future audiences. Given that her audiences are neither exclusively Latino nor gay, her role as translator, albeit a difficult one, is crucial. As her narrative addresses and navigates various cultures and lifestyles, as well as reinvents the past, it constructs new subjects for a hybrid audience and brings audiences to a meeting ground they might have never imagined without her performance. Her struggle to translate cumbersome issues of language, community, and sexuality impetuously disrupts the flow of her text throughout her work. Ultimately, as the critic José E. Muñoz eloquently argues, "Gomez's public performances of memory is a powerful disidentification with the history of lesbian stereotyping the public sphere."[19]

Despite the fact that (or maybe because) she was raised by Latino parents and was greatly impressed by the Latino entertainment world to which her parents exposed her, Gomez makes a provocative claim: she does not see herself as a "real Latina" because she cannot speak Spanish fluently; she claims that she has been totally assimilated into the "white supremacist social structure" that her parents encountered.[20] Gomez seems to equate the loss of cultural authenticity with the loss of language, and, at the United States' *fin de siglo*, Gomez shares this opinion with others. In a recent *Los Angeles Times* interview, she joked, "C'mon, I can't salsa. It's sad. Second-generation Latinos really feel a lot of angst over losing their language because it has to do with internalized racism."[21] Gomez's anxiety concerning her Latina-ness might also be fueled by the fact that "light-skinned Latinas often fail to fulfill exoticized racial expectations and must therefore continually confront challenges to their status as 'authentic' Latina subjects."[22] Because issues of internalized racism and sexism are rarely discussed and because Gomez knows so well the anxiety that Latinos can experience around such practices, some of her funniest material taps into the ambivalence and angst many second- and third-generation Latinos feel about issues of ethnic identity and identification. This material also demonstrates how these issues are complicated by and complicate issues of sexuality and class. In *Pretty, Witty, and Gay*, for example, Gomez explains that when she first arrived in San Francisco, knowing almost nothing about the city, she went to the Castro district looking for her people (Cubans) and to a Cuban-style restaurant that served beans and rice. Instead, to her delight, she found "Coco the Transvestite," as well as a lively gay and lesbian culture.

But others do not so readily agree with this notion that because Gomez, or any other Latina, cannot speak Spanish, she is not a true Latina. The theorist Rosa Linda Fregoso questions the notion of cultural authenticity and argues against the production of ethnic identity (specifically Chicano) built on "a political model of subjectivity grounded in a notion of a fixed self."[23] In this formulation, cultural identity appears as an "authentic essence, located in a core subject, whose identity is one of 'being.'"[24] Instead, Fregoso (expanding on Stuart Hall's theorizing on cultural identity) understands identity as a formation—one becomes a "subject in process" and is never a "fixed self."[25] This understanding allows one to recognize that the production of cultural identity is dynamic and subject to historical, geographical, and political change. Thus, what was once considered to constitute Latino identity is not completely lost in the past but does in some way inform the construction of a future identity, though it does not necessarily determine it. Fregoso's argument assumes that categories of race/ethnicity, gender, sexuality, and nationality are never biologically given but are located in history and are instead constructed through representation (or discourse). This assumption allows people (subjects) in their capacity as artists (and as everyday people) to reshape cultural/political identity. Fregoso's theoretical framework can be usefully applied to the construction of ethnic identity in general, but of course one has to make adjustments for each particular ethnic group under analysis. It seems that Gomez's anxiety about cultural authenticity is informed by this notion of the "fixed self," despite the fact that she constructs new Latina subjects in her performances. In this particular instance, the authentic essence of Latino identity is the ability to speak

Spanish—that which Gomez and others like her lack. Yet, Gomez, in constructing herself as a certain subject—a Queer Latina who desires to reclaim her Spanish language and Latino culture—works against the notion of a fixed cultural identity. She is a subject in the process of "becoming." As she inhabits multiple subject positions as a Queer Latina, Latina lesbian, and feminist, she is enacting what Fregoso discusses at length as "an alternative formulation of cultural identity," one that does not force Gomez to choose between a strictly Queer or Latino identity.[26] The tension Gomez jokes about as she is pulled by her two separate communities fuels her ambivalence, yet her identification with multiple communities (gay/lesbian and Latino/Chicano) allows her to turn what Fregoso so aptly describes as "the ambivalence of cultural identity into a politics of political identification."[27]

Gomez's representation of Latina identity as constructed in the 1950s (in *Memory Tricks*) and in the 1990s (in *Pretty, Witty, and Gay*) demonstrates how that identity has transformed over time. In her performance pieces and standup comedy, Gomez constructs, for a relatively diverse audience, representations of the categories Latina and Queer that challenge the status quo. She is honest about her desire to succeed within mainstream popular culture, and she sees herself as part of a social struggle against Hollywood's refusal to allow Latino/a performers to represent Latinos and Queers in a more complex manner. She has found that the more she attempts to whittle down her identity to a Hollywood cliché, the more complicated her representations become, as indicated in the title of one of her shows, *Half-Cuban, Half-Lesbian* (Gomez explains why she invented the title in an interview, discussed later).

Yet, despite, indeed, because of its tensions and contractions, Marga Gomez's work, like that of Marisela Norte, is important for its struggles against "the culture of the powerful"[28] for at least three major reasons: (1) Gomez's representation of racial/ethnic and sexual identity problematizes notions of a "homogeneous" North American national identity; (2) Gomez's performances of Latina experiences demonstrate the heterogeneity of this category; (3) Gomez's identification with both gay/lesbian and progressive Latino communities gives us insight into the way the construction of gendered, racial, and cultural identity and identification is negotiated by those theorizing outside of the university. It is necessary to discuss the way that these categories overlap in order to understand how we might organize new types of coalitions against racist, sexist, economically marginalizing, and homophobic practices. Last, Gomez's performance begins to map out common points of interest for those Latinos/as who do not feel "authentic" and for antihomophobic and antiracist individuals who want to respond to confused xenophobes who, as she jokes, "want all the PUERTO RICANS to go back to MEXICO."

The Politics of Location and Representation

In her provocative *Translated Woman: Crossing the Border with Esperanza's Story,* Ruth Behar foregrounds the discussion of the politics of location and representation throughout her text. This discussion is central to Behar's book, since she considers herself to be a "feminist ethnographer"[29] who is writing a feminist ethnography. Her text documents the life of a Mexquitic woman street peddler, who is given the fictitious name Esperanza.[30] Behar transcribes from audiotape, and translates from English to Spanish, a series of interviews, recorded from 1985 to 1989, in which Esperanza tells her life *historias.*[31]

The Chicana feminist ethnographer Pat Zavella has written about the ways in which ethnographers who come from aggrieved communities are beginning to cast a critical eye on the ways that they, in their position as ethnographers or interpreters, construct the identity of their "informants." She explains that:

> Increasingly, feminist and other field workers realize that we need to be sensitive to differences between our subjects and ourselves, aware of the possible power relations involved in doing research by, about and for women, and that feminist studies must include a diversity of women's experiences based on race, class, and sexual preference.[32]

Zavella highlights the racial/ethnic, class, and sexual preference differences and tensions that complicate feminist ethnography and that are being recognized by new ethnography. In the context of her situation—a Latina citizen of an economic center interviewing a so-called third-world woman living on the economic periphery—Behar "is forced to realize the extent to which the ethnographic relation is based on power," especially as her subject, Esperanza, talks back aggressively. Behar, positioning herself within this new school of ethnography, records the tensions she feels, in terms of power relations, between her and Esperanza. She also ensures that her readers know that Esperanza is keenly aware of the politics of location and that Esperanza knows how she herself is positioned in terms of her own relationship with Behar.[33]

It is both Behar's decision in her capacity as an economically upwardly mobile narrator to grant Esperanza subjectivity, and her meditation[34] on the politics of location and representation that make her book intriguing. It is also what distinguishes her work from that of other "travel writers" who cross the U.S.-Mexican border. Behar explains:

> Unlike all the other listeners of Esperanza's story, it was up to me, as the researcher with access to the resources of bookmaking, to transform her "spoken words into a commodity." In my multiple roles as priest, interviewer, collector, transcriber, translator, analyst, academic connoisseur, editor, and peddler of Esperanza's words on this side of the border, I had to cut, cut, and cut away at our talk to make it fit between the covers of a book, and even more important, to make it recognizable *as a story*, a certain kind of story, a life history. Although Esperanza in her own life is an immensely talented storyteller, the text of her life certainly did not come ready-made.[35]

Again, Behar highlights the fact that representation and narration are processes by stating that Esperanza's text did not come "ready-made." She demonstrates that she had to interpret more than just the oral language of Esperanza's stories. In this way, Behar helps to deconstruct any simple notion that translation occurs without reinvention or reconstruction. Yet, even with its self-reflexivity, Behar's work with Esperanza has not gone without criticism for its inherent "unequal power relationship."[36]

Behar's meditation on the politics of location and representation directly relates to my own social location as an academic who translates the spoken word of Chicana and Chicano writers/performers (who grew up in working-class neighborhoods) into academic discourse. Not long after I read Behar's book, I was confronted with these questions at a conference called "Feminist Multi-Insurgencies."[37] My presentation theorized about the Chicana spoken word, and on the spur of the moment I invited the spoken-word artist Marisela Norte to present with me; in intervals, she read excerpts from her collection *NORTE/Word* as I read my analysis. At the end of the presentation, Norte joked, "Well, I didn't realize I was doing all that, but if Michelle says so. . . ." Norte's comment inspired laughter among the listeners and anxiety in me. Someone from the audience then asked whether I could comment on the process and problems of interpretation and analysis. Given that two of the writers who are highlighted in my work have responded in person to my "readings" of their work, the problem struck a chord. Behar's *Translated Woman* had certainly helped me to understand the process of interpreting/rewriting texts. Additionally, I try not to judge Norte's (or other artist's) work by traditional aesthetic standards but instead attempt to understand how her work helps to illuminate how larger social practices affect women. However, I left the conference wondering whether that question would have been addressed to someone who did not write about "ethnic" culture in the United States. Was I being positioned as a "performance ethnographer" of sorts? If so, what were the assumptions and implications of that positioning?

A little more than a year after the conference, the opportunity to interview Marga Gomez arose, and I jumped at the chance. By that time I was already quite conscious of my uncomfortable role of "performance ethnographer." However, I was looking forward to the interview, as I had been inspired by scholars who, in the context of struggle for social change, saw the importance of and the need for open discussions with artists about the politics of representation.[38] I found Marga Gomez's work compelling: Her texts generate a provocative tension and contradiction in her representations of Latina sexuality and lesbian identity. I knew it would be important for my own theorizing to converse with Gomez in her capacity as an actual maker of Latina cultural production that addresses many of the questions I had been grappling with.

I structured the interview questions around issues that were important to me: hybrid identities, language, sexuality, and class. She was someone like myself. We had been "girl" rebels, whose suburban upbringing engendered an ambivalence about the hybrid identities we embodied as we lived betwixt and between cultures and languages. Though her work centers on and addresses lesbian subjects, her critique of the patriarchal control of women's sexuality spoke to me and, at the same time, forced me to recognize my own heterosexual privilege (she jokes about really "hip" straight people who appreciate and sometimes appropriate Queer aesthetics but hesitate to cross the line over to a Queer lifestyle).

I nervously drove the two hours from Santa Cruz to Marga's place in San Francisco. I was anxious because she was so well known and I had become a great fan. In addition, I wanted to prove to her that academics were "hip." By some miracle, I found a place to park my car near enough to her apartment on a slope with typical San Francisco Victorian houses.

I clutched my tape recorder for security as I struggled uphill to her apartment. When Marga opened the door, she was visibly surprised to see me, another dark-haired, brown-eyed Latina. I was surprised, too; she looks tall on video, but we were the same height. Luckily, we clicked. Given my name, Michelle, she told me, she was expecting the "granola" type Santa Cruz is famous for—no makeup, Birkenstocks—and certainly not a Chicana. But, instead, there I was, the exact opposite—dressed to impress—just as she was. True, I did not look like the "typical" graduate student (and she laughed when I explained that lipstick is part of my culture). I had also brought my copy of Nicolás Kanellos's *A History of Hispanic Theater in the United States* to share with her. Marga was writing *A Line around the Block* at the time, and I shivered when, as she was flipping through the pages, she found a photo of her father performing at the Teatro Hispano.[39]

Given that we are both engaged in the projects of rewriting and reinventing Latina identity and of tracing Latino theater history, and that, as native-born "Latinas," we are similarly positioned by racialized hierarchies in the United States, the power dynamics that structured the interview are quite different from those that structured Behar's and Esperanza's. We are both articulate public women, public in the sense that our critiques of patriarchy and sexist practices are available for public consumption. Of course, our critiques circulate in different modes and through different circuits, and, of course, Gomez has much more public exposure than most academic writers. In that regard, the interview became more of a dialogue, since we performed different, yet complementary, roles in the process of social change. Marga Gomez translates both her parents' "native tongue" and Hollywood's problematic politics of representation, which turns the empowerment of self-annunciation into a temporary "chic" trend, while I transcribe and reframe Marga Gomez's texts in the attempt to create a link between those who theorize racial and gender formation both inside and outside the academy. My ambition was to create an interview context in which we could mutually expand our theorizing of racial and gender formation. Embedded within our interview/conversation are the thorny questions of the politics of location.[40]

MHP: Your dad was a Spanish-language comedian, right?

MG: Well, he also was an impresario, he put huge shows together, and he also wrote songs. But what he was best known for was being a master of ceremony, and a comedian.

MHP: Since he spoke Spanish and you didn't, how did you understand him?

MG: Probably at the time I understood. Now, I don't have a lot of recollection of it. I don't know if I really did understand him that much when he did his show because by the time I started going to shows when I was six or seven, I think I didn't know Spanish so well anymore. So I think I understood some things, but probably not that much.

MHP: Wasn't it hard at home, then? How did you talk with your father?

MG: Well, no, he spoke English. On stage he spoke Spanish, but at home my parents spoke English to me. They weren't that concerned about me keeping the language. My father had more pride in being Cuban than my mother had pride in being Puerto Rican. He didn't want to learn English that well. He tried to make it in Hollywood. He had his breaks and he had a screen test, but he didn't make it. He was pretty stubborn about learning English, he didn't want to. I'll never know really why they, or he, let it be that I didn't learn Spanish. But I think there was so much pressure in the 1960s to totally assimilate that he probably thought he was helping me. My guess is my mother set the direction for that.

MHP: So he learned English in the U.S.?

MG: The story my mother told me was that he was in Cuba dancing on that strip of night clubs in Havana as a comedy act. A talent scout from Johnny Walker Red saw him. At that time he did a little comedy, a little dance. This scout said he was going to take him to New York, since he was doing really well in Havana. So he took my father, but I guess didn't realize that my father needed to speak English since most of the venues catered to Anglo people who would come to see "The Latins." That was the new thing, the new trend.

MHP: Where?

MG: I don't know the places, but there were a lot of clubs like that because it was a new type of show, and the performers really had to be bilingual. Or really just speak English with a Latin "flavor." And since my father didn't speak any English, he got fired from this gig. He then tried to get into the Teatro Hispano and Puerto Rican theater, but they wouldn't give him a break. And so one night he just jumped up on the stage and grabbed a microphone and started his comedy act and people really liked it, and after that they had to hire him.

He was a comic and then became a master of ceremony. Then he got involved in television. He got his diploma from a television broadcasting school in New York. And then he began creating his own television shows. In *Carpa Clash* I did a piece about my father. I changed the situation, but basically I copied a character he created for television called Caballero Thirteen. Mr. Thirteen. He was the narrator, an Alfred Hitchcock type. He'd come out of his coffin and then he would set up a scary story. He wrote the scripts himself. This was televised on Channel 9 or 13 in New York. This was in the 1950s, and there was a few hours of programming for Spanish-speaking audiences. In fact Spanish television is what changed everything for my father—besides his own drinking and bad choices. I think Spanish television killed the live variety show in New York because people just didn't bother going out anymore. They'd just stay home, and they watched people on television. Families were starting to fall apart; the pressure from trying to make it in this country; people got cynical and jaded, and along with the fact that they could watch television at home, they never went out anymore. So his show really started to fall apart. But that's what he did, he was a real force in the late fifties and sixties.

And so this piece that I'm going to write about him . . . yeah, it's very hard 'cause a lot of people are dead, I can't find people, and a lot of them were just out of it, nuts. So I'm going to try to do the research, but I might end up not making it so factual and just do the essence of who he was and what my experience was—mythologize him a little more. In *Memory Tricks,* the stories about my mother are things that actually happened. But with my father, I might not do it the same. I'm just thinking of having it be a little bit more abstract and using characters around his life. The thing is that I really love him, he treated me really wonderfully, but he really wasn't around. He wasn't there for me. Even though my mother was involved in her career, she still tried to fulfill the role of mother—deal with my school. My dad just showed up, was around for a couple hours, and then he went and did his show. He was just more of a mystery to me. And then of course my parents split up, I went with her, so I didn't really know as much about him.

You know, the research I'm doing about my father's life is difficult because I don't know Spanish. I have a few names in Puerto Rico. But the other thing is that a lot of people who knew my dad are still around. For some reason with my mom I wasn't thinking about those things, but after doing her piece I'm a little shy about doing my father's story. Some of the things he did to women were intense, and some of those women are still around. And there are probably kids around. So I can't . . . if I told his story, I would have to make up another person. So I'm still trying to balance the two—which do I want to do, the factual or the fictional, because it's very interesting—all the things he did—it makes a good story. But also it's hard to give up the fact that he actually lived, this is his name, these are the people. And if I do the factual, it's not going to be as honest. If I fictionalize it, I have the freedom to tell what happened. It will meet somewhere in between.

MHP: *Memory Tricks* has recently been optioned to *American Playhouse*. Part of its wide appeal is that almost everyone can relate to issues concerning family relationships, especially dysfunctional relationships.

MG: Yes, it's particularly popular with Latinos and Jewish people.

MHP: But the story you tell is so compelling because it is so specifically located in the history of U.S. Latino performance. As the daughter of Latino parents who immigrated to New York in the late 1940s, who left poverty to find success in the East Coast Latino entertainment scene, would you consider theirs an immigrants' success story? What were some of the challenges and obstacles faced by your parents?

MG: Well, I would call it an immigrant's quest-for-success story, but I would call it more a story of the failings of the American dream. That story focuses more on my mother. In her mind, and in the minds of our very small world, she was a success. She came to New York as a teenager with her mother, very poor. She had certain values: to be very beautiful, the most beautiful, to be the most sought after. She wanted to be an actress; to be an actress she had to take lessons, and to pay for the lessons she started dancing. She wound up being known as a dancer instead of an actress. She wanted to be a Hollywood star, but that wasn't going to happen because of her accent. Instead, she ended up dancing for Latino audiences, and that's how she met my father. People said they were the Lucy and

Ricky of their days; everybody loved them as couple, but of course that little honeymoon was over right away. I remember them sleeping in separate beds.

When I was around eight or nine years old, my mother decided to leave the Latino scene and started to dance in the Anglo night clubs. She was probably making more money in those places. She had an Anglo agent who sent her out to play Connecticut and that area. She was making more money than my father, and the marriage was lousy. By then they were pretty much living their own lives. But, yet, she was still very beautiful, and everyone thought, "Wow, she's got it all." And all she was doing, basically, was capitalizing on her looks and her dream to be an American; she really wanted to fit in, leave New York, leave Washington Heights. Well, eventually she met this guy, an Italian guy, but white enough, and he had made lots of promises that he was going to make a lot of money. She really wanted to move to Long Island, into the suburbs. When you made it, you get a big house in the suburbs. So that's what she did: she divorced my father; married this guy; got a big house in the suburbs; couldn't dance anymore, because this guy wouldn't let her; was never accepted by the other neighbors; and basically became a prisoner in this house. There was nothing else for her. She really cut off her culture, she cut off everything, just to have this stupid house in the suburbs, and to be the only Puerto Rican for miles. She really tried to deny who she was and deny who I was. In *Memory Tricks* I talk about her dying my hair red. So as my father continued in show business up to his last days, my mother gave it up. She gave up her career—in the traditional feminine role—for a man and for a white American man. So that was the failure of the American dream because she wasn't coming to this country with all her identity, with a real sense of herself. She was coming with a sense of somebody else she wanted to be and because of that she lost it all. And, then, as you see in *Memory Tricks,* her second husband just became more and more distant from her and then her life was really hell. The time before she got sick was really a nightmare for her, and really terrifying for her.

MHP: To go back to her early days as a dancer, what did it mean to be an exotic dancer in the fifties?

MG: You're the second person who's asked me that in a week. It's different today from what it meant back then. Now it means being a stripper; as far as I know, she was never a stripper. I think once you become a stripper, that's it. First she started out doing Afro-Cuban and merengues. She had beautiful little costumes—she had a cat costume—and she did burlesque numbers. I don't mean by burlesque that she would strip, but they were just dances. She would probably take off the cat suit and have a bathing suit type of costume underneath.

MHP: In terms of cultural mixing, it's interesting that she as a Puerto Rican woman was doing all these various dances.

MG: Well, those were the dances that the solo performers were doing then: merengues, Afro-Cuban, mambo. She did them all. At that time those dances were really hot. So, she was doing that—she was doing all kinds of numbers—with lighting and different types of effects. A real presentation there. So, when she became an exotic dancer, she started to play in the white clubs; that's when her stage name became Margo the Exotic. Dancers always had to change their styles according to the trends, and since Afro-Cuban dancers were no longer the rage, she became an exotic dancer. It was the new thing, and everybody was looking for exotic dancers. Exotic dancers could go to Japan. She had the opportunity to go to Japan, but I was too little, and she didn't want to leave me. So, I think she was dabbling in a few different dance routines and styles. But then she mostly started doing the exotic dancing. That would be the belly dancing with a little Middle Eastern music.

MHP: Interesting, a Puerto Rican woman performing Middle-Eastern dances.

MG: In those clubs, "exotic" meant the same thing; you could either be from Iran or from Puerto Rico, it's all considered exotic. Plus, she had bleached blonde hair, so it was pretty crazy.

MHP: I guess the question is, exotic for whom? But since we have a short amount of time, do you mind if I switch gears a little? You mentioned earlier that you observed that there is not a lot of documentation of Latino performance in this country. So do you see yourself as an historian of sorts, a chronicler of a different kind of history?

MG: I kind of wish that was true, but I don't know if I have the discipline to do all that work.

MHP: But I mean in a different way—a different kind of historian, what they call an organic intellectual. We have this term "organic intellectual," which is an intellectual not produced by the university.[41] So what I was trying to ask—since there is an impulse in mainstream culture to deny the full range of the contributions people of color have made to the economic, political, and cultural fabric of the U.S.—is if you see yourself telling about an experience that isn't considered history and telling it differently in a different form than we are taught history should be told in. Do you think about your project in that way?

MG: Well, that's what I hope to do, but I don't feel that's what *Memory Tricks* is. . . . *Memory Tricks* has just a hint, a suggestion of what was. For some people I guess that's big news. For me that's how life was. When I read *Mambo Kings* [by Oscar Hijuelos], I was very moved, because he captured a lot. For example, what it was like doing a gig, and taking the subway home; although my father always drove Cadillacs and my mother always took taxis home. The movie was a disgrace to the book, it was totally whitewashed, but I was inspired by that book, and I thought I would like to add to that. I would like to bring the details of my parents' life. But I'm finding it hard to get information. I just try to interview people, like my mother's old friends, and they are so reticent to talk. The thing is—I don't know if this is just a Latino thing—but we're really very private. So, a lot of people I talk to don't really want to say too much because they really believe in privacy. And, then, I have to honestly tell them that I'm going to do this film and do a piece, and that makes things even harder. There's someone who could tell me so much, but it's like pulling teeth. But even just a little is fun, and plus I have tons of pictures that I haven't even looked at yet and little clippings. Some of the material, though, that I'm going to put in these pieces about my father is going to be part imagination and intuition. If you can't remember the past, then you just make it up! So, it's going to be somewhere between history and myth.

MHP: Can you remember if your parents were involved in any actor's union or organizations?"

MG: Yes, they were in a group for *artistas*. I think my father was the president, and they made it up. But all they did was have parties, and then they got very criticized, because there were dues being paid and people thought all they did was do parties and didn't do very serious things. My parents really liked just having the meetings, and my dad really liked being president and my mother was vice president. It was like this club where they said, "Yes, we have to do something," but they weren't real serious about it. In his story I do want to recreate this little organization. Of course they were in AGVA, I think the letters stand for the Actors Guild for the Variety Arts. They were both in that.

MHP: What do you think is happening now in the development of Latino talent in the entertainment industry? What do you think has changed?

MG: Well, it's another chic, lesbian chic, Asian chic, and Latino chic. Everybody in Hollywood wants to have a hand in the Latino culture. I mean, Latinos have always been exploited and used by the industry and by advertisers. My father was really involved with that, in selling products, getting promotions going for whatever— Borden's, or cigarettes, or coffee. Usually things that are totally bad for your health. Miller Beer. In Hollywood, it's the same thing. They just want to make money, and so they think if they can make money off of us they'll use us. They had their *AKA Pablo* show, which was a disaster.

MHP: What was that?

MG: That was the Paul Rodriguez show about ten years ago. It was not written by Latinos, and he wasn't really ready for the show. He's a better actor now. That was a flop, and so what happened was since that was a flop, executives thought that Latino doesn't work on TV. So I've gone to meetings now where they want two different things. They want me to be a character for television who says something about being Latino, and then I go to other meetings where it's "You're Latino but it doesn't need to be the focus of the story." Which really for me would be more appropriate, because I feel so assimilated, so cut off that it's a source of shame and guilt for me. But at the same time, there's so many people like us [I told her my Spanish was choppy, too]. But it's hard because for television you have to be such a cliché almost. I don't know if it's serving us to do it.

For example, [sigh] do you know that piece *Death and the Maiden*? It's set in Argentina. It's ready to play in Los Angeles at the Mark Taper forum, with a Latina playing a Latina. But in New York they did it with Glenn Close playing a Latina. It's about a woman who's been tortured, then comes in contact with her torturers many years later. So, at the Mark Taper, they had a big controversy, because the big muca-mucas wanted to have a name, but then the people said, "No, this is bullshit, you can't try that in L.A." And now they are going to make a film of it and Sigourney Weaver is going to take Glenn Close's place. And I'm just sick. They are very concerned with names. It's a Catch-22. Now the names are Rosie Pérez, of course she can't do *Death and the Maiden* [imitating Pérez in a high Nuyorican accented voice], "No, get out of here, my people will defeat you." Then there's María Conchita Alonso. You can't really get too worried about her. They have to just open the doors. But there's no altruism in the industry. It's all about money. Someone breaks in once in a while despite all the obstacles because they never just give, and there is no way to control them. I mean we boycott the movies and they don't care. The only thing Latinos can do is somehow get behind Latino performers and really turn out for them. I don't know exactly how you do it, but I guess when there is a Latino film, go see it. For instance, a lot of Latinos went to see *Like Water for Chocolate*.

MHP: But *Like Water for Chocolate* is a film made in Mexico.

MG: Yes, it's not a Hollywood film. But *El Mariachi*, that's done pretty good, that guy has gotten a lot of attention now. But, of course, in that film, a lot of people did get their brains blown out; so, as long as you show that in a film I guess it will do okay. I think that it's still really hard out there, and there's a lot of mixed messages. They say they're really interested, yet they can't seem to have the balls to bankroll anybody and give everybody else a break.

MHP: Who are some of your connections in the world of Latino performers?

MG: Well, my major connections are Monica Palacios, Culture Clash, Luis Alfaro I'm getting to know through Monica, and Beto Ariaza. I've just gotten to know, she's not a performer exactly, Sandra Cisneros. That's really neat, because just as a writer, she's really inspiring.

MHP: How did you get to know her?

MG: She came to my show—just a comedy show I was doing at Josie's Cabaret—not this New Year's Eve [1994], but the New Year's Eve before, and she introduced herself. She was being interviewed at Herb's Theater, so I went to the interview, then afterwards I said, "Hi." Then I played in San Antonio, Texas, so I went and visited her there; we drank tequila and smoked cigars. I think that's probably it for my connections, everybody else is pretty peripheral. I've met Luis Valdez and José Luis Valenzuela. I met him at the Taper when he directed Culture Clash, and we had a real nice connection there.

MHP: I understand that your work is influenced by your involvement with grass-roots theater collectives, and I heard that you and Monica Palacios started Culture Clash together. How did that happen?

MG: Well, we didn't really form it. The person who formed Culture Clash was René Yañez; Richard Montoya [a member of Culture Clash] calls him "the Godfather." René was the director of the Galería de La Raza on 24th Street in the Mission district [of San Francisco]. Now he's at the Mexican Museum, and he's always got something going. Well, it was his job to organize something for Cinco de Mayo, and he wanted to do something different. Cinco de Mayo was always the same old thing. So, he wanted to do a comedy show, and he had a connection with Monica Palacios; they had both performed at the Galería and he knew Richard [Montoya]. He asked Monica, "Why don't you have Marga come?" So it was Monica, me, Richard, and Tony Burciaga.

MHP: That's Burciaga of *Drinking Cultura* fame?

MG: That's right, he's a visual artist and a poet. So the four of us had a meeting. Then Herbert Siguenza came and Rick Salinas came, and we had our first show. It was just each of us doing our own spot. The guys had never done standup before, and that's basically what it was. Each of us was doing standup comedy. Herbert was doing characters, Michael Jackson and Prince, and he was sort of in between the spots. Herbert would come out with different little outfits and do something like Tony Montana, or Scarface. That was the show.

MHP: When was this?

MG: This was maybe in '85 or '86. Monica and I stayed with the group for about two years and it was more or less like that. It didn't really take off until after we left, but I'm not saying it's 'cause we left. It was like we were all doing our own thing and then we would get together and do a Culture Clash show. Culture Clash was like a secondary occupation. It was really neat for me, because before that I had never played to Latino audiences. And one thing I had to learn was that Latino audiences are sometimes really religious [laughter]. I thought Latino audiences would think it was really funny to make fun of the Church. But it was just the opposite, and I was having real trouble with a lot of my material, because I was still new at it. A lot of my material was just a reaction against all the oppressive things of my childhood. So I was really going after the Church, and that was bad. We were doing a lot of shows for Republican Latinos, MAPA [Mexican American Political Association], and all those people. And Monica and I were just too feminist for these audiences. I don't even think we were doing any gay material, but we were not getting the same response as the guys. It just got depressing after a while. We had some good shows, and the women would always say "All right!" But it was just hard not to have everybody with you. Since we were all new, it was important for the group to get smaller, and that's what happened.

MHP: Do you think you influenced the group in a kind of feminist way?

MG: Monica was more outspoken. I was pretty unassertive. I was more passive-aggressive, and I'd blow up. I couldn't really articulate what was bothering me, but Monica would. They knew what was up, they came from the community, too, they had to deal with strong women. But it was still a learning process, and it was going to take them a while, and it was going to take us a while to feel comfortable. They continue, some people will say things about them. My experience has been pretty good this last time. In fact, they gave me all these male-bashing lines in the *Carpa Clash* show that everybody thought I wrote. But, no, I wrote my monologue, but all the things I said to insult them, they wrote for me.

MHP: So in this *Carpa Clash* show you play a character named Mimi. I haven't seen the show, but one reviewer writes that Mimi is the daughter of Mexican entertainers. Could you tell me about how that character evolved? Why did you decide to do present yourself as Mexican?

MG: Mimi is me. You know, I don't know how these reviewers get work [sigh]. I spent the first five minutes of a fifteen-minute monologue talking about being Cuban and Puerto Rican. This guy could have not been Latino. No matter how much you try to explain that these are different countries with different personalities, different histories, to them everybody's Mexican or everybody's Puerto Rican. It's the same to them; they think it's all Spanish. So, yeah,

Mimi is me. They told me that all the guys in *Carpa Clash* had a clown nickname. So, I figured I'd use Mimi. It's my nickname, from when I was a kid, and I like the name. It sounded kind of clowny, too.

MHP: Moving off the subject of reviewers and back to your work— your work is full of interesting tensions and contradictions.

MG: Thank you!

MHP: As you travel to different venues, different performance spaces, you construct your identity differently in response to different audiences. In other words, you represent your "self" or your identity differently to different crowds. Why do you do this?

MG: I'm not sure what you mean when you say that when I'm addressing Latino crowds that I'm not addressing my sexuality? Can you give me an example?

MHP: For instance, in the *Culture Clash* show, whose audience is primarily Latino, you tended to foreground your ethnicity and leave out discussions of lesbian sexuality. In contrast, when addressing Queer audiences, on the HBO comedy special, it seemed easier for you integrate comments about your ethnicity into your routine. This tendency to "shape" your identity is fascinating to me because it demonstrates that identity is fluid, not fixed, and mutable. But could you explain why issues of lesbian sexuality, but not sexuality in general, tend to fade out when you address Latino audiences?

MG: Oh, okay. Well, I hadn't really thought about it that way. The reason I didn't talk about lesbian issues in the Culture Clash show is because the producer told me that the audience was full of a bunch of college-aged kids on dates and since I was getting a break on television, I really didn't want to bomb. So I talked about growing up Catholic and having a chaperon named Hymenia Permanente. So I did talk about sexuality, but in a way that straight people could relate to. Since the HBO comedy special was focused on gay/lesbian comedy, I could joke openly about my sexuality. But what I've found is that jokes about relationships are popular with almost anyone, so I'm going to work on those for a while.

MHP: Recently a photo of you was featured in a special issue of *Time* magazine.[42] On the cover was the image of a mestiza who, the article explains, "was created by a computer from a mix of several races. What you see is a remarkable preview of the New Face of

America." Under her image, the caption reads "How Immigrants Are Shaping the World's First Multicultural Society." The funny thing is, we're not sure what this woman's ethnicity is or if she has one, nor is the late-twentieth-century U.S. the world's first multi-cultural society.

A few pages into the magazine we find an image of you. The difference is that this *mestiza*'s image is not computer generated but can be traced to an actual Latina, you. And your image is interestingly marked as hybrid. Poised on a variety show stage, your long-haired figure is illuminated by candles with images of Catholic saints on them and simultaneously holds a 1950s-style microphone as well as a rosary. Your pin-striped-panted leg is almost wrapped around the microphone, and the men's high-top sneaker (a reference to U.S. mass culture) looks as if it might come crashing down on the candles. Or maybe it's being energized by them. The caption labels you a "Latin actress." But, I don't think you speak Latin. Given that your image appears in this special issue, what would you say if I said that this representation constructs a new image of a U.S citizen or subject?

MG: Well, I don't think so much about this country as I do the planet, and sometimes I do feel very out of it—being an American, that is. Living in San Francisco or living in Santa Cruz is not like living in America. I don't know because I really always felt out of the main-stream, on the fringe. I don't know if I'm the new kind of citizen, because a U.S. citizen to me is really into being in a group, really into shared experiences like Super Bowls and all that stuff. That's not for me. I feel more like an expatriate who lives here [laughs].

MHP: Right, except that there are many of us who have a shared experience of feeling like we don't belong and whose communities have been disenfranchised from political and economic power. So I think that there is a different version of U.S. citizen emerging because of the historical conjunctures, and though you have concern for the planet, you've lived or experienced certain historical moments, from the sixties to the nineties, you've witnessed the world change in certain ways. You've seen how the influx of Latino immigrants has changed the cultural fabric . . . and we've all witnessed them, too, and experienced them, and this constructed image of what it means to be a true American—blond, blue eyes—excludes the full range of what constitutes "American," more specifically

North American. I think that we are more representative (not that any one image can represent everyone) but that your story is just as American as that of the constructed ideal blond, blue-eyed, straight subjects.

MG: I feel more, to use an old term, like a citizen of the underground.

MHP: Well, there's a quote by a poet, Bob Kaufman, he was from the Bay Area, and he used to say that "way-out people know the way out."[43] What he meant is that sometimes way-out people, people on the fringe, can sometime show us the way out—out of this homophobic, misogynist, racist climate in which we live. So what I mean that by people living on the fringe.

MG: Yes, I see where you're going. You know, I had a little rap I used to do, called "The Way Out." This was about the time of the NEA censorship and all that. I use to do it all the time, and I use to have go-go dancers behind me. I would sing a little Spanish and do it to Santana's tune "Evil Ways." I had sampled Mellow Man Ace, and he samples Santana. Olivia Records might have a video of it. It goes like this [Gomez starts to sing]:

> Check it homies, we got problemas grandes, porque our libertad is being [Gomez forgot the word] by a honky. Senator Helms, he hates the arts endowment. He's got a flag up his ass, hey don't have a cow man. Who told Jesse he's got taste? He's just a big pendejo, our culture is just too good to waste. Don't cut off my dinero. A mi no me importa, if I do not get a grant. The show must go on, 'cause we have a brand new dance. I warn you if you're prudish or fanatically devout, no mira este baile que se llama 'WAY OUT.' It's homo and erotic and you move your crotch about, it's a real ice-breaker and it's called the 'WAY OUT'" (and I'd have the dancers come on). "Carmen and Diane are here to show you, when you do the 'WAY OUT' people get to know you. First you lick your lips like a nasty thing, mirando y templando and flapping your left wing. Then you give your partner a gentle thrust, if you like rub your chichis, that means touch your bust. You can 'WAY OUT' on the job, and you can 'WAY OUT' in the car. Got the same sex cravings? The 'WAY OUT' will get you far. If you are in the closet but you feel like shouting, express yourself. Honey, do the way outed. I remember the day I WAY OUTed to my parents, they were angry, enojados—a little bit embarrassed.

But then my parents changed. Now they're real proud of me, y siempre me gritan 'Marga baila WAY OUTing.' This is my handle, this is my spout, this is how you do—the 'WAY OUT.' I hope you didn't mind the WAY OUT exhibition, we want to do it now, before they have a prohibition. I know that it's not a Disney creation; to me it's art, to others deviation.

I can't remember the rest of it, but I have it somewhere. I did that rap for a couple years, and people would always ask for it. But I lost the tape. I could start using it again, but, you know, it's not a topic anymore; but it was great 'cause everything came together, I was able to put some Spanish in there, even though I didn't know very much.

MHP: The titles of your shows are funny and highly suggestive [Marga laughs], especially titles like *Pretty, Witty, and Gay* or *Memory Tricks*. *Pretty, Witty, and Gay* suggests different things to different audiences; maybe Latinos think of *West Side Story*, but in the Castro district it means something else. What were you trying to say with that title?

MG: Oh, both things. I have a little bone to pick with *West Side Story*. When you watch it, it's hard not to laugh. There's the terrible accents and make-up jobs. But then at the same time I'm very attached to *West Side Story*, so I always wanted to do something about it in standup. The first time I did anything about *West Side Story*, I did a three-minute, twenty-second version of it. Did you ever see that? This is when I did my Spanish talk show host has-been named Filomena Fabulosa. She had a show called *Noche Line*. So that was my first experience satirizing *West Side Story*.

And still a lot of times events will play "I Feel Pretty" or "I Want to Live in America" [*sic*], some stupid song from *West Side Story*. That music will haunt Puerto Ricans 'til the end of time. So I decided it was time to get them back, get it back, get our shot. And a lot of times in standup you need to have little slogans to describe yourself, and I thought it was just a good sounding sound bit. So I decided to do the show that way. And to bring up shades of *West Side Story* was appropriate, too. That song was written at a time when the term "gay" meant something else, and of course its meaning has changed and can't really be used again. It just worked out nicely.

MHP: Some fans wanted me to ask you if you were you trying to make a political move by using *Pretty, Witty, and Gay* instead of *Pretty, Witty, and Lesbian*?

MG [laughs]: Well, I don't think they got the *West Side Story* connection. Did they think it should be *Pretty, Witty, and Lesbian*? To tell you the truth, I prefer the terms "gay" or "Queer." "Lesbian" to me just . . . it's just too charged. Monica Palacios does a whole bit about claiming the word "lesbian." To me, I just don't like it. I was involved in lesbian separatism. I just have had too much lesbian . . . it's not just a word that describes sexuality to me, it describes almost a very strict way of living. I identify more with gay men [laughter]. But that's a whole other performance piece.

MHP: Going back to your days in New York—you joke about how you could speak Spanish until the "pack of wild Irish women who raised me beat it out of me. Back in those days, we called those Irish women nuns." Did the nuns really beat it out of you? I wouldn't be surprised because in the U.S. there's a history of violence that surrounds language and issues of resistance.

MG: I don't know, they beat us, they just beat us. I was a very, very good girl in Catholic school, because I didn't want to get hit at all. I don't know if they would hit us exactly for speaking Spanish. But what they did was they really favored the Irish kids' class, because the neighborhood was Puerto Rican, a little Cuban and Irish. They always favored the Irish kids. They just made you feel bad for speaking Spanish, for being darker. It was a psychological beating, but, combined with the physical punishments we'd get for breaking a rule, it all became part of the same thing. I just wanted to survive and be on the nuns' good side. I'd do whatever it took. So the threat of punishment was really an encouragement to finally complete the process of total assimilation, and that's what I did. Total detachment from my roots—in which I feel my mother was a collaborator, she's the one who started the whole thing. I know it had to happen somewhere, because when I learned to speak, it was in Spanish, and in just a few years, it was gone.

MHP: I think that happens to a lot of people. Although there is nothing inherently wrong with speaking Spanish, we get rewarded not to, and the English-only laws reinforce prejudice against speaking Spanish. But you answered my next question: Was your school culturally and racially mixed?

MG: Yes, it was at least 50 percent Latino, if not more. There was this feeling from the nuns . . . this school probably was there in the forties or fifties, then suddenly in the sixties there was just this wave of all these little brown kids. I think they just couldn't stand it that their neighborhood was just changing. The school was pretty much in a white neighborhood.

MHP: So there were no African American students?

MG: Well, everything changes in the space of one block. So yes, there were African American students, in fact, that area was considered Harlem. But, there were a few black kids in the class. In a class of twenty kids there would be four or five black kids. They really got trashed unless they became total supernerds. They could never do nothing wrong or else they would get beat.

MHP: Because you grew up in Harlem, the press constructs you as a child of the city, which is true, but they do it in such a way that it seems as if you were underprivileged. But you went to private school and had nannies. Can you tell me about how issues of class figured in your inner-city experience?

MG: It was really bizarre, because the neighborhood was working class. Everyone was struggling and getting poorer and poorer as the years went by. We were rich in the eyes of the neighborhood and in our own eyes. I thought we were rich because my father drove Cadillacs, my mother had minks, she had housekeepers, and we took these trips to South America. We had tacky French furniture and statues. And I grew up with a false sense of being upper class when we were really not. They spent a lot of money on junk and suddenly there was no more money. My mother just married someone who strangled her financially. My father had one bad business thing after another. He died in poverty, on Medicare, in a little place. Since my mother didn't really have any of her own money, she ended up where she started. My mother is now in a nursing home. I wasn't able to put her in the one that I wanted, because I didn't have the money. They started really poor, grew up in poor circumstances—shacks, no running water. They came to this country, struggled, and had a few years of prosperity. My mother's lasted a little bit longer, but as the property of a man. So, you see, it's really hard to define my class position. I really did live as a rich kid for a few years, at least the years that are most formative. Everybody envied me, and I enjoyed that. I was a little brat.

MHP: How do issues of class come up in your work now?

MG: Issue of class? Well, I don't know, it's complex, it's not that simple. You have money, you have illusions. I think that the symbols are there, but they may not be obvious. In *Memory Tricks*, when I tell the story about my mom and her father . . . she was an illegitimate child and her mother would go and take her to see her father, that's when issues of class come in. He had money, she didn't have money. So you see she came from poverty. When somebody comes from poverty in Puerto Rico, it's sort of like being in a caste, and of course in the piece you can see she came to a bad end.

And even if I do manage to prosper, I'm still always going to have this sense that this is going to be taken away from me. I have so much anxiety about making money or being homeless. I mean you do have to take care of yourself, especially when there is no one else. I think the problem is that some people don't put a limit to it. People start to acquire and then they can't have enough. But there are certain basic things that you do need to provide for yourself as far as your health and old age.

MHP: Yes, it's especially difficult for women, especially working-class immigrant women, to get the kind of health care they deserve as they age.

MG: And that's why I worry.

MHP: You seem to be de-essentializing Latina and Queer identity. In other words, your work complicates any notion that Latina or lesbian identity is lived in any one way. Your new standup show is called *Half-Cuban, Half-Lesbian*. What are you suggesting with the title?

MG: *Half-Cuban, Half-Lesbian*? Well, it's always come up in my standup. I try to keep my standup simple, so I want to do jokes about being Puerto Rican. But I'm also half-Cuban. So I've tried to deal with that in standup. I don't even know that much about Cuban culture, although I know more now that I'm researching this for my father's piece.

MHP: But you know what it is to be Cuban American.

MG: Kind of . . . or more American Cuban, I guess. I don't remember how I put that title together, and of course I don't say half-Cuban, half-Puerto Rican, half-lesbian [pause]. I know why. It's because I played in Miami, so I wanted to get the message across to gain the audience of Cubans, but I did not need anybody there who was going to flip out when they realized I was gay. So that's the reason for the title, I wanted to hit my target audience. Not that my audience was just Cuban lesbians, but that anyone who thought this was pretty cool would come to the show. But I continue to use that title because it's catchy. Even though I don't like to define myself as a lesbian comic, it helps me take the worry out of a situation where I'm traveling hundreds of miles to face people. This way they know where I'm coming from.

And it's funny because it's like lesbian is almost a sort of ethnic root. In a way it is a culture unto itself, and the two meet in interesting ways. I think the title works whether people see it or not because a lot of people don't think of Latinos as being Queer at all. It's a message . . . and it also refers to the conflict that I've gone through with both cultures. The same goes with Puerto Rican. This is just easier, it just rolls off the tongue easier.

MHP: Have you seen the work of Luis Alfaro? I think he negotiates ethnicity and sexuality in different ways than you do. Alfaro refuses to separate his sexuality from his ethnicity. He explains that he cannot be Chicano without being gay and vice versa.

MG: Well, Luis is very uncompromising. I, on the other hand, come from show business parents. So I'm trying to remain true to myself, but at the same time I'm going to have my hand in a few different things. I do try do make things accessible, but still have some kind of integrity. I try to expand my audiences. And it's not out of any kind of idealism; it's dollars and cents. I'm trying to provide for myself, since no one else does. I'm honestly afraid of being old and homeless.

MHP: You once said that you've been received by the mainstream press because of your lesbian profile. Why do think issues of sexuality are more accepted than those of class, race, and ethnicity? Or is that the case?

MG: It's easier to follow because I'm a really assimilated Latina. So, I don't have that essential Latino quality.

MHP: But none of us do.

MG: Right. But it's not good, it's very hard to get sound bites out of me about being Latino. My stories are kind of short about it. I'm really trying to get back to it now, but the lesbian chic thing? Well, I've been living in the Castro, so I'm pretty much closer to this culture and to this community.

MHP: So you feel like this lesbian chic has made it okay to be lesbian now?

MG: Oh yeah, but we don't know how long that's going to last. There has been a taboo on homosexuality and bisexuality. But it's finally being lifted. For so long people of color have tried to get attention and get a dialogue going. With just being Queer we can't. We can't even write about this, we can't even talk about this or see what you do. So now it's almost like the first time it's in the open. That's why it's new and the information has got to get out up to the plateau. It's really how much we're going to plateau out, how much are they going to be able to take, and it's really a mainstream kind of thing, homosexuals that they're talking about. There is lesbian chic. k.d. lang came out and Martina [Navratilova], and that's made a big difference. They really can't argue with the way k.d. sings or the way Martina plays. Actually, I've gotten the most attention from the press for *Memory Tricks*. It's my struggles with my Latino heritage and my mother that I have gotten the most interest and attention for.

MHP: Marisela Norte is a spoken-word artist whose writing, at times, shares similar themes with yours. In one piece she has written that she is "the one who cuts the label out." My reading of that line is that she cuts the label out of the category Latina/Chicana in order to represent a different image of what it means to be Latina. You, too, do some "cutting out." I think that's important, given that some people don't realize that the category Latino is quite heterogeneous, that Chicano culture is different from Puerto Rican, from Cuban, and other Latino cultures.

MG: Oh yeah, but I still get mistaken for being Chicano, especially working with Culture Clash. At the end of Culture Clash shows, they have a question-and-answer session. One time Richard [a member of Culture Clash] said that Chicano is a state of mind; that's the way I feel about being Queer. It's not so much about who you sleep with; instead, it's this openness. So I thought, okay, I can be a Chicana, or I can even be a Chicano . . . I think I'll be a Chicano [laughs]. It happens constantly. And it works the other way. If I were a Chicano living in New York, then everybody would think I was Puerto Rican.

MHP: To me, the fascinating thing about your performances are that they mutate the dominant story of what it means to be Latina or

Queer in the U.S. They also alter the story of what it means to be a U.S. citizen in 1994. Even though you may not intend to make a huge political statement about such issues, well, maybe you do . . . or at least it can be interpreted that way.

MG: The only thing I do is be honest, and that has not been that easy. And that's what I try to stick to. I guess with my cultural identity, I do two things: I hold it up, and I try to strip it away at the same time. It's confusing. But I guess it's the honest approach.

MHP: Do you have any advice for aspiring comedians?

MG: Write down what you think is funny and don't steal jokes. Or just don't steal my jokes [laughter].

Why include a discussion of Marga Gomez's performance in a study that focuses mostly on Chicana and Chicano cultural production? Like Marisela Norte, Luis Alfaro, El Vez, and Jim Mendiola, her texts explicitly and implicitly theorize representation.

The fragmented history of Latino theater in the United States has contained a trans-Latino element: the mutual influence of diverse performers from Mexico, Puerto Rico, Cuba, and Spain forged a sense of hispanicity on stage, engendering—temporarily—a sense of common interest within an audience as diverse as the stage. Since Gomez's family's story parallels the rise and decline of theater in the United States, analysis of this story provides insights into the function of theater culture. Additionally, Gomez is in conversation with Chicano and Chicana artists such as Luis Alfaro. She was a charter member of one of the most well-known Chicano comedy groups, Culture Clash, and formed the first Latina lesbian comedy duo with the Chicana comedienne Monica Palacios. Last, employing a comparative approach to the study of Chicano performance compels us to discuss the construction of hybrid subjects, interrogate the social formation of femininity and masculinity, and recognize the cultural implications of the Latino diasporas in the United States that are continually reshaped by changing demographics. A discussion of Gomez's work compels us to locate sites where an important function of Latino stage—bringing together diverse audiences—continues.

5

"¿Soy Punkera, Y Que?"
Sexuality, Translocality, and Punk in Los Angeles and Beyond

> My theory had precedence. Stay with me on this. The Clash, for instance, jazzed up their music with this reggae influence—a direct reflection of their exposure to the Caribbean diaspora and its musical expression there in London. Nothing new—the usual white man appropriation of an exotic other story—anyway, the Sex Pistols, my theory went, were going to do the same with Norteño, the ole Tex Mex. I was going on the assumption that the Pistols probably heard the conjunto on KCOR or Radio Jalapeño on the bus ride down from Austin. But the point is, it worked. Talk about your revisionist histories! Greil Marcus is gonna flip!
>
> —Molly Vasquez, from Jim Mendiola's 1996 film, *Pretty Vacant*

> When Alice, lead singer for The Bags rock group, takes the stage in torn fishnet hose and micro-mini leopard-skin tunic, she explodes into convulsive, unintelligible vocals. The effect is a raw sexuality not for the fainthearted.   —*Los Angeles Times*, 1978

The xeroxed flyer advertising *Pretty Vacant*, Jim Mendiola's 1996 independent short film, depicts the much loved figure of the Mexican *La Virgen de Guadalupe* strumming, of all things, an upside-down electric guitar à la Jimi Hendrix.[1] As a U.S.-born Chicana who, in the 1980s, was rescued from the suburbs of Los Angeles by the Ramones, X, and Dead Kennedys, I must admit that I was captivated by this image and intrigued by the film's title, an obvious reference to the British Sex Pistols. A guitar juts out from *La Guadalupe* at a right angle, transforming the familiar oval shape of *La Virgen*'s image into the shape of cross, or an intersection

Promotional flyer for Jim
Mendiola's *Pretty Vacant.*
(Reprinted with permis-
sion.)

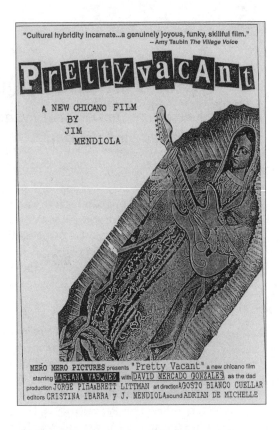

of sorts. What was this flyer suggesting by juxtaposing these deeply symbolic, yet seemingly unrelated, cultural icons? How did the title relate?
And why did this deliciously irreverent image prompt me to think of the
critically acclaimed graphic novella series *Love and Rockets* by Los Bros.
Hernandez?[2] And the title? *Pretty Vacant* is one of the "hit" songs of the
infamous 1970s British punk band, the Sex Pistols. Again, what is this
flyer suggesting? With all due respect, what and who lie at the intersection of *Guadalupe* and punk?

It turns out that the protagonist of *Pretty Vacant,* Molly Vasquez, like
the fierce Latina characters of the Hernandez brothers' *Love and Rockets*
graphic novella series and, most important, real-life Angelino Chicana
punk musicians, lives at that particular intersection.[3] The film depicts a
week in the culturally hybrid "Do-It-Yourself" world of "La Molly"
Vasquez, the off-beat, twenty-something, English-speaking Chicana feminist, *artista,* bisexual, *punkera* subject who lives in a working-class area

of San Antonio, Texas. Her love of the Sex Pistols leads her to the discovery of a well-kept secret that allows her, as a producer of 'zines and a beginning filmmaker, to *rewrite* rock 'n' roll history by inserting herself and Tejano culture into its narrative. All this while she prepares for a gig in her all-girl band, Aztlán-a go-go.

Pretty Vacant serves as a point of departure for my discussion of the emergence, during the late 1970s and early 1980s, of a punk "Do-It-Yourself" Chicana grass-roots feminist cultural production. This phenomenon circulated at the same time as other burgeoning Chicana activist and scholarly endeavors, as well as the East Los Angeles/Hollywood punk scenes, all of which still have not been examined in-depth. The film succeeds at what scholars of U.S. popular music have attempted—it shifts the paradigm that frames the reigning narrative of popular music produced in the United States.[4] Disrupting the status quo narrative of popular music production (in this specific case, U.S. punk) by granting a young Latina (more specifically, a Tejana) the authority to chronicle the history of punk, the film compels scholars to acknowledge the complexity of

A still shot from *Pretty Vacant* (1996), directed by Jimmy Mendiola, of "La Molly" Vasquez (played by Mariana Vasquez). (Reprinted by permission.)

popular music and popular music studies in the United States. Ultimately, the film viscerally unsettles long-held assumptions that unconsciously erase the influence of U.S. Latinos from popular music's sonic equation (and asks what is at stake in reproducing that erasure). The film opens a discursive space for my own analysis of the production of punk music by Chicanas in East Los Angeles and Hollywood during the 1970s and 1980s, and of the music's relation to punk communities beyond the United States. In examining the cultural production of Chicana punks, the chapter also illustrates how feminism and feminist thought are articulated in different keys. Feminist thought was and is alive and well in Chicana punk aesthetics.

Las Punkeras

What is fascinating about the film *Pretty Vacant* is the overlapping of the fictional character's art practices with the underanalyzed artistic production of Chicana musicians and visual artists who shaped the Los Angeles punk sensibility. In the late 1970s and early 1980s, Chicanas in local bands like The Brat (led by Teresa Covarrubias) and The Bags (fronted by Alicia Armendariz Velasquez) reconstructed the sound and subjects of British punk. These Chicana *punkeras* have a great deal to say about the artistic conditions of production, gender relations, and the punk aesthetic that emerged in the late 1970s and 1980s.[5]

Chicana/o punk, like punk everywhere, embodied a sonic response to the "excesses of seventies rock."[6] The rock chroniclers David Reyes and Tom Waldman note that "Indulgent guitar solos, pretentious lyrics, and pompous lead singers went against everything that Chicano rock 'n' roll represented from Ritchie Valens forward."[7] The appeal of punk to rebellious Chicana and Chicano youth makes sense for several reasons. First, the D.I.Y. (Do-It-Yourself) sensibility at the core of punk musical subcultures found resonance with the practice of *rasquache*, a Chicana/o cultural practice of "making do" with limited resources;[8] in fact, Chicana/o youth had historically been at the forefront of formulating stylized social statements via the fashion and youth subculture, beginning with the Pachucos and continuing with Chicana Mods in the 1960s. Second, punk's critique of the status quo, of poverty, of sexuality, of class inequality, of war, spoke directly to working-class East Los Angeles youth.[9]

In fact, the philosopher Bernard Gendron suggests that punk was introduced into the lexicon of rock discourse by Dave Marsh in 1971 after reviewing a Question Mark and the Mysterians show for *Creem* magazine: Marsh called their performance "a landmark exposition of punk rock."[10]

Question Mark and the Mysterians, a Mexican American musical group whose members were born in Texas, grew up just outside Detroit. In 1966, the band's national hit "96 Tears" propelled Rudy Martinez, Robert Balderrama, Frank Rodriguez, Jr., Eddie Serranto, and Frank Lugo (ages 15–21) into the rock 'n' roll limelight. Robert Martinez and Larry Borjas, also in the band, were drafted into the Vietnam War before they could enjoy their success.

In his exposition of punk, the rock critic Lester Bangs called "96 Tears" "one of the greatest rock and roll songs of all time."[11] Gendron explains that the rock critic Greg Shaw considered Question Mark and the Mysterians, along with Count Five, the Seeds, and the Troggs, to be one of the original punk bands.[12]

What rock critics have rarely written about is the sonic connection between the famous Farfisa organ hook of "96 Tears" and Tejano conjunto bands. The critic Ed Morales explains that in the 1960s, Texas conjunto bands augmented the accordion "with the organ . . . Mexican American conjuntos used Farfisa organs that had a tinny, cheesy, sound."[13] This sound, perfected by Question Mark and the Mysterians' Frank Rodriguez (also an accordion player) "became identified with garage rock and today has been elevated to exalted status by rockers."[14]

In the late 1970s, the media's obsession with British punk fueled a revision of punk's origins, and rock critics in the late 1970s recategorized Question Mark and the Mysterians as a "garage band." Gendron explains that "these former 'punks' [were] no longer punk, they were now merely influences on punk."[15] Recently, Dave Marsh asked, "Could '96 Tears' be the first postmodern rock record?" Perhaps, Marsh suggests, if they had possessed art school credentials, but since the song was recorded by children of Mexican American migrant workers, "all that Rudy Martinez gets credit for is creating a 'garage band' classic."[16]

It would not be surprising if Chicana and Chicano youth did not know about this earlier punk history. Yet, for all its familiar feel, punk's international sensibility also appealed to Chicanas/os, despite, or perhaps because of, the city's history of physically and economically segregating Chicanos from the wealthy West Side, thought to be by Los Angeles's dominant culture the place of important, "worldly" cultural invention.[17] It goes without saying that Chicana/o punk did not exist in isolation. The Chicano music chroniclers Reyes and Waldman observe that:

> Chicano punk groups were much more deeply embedded in the Hollywood rock scene than were the 1960s bands from East Los Angeles. On any given weekend in the late 1970s and early 1980s, Los Illegals, the Brat, and the Plugs would be playing somewhere in Hollywood. Before they crossed the LA River, however, they played at the Vex, an East LA club devoted to presenting punk rock bands.[18]

Vex emerged as a space produced by Chicano youth in East Los Angeles in order "to eliminate the barriers that inhibited Chicanos from playing in other parts of L.A., and that kept outsiders from coming to the neighborhood." Willie Herron, of Los Illegals, remembers, "We wanted to bring people from the West Side to see groups from the East Side."[19] At a historical moment when the confluence of cultures began to accelerate in the wake of global demographic and economic shifts, these Chicana/o youth transformed punk into a social site where popular music, national identity, sexuality, and gender dynamics were transformed. Bands like East L.A.'s The Undertakers used a form of youth subculture that circulated globally to bring together local, if segregated, youth.

She Says

> Punk allowed people to just get up there, and even if you were not feeling confident—which was not a problem I ever had—but I think for women who felt like they weren't sure of themselves, it was very easy to get up and do it anyway, because you weren't being judged on how well you played.   —Alicia Armendariz Velasquez, interview with author

Working-class Chicanas such as Alicia Armendariz Velasquez, Teresa Covarrubias, and Angela Vogel shaped independent, noncommercial music communities and subcultures in Los Angeles and responded to the shrinking of the public sphere and the increased privatization of daily life in contemporary U.S. culture through their musical practices. Although these women helped shape the sounds and concerns of the local independent music community, with a few notable exceptions almost no scholarly documentation of their participation exists. Perhaps these women do not register in nonacademic accounts because of the way they disrupt fixed, one-dimensional notions of identity.[20] In other words, Chicanas are not punk; women are not true musicians. Hence, fixed notions of Chicana identity framed by the dominant culture do not allow for recognition of these women in discussions of subcultural musical practices or in discussions focused on countering the shrinking of the public sphere.[21]

These women appropriated, reshaped, and critiqued imagery from unexpected sources, such as the British youth musical subculture, to invent local cultural practices that allowed them to express their realities in a public context. Chicanas as producers transformed punk and New Wave aesthetics into sites of possibility for transnational conversations concerning violence against women and the effects of the growing corporatization of public space. Given that most youth musical practices and communities are understood as male-dominated arenas, and rarely as Latino social spaces, these subcultures may seem an unlikely space for the development of a transnational conversation. Yet, it was a site of possibility for the young Chicanas who engaged these subcultures.

As transformative as this music was, however, it was certainly not without some of its own contradictions. The scholar José E. Muñoz illustrates this point in his meditation on some of the lyrics of X, one of the most critically acclaimed punk bands to come out of L.A. in the 1980s. With no small amount of unease, Muñoz relates that the title track of X's album *Los Angeles,* "narrates the story of a white female protagonist who had to leave Los Angeles because she had started to hate 'every nigger, and Jew, every Mexican who gave her a lot of shit, every homosexual, and the idle rich.'"[22] Although, as a teenager, Muñoz considered X his favorite band, the lyrics like those cited leave him with "a disturbed feeling" today. I, too, remember cringing at those lyrics as a teenager, as I do now, wondering why my favorite band had to write such horrendous words, especially since, at the time, I thought, mistakenly, that the lead singer, Exene, was Mexican American. As a high school student, however, I found it less difficult to digest those lyrics as I existed year after year in a mostly white, conservative, working- to middle-class public school, in which I experienced no small amount of anti-Mexican hostility, despite that fact that I had been born in California. X was my favorite band, and I truly believed that the lead singer of the band was Mexican American because her name was Exene Cervenka (which to my English-dominant ears sounded Spanish) and because she frequently made poetic allusions to Catholic iconography. In addition, to my young eyes, she looked like the Chicanas at the dance clubs in Hollywood, Whittier, and Long Beach that my friends and I frequented. Like them, Exene had dark hair and wore thrift-store chic and dramatic makeup. At the time I made sense of the song "Los Angeles" by imagining it was about one of my bigoted classmates. Nonetheless, this interpretation did not take away the sting I felt every time I heard the lyrics. Yet, I was able to hear beyond the sting and maintain my identification with punk primarily because, for me, as it did for Muñoz, the music functioned as "the avant-garde that I knew; it was the only cultural critique of normative aesthetics available to me."[23]

Years later, I was to find that my misrecognition of Exene as Chicana was not that off base. She had hand-printed the lyrics for the liner notes for The Brat's extended-play record, or EP, *Attitudes*. X had performed at Self-Help Graphics in East L.A.[24] Photos had been published of Exene hanging outside the Vex, in East Los Angeles.[25] The band members were friends with Los Lobos, the famed East L.A. group. One could argue that Exene's fashion style had been inspired by the young women in East L.A., and vice versa. I also discovered that Exene was not Mexican American. Exene had shortened her last name from Cervenkova, a much more Slavic-sounding name. Exene has never denied her connection to East L.A., but it has yet to be fully explored. The following section describes the practices of the young Chicanas who, in part, inspired Exene.

Staging the Bands

The Los Angeles bands discussed here produced their music on independent labels that circulated through grass-roots and alternative distribution circuits. These bands had little access to major distribution networks for at least two reasons: Most major record labels at the time could not imagine the market appeal of Chicano alternative music (much less Latino rock inflected by a grass-roots feminist ideology and punk aesthetic) and the women's stated primary desire was *not* to make it within the mainstream music industry at any cost but to create a place for public self-expression.[26]

This context, in addition to the larger social prejudices against "women in rock," helps to explain why young Chicanas' innovative use of alternative music to circulate critiques of social inequality and to express their rage against the domestic machine has often gone unrecog-

East L.A.'s favorite, The Brat. This image appeared on the cover of *Lowrider Magazine* in 1982. From left to right: Rudy Medina, Teresa Covarrubias, Lou Soto, Sid Medina. Photograph by Sean Carrillo. (Reprinted with permission).

nized: their recordings and visual images are extremely difficult to locate. This lack of distribution and exposure also occurred with other artists of the period, such as the spoken-word artist Marisela Norte, who also articulated a grass-roots critique of social inequality.[27] The cultural production of these young Chicanas paralleled the efforts of Chicana feminist theorists, even though their efforts rarely, if ever, intersected. As scholars of Chicana feminism wrote about multiply inflected subjectivity, the intersection of race, class, and gender, and the production of new Chicana subjects, these young women expressed these experiences in their music.[28]

The working-class Chicanas who helped create the local sound of the Los Angeles underground punk subculture were attracted to it for various reasons, but all of them experienced or witnessed violence against Chicanas at an early age, and most had been violently sexualized. In a series of interviews I conducted with Alicia Armendariz Velasquez and Teresa Covarrubias, both asserted that the visual and sonic language of the punk subculture allowed them to express their private rage about restrictions placed on and the violence done to their own bodies and to their mothers' bodies. In addition, their narratives document the effects of the shrinking of the public sphere because of the economic privatization that plagued the 1980s and that continues to this day. In other words, theirs is a story of transnationalism told from the bottom up, in the years leading up to accords like NAFTA, from the point of view of working-class women. Though each woman's experience was different, each was attracted to the punk subculture because it was a place where she could reimagine the world she lived in; it was a place where she could see herself as an empowered subject.

Despite the negative press the punk scene received (it was seen as extremely violent and racist), all of these women experienced the punk scene as a liberating space where the lines between gender and race were easily, if temporarily, blurred. It was a place where class differences and racial divisions were held temporarily in suspension. In fact, all the interviewees attested to the fact that, in Los Angeles, the scene was multicultural and reflected the mix of the Los Angeles population. In an era when representation of Latinas on English-language television and radio was even more rare than it is today, the Do-It-Yourself attitude and aesthetic held tremendous appeal for these artists.

In the Bag

Alicia Armendariz Velasquez (who used the stage name Alice Bag, of The Bags) is the daughter of Mexican immigrants. Growing up in East Los Angeles, she came of age in the late 1970s and "began singing professionally at the age of eight."[29] She, like Teresa Covarrubias, described her

In this rare photo we see, from left to right, Connie Clarksville (hairstylist to punks and scenesters), Alicia Armendariz Velasquez (a.k.a. Alice Bags), and Exene Cervenka (who was then part of X) performing in a benefit concert at The Masque, Los Angeles, February 25, 1978. This show was produced by *Slash Magazine*. Photograph by Jenny Lens. (Reprinted with permission.)

engagement with punk as a way out of an environment that she found too judgmental in terms of ethnicity and sexuality. She found no recourse in the mythic traditional Mexican family to discuss the domestic violence she witnessed as a child. Her embrace of punk culture occurred in "a period when Chicanas were questioning their traditional roles, increasing their participation within the political arena, and inscribing a budding Chicana feminist discourse and practice."[30] Although Armendariz Velasquez's path diverged from that of most Chicanas of the day, so profound was her influence on the L.A. punk scene that she was a featured artist in the recent photo exhibition and catalog *Forming: The Early Days of L.A. Punk*. Because The Bags "provided a blueprint for the hardcore sound popularized by Black Flag and other punk bands," the punk music chronicler David Jones considers Armendariz Velasquez the inventor of the West Coast hard-core punk sound.[31]

In 1978, Armendariz Velasquez was featured in a *Los Angeles Times* article, "Female Rockers—A New Breed."[32] Armendariz Velasquez, then known as "Alice Bag," along with Diane Chai, of the Alleycats, and Exene, of X, were considered the most groundbreaking women on the punk scene because their performances demolished narrow models of "women in rock": "the wronged blues belter à la Janis Joplin or the coy sex kitten typified by Linda Ronstadt. In tune with new wave's spirit of change, women punkers are rejecting the confining stereotypes and demanding more."[33] Although no explicit mention of Alice's ethnicity was made, McKenna describes her with code words reserved for ethnic others: "Alice, an exotic beauty whose frenzied vocal seizures generate such chaos that the Bags has earned a reputation for closing clubs."[34] In retrospect, we note that McKenna, perhaps unknowingly, cites two Chicanas, Ronstadt and Armendariz Velasquez, as wildly divergent models of "women in rock."

Often accused of being too aggressive on stage, Armendariz Velasquez performed in pink minidresses and severe makeup. In a clip from Penelope Spheeris's 1981 documentary film, *The Decline of Western Civilization,* we witness Armendariz Velasquez exploding onto the stage and wrestling the boys who jump onstage to join her during the show. The pink of Armendariz Velasquez's dress clashed with her performance and produced a complex statement about women's realities. Armendariz Velasquez did not reject femininity per se but rejected the equation of femininity with victimization and passivity. In fact, McKenna states, "women punkers like Alice Bag and Xene project an oddly incongruous sexuality. While not exactly neuter, their shock-level redefinition of the female role will take a while to be assimilated culturally."[35] Yet, Armendariz Velasquez's assertion that "female performers have always tended to be more reserved but all that is changing" foresaw and provided models for performers like Courtney Love, often noted, if not entirely correctly, for what has been called her unprecedented feminine rock aesthetic.[36]

Armendariz Velasquez also described the appeal of punk to young women in practical terms. She explains that while she detested the violence that surrounded her at home and public school, she could not help but internalize it. As lead singer of The Bags, she found an outlet: "all the violence that I'd stuffed down inside of me for years came screaming out . . . all the anger I felt towards people who had treated me like an idiot as a young girl because I was the daughter of Mexican parents and spoke broken English, all the times I'd been picked on by peers because I was over-

Alicia Armendariz Velasquez, in concert as Mothra Stewart as part of the band Stay at Home Bomb (Hollywood, 2003). Photograph by Jaime Cardenas Jr. (Reprinted with permission.)

weight and wore glasses, all the impotent rage that I had towards my father for beating my mother just exploded."[37] One of the best preserved and most accessible documents of Armendariz Velasquez's fearless performance as Alice Bag is The Bags's song "We Don't Need the English," on the 1979 *Yes, L.A.* recording.[38] With characteristic sardonic humor, Alice and the band loudly refute the notion that the only authentic punk scene was found in Great Britain. "We don't need the English, telling us what we should be / We don't need the English, with their boring songs of anarchy, telling us what to wear." The song opens by rejecting "the English, with their boring songs of anarchy," a direct reference to "Anarchy in the U.K.," by the infamous punk band the Sex Pistols. The song concludes by metaphorically barring the English from the "Canterbury," an infamous run-down apartment complex in Hollywood that served as a breeding ground for Hollywood punks.[39] Though Armendariz Velasquez did not write the song, the lyrics hold a different valence today when we consider that Armendariz Velasquez was bilingual in a city that often denigrated

Spanish-speaking ethnic minorities and that she has taught bilingual education for the Los Angeles Unified Public School District.

Although Armendariz Velasquez emerged as a performer in the 1970s Hollywood punk scene (unlike Covarrubias, who grew out of the East Los Angeles punk scene), she came to Chicana consciousness in the early 1990s. After performing as a Lovely El Vette for El Vez and the Memphis Mariachis, forming Cholita with Vaginal Davis, and performing as well as other L.A.-based bands, she fashioned a folk group, Las Tres, with Teresa Covarrubias and Angela Vogel, a former member of the East Los Angeles band the Odd Squad.[40] When Vogel left the band, the two remaining members formed the duo Goddess 13. In 2002, she formed Stay at Home Bomb with another East L.A. feminist rocker, Lysa Flores.[41]

East Los Angeles's The Brat

What fascinated Teresa Covarrubias, who was born to a working-class Mexican American family, about punk musical subculture was its Do-It-Yourself attitude, what she calls the "non-pretentiousness of it."[42]

Covarrubias discovered punk in the mid-1970s, when her older sister went on a backpack trip through Europe and began sending her punk fanzines from Germany and England. She recalls,

> What really attracted me to punk, was the notion that "Gee, I could do that." 'Zines had all these paste-up things and all these crazy little articles, and these girl bands and guy bands, and it just seemed like so open. It didn't seem like . . . you had to play really well. It seemed like a "from your gut" type thing, and I just fell right into it. You know, it was really raw, and it was in your face, and I really liked that, it kind of got me going.[43]

Inspired by this low-tech sensibility, one that she says "emerged" from the gut and seemed open to young men and women, she decided to form a New Wave band with Rudy Medina, called The Brat. The Brat is synonymous with East L.A. punk. In contrast to Armendariz Velasquez's family, which was fully supportive of her musical lifestyle, Covarrubias's family discouraged her. Although she found a place in the band to critique gender norms with song titles like "Misogyny," she found that sexism did exist in the scene, especially among her own bandmates. At times they

Teresa Covarrubias, 1981. Photo appeared on the cover of *Pro Fun* in an issue dedicated to "Journeys to Aztlán: Arts in East L.A." in June 1981. Photograph by Sean Carrillo. (Reprinted with permission.)

dismissed her creative opinions because she did not play an instrument. During those times, she explains,

> Because I couldn't get what I wanted, I started acting out in really self-destructive ways . . . because I just felt like I had no say . . . even now, women don't have a lot of faith in themselves, especially if you are going outside of the norm, when you're treading new ground. Everybody's always telling you what you can't do . . . people look at you and you're brown and you're a woman, and they think, "she can't do that." It's like they immediately assume less.[44]

Fortunately, visual documentation exists of Covarrubias's performances of her song "Misogyny." In 1992, the public television program *Life and Times* dedicated an entire segment, "Chicanas in Tune," to Covarrubias and Armendariz Velasquez.[45] "Misogyny" was originally written while

Covarrubias was in The Brat. The "Chicanas in Tune" clip captures Covarrubias's 1980 punk/New Wave mode and documents her performance as she swings to the beat in a shimmering early-1960s-style dress. Her voice is forced to compete with the guitar, but she holds the attention of her enthusiastic audience. The lyrics critique the position of women within patriarchal culture:

> A woman is a precious thing / Far beyond a wedding ring / You have kept her under your thumb / Creating the light-haired and dumb / You don't love her / You abuse her / You confuse her / You just use her / A woman's mind is a priceless Gift / You talk to her as if it's stripped / Women's beauty is in her mind / All you see is the sexual kind / You don't love her . . . / Blatant is misogyny / Scattered in our history / You will find it hard to kill / The strength from within a woman's will / You don't love her. . . .

The narrator breaks down the elements of misogyny by exposing their practice in everyday life in the following way: "you don't love her, you abuse her, you confuse her, you just use her." She critiques the strictures of matrimony that reduce women to property, to be possessed much like a wedding ring. And the narrator exhorts the listener to understand that a woman's strength lies in her mind and will and that it is a waste to value women *only* for their sexuality. Moreover, the power of the narrator's critique lies in her acknowledgment of the blatancy and frequency of women's abuse. Violence against women is so prevalent that its practices can be tracked throughout history and across geography, though its effects often go unacknowledged.

Though The Brat released a successful EP (extended-play recording), *Attitudes,* in 1980, they eventually broke up and morphed into Act of Faith, which released a self-titled compact disk, in 1991, and then broke up again. Covarrubias has continued to write and perform, in addition to continuing her duties as an elementary school teacher in the Los Angeles Unified School District.

Mex Goddesses

Armendariz Velasquez was part of a group of young singers who in the 1970s "blanch[ed] at being described as women's libbers—a tame, middle-aged scene by their standards [but] . . . could accurately be described as nihilistic feminists."[46] Meanwhile, at Hollywood punk shows in the 1980s, Covarrubias encountered a "punk elite" that was "really particular about what you looked like. If you didn't look right, they could be rude. There were a couple of times that they would tell me, 'you don't belong here.'"[47] In the early 1990s, however, with Angela Vogel, first as two-thirds of Las Tres and later as Goddess 13, she forged a sound that disrupted the exclusivity of white feminism and anti-Mexican punk. This sound, Armendariz Velasquez declares, "speaks to women of color about their experiences as women."[48] "Happy Accident," by Armendariz Velasquez, typifies the ways the group highlighted violence against women in their performance. The song's narrative centers on a battered woman's response to her partner's violent abuse:

Please believe me / I didn't mean it / All I saw was / the look in his eye / and I feared for my life / once again.

I didn't know / it was coming / all I know / is he done it before / sent me crashing to the floor / but no more.

Oh and / I can't say that / Oh no, no / I regret it / 'cause after all I had tried to leave every other way / And if I had the chance / to do it all again / I don't think it / would have a different end / I'm quite happy with this accident.

I didn't know / it was loaded / Yes, I knew where he kept all his guns / and I just grabbed the one / that was closest / So, if you ask / why I'm smiling / You may think / that a prison cell's tough / but I'm much better off / than before.

Oh and / I can't say that / Oh no, no / I regret it / 'cause after all it be him or me / you'd be talking to.

Though the narrative is bleak, the mid-tempo beat and clave accent create a "Chicana trova sound."[49] The contrast between the rhythmic sound of the music and the lyrics creates a punk-like disruption. The limited options the woman possesses in response to the domestic violence that has "sent [her] crashing to the floor" end up freeing her from one situation but contain her in another. She finds that a "prison cell's tough / but I'm much better off than before." This tragic all-too-real scenario speaks to the alarming rate of incarceration among women of color and to the quadruple bind of race, color, caste, and gender.[50]

Before Las Tres was reconstituted as Goddess 13 after Vogel left, the trio recorded a live performance at the Los Angeles Theater Center in 1993 and had recorded enough material to shop a compact disk to labels. However, the recording never saw the light of day because the two remaining women could not afford to buy the master tapes from the recording engineer. The band had been in hiatus since the mid-1990s but reunited for El Vez's 2002 Quinceañera Show and for the Eastside Review, a reunion of East Los Angeles boogie and rock 'n' roll bands from the 1940s on at Los Angeles Japanese American Cultural Center, in October 2002.

Vexed

Because "the Vex became a center for artistic activity of all kinds," punk musicians began to interact with visual and performance artists.[51] Teresa Covarrubias remembers that The Brat "did a show there with local artists. . . . It was through the Vex that I realized there were a lot of artists and poets in East L.A."[52] This must have been exciting for Covarrubias, considering that she was "an aspiring poet before she formed The Brat."[53] Equally important for young Chicanas gathering at Vex, whatever their artistic medium, themes of sexuality, antiwar protests, and antiracism ran throughout the narratives. In fact, Reyes and Waldman claim that bands like The Brat "produced enough original, exciting material to generate interest in the band throughout the LA punk underground. It was not long before punk fans from the West Side [of Los Angeles], maybe some of those who sneered at Teresa when she traveled to their part of town, came to see the Brat perform at the Vex."[54]

It can be argued that Chicana/o youth, marginalized by the West Side rock scene, enticed West Side youth, who otherwise refused to see Chicano culture as cosmopolitan or as worthy of their interest, and succeeded in creating integrated places in the most unexpected ways. As Sean Carrillo claims, "the punk scene had done the impossible. It accomplished what few cultural movements before had been able to do: it attracted all people from all over town to see Latino bands, and it brought musicians from all over the city to . . . deep in the heart of East L.A."[55]

Covarrubias and Armendariz Velasquez found punk to be an alternative oppositional movement to the Chicano movement, from which they felt excluded because of their position on gender issues, but they also felt alienated from white, middle-aged feminism. For these Chicanas from East L.A., punk subculture was not the end of their identity formation, but it was a path to a new way of being in the world and a way to expose the world to their reality.

Pistols Go Chicano, Hendrix Goes Tex-Mex: Plotting New Connections

Understanding U.S. punk within a U.S. Latino context produces exciting new questions, problematics, and contradictions around analyses of popular music. Equally important, including discussions of punk culture challenges the dominant paradigm that frames Chicano studies. So far I have examined Chicana shapings in "local" punk scenes of Hollywood and East Los Angeles. Instead of trying to define "the local" scenes, as the music scholar Keith Negus has advised, this chapter has explored "how the local is given meaning in a specific circumstance." My analysis has also included discussion of gender as a circumstance that gives meaning to the local.[56]

Returning to a discussion of Mendiola's *Pretty Vacant,* we can now explore punk sensibility in a different local context—that of San Antonio, Texas. For Negas, the local is "the relationship between music and place" and, I suggest, also the relationship between gender and generation.[57]

Mendiola, as a writer and filmmaker obsessed with the place of Texas in the Chicano imaginary, unexpectedly utilizes the sounds of British punk to narrate a day in the life of a young Tejana drummer and aspiring filmmaker. The film turns on three narrative strands that finally intersect at the climax of the film. The first strand involves Molly's avoidance of her father and his attachment to a nostalgia for Mexico that does not incorporate her (so refreshingly different from Moctesuma Esparza and Gregory Nava's representation of the pop star Selena as a devoted daughter). This nostalgia is illustrated when Molly's dad buys her an airplane ticket for the annual family reunion in Mexico that she does not want to attend.

The second strand invokes Molly's discovery of a well-kept secret that will allow her, as a producer of 'zines and a beginning filmmaker, to *re-write* rock 'n' roll history by inserting herself, and Tejano culture, into it. The third strand involves Molly's preparation for a performance of her all-girl band, Aztlán-a go-go, in which she is the drummer. Molly's father eventually catches up to her, and she ends up going to Mexico. But what she finds is not her father's version of *México viejo* but a dynamic, exciting youth culture composed of rockeros/as (young people who listen to and make rock en español) who are also concerned with social change.

Broadcast in Los Angeles on public television, in May 1998, the film successfully uses humor to deal with usually painful issues, including the problems that face daughters fighting patriarchal constraints; the frustration of having one's history erased; and the refusal to recognize the artistic and intellectual talents of racialized young women who are engaged in the struggle to create the conditions for the emergence of a world free from gendered, racialized, and economic oppression.

The film also provokes questions it does not necessarily address: What can Molly as the daughter of a Mexican maid and a working-class Tejano whose ideas are informed by the Chicano movement in its Texas manifestation and who lives at the geographic meeting place of Mexico and the United States and at the cultural intersection of Steve Jordan (known as San Antonio's "Chicano Jimi Hendrix of the accordion") and the Sex Pistols—tell us about this particular cultural moment, about new formations of politics of representation? And how does she speak to unequal economic conditions? What can Molly's character, who sees herself in both a local and an international milieu and as a gendered, racialized, and classed subject, tell us about transnational popular music and its potential for a feminist cultural politics? Gloria Anzaldúa, Norma Alarcón, and Sonia Saldívar-Hull describe a border feminist politics in which feminism "exists in a borderland not limited to geographical space" and "resides in a space not acknowledged by hegemonic culture." Border feminism illuminates the "intersections of the multiple systems of exploitation: capitalism, patriarchy, and white supremacy."[58]

The Molly character offers us some important insights into border feminism. From Molly, we learn that disempowered youth still make their presence felt in the realm of alternative, though not always oppositional, culture. We also see that rock returns to the United States from Mexico as rock en español in the hands of Chicana/o and Mexican youth who themselves are transformed by the music. Additionally, the film makes it clear that Chicana feminism cannot be contained by nationalism and national boundaries and that all forms of resistance to the values of the dominant culture have yet to be incorporated. Resistance still exists, not in mass movements but in local sites. In the realm of popular culture, *Pretty Vacant* illustrates that 'zines, popular music, and independent film enable conversations to occur across distant geographical locations between young people whose interests are not represented by corporate media. And, finally, the character of Molly reminds us that Chicana feminists' thinking has enabled the production of this film and helps us to locate sites of resistance to gendered norms and to the desires of the dominant culture in the most unexpected places.

Pretty Vacant takes place on the west side of San Antonio during the early 1990s. It is a setting far removed from both the time and place of the Sex Pistols' first fame in the 1970s. However, if one considers the influence of Question Mark and the Mysterians as described earlier, then perhaps punk's genealogy found its way home upon its arrival in Texas. Yet, it is Molly's investment in rewriting 1980s pop culture that drives her to revise and complicate circuits of musical diaspora (Molly literally recreates this Gilroy-style mapping in relation to Tex-Mex and its transatlantic meeting with the Sex Pistols in the film). This musical diaspora has been mapped out by the British scholar Paul Gilroy in his book *The Black Atlantic* and in Dick Hebdige's volume *Subculture: The Meaning of Style*. By documenting the "Tejanoization" of the Sex Pistols' music, Molly puts theory into practice. Always subverting stereotypical expectations of what constitutes the interest of Chicanas, the most recent issue of Molly's 'zine is dedicated to punk music. In this publication, she sets out to prove a secret that will forever transform rock 'n' roll history and make "Greil Marcus flip": her favorite British punk band, the Sex Pistols, had been Chicano-fied by their visit to San Antonio. Molly believes that the Sex Pistols had heard Steve Jordan's funky conjunto, "El Kranke," and that they were going to do a cover of the song for their performance.[59] If so, they might have unknowingly reproduced the connection between conjunto and 1960s punk forged by the driving force of the Farfisa organ in "96 Tears."

Molly's current edition of *Ex-Voto* is dedicated to her two musical obsessions, Esteven Jordan (the Jimi Hendrix of the accordion) and the Sex Pistols. She is determined to prove that Chicano music influenced the Sex Pistols during their performance in San Antonio. Devoted to the band that gives her inspiration for thinking about the world in new ways and for plotting new connections, Molly does research on the legendary final performance of the Sex Pistols at a cowboy club in San Antonio called

Randy's. According to Molly, it was their last and best performance. Snooping around the backstage area of Randy's, she finds a piece of paper:

> one hidden behind the stage. Get this—The Sex Pistols' play list! And even more amazing? Scribbled at the bottom?—Listen to this—"El Kranke," someone wrote "El Kranke"! one of Steve Jordon's songs! Shit, man, the Pistols were gonna end the show that night with some conjunto![60]

Inventing her alternatives around British punk is a response to her own limited options, which were circumscribed by Chicano patriarchy and U.S. racism. Her attraction to British punk is not about Great Britain but instead about her desire for an Other—she exoticizes Britain from a Tejana point of view, as a place where oppositional discourses and styles are produced, styles that she can later mine for their symbolic potential. This imaging of Great Britain is not that far off; her re-imaging is the inverse of European youth having their image of the U.S. framed by oppositional discourses articulated by some hip-hop production. Molly mentions that the Clash, an acclaimed anticapitalist punk British band popular in the 1980s, "for instance, jazzed up their music with this reggae influence. A direct reflection of their exposure to the Caribbean diaspora and its musical expression there in London."[61]

One way oppositional discourses emerging in the "third world" found their way to Great Britain was via the musical milieu of progressive black British immigrant and white British youth. Listening to these same imported British records, Tejana Molly tunes in to the embedded oppositional discourses layered within the music. Molly then narrates an even furthering layering of the British sound with conjunto, with its own oppositional history in Tejas. She explains: "I was going on the assumptions that the Pistols probably heard the conjunto on KCOR or Radio Jalapeño on the bus ride down from Austin. But the point is, it worked."

For Molly, her 'zine *Ex-Voto,* her band, and short films are the places where she engages what Norma Alarcón describes as the "struggle for histories actual and imaginary that give substance and provide an account of her/their position within culture and the political economy."[62] Molly's art practices are emblematic of both Chicana feminist art practices and the theoretical writings of the 1980s. She self-publishes her 'zine "cause no one was addressing my needs," just as Chicana feminists formed organizations like Mujeres Activas en Letras y Cambio Social (MALCS) and writers and artists created venues for their own work. Molly's 'zine catalogs the influences on her protofeminist subjectivity. She is still very much in formation. She combines the cut-and-paste aesthetic of punk with Chicana *rasquache* to create a form that expresses her social location. She prints essays titled, "Never Mind Che, Here's La Molly," ironically riffing off the song "Never Mind the Bullocks, Here's the Sex Pistols," while at the same time implicating Che Guevara, or at least the memory of him, in gendered power relations and disrupting the iconic Che as the signifier of social revolution. Her publication of readers' letters responding to her 'zine articles about "Emma Temayuca, the history of retablos, Love and Rockets, María Felix movies, Dolores Huerta, Ester Hernandez, the Ramones, and Sor Juana Inéz de la Cruz" speaks to the ways that the circulation of popular art forms are used to create community outside the bounds of ethnicity.

The Emergence of Chicana D.I.Y. Feminist Politics

Molly is linked to an earlier generation of Chicana politics, but the filmic representation of that connection is done in a complex, anti-essentialist manner through the composition of a scene that carefully locates Molly spatially and temporally. On her way to work at an independent record store called Hogwild, where she clerks, Molly leads us through local shots of San Antonio's Mexicano neighborhoods, the Alamo, and the city's freeways. At the record store, Molly informs us:

> I was born 21 years ago on January 23rd, 1973, a Saturday, the same day Raza Unida met for their first—and only—national convention, and across the Atlantic, David Bowie released "Ziggy Stardust": both movements didn't last, a radical Chicano political party and Bowie's particular strain of androgynous rock, but both had their influences, on me, to this day.[63]

Molly's birthday, January 23, 1973, is significant in the development of Chicana politics. In "Mujeres por La Raza Unida," Evey Chapa details the development of the Chicana caucus in relation to the January 23 national Raza Unida meeting. This caucus was formed by women who felt that more needed to be done to ensure women's participation in the party's electoral politics and positions of power. Chapa explains:

> We used already the evident commitment of many *mujeres* to the Raza Unida Party, . . . to implement the strategies for the development of Mujeres por La Raza Unida . . . a mini-meeting was held in Cristal (Crystal City Texas) attended by those who felt that words are not enough, that action is the only possible recourse. We formulated a strategy to discuss and survey the mujer issue with mujeres themselves. We canvassed opinions throughout the state . . . for five months they planned. . . . On August 4, 1973, in San Antonio, Texas, the first Conferencia de Mujeres por La Raza Unida was held. It was attended by almost 200 women from 20 different counties.[64]

The formation of the Chicana caucus within a larger political organization was an important move, but by the time Molly comes of age, the historical conditions that supported mass movements for social transformation and Civil Rights have changed. Yet Molly is a subject born out of the difficult struggles that did win important social advances. And that recognition allows her to narrate herself as being born of two movements, one concerned with social justice and organized around traditional male electoral politics, the other concerned with the critique of traditional masculinity located in the cultural sphere of popular music. Molly recognizes the value of both types of organizing. It is the existence and influence of these two movements, in fact, that has led Molly into the realm of cultural politics, to a place where she is now engaged in her own cultural work. She finds ammunition for imagining cultural transformation beyond the frame of cultural nationalism in the sphere of oppositional punk popular culture. In this domain, she imagines affiliation with other marginalized youth who also desire a different world. Yet, while working in the realm to which women have traditionally been relegated—that of the domain of culture reproduction—Molly does not reproduce traditional Chicano or patriarchal cultures. Nor does she produce the status quo values of the dominant culture. She creates something new (just as her flesh-and-blood analogues Covarrubias and Amendariz did), an alternative public sphere that includes her. Though corporate media chose not to give coverage to most oppositional movements during the Reagan-Bush era—

the historical moment when the globalization of capital accelerated and conservative political ideology dominated the public sphere—Molly's obsession with 1980s alternative popular culture speaks to the ways that young people fashioned an oppositional consciousness out of the limited resources available to them.

Beyond the Frame

The lens, her hands, her eye/body, the door, the house, the yard. She moves toward us, the viewers. The arrangement of elements within this frame evoke a sensation of both depth and movement. The lens of her Super-8 camera is at the front and center of the image. Behind the camera is a close-up of her face, her furrowed brow focusing. From there, hands, eye/body, door, and house recede from her camera lens until the frame is filled by the house, except for an open space to the right where the yard begins. The composition implies a double movement: We are pulled toward her center as she simultaneously moves away from the door. She is both the object and the subject of the gaze. She stands unconfined, outside the black, weathered door of the paint-chipped house behind her, outside the private domestic sphere. She has moved out into the day light, into the public sphere.

The black-and-white image just described circulates as a press photo for *Pretty Vacant.*[65] The photo functions as a visual allegory for the way Chicana feminists and artists—as women of color—have, at the turn of the century, turned a critical eye on the public sphere and, in so doing, have envisioned new subjects and subjectivities, as well as mapped out affiliations with racialized-as-nonwhite women within and across national borders.

Who is this young woman at the center of the frame?[66] What is she looking at? Who photographed the image of the woman? Where is she? When did this take place? Why is the image of this woman so provocative? As we address these deceptively simple questions, the many meanings of this image, which functions as a representation of Chicana artists, become clear.

In literal terms, the filmmaker Jimmy Mendiola physically photographed the image of "La Molly" during the filming of *Pretty Vacant.* In an abstract sense, Mendiola found inspiration for framing the image of Molly in this way from Chicana feminist writing and art practices.[67]

A D.I.Y. sensibility shapes his representation of Molly as well. Mendiola, like his character La Molly, came to the practice of film making via a D.I.Y. route. Though he majored in journalism at the University of Texas, Austin, Mendiola, in true punk fashion, wrote a screenplay and began shooting the film without formal film training, but with experience in local *teatro* at the Guadalupe Cultural Arts Center, in San Antonio. Like the best of the D.I.Y. punk bands, Mendiola made it work and earned a 1997 Rockefeller Intercultural Fellowship for his effort.

Mendiola was born in San Antonio, Texas, in 1965. His parents met in San Antonio in the early 1950s. His mother was born in a small south Texas town called Gonzales; his father is from San Antonio's west side, the Mexican American part of town. Neither of his parents went to college, despite the fact that his mother graduated second in her high school class. According to Mendiola, the expansion of the military during the cold war in the 1950s and 1960s led to the expansion of Kelly Air Force Base, in San Antonio. Civil service personnel were needed to fill jobs. For the first time in San Antonio, Mexican Americans were given the opportunity to make a decent wage with decent benefits. By the mid-1960s, a new and unprecedented and sizable middle class of Mexican Americans existed in San Antonio. Mendiola explains: "Both my parents got jobs at Kelly after graduating from high school. They were part of this generation. Our family moved to an economically better part of town when I was in second grade. My brother and I went to private Catholic Schools."[68]

What is particularly compelling about *Pretty Vacant* is that it demonstrates that punk aesthetics are not in opposition to Chicano aesthetics; in fact, both share the spirit of making do and express ideas and emotions that aren't necessarily "marketable" by utilizing the practice of cutting and mixing cultural references and sounds. Mendiola explains that while he was making the film, he came to a realization:

> Do-it-yourself punk rock aesthetic, as I was doing it and reading more about Chicano cultural practices, parallels the whole *rasquache* aesthetic. I was reading Tomás Ybarra-Frausto, particularly where he defines it as this populist creative strategy of making inventive use of what is available. And usually with no money and often times with no formal training. And I saw parallels between that aesthetic that informed a lot of Chicano art in the sixties and seventies with punk D.I.Y. I made this movie about punk rock and with this idea of critiquing a lot of these conventions of Chicano film, but what I ended up doing was redefining,

expanding, and critiquing punk itself because it's sort of seen as a white-boy type of musical and aesthetic. But it's not, a lot of people that I know, brown people, are into it and have been, and it's just a natural part of how we grew up.[69]

Like Chicana/o art, punk made a space for the critique of social inequality and racism, but mainstream representations of punk represent punk culture as a monolithic, white-boy-only fad. In fact, punk had various and competing strains; it was not one thing. Mendiola is interested in the ways youth of color "made the punk" scene in their image and changed it themselves. Mendiola's favorite example of this making over process is *Love and Rockets*, the graphic novella series by Los Bros. Hernandez. In fact, the young Tejana actress who plays La Molly grew up loving the British Sex Pistols. For Mendiola, the most valuable aspect of "punk aesthetics and the do-it-yourself mentality is this notion of making something that you'd like to see that wasn't out there. And that's what I absolutely did."[70]

Without question, the production of *Pretty Vacant* documents a break in filmic representation of Chicana subjects in films produced by Chicanos. Chicana feminist theorists have long documented and debated both the male-centeredness and patriarchal nostalgia generated by various forms of cultural production produced by Chicanos, including film, literature, *teatro, corridos,* and scholarship. Key films such as *The Ballad of Gregorio Cortez, Zoot Suit, Break of Dawn, Born in East L.A., La Bamba,* and *Mi Familia* (all which are readily available for public consumption at libraries and video stores) offer invaluable indictments of the collusion of the state's criminal justice system and capitalism and its effect of positioning Chicanos and Mexicanos as low-wage labor.[71] These films, however, tend to privilege a male subject in their narratives. The exception, as the filmmaker Lourdes Portillo confirms, is Herbert Bibberman's 1954 film *Salt of the Earth*. Produced outside the studio system and banned from general distribution because of its "communist" content, the film details the development of a Mexican American woman's coming to political agency around the well-known and successful miner's strike in Silver City, New Mexico. Yet, because most film narratives that star Latinas (including recent films such as *Selena* [1997], *U-Turn* [1997], *Out of Sight* [1998], starring Jennifer Lopez, and *From Dusk to Dawn* [1996], starring Salma Hayek) leave unquestioned patriarchal social structures, *Pretty Vacant* comes as a welcome relief.

Pretty Vacant emerges from a long history of Chicana and Latina independent filmmaking practices that began in the 1970s. For instance, Sylvia Morales, Lourdes Portillo, and, more recently, Ela Troyano, Francis España, and Francis Negrone have participated in producing films or videos that privilege engaging and complex Chicana and Latina subjects.[72] However, these women-of-color filmmakers have yet to break into Hollywood and have yet to benefit from mainstream distribution. *Pretty Vacant* follows this Chicana legacy of independent film making in both content and mode of distribution. *Pretty Vacant* begs important questions —about the relationship between the production of grass-roots Chicana feminism, Chicana feminist theory, Chicana art practices, and about film production and gender identity. This film is part of what Rosa Linda Fregoso calls a third wave of Chicano filmmaking.

The third wave, Fregoso explains,

> remain(s) committed to cultural politics insofar as their works deal with the Chicana/o experience . . . and is less interested in telling it all in one film, or in a grand narrative of Chicano history . . . indeed, these new film practices subvert the univocal or bifocal character of previous formulations of cultural identity by infusing these with multiplicity and difference.[73]

The film connects Chicana feminist theory with art through the story of a young Tejana *punkera* character who resists patriarchal control by producing art forms that allow her to enunciate her position in the struggle to imagine and create a different world. This world would be organized around just relations between men and women. It would be a place where the social construction of "race" is not used to legitimate economic injustice and where workers and artists are not subject to the policing structures of national borders. In fact, Molly's art production serves as an index of the 1980s explosion of Chicana writing and art. A useful way to interpret the film, then, is to read the figure of Molly as an allegory for the development of a Chicana feminist epistemology. The context for the Molly character was created by the efforts of all the Chicana feminists who came before her. She embodies the ideals set forth by these women. She is independent, confident in her cultural identity and sexuality, aware of existing power struggles and her place in them, and convinced of the importance of her world perspective as a young, working-class Tejana.

The still of Molly with the camera is extracted from a key sequence in the film's narrative. In that scene, Molly points the camera at her own art piece—her altar.[74] Molly's character has just given a summary of all of the self-made, low-budget *Ex-Voto* 'zine issues she has produced until that moment. She also explains why her current issue will be produced as a black-and-white Super-8 film. The sequence thus establishes Molly as a producer of various art forms and allows her to narrate how she constructed her social identity around particular forms of art and music. The sequence is also important because it explains the topic of her current 'zine issue—the Tejanoization of the British Sex Pistols—and it sets up the tension between the father and the daughter figures.

The photo image visually represents both the theme of the film and the theme of Chicana feminist writings of the 1980s: the decentering of patriarchal privilege through modes of art making. Though the first image we see is that of her father, the first voice we hear is Molly's, and it is her voice that we hear throughout the film. Because her voice-over directs the narrative of the entire film, the visuals are interpreted from Molly's point of view. A focus like this, on a character's interiority, is rarely found in mainstream representations of Chicanas. It is innovative and important in that it allows the daughter to narrate the father, rather than having the father figure narrate the daughter.

Molly's father—stout, in his late forties, Chicano, working-class, arms crossed—leers into her camera as Molly's voice-over informs us, tongue-in-cheek, "This is my dad, scary, huh?" She explains that "my dad had this thing about Mexico." The mise-en-scène of several frames suggests that the father, as an allegorical figure, represents a politics emerging from a previous generation of Chicano activism: that of Chicano nationalism (inflected by San Antonio's west side). This politics employed a grand narrative of Chicano history, one that traced its origins to Mexico, and was used as a defense against the racism of the dominant U.S. culture. It is a version of nationalism that recoups the rebellious daughter figure in the grand narrative. But the daughter figure resists. That Molly's interests and search for solidarity lie somewhere beyond the grand narrative does not lessen her commitment to antiracist struggles and economic justice. She just acts on it in a different way. Molly wages her struggle on two fronts: by redefining the relationship with her dad by questioning his values (and by extension the values of a manifestation of Chicanismo formed before she was born) and by producing her 'zine, *Ex-Voto*, a do-it-yourself journal that is inspired by anything Molly can get her hands on, "including old movimiento zines before they were called zines . . . old Caracoles are always good."[75]

Mendiola's framing of the Chicana character was greatly influenced by his engagement with critiques of representation produced by women-of-color feminist theorists. The filmmaker's serious engagement marks a specific moment in the production of Chicano film history; it registers the emergence of a third generation of Chicano and Chicana film makers, a generation whose aesthetic sensibility is, in part, enabled by the feminism of women of color. When asked about his influences, Mendiola explained that the writing of Rosa Linda Fregoso, especially her book *The Bronze Screen*, was one of his key inspirations:

> I just read it over and over and it influenced basic elements of the film— I was going to call the film "Un Acto," like the chapters in her book, where Fregoso conceives the notion of "actos of imaginative rediscovery. . . . I also came across a lot of Rosa Linda's early stuff that wasn't necessarily on film, and it was more on the critique of Chicano nationalism, and that spoke to me, because of my own real ambivalence about what it meant to be Chicano. People like bell hooks, I liked her film writings, her essays. Amy Tobin's film reviews in *The Village Voice*. She definitely has an outsider, a rock 'n' roll–like feminist perspective. And then Sandra Cisneros, who was almost just as important as Rosalinda. Especially Cisneros's *Woman Hollering Creek* and particularly the story "Bien Pretty." As far as Cisneros goes, she represented that very realistic bicultural lifestyle that I recognized in growing up in San Antonio in a way that I had never seen an artist do anywhere else.[76]

The implications of Mendiola's statement that "the critique of nationalism spoke to me" are complex. The fact that Mendiola finds the critiques of Fregoso and hooks liberating points to the ways that rigid definitions of manhood and masculinity mixed with homophobia, within politicized and artistic contexts, are detrimental not only to women but also to young straight men. In fact, in general, the appeal of Chicana feminist politics and feminist discourse to Mendiola demonstrates its utility for both men and women as a resource for re-imaging and transforming gender relations. Mendiola recognizes the material reality of masculine power and male privilege that women-of-color theorists critique. Admitting to his own privilege within the patriarchal order, Mendiola explains his relation to the theory:

I identified with the critique only to a certain extent because I'm not a woman, and I definitely recognize the privilege I have, but at the same time, it's [women-of-color feminist theory] like a tool. It was a very useful and appropriate tool to dismantle what I felt were problematic notions of Chicano, Chicano nationalism, and, again, I recognize it as being a tool and not necessarily an internal personally based ideology that doesn't apply to me.[77]

On the surface, it may seem problematic to interpret Molly's character as an allegory for the development of Chicana feminist epistemology—one that posits women of color as producers of knowledge—given that a man made the film. However, this interpretation actually provides an opportunity to refute the claim that Chicana feminist theory is essentialist and applicable only to women. This interpretation takes us away from a politics of representation rooted in biology. It is a theory that Mendiola, as a man, finds to be "a very useful and appropriate tool to dismantle" dysfunctional notions of masculinity. Because these writings have helped Mendiola understand the way his male privilege can disadvantage the art-making process, he attempts to prohibit this male privilege from interfering with his creative process. For instance, instead of taking sole credit for the development of the Molly character, Mendiola talks openly about the creative process between himself and the actress, Mariana Vasquez, who portrays the character. This back-and-forth process demonstrates that listening to the lessons of Chicana feminism pays off. Because the filmmaker gives agency to the fictional female character and does not silence the voices of the film's actress and editor, Christina Ibarra, the image of Chicana subjectivity that we see in this film is one that we rarely see represented in either Chicano or Hollywood film and one that possesses a strong appeal for many. Mendiola explains:

I went into the whole project with the idea of taking the notions of Chicano film, of all the usual expectations, and subverting each and every one or as many as I could. A primary one—making the main character a women, filming it in Texas and not California, playing around with punk rock as opposed to, like, the expectations of salsa. I just wanted to subvert all those elements and still, at the same time, be part of that legacy of Chicano oppositional film making. So I knew from the beginning it would be a woman, and I had my friend, Mariana, who I was good friends with. I wanted to do something with Mariana, and so I just wrote it specifically for her, with her in mind. Of course, I was influenced by the relationship of Maggie and Hopey from the *Love and Rockets* series, and my own personal notes. As far as writing for Mariana, it kept me from getting bogged down in my own autobiographical self-indulgence. There was a real freedom in writing for a woman, knowing that most people would not see that as me, so I didn't self-edit myself. . . . There was a real freedom in writing for a character, not a spokesperson for me. There were certain things there that women obviously weren't going to be into so—that's like the trick as a writer, to be true to a character. It didn't come down to a point of, I'm going to be treated like this woman because I'm a feminist. It was more like, there's this interesting person, who is this kind of person, what things would she be into and then trying to have everything—have that question dictate or have that answer dictate everything that I eventually gave her. . . . It was a negotiation. It was very easy because we're friends and I wrote it for her and she would read something and tell me if it didn't sound right. I think that was her way of saying, this person wouldn't say that. . . . I know none of us ever walked away dissatisfied with the compromises we made. The editor Christina told me what rang false and what rang true.[78]

Equally important, the collaborative relationship emerged from the way the film was conceived and shot. Mendiola was inspired by Vasquez's real-life obsession with Sid Vicious, of the Sex Pistols, and wrote the film for her. In the 1990s, Vasquez, the daughter of immigrant parents living in a working-class part of San Antonio, attended a high school in which very few of her fellow students were Anglo. Although Mariana was a young teen when her obsession with punk began, her otherwise conservative, Mexican, Spanish-speaking parents were open-minded when it came to her new choice of music and dress. Her cousins in Laredo had introduced her to the music, and she began to spend time with other first-generation Mexican American punk fans. No fellow students said, "You can't be punk, that's not Mexican." In fact, she remembers that cultural tensions developed between Spanish-speaking Mexican immigrants and monolingual English-speaking Mexican American students around issues of language. Vasquez, who in the late 1999s began studying film at Hunter College, in New York, explains that she met Mendiola while mingling at the appetizer table at an artist's reception:

I was really obsessed with the Sex Pistols, and I was telling them about the time I had carved this "S" into my like upper thigh. I was obsessed with the movie [*Sid and Nancy*]. I put myself in that whole thing, like I was living it. Well, I'm pretty sure that a lot of the stories that I told them went in and blended into this whole character of La Molly, and he started calling *me* La Molly. During filming we never used a script. He would just say, "Look like you're doing this" and "look like you're doing that" and you know and "act like you're doing this." And I'd never done film. It was all theater work that I had done. It sounded like a lot of fun, and so we did it. We shot it throughout the course of two or three years, and you can see that in the film. You can see there're subtle differences in my dress and in my body. . . . It was just get together when we could and do it. We did the first sound in San Francisco, but a lot of the stuff that we did didn't work. I did the voice-over in one take. We didn't have a lot of time. . . . I was never able to watch what was going on and then do it because he kept changing the script. I never had access to screening the movie. . . . The voice-over that I did do was just like a rough reading of the script that he had that day. So it was a little stressful on my part. . . . I think the character is a lot of me and the way he sees me, the way he feels about me in a little package.[79]

Vasquez explains how they worked together:

He would throw something out and I would say, "O.K., but what if I do it like this" and then we would just take if from there and it would work. It was very natural for me to play that character so I would just bring in myself . . . some of the words, some of the stuff that was written in the first couple of drafts, wouldn't have been true to the character. But not very much. I think it was more of him and his process of writing. We would just try out stuff, and some of it would work and some of it wouldn't. I know we worked really well together, and he was very open to my suggestions all the time! It was really good. He would guide me— there would be something that he really wanted to make a point of and then he'd tell me, "Here is where you go—I want it to be kind of like this," but that was more on the visual part but not in the—in terms of the reading, no. He was really good about that. He'd let me go, and all this stuff would come out. You know, he would ask me to put slang stuff —the way I talk—into the stuff that Molly would say.[80]

Pretty Vacant was released a few months before *Selena*—the first Hollywood "hit" film to feature a Mexican American female pop star protagonist. Unlike *Selena,* with its melodramatic narrative based on Selena's real life and tragic death, *Pretty Vacant* at least engages questions of gender representation taken up by Chicana feminist theorists.[81] Like the Latina punks Hopey and Maggie, whose lesbian relationship Jaime Hernandez depicts with great sensitivity in the *Love and Rockets* series, Mendiola's Molly represents a grass-roots feminist punk, still in formation, who draws inspiration from the signs of British punk, the *Love and Rockets* series itself, Tejano culture in general, and rock en español, to construct an "alternative" location away from patriarchal Aztlán, yet still oppositional to the racism of the dominant culture, a place from which to imagine new ways of being in the world, ways that speak to similar, but structurally different, conditions of working-class feminists, both straight and queer.

This film and the still pictured in the promotional flyer are provocative not because the young Tejana filmmaker is unique in her artistic endeavors but because they employ the numerous forms of cultural politics that were invented by Chicanas engaged in subversive art and identity formation, a perspective that has been underexamined, despite the fact that it has so much to teach us. We have still yet to understand fully how this Chicana feminism has so adeptly set the stage for future generations of artists and musicians.

What is equally fascinating is the potential for dialogue between Chicana feminist singer-songwriters in the United States and *rockeras* from Mexico, who, of course, are positioned differently by their respective nation-states in terms of racial hierarchies and class location and whose concerns are certainly not identical. In examining the flow of youth culture back and forth between Mexico and the United States, thorny and complex questions of race and class privilege emerge. Yet, as the musical culture demonstrates, the point of connection, of affiliation between the Chicanas and Mexicanas interested in transforming gender relations, stems from the shared recognition of their subordinated position within patriarchal culture. Their discursive interventions concerning gender and class relations point toward the possibility for transnational affiliation around critiques of violence against women, specifically against *mestizas* and women of color. The remarkable work of Julia Palacios and Tere Estrada on the history of women in Mexican rock points us in that direction.[82]

6

Bridge over Troubled Borders

The Transnational Appeal of Chicano Popular Music

El Vez has seven compact disks, several 45-rpm singles, and a book contract offer, and he is the subject of an in-progress independent film.[1] He has "r-o-c-ked across the U.S.A. and all over Europe" and is referred to as a "modern multicultural hybrid of Americana and Mexicano" and as a "Cross-Cultural Caped Crusader singing for Truth, Justice and the Mexican American way." *Rolling Stone* magazine considers him to be "more than an Elvis Impersonator. . . . He is an Elvis translator, a goodwill ambassador of Latin Culture" in the United States and Europe. He is the long-lost Chicano punk rock hero who has found his way home to Graciasland, Aztlán, USA; the Pocho Elvis, one who can't speak Spanish but "loves la, la, la raza," the Revolutionary Latin Lover who makes alienated Hispanics proud to be MexAmerican. He is the thin brown duke who makes explicit the connection among Elvis Presley, David Bowie, César Chávez, and Ché Guevara in Las Vegas–inspired *espectáculos* (spectacles).

Undulating in a skin-tight red vinyl jumpsuit that provocatively hugs the contours of his well-toned body, or strutting in his gold lamé charro suit, El Vez embodies the seemingly contradictory desires of a subject politicized by the Chicano movement, irreverent 1970s punk, and 1980s New Wave aesthetics. Part strip-tease, part Chicana/o studies, part Labor History, and part History of Popular Music course, El Vez's stage shows incite women to howl and young men (gay and straight) to growl, with a minimum of six "rip-away" costume changes per show. Not only does he shake his money maker in honor of James Brown (El Vez's "I'm Brown and I'm Proud" won first prize in the music video category of the 1998 International San Francisco Film Festival); he and the Memphis Mariachis

Robert Lopez, a member of one of the first L.A. punk bands, the Zeros, at Larchmont Hall, Los Angeles, July 8, 1977. The Zeros were also an all-Chicano group. The Weirdos also performed that day. This show was produced by *Slash Magazine*. Photograph by Jenny Lens. (Reprinted with permission.)

(his band) rev up their frenzied multicultural and multiracial audience to get down for the UFW and the Zapatistas' cause in Chiapas. He carries the namesake of his London-based fan club—"El Groover"—and he is regularly referred to as "the thinking man's Elvis," one who follows his Chicano movement and British punk roots and routes "back to a place we've never been." He is an exuberant Chicano sex symbol savior, a rock 'n' roll superstar persona created in the late 1980s by the musical genius Robert Lopez.

Despite having little formal musical training, Lopez is a virtual walking encyclopedia of rock and punk rock of the 1970s, the alternative popular music of the 1980s and 1990s, and Elvis Presley's extensive gospel, rockabilly, and ballad repertoire. Who else could turn "Suspicious Minds" into "Immigration Time" and make it clear that it is Mexican immigrants who are "Taking Care of Business" in the transnational economy? Who else could fuse Adam and the Ants and Santana with Rod Stewart's "Maggie Mae" or turn the international hit of the British band Oasis "Champagne Super Nova" into "Souped-up Chévy Nova" and improve on the original? In many ways, this multifaceted performance artist —whose father worked as master of ceremonies for the jai-alai games in Tijuana—is a child of "our extended Borderland culture: the frontera culture stretching from the shanty barrios of Tijuana/San Diego to the rich surf and turf of Santa Barbara (dominated by the megaspace of Los Angeles in the middle)."[2] Significantly, Lopez grew up in Chula Vista, California, then a predominately Anglo middle-class suburb of San Diego. Performing in the punk bands the Zeros and Catholic Discipline during the late 1970s and early 1980s, the teenaged Lopez actively participated in the development of oppositional punk music in Los Angeles.

Lopez, like many other disaffected Chicano youth (myself included) who were experiencing alienation from both the dominant and Chicano culture, was drawn to this scene because it was a site where identities outside ethnic stereotypes could be embodied. By the mid-1980s, Lopez was curating for the Luz de Jesús folk art gallery, located on the then low-rent Melrose Avenue in Hollywood—at the time a favorite site for punk youth to congregate. In the process of organizing a folk art exhibition honoring Elvis Presley, which included Elvis impersonators, he was inspired to develop his own translation of Elvis Presley: El Vez was born.

But what is it that makes Lopez's translation of Elvis into El Vez so impressive? The answer lies in his abilities as a transculturator of popular

The Zeros on stage at Larchmont Hall, Los Angeles, July 8, 1977. Photograph by Jenny Lens. (Reprinted with permission.)

culture.³ With relative ease, a serious dose of playfulness, and the well-developed critical arsenal of a camp artist supreme, he morphs Elvis into El Vez, thus enabling multiple layers of cultural hybridity and promoting complex instances of cross-cultural translation. Not only is Elvis reborn as a Chicano/Mexicano on the U.S.-Mexican border, but Elvis's music—which embodied a mixture of rhythm and blues and country music—is now partnered with mariachi, Caribbean, punk, and Latin punk rhythms. If this were not enough, with the strategic use of humor, rock 'n' roll, and a dash of T. Rex and New York Dolls glam rock (with its explicit exploration of gender subversion), El Vez's performance also calls into question traditional definitions of nationhood, masculinity, and the criteria by which human rights and citizenship are granted to or withheld from subjects of the nation and are affected by shifts in the global economy and hostile immigration policies.

Given that our historical moment is one of shrinking public outlets for the circulation and discussion of alternative and oppositional perspectives, Lopez's translation of Elvis into El Vez is significant in that he opens a discursive space—on the terrain of popular music, in the unlikely genre of Elvis impersonation—that enables both critique of the status quo and dialogue concerning progressive social transformation.⁴

In his fifteen-plus years traveling the world as a spectacular Chicano Elvis Presley translator (not impersonator), El Vez has wowed fans in every region of the United States, Canada, and Western Europe. Except for Los Bros. Hernandez' graphic novella *Love and Rockets,* El Vez has cultivated one of the broadest audiences of any contemporary producer of alternative Chicano pop culture. Fans everywhere have gobbled up copies of his numerous compact disks; who could resist such titles as *Fun in Español, Graciasland, G.I. Ay Ay! Blues, Son of a Lad from Spain (No from Mexico), Merry Mexmas,* or *Sno-way José.* He is even the sole subject of a documentary called *El Rey de Rock 'n' Roll.*⁵

But what explains the far-reaching appeal of a musician and performer so immersed in the humor and music of Chicano culture specific to Southern California? Perhaps it's that El Vez allows his audience to experience the visceral pleasures that progressive culture and politics can provide. This forward-thinking culture and politics emerge from a democratic belief that all races and creeds are created equal and have something of value to share. Unfortunately, this progressive impulse competes with a narrow nativist thought that seeks to exclude nonwhite and non-

Judeo-Christian communities. El Vez's performances ask his audiences, albeit momentarily, to be true to the democratic promise of inclusion and equality. In a time of major anti-immigrant hostility, El Vez's songs narrate the positive and vital contributions of Mexican immigrants to American life and explains that they are literally "taking care of business," as janitors, domestic workers, and nannies. Outside the United States, his narratives serve as an allegory for immigrant dynamics that occur across the globe.

Born to Juanita Cavada Lopez and Robert Lopez, of National City, California, Robert Lopez was raised in Chula Vista during the 1960s. His mother was a stay-at-home mom, while his father worked as a production technician at the local CBS affiliate and sometimes announced jai-alai games in Tijuana, Mexico. While Lopez's San Diego suburb was not known as a hub of Chicano youth movement activism, Lopez's extended family of civil servants and a Chicana activist aunt, who participated in San Diego's Centro de la Raza, exposed him to the movement's ideology. It would take a few years after graduating early from Chula Vista High school in the late 1970s for his aunt's activist lessons to appear in his music. Like many of his peers (Luis Alfaro, Culture Clash, Marisela Norte, Alicia Armendariz Velasquez, Teresa Covarrubias, Lysa Flores), Lopez was too young to be part of the first wave of Chicano cultural activism. Lopez was taken by another anti–status quo international youth movement that spoke to his experience as an outcast in his predominantly Anglo suburb—the punk music scene. Equally important was his admiration of glam rock artists like David Bowie and the New York Dolls, whose gender-bending antics thrilled and scandalized audiences.

Barely 15 years old, Lopez, with his cousins and brothers, formed the Zeros. The group was chronicled as one of the first punk bands to play Hollywood, and most accounts of West Coast punk acknowledge the Zeros' sonic influence. Punk appealed to many youth, who for myriad reasons (sexual orientation, class, race/ethnicity) did not fit into the mainstream and were critical of social relations. For many, punk was a first step leading to more nuanced critiques of poverty, racism, homophobia, and sexism. Equally important, punk was founded on a "Do-It-Yourself" approach to music. The early scene was about playing with one's guts and heart, not about musical proficiency. Any music fan could participate. Although Lopez was indignant about the unfair ways Chicanos and Mexicans were treated in the border region, it would take another 10 years for him to work those explicit themes into his music.

Between musical projects, Lopez attended Los Angeles City College and curated folk art exhibitions at the bohemian La Luz de Jesus gallery. As a buyer for La Luz's gift shop, Lopez traveled through Mexico, picking up Mexican history and mythology as well as curios for resale. As stated earlier, while curating a 1988 Lopez exhibition dedicated to Elvis Presley, Lopez was inspired to invent his own re-interpretation of the King, which he would call El Vez.

El Vez's first performances were musically accompanied by audiocassettes. Later, he had a rotating lineup of backup singers, the Lovely El Vettes (Alicia Armendariz Velasquez, Gwen Cardenas, Leena Marie Aguirre, and Lysa Flores, among others). Lopez knew that his Chicano reworking of Elvis had potential when he performed at Memphis's annual anniversary celebration of Presley's death. Not only was Lopez's interpretation a hit, but also he eventually won the admiration of the Reverend Al Green. In the early 1990s, Lopez got his big break when he was approached by a Danish promoter who was seeking acts for the Roskilde Music Festival. El Vez and his band, the excitable Memphis Mariachis, made such an impact that more promoters invited the band to perform across Europe. He hasn't stopped touring Europe and the United States since. For the past few years, Lopez has made his home in Seattle, performing with Teatro Zinani. He has also formed his own independent record label, Graciasland. Because of his broad appeal, Lopez regularly speaks about the reception of Chicano culture abroad at universities and colleges throughout the United States.

El Vez's musical metaphors continue a Chicano tradition of formulating public discourses that imagine a more kind, just, and equitable world. As he proclaims in "Oralé," his gospel redo of "Oh Happy Day," on *Boxing with God*, El Vez promises to bring peace by acting "like a bridge over troubled borders," bridging various segregated, yet interdependent, communities. Here, El Vez seeks to "double-cross the border—to trick the extensive machinery of containment, of discipline, and of exploitation that has historically made the border a proving ground not simply for citizenship but for humanness as well."[6]

Moreover, El Vez is a metaphor. No other musical icon says "American" like Elvis Presley. El Vez sonically demonstrates the "Americanness" of Chicanos and the "Chicano-ness" of American culture by grafting Chicano and Chicana experience onto Elvis's own blend of African American rhythm and blues, gospel, and country music. El Vez's *G.I. Ay, Ay! Blues* reminds audiences that Chicano soldiers have defended their nation and been overrepresented in U.S. wars since World War II. El Vez's title is particularly poignant, according to Jorge Mariscal, who notes that:

> [in view of the] likelihood of a protracted American occupation of Iraq and potential interventions against neighboring countries, Latino communities are once again sensing that their young men and women will be among those forced to pay the ultimate price. The names of the first killed in action and missing in Iraq included José Gutiérrez, José Garibay, Jorge Gonzáles, Ruben Estrella-Soto, Johnny Villareal Mata and Francisco Cervantes.[7]

El Vez advances a tradition of serious critique through humor, parody, and music, but what stands out against comic masters such as Lalo Guerrero, Teatro Campesino, and Cheech Marin is his relentless critique of traditional masculinity, sexism, and homophobia. In what is a thinly veiled critique of El Vez's feminist and pro-Queer ideals, critics have accused El Vez of simply making fun of Chicano culture. But, like his Manhattan audience, which on the day after 9/11 was soothed in a moment of danger and uncertainty by El Vez's call to be "bridge[s] over troubled borders," El Vez's musical metaphors can inspire those, Chicano and otherwise, who struggle to make North America live up to its democratic potential.

Through spectacular live and recorded musical performances, El Vez subverts the myth of "Elvis as the embodiment of the American Dream (and thus, by extension, as the embodiment of America itself)"[8] and interrogates the reactionary assumption that American national and cultural belonging and identity is (or should be) equated with exclusionary notions of whiteness. Superimposing Chicano cultural myths on top of the iconography, soundings, and lyrics that cluster around Elvis, El Vez's performance visually and viscerally demonstrates that Chicano history *is* American history, and vice versa. Hence, many of El Vez's lyrics—inflected by a Chicana and Chicano movement politics that the adolescent Lopez learned though his aunt—narrativize why immigrant and nonimmigrant populations in the United States that are racialized as nonwhite should be recognized as part of American national culture.

Lopez's own engagement with pop culture is subversive to the degree that he has hope for an America that has yet to live up to its democratic possibility and to the degree that he places much of his music in the service of this ideal.[9] His performances entice audience interest with a "flash," the image and soundings of Elvis. El Vez appropriates the signs of American pop culture to critique American society, but to accomplish this, he must "do" Elvis with a difference.

Elvis as Trace, El Vez as Screen

Lopez's self-described strategy of "superimposing" Latino culture onto popular culture allows others, including non-Chicanos, to recognize and identify with the difference that El Vez makes, even as it engenders contradiction. In an interview that I conducted, Lopez explains the positive reaction of non-Latinos to his performance of El Vez and irreverently draws on Chicano cultural nationalist discourse:

> Everyone's different, but you still have to be proud. It's the old idea, people will come and say, "I come to your show and I walk away proud to be Mexican, and I'm not, and I'm white" [which is no small feat in a state like California that constantly constructs Mexicans as inferior]. It's the idea of instilling pride, and you could fill in the blank. I mean I am El Vez, the blank Elvis, black, gay, straight, Asian, or whatever.[10]

However, El Vez could never be the blank Elvis—he has clearly overwritten Elvis with Chicana and Chicano culture.[11] Notwithstanding this fact, the body of El Vez, on stage, with its costumes and physical postures, acts as a projection screen where traces of multiple and different cultures and practices are made visible. He projects a critical multiculturalism that invites subjects to identify with the struggles of those most vilified by anti-immigrant campaigns. His statement "I am the blank Elvis, black, gay, straight, Asian, or whatever" might sound like a simple endorsement of a liberal pluralism or a watered-down nationalism that advances the ideology "that in the United States everyone is equal no matter their color, religion, or sexual orientation." However, in this case, El Vez implies something very different. By positing a "family of resemblance" that links the history of many Chicanos—a working-class past and/or present—to Elvis's own childhood of poverty, El Vez's performance connects Mexican American working-class histories to those of most other Americans and highlights the fact that any notion of multiculturalism is incomplete without understanding how class and racial position makes some residents of the United States more equal than others. Furthermore, El Vez does not equate social constructions of racial and class difference with inferiority or superiority. Instead, he suggests that one can be proud of difference, that one should not suppress it, and that one should not have to face consequences for being different.

One advantage of this strategy, especially for an artist who performs on the fringes of the entertainment industry, is that it avoids alienating his audience. In addition, by superimposing images of Ché Guevara, *La Virgen de Guadalupe,* and César Chávez onto the trace images of Elvis Presley, James Brown, and David Bowie, El Vez enacts complex strategies for getting people from different walks of life interested in Chicano history and progressive politics, in this case a politics not based on an assumed biological identity. By deploying the mass appeal of a working-class form of popular culture—"rock 'n' roll"—his performances address serious questions of social inequality in an unconventional, flashy style in order to bring in alternative ideas about social structure "though the back door" when audiences' guards are down.

Lopez's re-presentation of Elvis is important, then, because El Vez embodies an aesthetics of resistance grounded in popular culture and music, yet does so in no simple terms. To incorporate the iconography of Elvis (as a supreme icon of Americana) into the milieu of Chicano culture disrupts the demand of Chicano nationalism for a return to an uncorrupted mythic indigenous past. On the other hand, non-Chicano Elvis fans rarely associate Elvis with Mexican or Chicano culture (or understand how Chicano culture has affected "white" America), although few can deny Elvis's connection to southern black culture. Enacted on the accessible terrain of popular music, El Vez's aesthetics of resistance is double-edged, for it transforms the dominant culture's imposition of social codes that attempt to define "Mexican immigrant" or "Mexican American" identity and place in society, as well as subaltern demands to reduce Chicana and Chicano identity to an essentialized, fixed form. His aesthetic of resistance disrupts both the dominant and the subaltern dictates for strict, unyielding definitions of identity, sexuality, and citizenship and suggests that breaking with Chicano nationalism does not signify a break with Chicano politics.[12]

It's *"Immigration Time"*

These dimensions of Lopez's performance aesthetics can be found in the song "Immigration Time," which substitutes for the lyrics of Elvis's version, "Suspicious Minds" (a song that thematizes emotional entrapment within a dysfunctional relationship), a contemporary immigrant narrative that recalls the predicament of displaced Mexicans. Included on the compact disk *Graciasland* (El Vez's reappropriation of Paul Simon's *Graceland*), the lyrics of this song highlight inherent contradictions in official myths that frame a "melting pot" democracy in the United States:[13]

> I'm caught in a trap, I can't walk out / Because my foot's caught in this border fence / Why can't you see, Statue of Liberty / I am your homeless, tired and weary / We can grow on together, it's Immigration Time / And we can build our dreams, it's Immigration Time /

> Yes I'm trying to go, get out of Mexico / The promised land waits on the other side / Here they come again, they're trying to fence me in / Wanting to live with the brave and the home of the free / We can grow on together, it's Immigration Time / And we can build our dreams, it's Immigration Time /

> All that I have I will share, I'm not asking a lot, / You're the one that's supposed to care, we're the melting pot / But you lied to me / Woe—my, my / Woe—yeah yeah / I'm caught in a trap, I can't walk out / Because my foot's caught in this border fence /

> This is the land of opportunity / An American Dream / That can be shared with everyone / Regardless of race, creed, national and sexual origin / Anything / This belongs to everybody /[14]

In changing Elvis's lyrics "I'm caught in a trap / I can't walk out / Because I love you too much baby" to "I can't walk out / Because my foot's caught in this border fence," the song conjures Elvis's version—the back-beat remains the same[15]—yet thematizes the increased militarization of the Mexico-U.S. border.[16] "Immigration Time" thus highlights the nation's contradictory immigrant policy and its connection to an economy fundamentally based on hyperexploited undocumented workers.

In addition, by imagining a conversation between an undocumented immigrant and the Statue of Liberty from the perspective of the former, El Vez's lyrics also provide an oppositional image of the plight of undocumented racialized immigrant workers. This hypothetical conversation is significant given that the song circulated in California at the same time as the Proposition 187 television campaign and its attendant propaganda. The Proposition's advertisements portrayed immigrants as dehumanized, invading "aliens" and ignored studies proving that undocumented workers boost California's economy[17] to justify its call to further reduce the basic human rights of undocumented immigrant workers and their children.[18] Within this context, El Vez's performances, live and recorded, enabled and enable a site where counterrepresentations of undocumented racialized immigrant voices (voices rarely, if ever, consulted in national or international debates) are considered.[19]

In "Immigration Time," the immigrant voice boldly asserts his humanity by evoking "our dreams" to "build" and "grow on together." At the same time, he indicts the inhumane forces that make his dream impossible today, and he alludes to the cyclical deportation of Mexicans, suggesting: "Here they come again, they're trying to fence me in." These forces include "*la migra*," the U.S. Customs and Border Protection, which polices the border and literally chases, corrals, and deports racialized immigrants like animals. With his images of border entrapment, El Vez evokes remembrances of internal colonialism and suggests that immigrant workers—economic refugees—are literally trapped in the fences erected along the transnational border of San Ysidro. He also implicates the global economic structure of labor exploitation that traps immigrants without documentation, a structure that requires cheap, alienated labor to maintain prosperity.

El Vez thus remakes and alters the master's tools to "dismantle the master's house." In this song, the singing subject stakes his claim to inclusion in the national body along the lines of a modified civil rights discourse by invoking the traditional symbol and ideology of "Lady Liberty." He reminds the Statue of Liberty of her obligation to accept all "your tired and your poor," regardless of their point of entry, be it Ellis Island or San Diego county, and if this were not enough he condemns her for her deception, stating: "You lied to me." He also draws attention to both the tragedy of her "conscious" differential treatment of Mexican immigrants and the tragedy of those who are "fenced in" and forced out. This critique is strengthened because he contrasts his position to hers;

unlike Lady Liberty, who selectively opposes the American Dream for Mexicans, he offers to "share all that he has" with America. Equally important, the racialized immigrant protagonist recognizes a shared experience of displacement with other U.S. citizens and suggests that she is either blind or indifferent to U.S. citizens who are also "homeless, tired," and dispossessed. Finally, as a retort to the position of arch-conservatives who would deny him his place in the United States, he triumphantly employs their own arguments against them, exclaiming, "This is the land of opportunity / An American Dream / That can be shared with everyone / Regardless of race, creed, national and sexual origin / Anything / This belongs to everybody." Yet, by equating American identity with the ability to spend within the parameters of capitalism—"I got my green card, I want my gold card"—the immigrant runs the risk of falling into another trap, that of reproducing the ideology that excluded him in the first place.

Remapping Aztlán, Remapping Graceland

A telling example of El Vez's cultural translation, or transculturation, is found in the compact disk *Graciasland,* which is "produced, written, rewritten, arranged and mixed by El Vez."[20] *Graciasland* riffs off Paul Simon's homage to Elvis, *Graceland*. In the song "Immigration Time," he also puns Disneyland, "the promised land in Anaheim," and instead invokes Aztlán. The compact disk maps a new cultural geopolitics: It marks a trail from Elvis's Graceland in Memphis, Tennessee, to Califas, Aztlán, acknowledging César Chavez, the United Farm Workers, and Emiliano Zapata along the way. The third cut of *Graciasland,* "Aztlán," and the last, "Immigration Time," can be read as companion pieces, since they both thematize issues of nation, citizenship, displacement, immigration, nation, sexuality, and hybridity within an international context. The musical arrangement of "Aztlán" follows Paul Simon's song "Graceland."

> The river Río Grande is carving like a national scar
> I am following the river making wetbacks
> Where my parents crossed to be now where they are
> I'm going to Aztlán, where I wanna be I'm going to Aztlán[21]
> Homeboys, Chicanos, Latinas and we are going to Aztlán
> My traveling companions, La Virgen, Miss Liberty
> A map and my M.E.Ch.A. book[22]

Well I've reason to believe, we all have been deceived
There still is Aztlán
Miss Liberty tells me Aztlán's gone, as if I didn't know that
As if I didn't know my own back yard, as if I didn't know
To get in you need a card
And she said losing home is like a bullet in your heart
I am looking for a place, a myth of my people where I won't get
torn apart
I'm going to Aztlán, Aztlán
Where I want to be, I'm going to Aztlán
Homeboys, Chicanos, Latinas with greencards
and we are going to Aztlán
With my traveling companions
Through Califas,[23] Arizona on the way to Texas
But I've reason to believe, we all will be received, in Aztlán
There is a girl in San Antonio who call herself
the human mortar, eleven generations she's lived there
It's just the land and name that's changed its borders
She is the cement that is Aztlán
And I say who ever has seen this place
I am looking for a land that once belonged to Mexico
But now holds no time or space
In Aztlán, Aztlán, I'm going Aztlán
For reasons, I've explained, I'm not a part of Spain,
I'm part of Aztlán, and I'm trying to get back to a place I've never
been, I'm trying to cross over,
Well I've reason to believe, we all have been deceived,
There still is Aztlán.[24]

El Vez's lyrics invoke the primary icon of Chicano nationalism:—Aztlán. The lyrics and the music undercut any serious move toward the Chicano nationalism of the 1970s: El Vez employs a Paul Simon song about Elvis's music to disrupt the homogeneous mythic imagery of Aztlán, to tell a story about contemporary America. If, in the late 1960s and early 1970s, Aztlán was the Chicano movement's version of Eden, then Aztlán was the place where Chicanos would not be treated as second-class citizens in terms of jobs, education, housing, and health care, as they still are in a territory that belonged to Mexico before the signing of the Treaty of Guadalupe-Hidalgo, in 1848.[25] Yet, despite the desire for social equality,

El Vez, The Mexican Elvis
(a.k.a. Robert Lopez).
Throne designed by Jon
Bok. Photograph by Mar-
cus Cuff. (Reprinted with
permission.)

the myth of Aztlán rejected difference and *mestizaje*. El Vez's 1990s revision of Aztlán maintains the desire for social equality, yet embraces difference, *mestizaje*, undocumented immigrants, all people of color, Latinas, and "anyone regardless of sexual orientation."[26] Cautious of nationalism's fascist potential, El Vez considers: "when is pride good? Or when
does pride become nationalistic, because it can come close to the Nazis'
obsession with pride?"[27] Instead of excluding subjects like Elvis, Marisela
Norte, Luis Alfaro, and Marga Gomez, El Vez's reimagining of Aztlán
welcomes them.

"Aztlán" is written in the tradition of the American "road" song. The
lyrics begin at the U.S./Mexico border, likening the Río Grande to a national scar. This framing of the border area resonates with Gloria Anzaldúa's representation of the border as an "open wound."[28] El Vez then
guides us through Aztlán with deeply symbolic icons: "La Virgen, Miss

Liberty and his M.E.Ch.A. [Movimiento Estudiantil Chicano de Aztlán] book." Positioning "Miss Liberty" between "La Virgen" and the "M.E.Ch.A. book" may suggest that mainstream culture is still at the center, but it also suggests that through the process of transculturation, the dominant culture has become as hybrid as Chicano culture. The lyrics also call attention to the pain of geopolitical displacement—"losing home is like a bullet in your heart"—when they address the effects of the Treaty of Guadalupe-Hidalgo. The lyrics acknowledge the communities of Mexican nationals who became Mexican Americans overnight; it was "just the land and name that's changed its borders."

At the end of El Vez's tour of Aztlán, the lyrics express a desire to cross over: "I'm trying to get back to a place I've never been, I'm trying to cross over." The lyric speaks to many different types of crossings. As a Chicano, he could want to cross into the mainstream and still be respected as a Chicano, or, more important, to cross over into economic equality. To cross over in the music industry, one must sell units—or make the charts—in more than one market segment. For instance, it is a rare recording that sells both in rock—marked as white—and hip-hop—marked as black—markets. But when one does, it points to the ability of musical forms to speak across markets or racialized divides, perhaps creating the conditions for a cross-cultural heterotopia in the United States.

"Taking Care of Business," Every Day

El Vez's version of "Taking Care of Business" also disrupts recent national constructions of Mexican, Latina, and Latino immigrants as a dehumanized army of social parasites that are "invading" the nation and depleting resources and employment opportunities.[29] He achieves this by translating the original version of "Taking Care of Business" into a tribute offered to those racialized immigrants who have been structurally relegated to service positions, jobs that literally take care of business. When El Vez performs "Taking Care of Business" live, against the backdrop of the North American Trade Agreement (NAFTA) and Proposition 187, he usually prefaces it by asking, "What would happen if all the Latinos and all the immigrants in the United States decided not to work, what if they all went on strike? Business would shut down, because no one would be around to take care of business, vegetables would rot in fields, parents wouldn't be able to go work because they'd have to take care of their own children." For those in the Southwest who have never considered their own reliance on immigrant labor, the song illuminates the everyday contributions of Latinos:

> We get up every morning, from the alarm clock's warning / do the menial jobs that run this city / there's a whistle up above and we're cleaning and we scrub / do your lawn, to make you look pretty / and if our bus is on time, getting to work way before nine / to stock and slave, $2.15 is our pay / and you're getting all annoyed / blaming us for unemployed / they're jobs you wouldn't take any way /
>
> and we're TAKIN' CARE OF BUSINESS—every day / TAKIN' CARE OF BUSINESS—oralé / TAKIN' CARE OF BUSINESS—we're the maid / TAKIN' CARE OF BUSINESS—and getting underpaid! / work out! /
>
> for an easy addition you get workers for your kitchen / paid under table, they won't tell'o / If you need a handyman, you can go to Standard Brands / and get one of those stand around fellows / you see us slaving in the sun, from *la migra* we must run / you tell us that you like it this way / and you're getting all annoyed, blaming us for unemployed / they're jobs you wouldn't take any way /
>
> all we want is good job / so we can stand on our own two feet / we crawling up from the bottom, we're proud labor that just won't hide / You wouldn't want to be a farmworker and be sprayed with pesticide / Oww /
>
> and we've been TAKIN' CARE OF BUSINESS [TCB]—every day / TCB—oralé / TCB working fields / TCB—and cooking all your meals / TCB—kitchen crew / TCB—nannys too / TCB—blowing leaves / TCB—no green cards up our sleeve[30]

For those who are not aware of who is "taking care of business," El Vez clarifies that it is Mexican or Central American working-class undocumented immigrants, and these workers, who enable a middle-class lifestyle for some, are those who are persecuted by "*la migra*." El Vez's lyrics thus expose important class issues, because the song makes clear it is those workers, who are making their way up "from the bottom," who get scapegoated. His description of the real lives, spent "cleaning and scrubbing," of undocumented and documented labor defies the right-wing ideology that criticizes, attacks, and belittles Latino, working-poor immigrants as do-nothing social parasites. This description also rebukes the argument of conservatives, of various economic classes and ethnicities, who contend that undocumented immigrants "take" jobs way from citizens and permanent residents by reminding us that the jobs that business makes available to undocumented workers are the "menial" ones without benefits and decent pay, jobs those who criticize "wouldn't take anyway."

The lyrics suggest that owners and managers are the ones who decide that the vital jobs that maintain white citizens' lifestyles—child care, construction work, harvesting of food—merit only $2.15 per hour in pay despite the hard labor and exposure to lethal toxic chemicals they entail. The words also lay out the dependence of overdeveloped economies on hyperexploited labor to maintain low-cost comforts, services, and products (e.g., manicured lawns, somewhat affordable housing for the middle class, cheap food). In essence, the song paints the interdependence of citizens and undocumented immigrant workers in the United States in socioeconomic terms and exposes the hypocrisy of annoyed middle-class citizens who object to granting basic human rights to individuals who are not recognized by the state; these bothered citizens want the financial benefits of cheap immigrant labor, but they do not want the immigrants themselves, or their children; they want their own business taken care of quickly and cheaply but do not care if the workers have time to take care of their own personal business of survival.

Kinging Elvis, or El Vez Kinging

As El Vez takes on the cause of immigrant Mexican labor, he generates a remarkable critique and revisioning of traditional masculinity. El Vez's still-frame assemblages "turn masculinity into theater" as much as his stage shows.[31] A photo included in the inset of *G.I. Ay, Ay! Blues* appears as an homage to Elvis, Ché, and the Zapatistas and provides an excellent example of El Vez's transculturation of important signs and what the scholar Judith Halberstam names "kinging." This image visually represents his break from traditional Chicano aesthetics and his invention of one that uses old signs in new ways. Here, El Vez's image of manhood subverts traditional representations of masculinity. Traditional masculinity,

Publicity photo of El Vez
(a.k.a. Robert Lopez) for
his Rockin' Revolution
Tour. 1996. Photo by Ran-
dall Michelson. (Reprinted
with permission.)

especially as embodied by a revolutionary soldier, and usually represented as somber, impenetrable, intimidating and aggressive, is undercut by the photo. Within the frame, El Vez's body is staged as the object of the desire in this image; the viewer (male or female) is implicated because El Vez points back to us with his index fingers. His posture is open—hips loose, and his arms, up and away from his body, suggest that he might be vulnerable to attack, or pleasure. The gun, symbol of war, conquest, and masculine power, an extension of phallic power, does not threaten us; it is not pointed toward us. Unthreatening, it rests behind his neck. Instead of communicating intimidation, his gaze, focused beyond the camera, has an erotic charge, with its "come hither" beckoning. For those invested in traditional representations of manhood, then, this image is unsettling, which is evident in the complex reception of, and even resistance to, El Vez.

When I first saw El Vez's performance, at a small club in Santa Cruz, California, I was impressed by his cabaret-like show, complete with several costume changes, and the fact his translation of Elvis Presley could be interpreted as a very Queer performance of heterosexual masculinity. It was El Vez's over-the-top, joyfully flamboyant gold lamé mariachi suit that first alerted me to El Vez's gender drag. El Vez's multiple form-fitting costumes, especially his mariachi suit (a traditionally form-fitting outfit) and the cabaret style both signify long-established Mexican entertainment culture, not necessarily Queer culture. Coco Fusco reminds us that since the 1940s and 1950s, "the cabaret functions for many Latinos not only as venue but as tradition."[32] (Chapter 4 discusses this tradition.) But it is the way Lopez fuses Elvis with the androgyny of early David Bowie and glitter rock aesthetics that gives him away to audiences in the know.

What I first interpreted as a campy rendition of masculinity is closer to Halberstam's "kinging." Kinging, according to Halberstam, is different from camp in the following way. While both camp and kinging are about flamboyant, hyperbolic, performances of gender, camp refers historically to parody of femininity, while kinging refers to parody of masculinity. Different from male impersonation, which strives for the appearance of realness, kinging is the practice of making masculinity theatrical, of exposing masculinity as a construct. Its goal is to denaturalize masculinity. Kinging counters "the idea that masculinity 'just is,' whereas femininity reeks of the artificial."[33] Through an analysis of different modes of kinging, Halberstam illustrates that masculinity is not necessarily attached to a particular gender or race.

Though Halberstam proposes "kinging" as a performance practice different from "camp" to "avoid always collapsing lesbian history and social practice associated with drag into gay male histories and practices," she makes it clear that kinging, or the theatrical performance of masculinity, is not practiced only by women or lesbians.[34] Enter El Vez. El Vez's performances of masculinity illustrate Halberstam's assertion. And perhaps this is why some are uncomfortable with El Vez's performances, for "if non-performance is part of what defines white male masculinity, then all performed masculinity stands out as suspect and open to interrogation."[35]

Although El Vez's performance can be read as Queer, it can be read differently within particular contexts. Outside Queer contexts, El Vez's performance of outrageous masculinity might be a safer way to be "out" in contexts that do not traditionally condone what the film scholar Sergio de la Mora calls "queen homosexuality."[36] El Vez's performance of masculinity suggests that he is out but not necessarily visible within contexts that prefer not to interpret his performance as Queer and where a less rigid version of masculinity is permitted (e.g., within Latino or other ethnic communities).[37]

According to de la Mora, "Within Mexican cultural production, the cabaret is associated with the brothel" and "is the privileged space for articulating gender/sexual identities."[38] The context of the cabaret permits "the free play of dominant cultural images that associate masculinity with an overwhelming sexual drive" and is a "veritable altar erected to virility."[39]

De la Mora argues that homosexuality is relegated to these spaces, but only through the figure of what de la Mora calls "the queen homosexual," or drag queen, "men who have betrayed their masculinity by 'acting like women.'"[40] Within Mexican cultural production, the figure of the homosexual queen is endowed with the "most misogynist characteristics heterosexual males attribute to 'femininity,' including weakness, frivolity, and narcissism."[41] Almost never is "kinging" associated with this social space.

El Vez, however, brings the kinging aspect to the cabaret. El Vez's performance turns on his "sexual drive and virility" by enacting his "sexual potency . . . the qualifying/quantifying category with which a Mexican male constructs his gender identity" on the gorgeous El Vettes as feminine foils (the El Vettes, El Vez's backup singers, are always women who camp femininity).[42] However, El Vez subverts traditional masculinity by "opening up his body for objectification and thus signals a collapse of the conventional gendered hierarchy of looking."[43] For instance, when El Vez performs his "boylesque" version of "Quetzalcoatl," an homage to the Aztec legend of Quetzalcoatl via Elvis's "Heartbreak Hotel" (who would imagine that "Heartbreak Hotel" could be made to rhyme with "Quetzalcoatl"?), El Vez begins his performance fully dressed in a shiny black outfit and begins, "I'm going to tell you the tale of Quetzalcoatl, but first let me show you *my* tail." The Lovely El Vettes strip away pieces of his costume throughout the song, while simultaneously helping him put on his Quetzalcoatl costume, which consists of two gold armbands, a gold collar, and an intricately designed loincloth. At the climax of the song, the El Vettes crown El Vez with a colorful feathered headdress. Any pretense of heterosexual masculinity evaporates at that instance.

In examining the performance of El Vez, it makes sense to expand the metaphor of kinging in multiple ways. El Vez's performance not only exposes the theatricality of masculinity, but also, by deploying Elvis, the king, as a trope for what it means to be a working-class American, exposes the theatricality of national identity in general. Specifically, he exposes the theatricality of "Americanness" and "Mexicanness." El Vez is not necessarily kinging on white masculinity but is instead kinging the notion that the ideal American is always white and male. In addition, El Vez is also kinging on a particular version of Mexicanness, one that charac-

Lysa Flores and Cristi Guerrero as the El Vettes. 1996. Photography by Timothy McCleary. (Reprinted with permission.)

terizes Mexicans as frivolous, fun-loving, and anything but serious. Yet, through his critique of anti-immigrant hostility, El Vez turns that around, as well. El Vez satires the expectations non-Latino audiences have for Latino performers by dressing in exaggerated Mexican costume (although quite customized) and by speaking with a fake Mexican accent that usually gets lost by the end of the show but that forces audiences to confront racial hierarchies, albeit through humor.

Ambassador of Latin Culture? El Vez in Germany

It is important to note that "Immigration Time" speaks to an audience far outside the Chicano and Latino immigrant community as it addresses the effects of transnational capital on low-wage workers in general. The song narrates what is happening to employees at the bottom of the economic ladder—they are being told to work harder, work overtime, take care of business, all the while losing employment protections. Of course, when business cycles are in decline, workers without proper documentation are harassed and deported. El Vez's ability to superimpose issues of immigration, labor, and national belonging on top of songs associated with Elvis resonates well abroad in performances that sustain his artistic production in the United States; it also takes Chicana culture and his critique of the status quo out of a local context and situates it within an international one. El Vez's performances thus enable the possibility of building alliances in communities "with and between others . . . who are subject to and subjects of the state" on the basis of "'horizontal affiliations'—a process by which marginalized groups recognize shared stakes in the struggle to create counterhegemonic practices and communities."[44] It is worth noting that Lopez is well aware of these repercussions of his music. In our interview, for instance, he reflected on the reaction of Turkish youth in Germany to his music. He observed that:

> [performing in Europe] is great. [Ethnic] Turkish kids [who speak English] come to me and go, "I love when you sing about 'Immigration Time' because I know what you are. My family came here and we're immigrants and we're just trying to be here, we're in Berlin here trying to make a living and trying to be part of this society." It's something . . . we were in Slovenia, and the people, some Croatian kids, say, "I know when you sing about Zapata because that's happening now, too."[45]

In theorizing about the international reception for his performance, Lopez recognizes that even though his performance originated in southern California, "it took on a whole new meaning in Europe, because the song . . . has something to do with their lives." He elaborates: "It's lost something in the translation and gained something else, too. It's the whole process of changing and meaning something else to someone else."[46]

Although the specifics of Chicana and Chicano cultural symbols and experiences may be lost in translation, what is gained is the possibility of recognizing that young Turkish Germans are positioned similarly to Chicanas and Chicanos by capitalism and nationalism. Hence, "Immigration Time" and "Taking Care of Business" speak to the frustrations of many young ethnic Turks who are also dealing with issues of transnational immigration, citizenship, labor, social mobility, and cultural diversity in a contentious social ambient.[47] Of course, there are historical circumstances that allow for these identifications to take place. After the Berlin Wall was built, in the early 1960s, West Germany lost access to the cheap labor pools available in East Germany and invited Turkish temporary guest workers to fill its labor needs.[48] As in the Bracero program, launched in the Southwest in 1942, which contracted with Mexican nationals to work in the United States under temporary arrangements, only Turkish men were granted work visas. Thus, Turkish workers were excluded by German labor processes that were similar in structure to those found in the Bracero policy.[49] Then, in the late 1960s, wives of guest workers were granted work visas, as well. The children of the Turkish guest workers, although they were born in Germany, did not receive automatic citizenship, since German citizenship required having German ancestry.[50] As these children came of age, in the 1980s and 1990s, they began to question their relation to the nation-state. Although they were considered to be foreigners and had experienced anti-immigration violence, they had grown up in Germany, not Turkey.[51] Many felt that they should be recognized as part of German culture.

We hear the echo of "Taking Care of Business," with its concern for immigrant labor in the United States, in the words of a Turkish working woman in Germany. Commenting on the anti-Turkish sentiment in Germany after the fall of the Berlin Wall, Sasian Ozakbyiyik bitterly explains that "we were welcomed with open arms . . . none of the Germans wanted to do the jobs we did and now they don't want us." Her daughter continues, "We were the builders of Germany's economic miracle. So we have a right to live here."[52] Though the context is different, these sentiments are also expressed in El Vez's "Taking Care of Business."

"Working Over Time" and Place, Oralé!

The popularity of El Vez's music in Europe, though it may play into Western Europe's fascination with so-called exotic others, demonstrates that oppositional forms of Chicana and Chicano culture (including the related form of rock en español) have a role to play in cross-cultural contestatory musical practices of racialized immigrant European youth.[53] Though not an immigrant worker himself, Lopez, in his music, helps to humanize the struggle of racialized global immigrants who are displaced by global restructuring and hostile immigration policies. When young Turkish-Germans recognize the social and political resemblance between their situation and that of many Latinos in the United States, the progressive potential of subversive forms of popular culture is revealed. While nation-states regularly question identities—who is a citizen, who a worker?—and while capital increasingly requires that identities be as fluid as possible in order to make labor more pliable so that capital can maximize its profits, artists such as Lopez open up the possibility of creating the newest links of resistance by mixing histories and aesthetic styles within a progressive and pro-democratic performance form. This form, as it travels, tells racialized immigrants that they are not alone. This can be the first step toward solidarity.

El Vez's performances manipulate the affective power of Elvis-as-icon to advance the discourse of a renovated Chicano cultural politics that is not bound to the closures of cultural nationalism; El Vez harnesses the ability of the figure of Elvis to travel easily (outside the South) across socially constructed boundaries of all sorts to attract and forge a mixed audience, one that may have never been exposed to an oppositional politics. Ultimately, the performance of Lopez's El Vez translates and transforms nationalist codes (both dominant and Chicano) that insist on cultural and racial purity. As they recycle forms of mass popular culture, El Vez and his fans, both here and abroad, make visible both the possibility of a new understanding of community—one that responds to an exploitative transnationalism—and an international political agency and musical sensibility of social subjects that, because of their unique histories and social predicaments, do not possess the luxury of ethnic or national absolutism.

Epilogue

"Call Us Americans,
'Cause We Are All from the Américas":
Latinos at Home in Canada

I'm twenty years old and I still look at myself in the mirror every morning wondering who the hell I am. Am I Mexican? Am I Canadian? Am I just plain Latino? Am I Mexican-Canadian? Am I Latin-Canadian? — *¿Qué Pasa con la Raza, eh?*

Well I've never been to Spain / So don't call me an Hispanic /. . . that name, refuse it / Never going to choose it / I just can't use it.
—El Vez and the Memphis Mariachis

DON'T CALL US HISPANIC, 'CAUSE WE AIN'T NEVER BEEN TO SPAIN . . . IF ANYTHING, CALL US AMERICANS, 'CAUSE WE ARE ALL FROM THE AMERICAS. — *¿Qué Pasa con la Raza, eh?*

As post-9/11 xenophobic discourse justifies the increased surveillance and militarization of the territory that divides the United States and Mexico for the sake of security, support for the demilitarization of the border for the sake of human rights receives little attention in the mainstream media.[1] General public debate about the need for undocumented migrant labor to support local economies of many regions throughout the United States has been stymied by a post-9/11 nativist impulse. In this context, we come to realize the value of the cultural production discussed throughout this book, as examples of public culture. Crucially, the artists in this study contribute to public, if not mainstream, debates about these issues in the most unexpected forms of popular culture.

The particular Chicano and Latino performance discussed in these pages are important because they construct transnational imaginaries within the Americas that are shaped by a particular historical moment, politics, and humor. Ultimately, Chicana and Latina artists deeply rooted in a local context invent and advance a critical transnational and translocal imaginary via performative modes of humor.

In this book, I have located a remarkably untapped reservoir of materials that treat the dynamics of race/ethnicity, class, gender, and sexuality by critically analyzing experimental forms and sensibilities of Chicana/Latina popular culture. I have contextualized these experimental forms (performance, feminist standup comedy, as well as D.I.Y. film, popular music, and spoken word) by exploring the practices of early-twentieth-century U.S.-based Latino performance, as well as the legacy of the Spanish Fantasy Heritage, to demonstrate how contemporary artists challenge them. I have also suggested that the artists' innovative use of noir and punk sensibilities explode stereotypes that would forever locate Latinas and Latinos in a mythic, pastoral past, making way for the emergence of new representations that locate us in the present and the future.

In my treatment of artists who possess a deep commitment to progressive social change and who, through their work, strive to create a more equitable world, I have argued that the notable cultural production of Marisela Norte, Luis Alfaro, Marga Gomez, and Jim Mendiola is seriously playful, yet deeply moving. Humor, whether ironic, sarcastic, sincere, or campy, is their weapon of choice. Their work pokes fun at the idea that the current status quo is fixed and immutable and guides us to places we've never been. These artists show audiences how to implant, into the matrix of popular imagination, critiques of sexism, racism, homophobia, and anti-immigrant hostility through humor. In our post-9/11 climate of fear, humor opens up desperately needed public sites of critical dialogue. Their use of humor as an aesthetic strategy becomes an important tool to work through moments of crises and to re-imagine status quo power relations within and beyond national borders.

I have also demonstrated that Chicana/Latina popular culture is important for the labor it performs when it travels throughout, and outside, the United States. In looking back to the future, I would like to consider a broader notion of diasporic Latino cultural work by bringing the Canadian and Mexican borders into conversation in terms of Latino cultural production.

By examining the play *¿Qué Pasa con la Raza, eh?*, performed by the Latino Theater Group in Vancouver, British Columbia, this epilogue illuminates the new hemispheric and local connections that the interventions of Chicana cultural production make between unlikely communities and audiences, as well as the actual connections among various artistic scenes. This chapter suggests that particular forms of local Chicana/o brands of humor resonate hemispherically, because they captures the mechanics of transnationalism as it affects everyday local life. Ultimately, the cultural production of Chicana and Latina artists is important to those who teach, study, and live within an American context as their cultural production demonstrates how transnational/translocal movements affect students' everyday lives and their own identities within and without a U.S.-centered context. Exploring more inclusive conceptions of America is crucial now that many college-age Latinas and Latinos (both U.S.-born and noncitizen) are sacrificing their lives fighting the U.S. war on terrorism.[2]

This discussion of *¿Qué Pasa con la Raza, eh?* serves as a metaphor that ties the themes of previous chapters together. The themes of traveling, sexuality, identity formation, cultural politics, and transnational and translocal cultural dynamics are addressed in the play, albeit through a farcical mode. Additionally, the play offers an example of what a critical aesthetic culture of *las Américas* might look like. Perhaps it is a construction of culture that José Martí imagined as *"Nuestra America"* [Our America] in his wildest dreams for the future.[3]

As a scholar trained in the southwest, I had never conceptualized Canada as participating in a larger culture of the Americas. However, my analytical framework was changed forever during my first drive across the northwestern border. Moving to Seattle in 1998 after living my entire life in the Southwest was a major culture shock. Homesick for the thrills of a multicultural West Coast city, my partner and I decided on a day trip and drove about two hours north to Vancouver, British Columbia. When we approached the border, I was shocked—expecting the militarized bleakness of the San Ysidro/Tijuana border, I was surprised to see a lush green parkway with picnic tables. I did understand that climate made the northern border visually different from the dusty desert I was familiar with. But what astounded me was the giant ivory peace arch that stood in the middle of the parkway.[4] Its pleasing aesthetics posed a stark contrast to the army of INS agents that guards the southern border crossing. Once we were waved in, we drove straight into downtown and picked up a copy of the local newspaper. And, to my surprised delight, I read an advertisement for the Latino Theater Group. It was to perform *¿Qué Pasa con la Raza, eh?* This trip and the Canadian-based performance of this play forced me to retheorize the production of Chicano and Latino culture, especially as it transforms and is transformed by youth communities on both sides of the U.S./Canadian border.

Latinos at Home in Canada

The Chilean-born director Carmen Aguirre, the daughter of political exiles and an active theater artist in Vancouver's independent media scene, initiated the city's Latino Theater Group (LTG) in 1999.[5] (After attending a conference in Brazil on Augusto Boal's Theater of the Oppressed, she was inspired to form a community theater workshop focused on Latino issues. The group first acted out improvisational street performances that called for audience participation to resolve enacted crisis situations. As the group coalesced, a collective playwriting process began, from which *¿Qué Pasa con la Raza, eh?* emerged. Since each member developed and performed a character based on his or her own experiences, the play's structure requires innovation and openness as it registers multiple Latino-Canadian experiences—specifically those of Guatemalan, Chilean, Salvadoran, and Mexican Canadians, as well as of ethnically mixed Latino-Canadians. Hence, the frenetic pace and nonlinear structure moves back and forth in time, just like the performer's memories that constitute the play.

In order to understand the significance of *¿Qué Pasa con la Raza, eh?* within its Canadian context, it is important to note that, for the most part, the cultural production made by Latin Americans in Canada has been framed by the notion of exile.[6] Although the first wave of Chileans arrived after Salvador Allende was democratically elected, the second major wave of immigration of Latin Americans to Vancouver was composed of highly educated Chilean and Argentine leftists fleeing from persecution by the Pinochet dictatorship and the military juntas. During the 1970s and 1980s, Canada granted asylum to political refugees from all over Latin America.[7] The nature of Latino/Latin American communities in Vancouver has been shaped by their progressive politics. According to Aguirre, however, the recent increase in undocumented immigration from central American and the Caribbean has made the Latino/Latin American community more heterogeneous.[8] More recent research documents Canada's reliance on noncitizen labor.[9]

Reflecting this change, the protagonist of *¿Qué Pasa con la Raza, eh?* is not a political exile but an economic immigrant.[10] In addition, each of the play's characters represents a different stage of the Latin American and Latino community's integration into the greater Vancouver community. Some of LTG members—whose ages run from sixteen to twenty-seven—are the children of exiles. Their relationship to Latin America and to Canada, and to English (the language of the play), differs significantly from that of their parents. However, one LTG member explains: "The only way people see Latinos is through the point of view of adults, and they have a totally different view from youth."[11] Aguirre comments further, "Their parents describe them as Canadian but they're not accepted by the mainstream, which sees them as Latino. So these kids are stuck in the middle, trying to find their own ground."[12] This play constructs a narrative that enables young Latinos to assert their rightful place in the local and national context (Vancouver, Canada) by making visible their connection to the larger geopolitical space and history of *Las Américas*.

Welcome to the Américas

Six dancers, most under the age of twenty-five, jump on stage and begin to hip-hop to "Mexican Power," by the Chicano rappers Proper Dos, as "Never Been to Spain," by El Vez, fades out.[13] A series of slides of the internationally acclaimed Chicano comic novel series *Love and Rockets* by Los Bros. Hernandez flashes behind them.[14] Another slide reads:

THE LATINO THEATER GROUP WAS CREATED IN 1994 TO EXPRESS OUR LATINO SELVES THROUGH THEATER. . . . WE'RE A SOULFUL BUNCH, FULL OF LATINO PRIDE AND LOTS OF STORIES TO SHARE WITH YOU. . . . LIKE, DID YOU KNOW THAT NOT ALL OF US ARE ACTORS! NO, WE'RE ALL LIKE ECONOMISTS AND CASHIERS AND CHILD CARE WORKERS AND HIGH SCHOOL STUDENTS AND COLLEGE STUDENTS AND COMPUTER GEEKS AND SO ON AND SO ON. . . . IN OTHER WORDS, WE ARE THE REAL THING FROM THE REAL VANCOUVER LATINO COMMUNITY HERE TO TELL YOU SOME REAL STORIES BASED ON OUR REAL LIVES. . . . WELCOME TO THE FIREHALL, IN THE DOWNTOWN EASTSIDE OF VANCOUVER, IN THE NORTHWESTERN

TIP OF THE AMERICAS, THIS CONTINENT THAT CONTAINS US ALL
. . . AND REMEMBER, DON'T CALL US HISPANIC, 'CAUSE WE AIN'T
NEVER BEEN TO SPAIN. . . . IF ANYTHING, CALL US AMERICANS,
'CAUSE WE ARE ALL FROM THE AMERICAS.

When we think about the culture of *Las Américas, con acento,* Canada rarely comes to mind.[15] However, the performance of *¿Qué Pasa con la Raza, eh?* by the LTG locates Vancouver, British Columbia, on both the cultural and the geographical map of *Nuestra América* [Our America]. In fact, an inverted borderless map that locates Chile at the top and Canada at the bottom of the *Américas* remains center stage throughout the performance; at its conclusion, text projected on the map states: "THE BORDERS HAVE BLURRED, NORTH IS DOWN AND SOUTH IS UP: WELCOME TO THE AMERICAS." *¿Qué Pasa con la Raza, eh?* advances an alternative story concerning the culture of *Las Américas.* Written as a farce, the play thematizes the life stories of Latino-Canadian youth. Like the map, the play seeks to disrupt outdated cultural conceptions about who constitutes Canada as it defines a citizenship of *Las Américas.* The upside-down map that remains visible throughout the performance serves to remind the audience that the characters, although in Canada, still remain part of *Las Américas.* The inverted map also symbolically turns on its head the connection among Canada, the United States, and Mexico (and the rest of Latin America); it suggests that the audience will be given a glimpse of what economic restructuring, as exemplified by the North American Free Trade Agreement (NAFTA), looks like from the perspective of those on the bottom.[16]

¿Que Pasa con la Raza, eh? begins at the U.S.-Mexican border, where a coyote, ironically named Santo (Saint), guides a group of undocumented immigrants across the Rio Grande to "el Norte."[17] Only one immigrant, the Guatemalan Rata, makes it though the doomed crossing. Rata makes his way up the West Coast, and, once he is in Vancouver, the narrative is propelled by his impending deportation and by his friends' attempts to save him by organizing a marriage of convenience to ensure his Canadian citizenship. Characters enlisted in his aid include Sombra (Shadow), who left Guatemala after her parents were "disappeared"; Skin, a Canadian-born Chilean activist; Zap, a Mexican Canadian bachelor; Dandelion, a Canadian-raised Jewish-Argentine environmentalist; and Julio, a recent political refugee from Guatemala. All of the characters are in their early to mid-twenties, except for Julio, who is in his thirties, and almost all are in search of romance.

Publicity photo of the Latino Theatre Group (Vancouver, British Columbia). 1999. (Reprinted with permission from Carmen Aguirre.)

Composed collaboratively and based on real-life *testimonios* (testimonies), the play distills the experiences of forty LTG members. The two-act play mixes farce and performance art, and each scene is punctuated by short dance breaks. Because the play takes its cue from the Theater of the Oppressed, the combination of forms and content reflects the interests and experiences of the group. Theater of the Oppressed, a process rather than an aesthetic or particular practice, assists disempowered communities in solving social crises by providing a cultural space for dialogue and exchange of ideas.[18] By creating "a reflection on reality and a rehearsal for future politics," Theater of the Oppressed transforms everyday passive spectators into social actors.[19] It is popular, in the democratic sense of the word, in that it is a grass-roots process. In *¿Qué Pasa con la Raza, eh?* the group must collaborate to prevent Rata's deportation.

¿Qué Pasa con la Raza, eh? serves as a launching point to examine the way the themes, iconography, and sounds of Chicano popular culture

resonate in the northern reaches of the hemisphere (and contribute to a larger culture of *Las Américas*) within a framework of what the scholar Angie Chabram-Dernersesian calls a critical transnationalism, one that considers "geopolitical and linguistic complexities" within *"Las Américas,"* complexities "that arise from making strategic connections with other people of color in *Las Américas."*[20] This conceptual framework points to a nuanced understanding of the cultural effects of late-twentieth-century neoliberal economic restructuring on the continent of North America and compels people of color in the Americas who are interested in issues of social justice to find the common ground for a transnational conversation. The characters in the play immediately invite a transnational conversation with Chicanas and Chicanos by invoking, during the opening scene, the Chicana/o edict "don't call us Hispanic" and by reiterating El Vez's lyrics "'cause we ain't never been to Spain." These gestures also urge Chicanos and other progressively minded U.S. Latinos to examine their relation to Latino diasporas and communities north of the border.[21]

Don't Call Us Hispanic

To those familiar with the history of Chicanos in the United States, it comes as no surprise that the memories that constitute *¿Qué Pasa con la Raza, eh?* resonate with the major themes addressed in Chicana and Chicano literature, *teatro*, music, and visual art, themes that include migration and immigration, border crossings, cultural identity crisis, critiques of transnational labor exploitation, and the struggle for social justice. These themes remind us that it is impossible to take for granted the meanings of nation and citizenship. In fact, Chicana and Chicano cultural production emphasizes that the "concept of citizenship does not exist in a vacuum; rather, it is related to other aspects of a society, particularly where a society is marked and divided by racism and when race and national origin have determined who is awarded citizenship."[22]

¿Qué Pasa con la Raza, eh? echoes these themes as its narrative turns on a crisis of citizenship, albeit Canadian citizenship. The excerpts that follow demonstrate the way the play illuminates the particular, yet familiar, conflicts and tensions that shape the lives of young Latinos north of the U.S. border in a historical moment when "accords like NAFTA have

engendered profound disruptions that evoke the prospect of deepening social immiseration and marginalization on the one hand and the potential for cross-national popular organizing and resistance on the other."[23]

Mary Pat Brady argues that certain Chicana narratives provide "highly charged political critique of border mechanics," that is, of the U.S.-Mexico border's site-specific practices of terror and exclusion. *¿Qué Pasa con la Raza, eh?*, like the narratives Brady cites, takes the "U.S.-Mexico border seriously, seeing it as a process, not a static place" that impacts the lives of the characters.[24] The play begins in 1996 with a tragically familiar U.S.-Mexico border crossing. Here, the coyote figure, Santos, is rendered as a greedy smuggler who extorts money and possessions from his five terrified clients, including Rata. Santos, however, sees himself as "a guide, messenger, coyote, messiah." The role of the coyote (the person who smuggles undocumented workers across the border) as indispensable to border economies has intensified during the latest phase of restructuring. As an attempt to rally customers, Santos reproduces the utopic myth of "*el Norte*" that these economic immigrants desire by proclaiming:

> Imagine a land where there are no twelve-hour lineups, where you pay phone bills sitting at home, through the internet—I know you don't know what that means . . . everybody in the North has a computer. . . . Everyone in the North has or can find a job. Everyone is employed. They have positions for turkey watchers at the supermarkets during Christmas time. You can get a job waxing apples.

To a certain extent, Santos tells the truth when he explains that beyond the Rio Bravo lies "a land of great opportunity and wealth. Yes, riches beyond your wildest dreams." What he fails to mention is that those great opportunities and wealth are much easier to acquire if one holds the privilege of citizenship or legal residence and that they do not necessarily trickle down to undocumented workers. He makes no mention of the massive inequalities that exist in the North, or of the constant vulnerability to deportation.

¿Qué Pasa con la Raza, eh? constructs a border crossing experience gone bad to portray the exclusionary mechanisms of "nation" at work and to articulate the meaning of nation and citizenship from the perspective of the disempowered who are denied them. The crossing turns for the

worse when Santos orders his five clients to strip and hand over their jewelry and wallets; he claims he wants to keep them dry. The women reluctantly do so but then panic when searchlights appear, accompanied by the sounds of helicopters and dogs. Chaos breaks out, and Rata screams for them to "shut the fuck up! I want to get across." When the crossers emerge on the other side, they find that two parents have been lost to the river. Their daughter begins to wail, and another young crosser becomes hysterical and has a laughing attack. Santo silences the hysterical crosser by punching her in the face and raping her, while Rata merely turns away. The rape is interrupted by two U.S. Border Patrol agents, Rodrigo and Federico. They arrest all of the border crossers except for Rata, who slips away. Forced to their knees at gunpoint, the girls plead with the agents: "But you're one of us, both of you, are just like us . . . you're not gringos, you're Latinos, aren't you ashamed? . . . we have done nothing wrong. . . . This land is ours and was taken from us." Insulted that the "lettuce-pickers" see a connection with them, the agents reply, "We are American citizens and proud of it. Born and raised. One more word out of any of you and we'll set you on fire. Let's go." This scene, not unlike the U.S. film *El Norte*,[25] explores the very real tensions between the U.S.-born and the undocumented that exist within Latino communities.[26]

While the crossers understand their connection to the Mexican Americans in a much larger context—the history of colonization—the Mexican American Border Patrol agents, at the height of anti-immigrant hysteria and caught up in the privileges of citizenship, allow a nativist nationalism to override that possibility of solidarity. Rata eventually crosses over the "easy" border to Vancouver, but not before almost hitching a ride from a "friendly" Chicano trucker who picks up recently crossed immigrants. He finds Rata walking on the road and urges him to "get in my truck before you end up . . . back where you came from. . . . We all look out for each other out here." He advises him to "follow the coast, hitch rides, I hear you can pretty well walk right into Canada." However, he does not let Rata on until Rata pays him. As Rata hands over the money, the trucker thanks him with "We're all in this together, brother. *i Viva la raza!*" Rata hops into a truck packed with other undocumented workers that is stopped by a highway patrol car before it can leave. Rata jumps off and sneaks away as the others faint from the heat in the enclosed truck. By framing the experience of young Latino-Canadians in this way, *¿Qué Pasa con la Raza, eh?* parallels what Manuel Pastor Jr. asserts is a recent trend in "cultural production aimed at understanding the Chicano experience"; that is, it "is rooted increasingly in the notion of *frontera* (border)" and concerned with the "defense of the rights of undocumented immigrants, an agenda based implicitly on a nation of transnational (or non-citizen) human rights."[27]

Rata finally settles into the Latino community in Vancouver in 1999. As an economic immigrant, Rata rejects his new friends' progressive politics. He describes himself as a free agent, "a man of the world" who passed over "L.A. and El Paso" because he "needed a new land." He fantasizes in front of his friends about buying a low-rider limousine complete with hydraulics, a pool in the back, and a boom system. He explains to them, "I want to drive it all the way to Chile so that I can have a limo business there." Rata has no desire to volunteer for community politics and fund-raisers organized by his friends and cannot understand why they "don't want to keep any money for yourselves. . . . Volunteer? I didn't come all the way over here to give my money away." The irony is that as he espouses the virtues of American individualism, he depends on community to help him acquire the documentation he needs.

The Canadian-born Skin, the most idealistic character and the most critical of Canadian nationalism and racism, pleads with their environmentalist friend Rocio Bernstein, nicknamed Dandelion, to marry Rata. Dandelion wants to know why Skin will not marry him herself, and Skin, exasperated, fumes, "Don't mock me. . . . I renounced my Canadian citizenship, . . . I'm not going to be suckered in like you idiots to this imperialistic, capitalist, racist, whitewash, superiority-complex country." In a speech that gets her elected the president of the college organization "Shades of Revolution" (formerly called Rainbow Nation, a name she rejects), Skin reveals the source of her anger:

> I don't feel like I'm part of the multicultural mosaic when I'm surrounded by bleeding hearts who suffer from amnesia about the history of their country. . . . We are living in Vancouver. A place where white supremacists beat an old Sikh brother to death, where they chase black brothers out of the Ivanhoe with baseball bats, where they beat the crap out of Filipino brothers in Squamish, where everywhere I look I'm portrayed as a fuckin' drug dealer 'cause I'm Latino. (12)

As Skin recounts these true incidents of racial hate crimes, she provides a relatively unknown counterhistory of life for people of color in Vancouver.[28] For Skin, the sole way of combating hate crimes against people of color in the Americas is though a coalition politics that recognizes Canada's role in the legacy of imperialism that has ravaged indigenous people throughout the Americas. In calling for solidarity across racial, ethnic, and national lines in antiracist struggles, Skin reiterates the desire of radical U.S. women of color, in particular that of Chicana feminists, for what Sonia Saldivar-Hull calls "border feminism."[29] Though Skin may not recognize herself as a border feminist, the character's activism in Canada on behalf of revolutionary struggles in Latin America parallels the transnational efforts of border feminism. Yet, despite her valiant efforts, she cannot immediately change Rata's quandary: Without the privilege and protection of the citizenship that she renounces, Rata will be deported to meet a more dangerous fate in Guatemala.

The second act begins with an apparition of the Mexican *Virgen de Guadalupe*. Zap, short for "Zapatista, Emiliano Zapatista, Chiapas, Mexico, Resistencia," prays to the *Virgen* for help in solving what he calls "his cultural identity crisis," even though Rata cannot understand why he has a problem: "You've got this land, this land's got you. Simple. You're Canadian." But Zap is caught in a situation explored by many Chicana and Chicano narratives. Zap feels trapped "between two worlds"; his national and cultural identity are at odds: "I'm twenty years old and I still look at myself in the mirror every morning wondering who the hell I am. Am I Mexican? Am I Canadian? Am I just plain Latino? Am I Mexican-Canadian? Am I Latin-Canadian?" As Zap considers the multiple identities he might embody, "Mexican, Canadian, Mexican Canadian, etc.," he laments that he is so "mixed up." Though Zap is confused, he is on the verge of realizing that cultural identity is a process of becoming, that it is not a given.[30] He is what Guillermo Gomez-Peña calls "a child of crisis and cultural syncretism."[31] His presence engenders what Teresa McKenna calls a "new culture that repudiates both a monocultural and a binary existence."[32] Zap is in the initial stages of constructing a border identity, an identity that will allow him to negotiate life in Canada as a racialized other, where Latinos are categorized as a visible minority. After trying and failing, Zap realizes that he cannot resolve his identity through interracial dating. Although he likes the Canadian "suburban Brady Bunch meets Melrose Place white girl" who wants him to "do his best Spanish accent in English" and talk about "Che and the revolution," he realizes that she demands a performance of a racist stereotype of Mexicanness—as do the customers in his aunt's Mexican restaurant, for whom he is required to speak with a fake Spanish accent and play the maracas as he buses their tables.[33] He contemplates attending "a cross-cultural support group" but instead goes to Latin Lovers Dating Service, where he finally meets a Canadian *mestiza* like himself.

For all of the play's open discussion of sexuality and safe sex, it makes only passing references to Queer practices. When his friends kid Rata about marrying Zap to retain his citizenship, Rata responds, "I'm not even going to pretend I'm a fag." Skin tells Rata to "shut up," and Zap admonishes him "not to be such a homophobe." Rata is reassured by the fact that (at the time) Canada prohibits same-sex marriages for its citizens: "It's illegal" for "two Latin American males" to get married.

In the final third of the play, Sombra decides to confront Rata's childhood friend Julio about her disappeared parents. She and the group question him at the sugar refinery where he works: She holds a picture to his face and demands, "Where are they?" Julio, who "wants to suffer from amnesia," denies he knows anything. He suddenly flashes back to Guatemala, where he sees his support of and participation in a bloody dictatorship as heroic: "Who do you think saved Guatemala from the Communists?" He continues the torture scene, describing to his victim that what he likes most is "watching your expression of fear." But what compels him is his ability to proclaim a sentence worse than death: "You never existed." When he returns to the present, he admits, "There were so many. They might be in a ditch, a river, or who knows where." Julio trashes the photo and tries to leave, but the group stops him: "you have to pay for what you've done." They beat him in slow motion and dance around him to the rock en español song "Matador" [Killer], by the Argentine Los Fabuloso Cadillacs [the Fabulous Cadillacs]. When they are done, Sombra begins a monologue:

> My parents may never make it into the history books, but you will. The whole world will know what you've done. 'Cause I remember. . . . If you wanted to destroy the cause and the desire for people to live better, you should have killed me. You should have killed us all, because I have my memory. I have my humanity.

Refusing to forget her parents and their desire for a better way of living, and confronting this past in public, Sombra walks out, with the support of her friends, in the shadow of this past. Again, the incident the character describes is one that more than a few Latino immigrants face. For

Sombra, asylum and the privilege of Canadian citizenship do not necessarily mean safety from the torturers she fled.[34]

This Is for la Raza

¿Qué Pasa con la Raza, eh? emphasizes the heterogeneity of experiences and values within Vancouver's Latino community in order to resist stereotypical U.S. representations of Latinos that spill into Canada and often influence the way non–Latino Canadians see them. A recent controversy involving stereotypical views of Chicanos among members of the Toronto Police Association points to the ways that images that originate in the United States inundate Latino Canadian youth;[35] a provincial election poster depicting "a gang from East L.A." urged voters to "help fight crime by electing candidates who are prepared to take on the drug pushers, the pimps, and rapists."[36] Members of the LTG affirm that the circulation of images that equate Latinos and criminality affect their everyday realities: "Day after day, you see it in the media: Latinos, drug dealers, Latinos, drug dealers. Then I'll be walking around or standing on a street corner, and I can feel that . . . I'm not kidding—not one day goes by without at least one white person asking me to sell them drugs."[37] However, the group finds offensive any suggestion that they are making victim art and uses farcical humor as a strategy to avoid such representation. Aguirre explains that by using farce, "we are really highlighting the fact that we're laughing at ourselves and our community . . . the show is all about resilience"[38]

¿Qué Pasa con la Raza, eh? also uses imported images to construct a larger consciousness about North American Latinos living in *Las Américas*. However, it is in alternative and oppositional Chicano and Latino popular culture that the play finds the language to shape oppositional representations of Latino-Canadian youth. U.S. Latino rap and hip-hop by Lighter Shade of Brown, Kid Frost, El Vez, Mellow Man Ace, and Proper Dos reinforce the theme of each scene.[39] The play's use of Chicano and U.S. Latino cultural production to underscore characters' experiences not only speaks to the way that cultural production travels and resonates across national borders but also points to the innovative ways Latino Canadian youth culture interprets and customizes forms of oppositional culture. *¿Qué Pasa con la Raza, eh?* successfully navigates what George Lipsitz calls "a dangerous crossroads, an intersection between the

undeniable saturation of commercial culture in every area of human endeavor and the emergence of a new public sphere that uses the circuits of commodity production and circulation to envision and activate new social relations."[40] Why should Latino Canadian youth culture turn to the popular forms of Chicano youth culture? Perhaps, as María de los Angeles Torres reminds us, it is for the same reason that Mexicans in Mexico find inspiration in it: "Mexicans in the United States have developed unique cultural and political skills as a result of the struggles they have had to wage against racism . . . home countries can rely on these skills in developing cultural and political projects that offer an alternative to pervasive and often popular global market culture."[41]

The best of Chicano and Chicana cultural production responds compellingly to the historical moment from which it emerges. *¿Qué Pasa con la Raza, eh?* shares this quality in its desire to document a particular time, place, and sensibility in Latino youth culture. The play references themes found in the best of what has been called the third wave of Chicana and Chicano cultural production, a wave that finds no shame in expressing its love affair with U.S. youth pop culture and that interprets it in unexpected ways.[42] *¿Qué Pasa con la Raza, eh?* attempts to activate new social relations between Latino youth in the United States and in Canada by thinking beyond the nation and by employing Chicano popular music and images, distributed though commercial circuits, to narrate the experiences of Latino youth in Canada. The ease with which Chicano themes speak to their situation illuminates their experience as part of a larger North American context. This is not to argue that young Latino Canadians will, over time, become "Chicana or Chicano." We must remember that Chicano iconography emerges out of and responds to the specific historical and political context of the United States, specifically the annexation of most of the U.S. Southwest from Mexico.[43]

The play translates the symbolic meaning of Chicano iconography to fit its own specific location, especially since Latinos in Canada have a different historical relation to legacies of European and U.S. imperialism. In the end, Chicano cultural production acts as a partial mirror that helps the play express their experiences. For instance, the title *¿Qué Pasa con la Raza, eh?* reads as an analogue for the way that Chicano culture gets transculturated in Vancouver. The "eh?" in the title marks the inflection of Canadian English. Diane Taylor, elaborating on the Cuban anthropologist Fernando Ortiz's definition of the term, explains that transculturation "suggests a shifting or circulation pattern of cultural transference . . .

it involves the shifting of socio-political, not just aesthetic borders; it modifies collective and individual identity; it changes discourse, both verbal and symbolic."[44] In recognizing that the transculturation of Chicano cultural production occurs outside the United States and provides important feedback from English-speaking Latinos who live outside the United States, Chicano cultural studies is compelled to move beyond a U.S.-Mexico framework into an hemispheric one. It also compels students of Chicano and Latino studies to see their concerns reflected in the world, the required initial step toward Chabram's "strategic connections with other people of color in the Americas."[45]

The play concludes at the Ukrainian Hall where, historically, the Chilean exile community has held its *peñas* (fund-raising events and cultural celebrations) to support progressive struggles in Chile.[46] Rata and Dandelion are wed at the hall a day before Rata is to be deported, thereby preventing his departure. As an allegory, the wedding suggests that the fate of recent undocumented immigrants is linked to that of the Canadian-born Latinos and vice versa. As "La Raza," by Kid Frost, plays, the newlyweds toast "Que viva los novios" shifts to "Que viva la Raza" (long live the people), and all the performers, echoing the opening scene, begin to dance, inventing new moves for the "land of a thousand dances," in our new *América*.

By invoking El Vez and locating the members of LTG as American, *¿Qué Pasa con la Raza, eh?* employs Chicano popular culture to invent a critical transnational culture, one that reinforces a continental and, by extension, a hemispheric connection based on oppositional cultures of *Las Américas,* instead of a connection based on nation. At the heart of the play is a critique of citizenship and, by extension, nation, nationalism, and transnational exploitation. The play articulates this critique by Latinos under the age of twenty-five living in Vancouver through modes of Chicano popular culture and by representing the trials and tribulations of their everyday lives. Ultimately, the play speaks to the power of popular theater to articulate in everyday terms an oppositional narrative of Américan identity.[47] In the LTG's actors' demand to be called American, despite their citizenship status, "'cause we are all from the Americas," we hear the echo of José Marti's dream for Our America, *"Nuestra America."*

Notes

NOTES TO THE INTRODUCTION

1. Ruben Martinez, *Diva L.A.: A Salute to L.A.'s Latinas in the Tanda Style,* program notes for performance by Ruben Martinez, presented at the Mark Taper Forum's Mainstage, Los Angeles, California, July 2, 1995.

2. *Tanda* is translated as variety or vaudeville show.

3. For a collection of U.S. Latino and Latin American performances that were performed in London in 1996, see Coco Fusco, ed., *Corpus Delecti: Performance of the Americas* (London: Routledge, 2000).

4. Walter D. Mignolo, "Capitalism and the Geopolitics of Knowledge: Latin American Social Thought and Latino/a American Studies," in *Critical Latin American and Latino Studies,* ed. Juan Poblete (Minneapolis: University of Minnesota, 2003), 45.

5. Angie Chabram-Dernersesian, "Chicana/o Latina/o Cultural Studies: Transnational and Transdisciplinary Movements," *Cultural Studies* 13, no. 2 (1999): 183.

6. For a complex discussion of the ways U.S. Latino studies and Latin American studies might approach such studies, see George Yúdice, "Rethinking Area and Ethnic Studies in the Context of Economic and Political Restructuring," in *Critical Latin American and Latino Studies,* ed. Juan Poblete (Minneapolis: University of Minnesota, 2003), 76–102.

7. Kaplan's study suggests that use of travel as a metaphor and a social practice mostly contributes to the cultural capital of privileged western subjects, usually bourgeois white men. See Kaplan's *Questions of Travel: Postmodern Discourses of Displacement* (Durham: Duke University Press, 1996).

8. See Otto Santa Ana, *Brown Tide Rising: The Metaphors of Latinos in Contemporary American Public Discourse* (Austin: University of Texas Press, 2002); and also Linda McDowell, *Gender, Identity, and Place: Understanding Feminist Geographies* (Minneapolis: University of Minnesota Press, 1999).

9. The literary critic Lauro Flores proposes the notion of a "floating borderlands," a geocultural rather than a strictly geographical concept, to account for the "cultural purpose and identity" of Latinas and Latinos who live outside of

the Southwest or Puerto Rico. Lauro Flores, "Introduction," in *The Floating Borderlands: Twenty-Five Years of U.S. Hispanic Literature*, ed. Lauro Flores (Seattle: University of Washington Press, 1998), 4.

10. Carl Gutiérrez-Jones, "Humor, Literacy and Trauma in Chicano Culture," *Comparative Literature Studies* 40, no. 2 (2003): 113.

11. Alberto Sandoval-Sanchez, *José, Can You See? Latinos On and Off Broadway* (Madison: University of Wisconsin Press, 1999), 122.

12. See Stuart Hall, "Notes on Deconstructing the 'Popular,'" in *People's History and Socialist Theory*, ed. R. Samuel (New York: Routledge and Kegan Paul, 1981), 239.

13. See Arlene Dávila, *Latinos, Inc.: The Marketing and Making of a People* (Berkeley: University of California Press, 2001); Angharad N. Valdivia, *A Latina in the Land of Hollywood and Other Essays on Media Culture* (Tucson: University of Arizona Press, 2000); Frances Negrón-Muntaner, *Boricua Pop: Puerto Ricans and American Culture from* West Side Story *to* Jennifer Lopez (New York: New York University Press, 2004); Chon A. Noriega, *The Future of Latino Independent Media: A NALIP Sourcebook* (Los Angeles: UCLA Chicano Studies Research Center Publications, 2000); and Chon A. Noriega and Ana M. López, eds., *The Ethnic Eye: Latino Media Arts* (Minneapolis: University of Minnesota Press, 1996).

14. Glenn Jordon and Chris Weedon, *Cultural Politics: Class, Gender, Race, and the Postmodern World* (Cambridge: Blackwell, 1995), 5.

15. Rosa Linda Fregoso, *The Bronze Screen: Chicana and Chicano Film Culture* (Minneapolis: University of Minnesota Press, 1993), 31.

16. Mary Romero and Michelle Habell-Pallán, "Introduction," in *Latino/a Popular Culture*, ed. Michelle Habell-Pallán and Mary Romero (New York: New York University Press, 2001), 3. See also Juan Flores, "The Latino Imaginary: Dimensions of Community and Identity," in *Tropicalizations: Transcultural Representations of Latinidad*, ed. Frances Aparicio and Susana Chávez-Silverman (Hanover, N.H.: University of New England Press, 1997), 183–193; and Angie Chabram-Dernersesian, "Latina/o: Another Site of Struggle, Another Site of Accountability," in *Critical Latin American and Latino Studies*, ed. Juan Poblete (Minneapolis: University of Minnesota, 2003), 76–102.

17. Fregoso, *The Bronze Screen*, 31.

18. See, especially, the following influential works: Alicia Arrizón, *Latina Performance: Traversing the Stage* (Bloomington: Indiana University Press, 1999); David Román, *Acts of Intervention: Performance, Gay Culture, and AIDS* (Bloomington: Indiana University Press, 1998); José E. Muñoz, *Disidentifications: Queers of Color and the Performance of Politics* (Minneapolis: University of Minnesota Press, 1999); Yvonne Yarbro-Bejarano, *The Wounded Heart: Writing on Cherríe Moraga* (Austin: University of Texas, 2001); and Juana

María Rodriguez, *Queer Latinidad: Identity Practices, Discursive Spaces* (New York: New York University Press, 2003).

19. In their important book *Racial Formation in the United States: From the 1960s to the 1980s,* Michael Omi and Howard Winant define racial formation as a "process by which social, economic and political forces determine the context and importance of racial categories and by which they are in turn shaped by racial meaning." Michael Omi and Howard Winant, *Racial Formation in the United States: From the 1960s to the 1980s* (New York: Routledge, 1986), 61.

20. There are many important artists who share this sensibility and deserve recognition: Monica Palacios, Culture Clash (Ric Salinas, Herbert Siquenza, and Richard Montoya), Sean Carrillo, Diane Gamboa, Josefina Lopez, Michele Serros, Chicano Secret Service, Taco Shop Poets, and Alma Lopez, among others.

21. Alicia Gaspar de Alba, *Chicano Art Inside/Outside the Master's House: Cultural Politics and Cara Exhibition* (Austin: University of Texas, 1998), xv. See also Charles Tatum, *Chicano Popular Culture: Que Hable el Pueblo* (Tucson: University of Arizona Press, 2001).

NOTES TO CHAPTER I

1. I attended this performance of *Deep in the Crotch of My Latino Psyche* in December 1993, at the Highways Performance Space, in Los Angeles. I thank Monica Palacios and Luis Alfaro for clarifying the details of the show.

2. See Carl Gutiérrez-Jones, *Rethinking the Borderlands: Between Chicano Culture and Legal Discourse* (Berkeley: University of California Press, 1995).

3. Neil Foley, review of *The Spanish Redemption: Heritage, Power, and Loss on New Mexico's Upper Rio Grande,* by Charles Montgomery, in *American Historical Review* 108, no. 4 (October 2003): 1156.

4. Ibid.

5. Mario García, "A Chicano Perspective on San Diego History," *Journal of San Diego History* 18, no. 4 (fall 1972): 19.

6. See Carey McWilliams, *North from Mexico: The Spanish-Speaking People of the United States* (1948; reprint, New York: Greenwood Press, 1968); David Weber, "The Idea of the Spanish Borderlands," in *Columbian Consequences: The Spanish Borderlands in Pan-American Perspective,* ed. David Thomas (Washington, D.C.: Smithsonian, 1991), 3–20; and Lisbeth Haas, *Conquests and Historical Identities in California, 1769–1936* (Berkeley: University of California Press, 1995). Haas explains that, "[w]hen Mexican playwrights working in the U.S. wrote about regional history, two major influences were at work: Spanish language theater and Hollywood film. *Ramona,* for example, was adapted to the stage and film from Helen Hunt Jackson's enormously popular 1884 novel *Ramona: A Story.* The Spanish-language version created by Los

Angeles playwright Adalberto Elias González, titled *Los Amores de Ramona,* broke all box office records in June 1927, drawing more than fifteen thousand people after only eight performances" (156).

7. Leonard Pitt and David J. Weber document Bolton and Bannon's deployment of the Spanish fantasy heritage.

8. Helen Hunt Jackson, *Ramona* (1884; reprint, New York: Avon, 1970).

9. Garcia, "A Chicano Perspective," 17.

10. Leonard Pitt, *The Decline of the Californios: A Social History of the Spanish-Speaking Californians, 1846–1890* (Berkeley: University of California Press, 1966).

11. This Hispanophobia emerged out of the Anglo world's Black Legend, which posited the Spanish as inherently unredeemable and racially inferior to the English. See Raymond Paredes, "The Origins of Anti-Mexican Sentiment in the United States," *New Scholar* 6 (1974): 139–165.

12. Pitt, *The Decline of the Californios,* 280.

13. Rosaura Sánchez, *Telling Identities: The Californio Testimonios* (Minneapolis: University of Minnesota Press, 1995).

14. Ibid., 23.

15. Ibid., 20.

16. Ibid., 30.

17. Ibid., 29.

18. Paredes, "The Origins of Anti-Mexican Sentiment." For more on Lummis, see Mike Davis, *City of Quartz: Excavating the Future in Los Angeles* (1990; reprint, New York: Verso, 1992). In the late 1800s, Lummis took the myth and used it to promote real estate in Southern California. Davis writes: "The mission literature depicted the history of race relations as a pastoral ritual of obedience and paternalism. . . . Any intimation of the brutality inherent in the forced labor system of the missions and haciendas, not to speak of the racial terrorism and lynchings that make early Anglo-ruled Los Angeles the most violent town in the West during 1860s and 1870s, was suppressed. If Jackson's *Ramona* transformed selected elements of local history and romantic myth (still popular to this day), Lummis was the impresario who promoted the myth as the motif of an entire artificial landscape" (26).

19. Weber, "The Idea of the Spanish Borderlands," 5.

20. Sánchez, *Telling Identities,* 10.

21. See also Genaro Padilla, *"My History, Not Yours": The Formation of Mexican American Autobiography* (Madison: University of Wisconsin Press, 1993).

22. Sánchez, *Telling Identities,* 31.

23. David J. Weber, "John Francis Bannon and the Historiography of the Spanish Borderlands: Retrospect and Prospect." Chapter in *Myth and the His-*

tory of the Hispanic Southwest (Albuquerque: University of New Mexico Press, 1988), 55–88, passim.

24. Ibid.

25. Herbert Bolton, *The Spanish Borderlands: A Chronicle of Old Florida and the Southwest* (New Haven, Conn.: Yale University Press, 1921), vii.

26. Weber, "John Francis Bannon," 65.

27. Ibid., 60. See Juan Flores and George Yúdice, "Living Borders/Buscando América: Languages of Latino Self-Formation," *Social Text* 8, no. 2 (1990): 57–84; and D. Emily Hicks, *Border Writing: The Multidimensional Text* (Minneapolis: University of Minnesota Press, 1991), for their theorization of the borderlands.

28. Weber, "John Francis Bannon," passim.

29. See Patricia Nelson Limerick, *The Legacy of Conquest: The Unbroken Past of the American West* (New York: Norton, 1987).

30. Weber, "John Francis Bannon," 61.

31. Ibid.

32. Ibid., 66, quoting John Francis Bannon, *Spanish Borderlands Frontier, 1513–1821* (New York: Holt, Rinehart and Winston, 1970), 3.

33. See Américo Paredes, *Folklore and Culture on the Texas-Mexican Border,* ed. Richard Bauman (Austin: Center for Mexican American Studies, University of Texas at Austin, 1993), xi.

34. Haas, *Conquests and Historical Identities in California,* 11.

35. Paredes, *Folklore and Culture,* 6.

36. Quoted in Weber, "John Francis Bannon," 66.

37. See Nicolás Kanellos, *A History of Hispanic Theater in the United States: Origins to 1940* (Austin: University of Texas Press, 1990). Kanellos writes: "Although they did not make it to Hawaii, Mrs. Fabregas's tours extended to the outer reaches of the Spanish-speaking world, including the Philippines and Guam" (19). Also, "[b]y the turn of the century, professional companies were actively touring the Southwest and to Tampa, a little later to New York, with various companies and individual artists putting down roots and becoming residents. But the touring tradition continued to thrive into the beginnings of the Depression, with the railroads facilitating the linkages between Mexico City, San Antonio, and Los Angeles, the steamships carrying troupes back and forth between Cuba, Key West, Tampa and New York" (198).

38. I would like to thank Vicki Ruiz for telling me about the Mexican Players and Matt García for guiding me through their archive in the Pomona Public Library.

39. Weber, "The Idea of the Spanish Borderlands," 8.

40. Ibid.

41. See Matt García, "'Just Put on That Padua Hills Smile': The Mexican

Players and the Padua Hills Theatre, 1931–1974," *California History* 74 (fall 1995): 254–359, for a history of the Mexican Players. For an expanded analysis of the Padua Hills Theater in the context of California history, see Matt García, *A World of Its Own: Race, Labor, and Citrus in the Making of Greater Los Angeles, 1900–1970* (Chapel Hill: University of North Carolina Press, 2002).

42. See chapter 1 of David Gutiérrez, *Walls and Mirrors: Mexican Americans, Mexican Immigrants, and the Politics of Ethnicity* (Berkeley: University of California Press, 1995) for a discussion of how elite Mexicans participated in recasting their past as a Spanish one.

43. McWilliams, *North from Mexico,* 36.

44. By understanding that the Mexican Players' audience was Anglo, we can theorize about the construction of whiteness and Mexicanness in that context, as contrast to when the audience is Latino and there is a horizontal relationship built, as in the work of teatro and contemporary performance artists.

45. Francisco Balderrama and Raymond Rodríguez, *Decade of Betrayal: Mexican Repatriation in the 1930s* (Albuquerque: University of New Mexico Press, 1995), presents a thorough discussion of the repatriation.

46. See Pauline Deuel, *Mexican Serenade: The Story of the Mexican Players and the Padua Hills Theatre* (Claremont, Calif.: Padua Institute, 1961). Deuel gives a description that shows us what the cultural-political atmosphere of the theater was like: "At Padua Hills they were all comedies, for that is in keeping with the happy spirit of the theater and dining room. Even the productions with a serious note have much comedy relief and the songs and dances are bright and cheerful. This relaxed atmosphere helps the play-goer to live with the action, to identify himself with the pleasant people on the stage and to know that they are his friends. It generates a feeling of good-will toward them that often inspires a broader understanding of Mexico and the Mexican public. Whatever success these plays have had in promoting better relations between our country and its southern neighbor is sufficient reward for the effort, because the PI is sincerely dedicated to the mutual acquaintance of these two nations and their international friendship" (54).

47. García, "'Just Put on That Padua Hills Smile,'" 256–258.

48. Garcia, "'Just Put on That Padua Hills Smile,'" 245–261; see also Alicia Arrizón, "Contemporizing Performance: Mexican California and the Padua Hills Theatre," *Mester* 22, no. 2–23.1 (fall 1993–spring 1994): 6.

49. García, "'Just Put on That Padua Hills Smile,'" 246.

50. The success of real estate promoters' use of the Spanish Fantasy Heritage as a marketing tool is evident in the large number of Mission Revival–style homes being built to this day in California. Carey McWilliams and Mike Davis note that this was not a unique thing to do at the time, since those discourses had been used to attract both tourists and homebuyers since the turn of the century. And it was popular in theaters and movies in Los Angeles. It became such a suc-

cess as an escape that it was a successful marketing tool. The architecture remains popular.

51. See Gutiérrez-Jones, *Rethinking the Borderlands,* for an insightful analysis of how Helen Hunt Jackson's perennially popular novel *Ramona* (1884), as well as film and theatrical performances, shape contemporary notions of *mestizo* stereotypes.

52. Arrizón, "Contemporizing Performance," 7.

53. García, "'Just Put on That Padua Hills Smile,'" 249.

54. Ibid., 248.

55. Ibid., 249.

56. Ibid., 250.

57. See Balderrama and Rodríguez, *Decade of Betrayal,* and George J. Sánchez, *Becoming Mexican American: Ethnicity, Culture, and Identity in Chicano Los Angeles, 1900–1945* (New York: Oxford University Press, 1993), chapter 10.

58. Deuel, *Mexican Serenade: The Story of the Mexican Players and the Padua Hills Theatre,* 2.

59. Julianne Burton, "Don (Juanito) Duck and the Imperial-Patriarchal Unconscious: Disney Studios, the Good Neighbor Policy, and the Packaging of Latin America," in *Nationalisms and Sexualities,* ed. Andrew Parker, Mary Russo, Doris Sommer, and Patricia Yeager (New York: Routledge, 1992), 25. For an insightful analysis of the Good Neighbor policy in relation to Latino performance, see Alberto Sandoval Sánchez's *José, Can You See? Latinos On and Off Broadway* (Madison: University of Wisconsin Press, 1999).

60. Allen Woll, *The Latin Image in American Film,* rev. ed. (Los Angeles: UCLA Latin American Center Publications, 1980), 55.

61. Nicolás Kanellos, *The Hispanic Almanac: From Columbus to Corporate America* (Detroit: Visible Ink Press, 1994), 504.

62. Kanellos, *The Hispanic Almanac,* 503.

63. García, "'Just Put on That Padua Hills Smile,'" passim.

64. Ibid., 256.

65. Ibid.

66. See Gutiérrez-Jones, *Rethinking the Borderlands,* 56–69; he calls this the process of "mission denial."

67. García, "'Just Put on That Padua Hills Smile,'" 251.

68. Ibid., 252.

69. See note 26 in García, "Just Put on That Padua Hills Smile,'" 358.

70. Ibid., 259.

71. See Yolanda Broyles-González, *El Teatro Campesino: Theater in the Chicano Movement* (Austin: University of Texas Press, 1994), 74.

72. Broyles-González, *El Teatro Campesino,* 54.

73. According to Weber, "the romanticized version of the Hispanic past"

provided the fabric from which Anglo immigrants new to California could tap into a sense of belonging because, "it permitted rootless English-speaking immigrants to identify with the region's early European settlers." Weber, "The Idea of the Spanish Borderlands," 6. Linked to regional boosterism, the success of the group is no surprise.

74. Arrizón's article "Contemporizing Performance" asserts that the representation of Mexican culture approved by the Garners reified gender and ethnic identities.

75. Limerick, *The Legacy of Conquest*, introduction.

76. Ibid., 19.

77. Héctor Calderón and José D. Saldívar, *Criticism in the Borderlands: Studies in Chicano Literature, Culture, and Ideology* (Durham: Duke University Press, 1991), 4.

78. Limerick, *The Legacy of Conquest*, 19.

79. Haas, *Conquests and Historical Identities in California*, 148. Also see Kanellos, *A History of Hispanic Theater in the United States*, 17–21.

80. Kanellos, *A History of Hispanic Theater in the United States*, 11.

81. Ibid., xv.

82. Haas, *Conquests and Historical Identities in California*, 138.

83. Paul Gilroy, *"There Ain't No Black in the Union Jack"*: The Cultural Politics of Race and Nation (Chicago: University of Chicago Press, 1987), 157.

84. Haas, *Conquests and Historical Identities in California*, 147–148.

85. Ibid., 158–159.

86. See Tomás Ybarra-Frausto for an excellent discussion of Rasquachi aesthetics: Tomás Ybarra-Frausto, "Rasquachismo: A Chicano Sensibility," in *Chicano Art: Resistance and Affirmation, 1965–1985*, ed. Teresa McKenna, Richard Griswold del Castillo, and Yvonne Yarbro-Bejarano (Los Angeles: Wight Gallery, University of California, Los Angeles, 1992), 155–162. The performance group Culture Clash, founded in the 1980s, follows in the wake of and revises carpa entertainment dating back to the early part of the twentieth century.

87. Broyles-González, *El Teatro Campesino*, 7. See also Luis Valdez and El Teatro Campesino, *Luis Valdez—Early Works: Actos, Bernabé and Pensamiento Serpentino* (1971; reprint, Houston: Arte Publico Press, 1990).

88. See Lisa Lowe, *Immigrant Acts: On Asian American Cultural Politics* (Durham: Duke University Press, 1996).

89. See Frantz Fanon, *The Wretched of the Earth* (1961; reprint, New York: Grove Press, 1968).

90. See Rosa Linda Fregoso, *The Bronze Screen: Chicana and Chicano Film Culture* (Minneapolis: University of Minnesota Press, 1993).

91. See Angie Chabram-Dernersesian, "I Throw Punches for My Race, But I Don't Want to Be a Man: Writing Us—Chica-nos (Girl, Us)/Chicanas—into the

Movement Script," in *Cultural Studies,* ed. Lawrence Grossberg, Cary Nelson, and Paula Treichler (New York: Routledge, 1992), 81–95.

92. Jorge Huerta, *Chicano Theater: Themes and Forms* (Ypsilanti, Mich.: Bilingual Press/Editorial Bilingüe, 1982).

93. Diane Rodríguez, personal interview, August 15, 1996.

NOTES TO CHAPTER 2

An earlier version of this chapter was published in *Women Transforming Politics,* edited by Kathy Jones, Cathy Cohen, and Joan Tronto. New York: NYU Press, 1997. Reprinted by permission.

1. Marisela Norte, "Dance in the Shadows," *NORTE/word,* Lawndale, Calif.: New Alliance Record Company 062/Cro2, 1991, compact disk.

2. See Norte's image in "The Muse on the Bus," *Buzz Magazine* (October 1995): 85. See also Cynthia Rose, "Word UP," *Face Magazine,* no. 51 (December 1992): 23.

3. Norte, "976-LOCA," in *Recent Chicano Poetry/Neueste Chicano-Lyrick,* ed. Heiner Bus and Ana Castillo (Bamberg, Germany: Universitätsbibliothek Bamberg, 1994), 106–127.

4. For the development of an official folkloric imagery invented for Los Angeles's Olvera Street, see Raúl Homero Villa, *Barrio-Logos: Space and Place in Urban Chicano Literature and Culture* (Austin: University of Texas Press, 2000), 59–61.

5. Marisela Norte, public lecture, Arte y Cultura Lecture Series and Exhibit, Carnegie Art Museum, Oxnard, California, October 17, 2003.

6. For more on the influence of María Félix in Mexican film, see Susan Dever, *Celluloid Nationalism and Other Melodramas: From Post-Revolutionary Mexico to Fin de Siglo Mexamerica* (Albany: State University of New York Press, 2003).

7. Marisela Norte, "Club Sufrimiento 2000," in *NORTE/word.*

8. Seshu Foster, "The Spine of Califas," Latino L.A. web magazine, www.latinola.com/story.phy?story=845, accessed March 20, 2003.

9. David E. James, "Poetry/Punk/Production: Some Recent Writing in LA," in *Postmodernism and Its Discontents: Theories, Practices,* ed. E. Ann Kaplan (London: Verso, 1988), 171.

10. Ibid.

11. "Originally set up by Mike Watt (of the Minutemen and Firehouse . . .) it was subsequently acquired by SST, the label founded by members of the seminal punk band Black Flag." From C. Parker, "Spoken Word: Hollywood Babylon," *Wire* Magazine 121 (March 1994): 24.

12. See review of "State of Language" by the Hammerman, in *Shattersheet,*

no. 17 (February 1987): 9. The event was sponsored by the Social and Public Art Resource Center (SPARC).

13. Marisela Norte, "En Sueños," *La Línea Quebrada/The Broken Line* 2, no. 2 (March 1987): n.p.

14. Program notes, "The Eastside Revue: A Musical Homage to Boyle Heights," October 12, 2002. The event was held in conjunction with the exhibition "Boyle Heights: The Power of Place," Japanese American National Museum, Los Angeles, California, October 12–February 23, 2003.

15. A City of Los Angeles Cultural Affairs Department press release for the Gamboa 84 exhibition, which opened, on April 15, 1984, at the Los Angeles Photography Center, documents that Marisela Norte would perform her play *Exito* and that The Brat and The Odd Squad would be musical performers for the night. Other performances included Harry Gamboa's *Shadow Solo,* performed by Sean Carrillo and Humberto Sandoval. *Pseudoturquoiser* was performed by Gronk. Diane Gamboa provided *Cold Blooded* paper fashions. Press release from the Tomás Ybarra-Frausto Research Material, 1965–1997, collection at the Archives of American Art, Smithsonian Institution. On November 2, 1984, Norte performed "Sleepwalk" at the Día de los Muertos celebration at Club Lingerie, a Hollywood nightclub. Musical performers included Lil' Ruben G. and Thee Latin Soul Revue, Con Safos, Las Angelinas, Wildcards, and others. In 1982, an ASCO event included a performance of the play *La Condición Feminina,* written by Marisela Norte and María Elena Gaitán. Teresa Covarrubias, Sean Carillo, and others performed in Harry Gamboa's fotonovela *Random Rumor.* See flyer for ASCO, Tomás Ybarra-Frausto Research Material, 1965–1997, collection at the Archives of American Art, Smithsonian Institution.

16. Norte, public introduction to The Brat, "The Eastside Revue: A Musical Homage to Boyle Heights," October 12, 2002.

17. For an excellent discussion of how Chicana artists made do with limited resources, see Laura Pérez, "Spirit Glyphs: Reimagining Art and Artist in the Work of Chicana Tlamatinime," *Modern Fiction Studies* 44, no. 1 (1998): 36–76.

18. Sean Carrillo, public lecture, Chicana/o Punk Aesthetics colloquium, University of California at Santa Barbara, May 5, 2003.

19. In the spirit of making do and inventing culture with minimal resources, Sean Carrillo, self-appointed minister of East Los Angeles culture, appointed Marisela Norte to be the East L.A. ambassador of culture in 1983. Carrillo had made a rubber stamp that said "East L.A. Ministry of Culture." Once appointed, Norte began sending mail art and resumes with the stamp. Marisela Norte, transcript, public lecture, Carnegie Museum of Art, October 2003, and Sean Carrillo, e-mail correspondence with author, November 9, 2003.

20. Norte, "976-LOCA," in *Recent Chicano Poetry/Neueste Chicano-Lyrick,* 106–127.

21. D. Emily Hicks, *Border Writing: The Multidimensional Text* (Minneapolis: University of Minnesota Press, 1991), 112.

22. Victor Valle, e-mail correspondence with author, February 2002.

23. See Raúl Homero Villa, *Barrio-Logos: Space and Place in Urban Chicano Literature and Culture* (Austin: University of Texas Press, 2000), 110, 113.

24. Cultural politics in and of themselves are not necessarily progressive. A clear example of a conservative engagement of cultural politics is former California governor Pete Wilson's Proposition 187 anti-immigrant campaign. The campaign's infamous television advertisements dehumanized people I recognize as "undocumented workers" and constructed them as "illegal aliens," thus framing border-crossing job seekers in a way that erases the vital role they play in California economy. Instead of featuring the undocumented workers picking crops in our agricultural fields, keeping houses, caring for children not their own, sewing in unsafe shops, or washing dishes in the back of restaurants—typical employment sites where they commonly work for below standard wages—the ads showed helicopter footage of these workers running for their lives across an interstate freeway located near the border checkpoint. Designed to play on the economic insecurities of "legal citizens," the image suggests that California's economic crisis is caused by assumed "parasitic aliens," omitting the fact that people do not take jobs but instead are given them. The ad also ignored the larger reasons for the economic crisis, a major one being the defunding of federally supported defense contracts that once upheld California's economy.

25. Other writers, such as Gloria Anzaldúa, Ana Castillo, Gina Valdez, and Helena Maria Viramontes, to name a few, make similar moves in their writing.

26. Norte, "En Sueños" remix, public lecture, University of Washington, 2000.

27. Cynthia Rose, "Word UP!" *Face* 51 (December 1991): 23.

28. Ibid.

29. Writers in Focus, *The Road to Aztlán: Art from a Mythic Homeland*, program notes, Los Angeles County Museum of Art, June 22, 2001.

30. Marisela Norte, "Dance in the Shadows," *NORTE/word.*

31. Ironically, it was on one of those trips that she first encountered the East L.A resident Harry Gamboa's photography. See Norte's interview of Gamboa in "Harry Gamboa Jr.: No-Movie Maker," *Revista El Tecolote Literaria/El Tecolote Literary Magazine* (July 1983): 3, 12. In the interview, Norte also describes how she knew Patssi Valdez as a child in East L.A.

32. See Christopher Buckley and Gary Young, eds., *The Geography of Home: California's Poetry of Place* (Berkeley, Calif.: Heyday Books, 1999), 266, for Norte's bio.

33. Metropolitan Transit Authority (MTA) Art website, 1997. http://mta.net/other_info/metroart/temp/ma_pep1.htm, accessed March 1, 2002.

34. Author bio in *Southern California Women Writers and Artists,* Raras Aves series (Los Angeles: Books of a Feather, 1984), 162.

35. Norte, public lecture, Arte y Cultura Lecture Series and Exhibit, Carnegie Art Museum, Oxnard, California, October 17, 2002.

36. Ibid.

37. Norte, "Harry Gamboa Jr.: No-Movie Maker," 12.

38. Liner notes, *NORTE/word.* Another important influence on Norte's creative impulses are the published diaries of Anaïs Nin. Though Norte had kept diaries since she was a preteen, it never occurred to her that that form of writing would be of interest to the general public until she devoured Nin's. Over the years, the writing of José Montoya, Willa Cather, Truman Capote, Tennessee Williams, Dorothy Allison, and Ana Castillo inspired her to continue writing. However, the strongest forces shaping her work so far are "living in L.A. as a single woman and having made choices along the way that she never thought she could [make]" (personal interview with author, July 1995).

39. Liner notes, *NORTE/word.*

40. Marisela Norte, personal interview with author, July 1995.

41. Victor Valle, e-mail correspondence with author, February 12, 2003.

42. See Ondine Chavoya's articles for more on ASCO: "Internal Exiles: The Interventionist Public and Performance Art of Asco," in *Space, Site, and Intervention: Situating Installation Art,* ed. Erika Suderburg (Minnesota: University of Minnesota Press, 2000), 189–208; "Orphans of Modernism: The Performance Art of Asco," in *Corpus Delecti: Performance Art of the Americas,* ed. Coco Fusco (New York: Routledge, 2000), 240–263; and "Pseudographic Cinema: Asco's No-Movies," *Performance Research,* special issue, "On America," ed. Nick Kaye, 3, no. 1 (1998): 1–14.

43. Juan Garza, personal correspondence with author, September 1995.

44. Linda Burnham, "Marisela Norte," *High Performance* 35 (1986): 66. Norte toured *La Condición Feminina* and *Exito* during the early 1980s. According to ASCO program flyers, Norte performed *La Condición Feminina* with Maria Elena Gaitan as part of a fundraiser for the Main St. Gallery and Theater on November 14, 1982. The program was directed by Patssi Valdez and Victor Herrera Lutz. Norte and Gaitan also performed the play at the Hispanic Urban Center as part of an ASCO group show on October 1, 1982. The performance was dedicated to the victims of the Beirut massacre. Norte performed *Exito* as part of an ASCO group show at the Galería de la Raza in San Francisco in July 1983. "Se Habla Inglés" was also performed as part of an ASCO group show at Otis/Parsons gallery in Los Angeles on April 22, 1983. All flyers held in the Tomás Ybarra-Frausto Research Material, 1965–1997, collection, Archives of American Art, Smithsonian Institution.

45. Marisela Norte, personal interview with author, July 1995.

46. Marisela Norte, "Peeping Tom Tom Girl," *El Tecolote Literario* (July 1983): 9.

47. George Lipsitz, "We Know What Time It Is: Race, Class, and Youth Culture in the Nineties," in *Microphone Fiends: Youth Music and Youth Culture,* ed. Andrew Ross and Tricia Rose (New York: Routledge, 1994), 17–28.

48. *NORTE/word* (Los Angeles: New Alliance Record Company 062/Cr02, 1991). Frustrated by the lack of respect for women writers who did not fit stereotypes in both the Chicano/Latino and the Anglo artistic communities, Norte took a self-imposed exile from public readings in 1989. Despite her absence from the reading scene, her grass-roots following thrived. While she was working as an administrative assistant at the Los Angeles Medical Association, in 1991, Harvey Kubernik, well known in Los Angeles for producing spoken-word recordings, asked her to contribute to a compact disk compilation emphasizing material from African American and Chicano/Latino writers from L.A. The disk is titled *The Black and Tan Club*. Despite the hybrid nature of her narratives, which merge prose, poetry, lyrical, and rap forms, along with her tendency to experiment with them in live performances, Norte discovered, while recording material for Kubernik's compilation, that the audio recording was an ideal medium for her writing. Later that same year, New Alliance Records released *NORTE/word*, Norte's first compact disk collection of spoken-word narratives. However, the narratives are particularly engrossing in the written form.

49. For an invaluable discussion concerning the formation of "new subjects for political identification," see Angie Chabram-Dernersesian, "I Throw Punches for My Race But I Don't Want to Be a Man: Writing Us—Chica-nos (Girl, Us)/Chica*nas*—into the Movement Script," in *Cultural Studies,* ed. Lawrence Grossberg, Cary Nelson, and Paula Treichler (New York: Routledge, 1992), 81–95.

50. Quotation by Harvey Kubernik in C. Parker, "Spoken Word: Hollywood Babylon," *Wire* 121 (March 1994): 23.

51. Thomas Swiss, "Essay Reviews: Sweet Nothings: An Anthology of Rock and Roll in American Poetry and Aloud: Voices from the Nuyorican Poets Café," *Popular Music* 15, no. 2 (May 1996): 233–240.

52. Ibid., 235.

53. C. Parker, "Spoken Word," 26.

54. In fact, Norte joined the Bus Riders Union of Los Angeles to help reform the city's remiss bus service.

55. Harry Gamboa, Jr., "Marisela Norte," *La Opinion* (*La Comunidad* section, 17 October 1982), 11.

56. Marisela Norte, interview with ASCO for Chicano Art and Culture in California Conference (CALIFAS), University of California, Santa Cruz, April 16–18, 1982; transcript available in the Harry Gamboa, Jr., Papers, 1968–1995,

Department of Special Collections and University Archives, Stanford University Library.

57. Norte, UCSC interview 1984.

58. M. H. Abrams, *A Glossary of Literary Terms,* 5th ed. (San Diego: Harcourt Brace Jovanovich, 1988), 91.

59. Marisela Norte, quoted in Don Snowden, "A New Spin on Words and Music," *Los Angeles Times,* December 3, 1991, F6.

60. Marisela Norte, "El Club Sufrimiento 2000," in *NORTE/word.*

61. For examples of the way the dominant culture has represented Chicanos, see A. G. Pettit, *Images of the Mexican American in Fiction and Film* (College Station: Texas A and M University Press, 1980).

62. My use of the term "Latina" refers to Mexicana, Central American, South American, and Puerto Rican women, all of whom can be found, in varying degrees, working in Los Angeles's industrial sections. Because it is not my intention to flatten and uncomplicate Latina identity, I use the terms "Chicana" and "Mexicana" when describing geopolitical particulars.

63. Douglas Monroy, *Thrown among Strangers: The Making of Mexican Culture in Frontier California* (Berkeley: University of California Press, 1990).

64. Marisela Norte, "Peeping Tom Tom Girl," in *NORTE/word.*

65. See Rosaura Sanchez, "The History of Chicanas: Proposal for a Materialist Perspective," in *Between Borders: Essays on Mexicana/Chicana History,* ed. Adelaida R. Del Castillo (Encino, Calif.: Floricanto Press, 1990). Sanchez explains that Chicana history "need not postulate direct links between us and La Malinche" (13). In discussing this cultural paradigm, my intent is not to reproduce the notion that a "direct link" exists but, instead, to begin to show that the paradigm is both constructed and contested. In her excellent article "The Female Subject in Chicano Theater: Sexuality, 'Race,' and Class" (*Theater Journal* 38, no. 4 [1986]), Yvonne Yarbro-Bejarano demonstrates how the images of *La Virgen* and *La Malinche* have been both constructed and challenged in Chicano cultural production.

66. Norma Alarcón, "In the Tracks of the Native Woman," *Cultural Studies* 4, no. 6 (1990).

67. Tomás Almaguer, "The Cartography of Homosexual Desire and Identity among Chicano Men," *Differences* 3, no. 2 (summer 1992): 82.

68. Yarbro-Bejarano, "The Female Subject in Chicano Theater."

69. For a cultural genealogy of *La Malinche* discourse see Jean Franco, "La Malinche: From Gift to Sexual Contract," chapter in *Critical Passions: Selected Essays,* ed. and with an introduction by Mary Louise Pratt and Kathleen Newman (Durham: Duke University Press, 1999), 66–82.

70. *NORTE/word.*

71. For examples see Rudolfo Anaya's *Bless Me, Ultima* (Berkeley: Tonatiuh-

Quinto Sol International, 1990), or Edward Rivera's *Family Installments* (New York: Morrow Press, 1982).

72. Marisela Norte, "Shelf Life," *Caffeine* 1, no. 2 (April 1993): 23–26.

73. In some nineteenth-century literature written by European women such as George Sand and Madame de Stael, the idea of the home is constructed as a place of refuge and retreat. Constructed in a positive light, the idea that the home was a place of refuge from the harsh reality of the public realm helped support the power structure of the middle-class family. Norte writes about family life in a different historical, social, and geographical context and constructs the home as a space of negative withdrawal and suppression.

74. Norte, "Shelf Life." That this Latina body temporarily escapes to Chinatown points to the interaction between diverse ethnic communities residing in Los Angeles.

75. I transcribed this from a recording of a live performance at the Centro Cultural, Balboa Park, San Diego, California, May 1992. In print it looks as if Norte is contradicting herself when she states that "she never dared sneak out of" her bedroom but then states that she managed to slither out of her bedroom into bar rooms. However, on the CD, the tone of her voice indicates that she is being ironic when she states that "she never dared sneak out." Being misunderstood is the chance she takes for being ironic.

76. Michel Foucault, "Of Other Places," *Diacritics* (spring 1986): 24.

77. Edward Soja, *Postmodern Geographies* (New York: Verso, 1989), 14.

78. Ibid.

79. I am tempted to replace the term "character" with that of "narratrix" because of the term's implications. Norte conflates the term "narrator" with "dominatrix" to create a new term that suggests that the characters who voice her narratives are in a position of power. "Narratrix" implies an engagement in the struggle for the domination over words. These narratreces, who have thus far been misrepresented through language, are fighting to represent themselves in the realm of language.

80. Marisela Norte, "Se habla inglés," first published in *Raras Aves: Southern California Women Writers* 6, no. 7 (1983): 92, and later recorded on *NORTE/word*.

81. Norte, "Se habla inglés."

82. Ibid., 89–90.

83. Ibid., 92.

84. Ibid., 93.

85. Jennifer González and Michelle Habell-Pallán, "Heterotopias: Navigating Social Spaces and Spaces of Identity," *Inscriptions: Enunciating Our Terms* 7 (1994): 80–104. For more on the effects of the border see Alicia Schmidt Camacho, "The Violence of Citizenship: Border Crossing and Cultural Conflict in

Marisela Norte's El Paso," in *Steel and Glass: Latin American Women Write the City,* ed. Anne Lambright and Elisabeth Guerrero (forthcoming 2004); and Démian Pritchard, "Policing the Border: Politics and Place in the Work of Miguel Méndez, Marisela Norte, and Leslie Marmon Silko" (Ph.D. diss., University of California, San Diego, 2003).

86. Marisela Norte, "Act of the Faithless," in *NORTE/word.*

87. González and Habell-Pallán, "Heterotopias," 87.

88. Norte, "Act of the Faithless."

89. Ibid.

90. George Lipsitz, *Time Passages: Collective Memory and American Popular Culture* (Minneapolis: University of Minnesota Press, 1990), 265.

91. Marisela Norte, "Three Little Words," *Dis Closure* (Los Angeles: New Alliance Record Company, 1992).

92. Paula Rabinowitz, *Black and White and Noir: America's Pulp Modernism* (New York: Columbia University Press, 2002), 64.

93. For an excellent analysis of the working conditions of Chicana domestic workers, see Mary Romero, "Nanny Diaries and Other Stories: Imagining Women's Labor in the Social Reproduction of American Families," *DePaul Law Review* 52, no. 3 (2003): 809–847; and Mary Romero, *Maid in the U.S.A.* (New York: Routledge, 2002).

94. *ASCO Means Nausea in Spanish: A 13-Minute Documentary,* dir. Juan Garza, 1995.

95. Rabinowitz, *Black and White and Noir,* 62–63.

96. Ibid., 64.

97. Ibid.

98. Ibid.

99. Christine Gledhill, "Klute 1: A Contemporary Film Noir and Feminist Criticism," in *Women in Film Noir,* ed. E. Ann Kaplan (London: BFI, 1994), 16.

100. Ibid., 17.

101. Marisela Norte, *Exito,* in *Spectacle: A Field Journal from Los Angeles,* no. 1 (1984): 18–21. *Spectacle* is one of the numerous self-published 'zines of the 1980s.

102. George Lipsitz, *American Studies in a Moment of Crisis* (Minneapolis: University of Minnesota Press, 2001).

103. The *tandas de variedad* were the Mexican equivalent of American vaudeville shows. Popular during the 1920s and 1930s, they entertained the U.S. Spanish-speaking population until Depression-era deportation and repatriation policies eroded their audience base.

104. "Untitled," performed at *Diva L.A.: A Salute to L.A.'s Latinas in the Tanda Style,* conceived and directed by Luis Alfaro and Diane Rodriguez, Mark Taper Forum, Los Angeles, California, July 2, 1995.

105. Stuart Hall, "New Ethnicities," *ICA Documents* 7 (1989): 27–31.

NOTES TO CHAPTER 3

An earlier version of this chapter was published in *Ollantáy Theater Magazine* 4, no. 1 (January 1996). Reprinted by permission.

1. On the advice of George Mariscal, I attended Alfaro's show with the intention of inviting him to perform at UC San Diego. Alfaro introduced me to Marisela Norte, who had happened to attend that performance, and I decided to invite them both.

2. Luis Alfaro, personal correspondence with author, 1991.

3. Jan Breslauer, "Voice for a Silent Minority: Performance Artist Luis Alfaro Finds Stage Doors Opening for His Provocative Works Meshing Latino and Gay Experiences," *Los Angeles Times,* July 21, 1991, calendar section, 47.

4. Personal correspondence with author, 1991.

5. Breslauer, "Voice for a Silent Minority," 54.

6. For an in-depth discussion of both how the Chicano movement addressed these issues and how Chicanos were not a monolithic entity, see David G. Gutiérrez, "*Sin Fronteras?*: Chicanos, Mexican Americans, and the Emergence of the Contemporary Mexican Immigration Debate, 1968–1978," *Journal of American Ethnic History* 10, no. 4 (1991): 5–37.

7. For a useful discussion of Chicano theater and cultural nationalism, see Yvonne Yarbro-Bejarano, "The Female Subject in Chicano Theater: Sexuality, 'Race,' and Class," *Theater Journal* 38, no. 4 (1986): 389.

8. Ibid.

9. Ibid.

10. Ibid., 390.

11. See David Román, "Teatro Viva!: Latino Performance and the Politics of AIDS in Los Angeles," in *¿Entiendes? Queer Readings, Hispanic Writings,* ed. Emilie L. Bergmann and Paul Julian Smith (Durham: Duke University Press, 1995), 346–369.

12. Roman, "Teatro Viva!" 349.

13. See Kate Millet, *Sexual Politics* (1970; reprint New York: Simon and Schuster, 1990); bell hooks, *Talking Back: Thinking Feminist, Thinking Black* (Boston: South End Press, 1989); Donna Haraway, *Simians, Cyborgs, and Women* (London: Free Association Books, 1991); and Lisa Lowe, *Immigrant Acts: On Asian American Cultural Politics* (Durham: Duke University Press, 1996), 60–83. My understanding of Millet's theory of sexual politics is supplemented by hooks's, Haraway's, and Lowe's discussions of how race and class complicate sexual politics. For Millet, the term "politics" refers to "power-structured relationships, arrangements whereby one group of people is controlled by another" (10). Alfaro's work demonstrates that there are multiple power relationships that a subject must negotiate.

14. For a discussion of contemporary Chicana articulations of sexual poli-

tics, see Ramón A. Gutiérrez, "Community, Patriarchy and Individualism: The Politics of Chicano History and the Dream of Equality," *American Quarterly* 45, no. 1 (1993): 44–72.

15. Yarbro-Bejarano, "The Female Subject," 391.

16. Román, "Teatro Viva!" 349.

17. See Jorge Huerta, *Chicano Theater: Themes and Forms* (Ypsilanti, Mich.: Bilingual Press/Editorial Bilingüe, 1982), and his *Chicano Drama: Performance, Society, and Myth* (New York: Cambridge University Press, 2000).

18. Huerta, *Chicano Theater,* 3.

19. Román, "Teatro Viva!" For an in-depth discussion of Latino theater in the United States, see Nicolás Kanellos, *A History of Hispanic Theater in the United States: Origins to 1940* (Austin: University of Texas Press, 1990). The Chicano oppositional theater movement itself must be understood in relation to other U.S. and European political theater movements; see Bruce A. McConachie and David Friedman, eds., *Theater for Working-Class Audiences in the United States, 1830–1980* (Westport, Conn.: Greenwood Press, 1985). They have edited a collection of essays about the history of U.S. working-class theater, a theater, like the Latino theater, that is often ignored by theater historians. Also see Eugene Van Erven, *Radical People's Theater* (Bloomington: Indiana University Press, 1988). Van Erven situates radical people's theater in an international context. He begins his analysis in 1968 by examining the worldwide student movements that inspired many theater projects.

20. See Elizabeth Martínez, "A Call for *Chicanisma," CrossRoads* 29 (March 1993): 6. Martínez observes that gay and lesbian issues are still not fully accepted. She acknowledges that while "a few Chicana feminists raised their voices in the late 1960s and early 1970s, an almost total silence hung over gay and lesbian advocates. No openly gay person could be a movement leader. Today homophobia persists, and most progressive straight Chicanos as well as Chicanas still fail to perceive gay and lesbian rights as the struggle of another oppressed social sector, or homophobia as a sometimes murderous force of discrimination" (7).

21. Yarbro-Bejarano, "The Female Subject," 396.

22. Ibid.

23. Ibid., 397.

24. Ibid., 401.

25. Tomás Almaguer, "Chicano Men: A Cartography of Homosexual Identity and Behavior," *differences* 3, no. 2 (1991): 76.

26. Yvonne Yarbro-Bejarano, *The Wounded Heart: Writing on Cherríe Moraga* (Austin: University of Texas Press, 2001), 49. A new body of scholarship on the subject is also being produced by Chicano scholars. See Sergio de la Mora, "Fascinating Machismo: Toward an Unmasking of Heterosexual Masculinity in Arturo Ripstein's *El Lugar Sin Límites," Journal of Film and Video* 44, no. 3

(fall–winter 1992–1993): 83–104, as well as de la Mora's *Virile Nationalism: Masculinity and Sexuality in Mexican Cinema.* (Austin: University of Texas Press, forthcoming 2005). Also see Lionel Cantú, "De Ambiente: Queer Tourism and the Shifting Boundaries of Mexican Male Sexualities," *GLQ: A Journal of Lesbian and Gay Studies* 8.1–2 (2002): 139–166; Cantú, "A Place to Call Home: A Queer Political Mexican Immigrant Men's Family Experiences," in *Queer Families, Queer Politics: Challenging Culture and the State,* ed. Mary Bernstein and Renate Reimann (New York: Columbia University Press, 2001); and Cantú, "Entre Hombres/Between Men: Latino Masculinities and Homosexualities," in *Gay Masculinities,* ed. Peter Nardi (Thousand Oaks, Calif.: Sage, 2000). See also David William Foster, ed., *Chicano/Latino Homoerotic Identities* (New York: Garland, 1999).

27. Román, "Teatro Viva!" 354. According to Sergio de la Mora, professor of Chicano Studies at University of California at Davis, who researches the film and literary representation of Chicano and Mexicano gay sexuality, Teddy Matthews established reading groups for gay Latino men in 1989 at Modern Times Bookstore in San Francisco. Matthews died from an AIDS-related illness.

28. Luis Alfaro, "Pico-Union," in *Men on Men 4,* ed. George Stambolian (New York: Plume, 1992), and Alfaro, "Deseo es Memoria," in *Latino Heretics,* ed. Tony Diaz (Normal, Ill.: Fiction Collective Two, 1999): 100–103.

29. Almaguer, "Chicano Men," 76.

30. Luis Alfaro, *Downtown,* New Alliance Records, 1993, compact disk. See Román, "Teatro Viva!" for an in-depth discussion of how the privileging of a male heterosexual subject in Chicano *teatro* worked hand-in-hand with cultural nationalism to exclude female and queer subjects.

31. See Angie Chabram-Dernersesian, "I Throw Punches for My Race, But I Don't Want to Be a Man: Writing Us—Chica-nos (Girl, Us)/Chicanas—into the Movement Script," in *Cultural Studies,* ed. Lawrence Grossberg, Cary Nelson, and Paula Treichler (New York: Routledge, 1992), 81–95, for an invaluable discussion of the production of Chicana counterdiscourse.

32. Luis Alfaro's recent CD, *Downtown,* and his written piece "Pico-Union" are based on his live performances.

33. Alfaro's work has also been performed throughout California in places as diverse as the Los Angeles Theater Center and the South Coast Repertory Theater, in Orange County, and at art galleries, bookstores, cafés, community cultural centers, and universities, as well as at the legendary Lollapalooza music festival. For an announcement of Alfaro's participation in the event, see *Teeth: The Official Magazine of Lollapalooza* (1994): 13, designed by and produced by the *Los Angeles Reader.*

34. The Latino gay and lesbian arts organization VIVA! was cofounded by Alfaro and a fellow performance artist, Monica Palacio, in 1988, to keep these is-

sues visible. Also see David Roman's *Acts of Intervention* (Bloomington: University of Indiana Press, 1998), for the ways queer activists make these issues visible.

35. Alfaro's *Downtown* was performed as "*Pico-Union*" and billed with Chloe Webb's *Walkin' the Walls* and Rocco Sisto's rendition of Dario Fo's *The Tale of The Tiger*. It was performed at the Los Angeles Theater Center from July 25 to September 8, 1991.

36. Note Alfaro's use of the more general figure of "The Virgin Mary" instead of the culture specific *La Virgen de Guadalupe*. It may be that Alfaro deliberately uses the Virgin Mary to connect with non-Chicano audiences, even though it is the image of *La Virgen* that graces the back cover of his CD. See Angie Chabram-Dernersesian's discussion of Yolanda López's important feminist re-presentation of the image of *La Virgen de Guadalupe* in her "I Throw Punches for My Race." See also Alma López's digital revision of *La Virgen* and the subsequent controversy at http://www.almalopez.net/.

37. Yarbro-Bejarano, *The Wounded Heart*, 67.

38. This gay Chicano narrator is part of the Chicano community, but at the same time his gay identification excludes him from it in much the same way that he, as a Chicano, is positioned both inside and outside the gay community.

39. Alfaro, "Virgin Mary," recorded on *Downtown*.

40. Paul Gilroy, "Diaspora Crossings: Intercultural and Transnational Identities in the Black Atlantic," in *Negotiating Identities: Essays on Immigration and Culture in Present-Day Europe,* ed. Aleksandra Ålund and Raoul Granqvist (Amsterdam: Rodopi, 1995), 105.

41. Alfaro, "Virgin Mary."

42. Ibid.

43. Ibid.

44. Ibid.

45. Ibid.

46. Ibid.

47. The presence of the Crips, an African American gang, in this neighborhood illustrates the tension between different ethnic groups in Los Angeles. The narrative tells of the common and turbulent ground they share, literally and figuratively.

48. Alfaro, "Virgin Mary."

49. See Yarbro-Bejarano, *Wounded Heart,* 61. See also Theresa Delgadillo's fascinating discussion of the empowering aspects of Chicana spirituality, in "Forms of Chicana Feminist Resistance: Hybrid Spirituality in Ana Castillo's *So Far from God,*" *Modern Fiction Studies* 44, no. 4 (winter 1998): 888.

50. Even the Angelino journalist and poet Rubén Martínez, albeit tongue-in-cheek, acknowledges the influence of the images broadcast in the 1970s television series *The Brady Bunch* in figuring late-twentieth-century Latino identity. See his

"East Side, West Side: Taking the Best from a Childhood of Spanish, Prayers, and Rock 'n' Roll," *Los Angeles Times Sunday Magazine,* May 3, 1992, 12.

51. Alfaro, "Virgin Mary."

52. Alfaro, "Chicana Liberation," recorded on *Downtown.*

53. For an in-depth discussion of what Chicana liberation entails, see Angie Chabram-Dernersesian, "I Throw Punches for My Race."

54. The Romanian playwright Radu Apostal translated *Drept ca o linie (Straight as a Line).* *Drept ca o linie* was performed at the "Ion Luca Caragiale" National Theatre Festival, winter 2002.

55. Guillermo Gómez-Peña, "1995—*Terreno peligroso*/Danger Zone: Cultural Relations between Chicanos and Mexicans at the End of the Century," in *Borderless Borders: U.S. Latinos, Latin Americans, and the Paradox of Interdependence,* ed. Frank Bonilla, Edwin Meléndez, Rebecca Morales, and María de los Angeles Torres (Philadelphia: Temple University Press, 1998), 134–135.

56. Reviews and analysis are available in both Spanish and English. In English, see Jan Breslauer, "U.S., Mexican Artists Draw Connections in 'Danger Zone,'" *Los Angeles Times,* February 8, 1995, sec. F, 1, 8; Shifra Goldman, "Performances in the Danger Zones I," *Art Nexus,* April–June 1996, 62–66; Shifra Goldman, "Performances in the Danger Zones II," *Art Nexus,* July–September 1996, 52–56; and David Ulin, "The Ballad of Luis Alfaro," *Los Angeles Times Magazine,* November 15, 1998, 14ff. In Spanish, see Jorge Cisneros Morales, "El Performance como Crónica Social," *El Nacional* (Mexico City), February 17, 1995, sec. Cultura, 32; Felipe Ehrenberg, "Territorios Harto Peligrosos," *La Opinión* (Los Angeles), February 3, 1995, sec. E, 9; Guillermo Gómez-Peña, "Terreno Peligroso," *Reforma* (Mexico City), February 18, 1995, sec. Gente!, 12ff.; Guillermo Gómez-Peña, "Terreno Peligroso (Las Relaciones entre Chicanos y Chilangos)," *La Opinión* (Los Angeles), February 3, 1995, sec. E, 7ff.; Elda Maceda, "Artistas Mexicanos y Chicanos Pisan 'Terreno Peligroso,'" *El Universal* (Mexico City), January 28, 1995, n.p.; Rubén Martínez, "El Evangelio Según San Lucas," *Reforma* (Mexico City), February 18, 1995, sec. Gente!, 12ff.; Rubén Martínez, "El Terreno Peligroso en Que Vivimos," *La Opinión* (Los Angeles), February 3, 1995, sec. E, 15; Josephine Ramírez, "Nuestros Performances Vivieron una Traducción Cultural," *El Universal* (Mexico City), February 23, 1995, sec. Cultural, 2; Lorena Ríos Alfaro, "Terreno Peligroso/Danger Zone, Arte Acción en el Foro X'Teresa," *Uno Más Uno* (Mexico City), February 23, 1995, sec. Ciencia, Cultura y Espectáculos, 20; Blanca Ruiz, "X Teresa, Un 'Terreno Peligroso,'" *Reforma* (Mexico City), December 27, 1994, sec. Cultura, 1; Blanca Ruiz, "Van a 'Terreno Peligroso,'" *Reforma* (Mexico City), January 28, 1995, sec. Cultura, 14; Lorena Woffler, "Atajos Para un Encuentro en Terreno Peligroso: ¡En Sus Marcas, Listos! . . . El Diálogo Comienza," *La Opinión* (Los Angeles), February 3, 1995, sec. E, 8, 13; and no author, "Terreno Peligroso, Per-

formance Sobre México y LA," *La Jornada* (Mexico City), February 23, 1995, sec. Cultura, 25.

57. Gómez-Peña, "1995—*Terreno peligroso*/Danger Zone," 136.

58. Ibid.

59. See Coco Fusco, *Corpus Delecti: Performance Art of the Americas,* ed. Coco Fusco (New York: Routledge, 2000).

60. Alfaro's homage to his favorite childhood "sport," *Ladybird: The Life and Times of a Roller Derby Queen,* toured San Diego, Imperial County, and Tijuana schools, community centers, and libraries from January 28, 2002, to March 8, 2002, under the auspices of the La Jolla Playhouse.

61. For a complimentary analysis of Alfaro's X-Teresa performance, see Antonio Prieto-Stambaugh, "Incorporated Identities: The Subversion of Stigma in the Performance Art of Luis Alfaro," in *Chicano/Latino Homoerotic Identities,* ed. David William Foster (New York: Garland, 1999): 147–157, and Prieto-Stambaugh, "La Actuación de la Identidad a Través del Performance Chicano Gay," *Debate Feminista* 7, no. 13 (1996): 285–315.

62. Interview with author, Los Angeles, August 7, 1996.

63. Personal interview with Alfaro, Los Angeles, August 1996.

64. Stuart Hall, "New Ethnicities," *ICA Documents* 7 (1989): 27–31.

65. Luis Alfaro and Diane Rodríguez, *Los Vecinos: A Play for Neighbors,* performed under the auspices of Cornerstone Theater's Community Collaborations (December 4–21, 1997).

66. Laurie Winer, "A Usually Reliable Company Disappoints Its 'Neighbors,'" *Los Angeles Times,* December 16, 1997, F1.

67. Yarbro-Bejarano, *The Wounded Heart,* 77.

NOTES TO CHAPTER 4

An earlier version of this chapter was published in *Latinas on Stage: Practice and Theory,* edited by Alicia Arrizón and Lillian Manzor (Berkeley: Third Woman Press, 2000). It is reprinted here by permission of Third Woman Press/Norma Alarcón.

El Vez's pun "I don't speak Spanish but I try my best eso si que es! (S.O.C.K.S.)" is long-standing joke in Spanish-speaking communities within the United States about how to teach Spanish phonetically to an English-language speaker using the sounds he or she is familiar with. The proper saying goes "eso si que si!" which means "this is how we do it," not "socks," which is *calcetines.* The pun is funny because El Vez repeats the Spanish saying incorrectly in order to make a play on words.

1. Culture Clash performed *Carpa Clash* in the spirit of the original *carpas.* *Carpas* (literally, tents) were used by Mexican troupes that toured Chicano communities in the Southwest in the 1920s and 1930s. The troupes were named for

the portable theaters in which they performed vaudeville productions, which included sketches about current topics, as well as songs and dances.

2. The following anthology includes an excerpt from Gomez's *A Line around the Block*: Kathy A. Perkins and Roberta Uno, eds., *Contemporary Plays by Women of Color: An Anthology* (New York: Routledge, 1996).

3. Monica Palacio has also developed an impressive body of work on her own. Please see the informative analysis in Alberto Sandoval Sanchez, *José, Can You See? Latinos On and Off Broadway* (Madison: University of Wisconsin Press, 1999); Alicia Arrizón, *Latina Performance: Traversing the Stage* (Bloomington: University of Indiana Press, 1999); and M. Teresa Marrero, "Out of the Fringe: Desire and Homosexuality in the 1990s Latino Theater," in *Velvet Barrios: Popular Culture and Chicana/o Sexualities,* ed. Alicia Gaspar de Alba, fwd. Tomás Ybarra-Frausto (New York: Palgrave, 2003).

4. Yvonne Yarbro-Bejarano, *The Wounded Heart: Writing on Cherríe Moraga* (Austin: University of Texas Press, 2001), 25.

5. Arrizón, *Latina Performance,* 141.

6. Carl Gutierrez-Jones, "Humor, Literacy and Trauma and Chicano Culture," *Comparative Literature Studies* 40, no. 2 (2003): 113.

7. Yarbro-Bejarano, *The Wounded Heart,* 28.

8. Ibid., 24.

9. Sandoval-Sanchez, *José, Can You See?* 122.

10. Judith Butler, "Imitation and Gender Insubordination," in *Inside/Out: Lesbian Theories, Gay Theories,* ed. Diana Fuss (New York: Routledge, 1991), 20.

11. Nicolás Kanellos, *A History of Hispanic Theater in the United States: Origins to 1940* (Austin: University of Texas Press, 1990), 198.

12. According to Kanellos: "By 1940 Teatro Hispano fixed its relationship to the predominantly working-class community, which had now become Puerto Rican in the majority." See Kanellos, *A History of Hispanic Theater in the United States,* 135.

13. Ibid., 200.

14. Kanellos, *A History of Hispanic Theater in the United States,* 130–136.

15. While rooted in the immigrant and working-class backgrounds of its actors and actresses, vaudeville spoke to a broad national audience, and vaudeville on the Spanish-language popular stage contributed to the shape of ethnic and American identities during its height before the arrival of sound cinema. See Lisbeth Haas, *Conquests and Historical Identities in California, 1769–1936* (Berkeley: University of California Press, 1995), 144.

16. Marga Gomez, *A Line around the Block,* John Anson Ford Theater, Los Angeles, California, April 14, 1995.

17. See Yvonne Yarbro-Bejarano, "The Lesbian Body in Latina Cultural Production," in *¿Entiendes? Queer Readings, Hispanic Writings,* ed. Emilie Berg-

mann and P. Julian Smith (Durham: Duke University Press, 1995), 81–197, for a discussion of the way Latina lesbian performers deconstruct body parts in order to reconstruct new lesbian subjects. See also Gloria Anzaldúa, *Borderlands/La Frontera: The New Mestiza* (San Francisco: Spinsters/Aunt Lute, 1987).

18. For an excellent reading of Carmelita's lingual abilities, see José E. Muñoz, *Disidentifications: Queers of Color and the Performance of Politics* (Minneapolis: University of Minnesota Press, 1999), 123. See also Carmelita's collected work in Alina Troyano, *I, Carmelita Tropicana,* ed. Chon A. Noriega (Boston: Beacon Press, 2000).

19. Muñoz, *Disidentifications,* 3.

20. See bell hooks, "Dialectically Down with the Critical Program," in *Black Popular Culture,* ed. Gina Dent (Seattle: Bay Press, 1992), 48.

21. See Jan Breslauer, "Pretty, Witty, and Mainstream: Lesbian Comedian Marga Gomez Says There Are Signs of Acceptance," *Los Angeles Times,* October 13, 1994, Calendar section, 1ff.

22. Juana Maria Rodríguez, *Queer Latinidad: Identity Practices and Discursive Spaces* (New York: New York University Press, 2003), 20.

23. Rosa Linda Fregoso, *The Bronze Screen: Chicana and Chicano Film Culture* (Minneapolis: University of Minnesota Press, 1993), 31.

24. Ibid.

25. Ibid.

26. Ibid.

27. Ibid.

28. See Stuart Hall, "Notes on Deconstructing the 'Popular,'" in *People's History and Socialist Theory,* ed. R. Samuel (New York: Routledge and Kegan Paul, 1981), 239.

29. Ruth Behar, *Translated Woman: Crossing the Border with Esperanza's Story* (Boston: Beacon Press, 1993), xiii.

30. Mexquitic is located in Mexico, near San Luis Potosí.

31. Behar, *Translated Woman.* Behar is constructing an identity for Esperanza. We must recognize that Esperanza is not a person but a textual figure, a figure that is based on a living person. We know that the woman on whom the story is based exists because we see her pictures and recognize that many women live in similar conditions.

32. Patricia Zavella, "Feminist Insider Dilemmas: Constructing Identity with 'Chicana' Informants," *Frontiers: A Journal of Women's Studies* 13 (1993): 55.

33. Behar explains that "By asking me to become her comadre, Esperanza had opened up a terrain for our exchange. Women ethnographers have often found themselves positioned in the daughter role in relation to the people with whom they work. In giving me the role comadre, Esperanza also made me 'fictive kin,' but in way that both highlighted and formalized the contradictions of the racial and class differences between us" (Behar, *Translated Woman,* 6).

34. Behar's mediation occurs throughout the text, but especially in the auto-biographical section "Biography of the Shadow"; see Behar, *Translated Woman*, 320–344.

35. Ibid., 12.

36. Edén Torres, *Chicana without Apology: The New Chicana Cultural Studies* (New York: Routledge, 2003), 140.

37. "Feminist Multi-Insurgencies," UC Santa Cruz, October 1993. I thank Carla Freccero for inviting me to present at this conference.

38. See Stuart Hall, "New Ethnicities," *ICA Documents* 7 (1989): 27–31.

39. Kanellos, *A History of Hispanic Theater in the United States,* eighteenth plate in the photo section.

40. Marga Gomez, interview with author, San Francisco, California, February 28, 1994.

41. See Raymond Williams, *Marxism and Literature* (New York: Oxford University Press, 1977), 108.

42. See "The New Face of America," *Time* special issue (fall 1993): 56.

43. See Maria Damon, "Unmeaning Jargon," *South Atlantic Quarterly* (fall 1988): 708–709.

NOTES TO CHAPTER 5

An earlier version of this chapter was published in *Rockin' Las Americas: The Global Politics of Rock in Latin/o America,* edited by Deborah Pacini Hernandez, Héctor Fernández L'Hoeste, and Eric Zolov (Pittsburgh: University of Pittsburgh Press, 2004). Reprinted by permission of the University of Pittsburgh Press.

1. I am grateful to the editors of *Rockin' Las Americas* for inviting me to present this research as part of the Rockefeller Foundation Research Residency Team in Bellagio, Italy, in the summer of 2002. I began and presented research on this chapter as a University of California President's Postdoctoral in 1997–1999. Portions of this draft have been presented at the following meetings: National Association of Chicana and Chicano Studies, 1998; American Studies Association, 1999; Modern Language Association, 2000; and Latin American Studies Association, 2000. I thank Lisa Lowe for her wonderful early comments, Rosa Linda Fregoso for her Tejana insight, George Mariscal for clarifying the nuances of Chicana/o cultural nationalism, and Jocelyn Guilbault for her valuable feedback on a grant version of the chapter.

2. For discussion of Los Bros. Hernández, see José D. Saldívar, "Postmodern Realism," in *The Columbia History of the American Novel,* ed. Emory Elliott (New York: Columbia University Press, 1991), 521. See also William A. Nericcio, "A Decidedly 'Mexican' and 'American' Semi[er]otic Transference: Frida Kahlo in the Eyes of Gilbert Hernandez," in *Latino/a Popular Culture,* ed.

Michelle Habell-Pallán and Mary Romero (New York: New York University Press, 2002).

3. *Pretty Vacant,* written, directed, and photographed by Jim Mendiola, ed. Cristina Ibarra and Jim Mendiola. Mendiola's films include *Come and Take It Day* (2001) and *Speeder Kills* (2003). Cristina Ibarra directed *Dirty Laundry: A Homemade Telenovela,* in 2001.

4. See the chapter titled "'Thank God for Punk,'" in David Reyes and Tom Waldman, *Land of a Thousand Dances: Chicano Rock 'n' Roll from Southern California* (Albuquerque: University of New Mexico Press, 1998); George Lipsitz, *Dangerous Crossroads: Popular Music, Postmodernism, and the Poetics of Place* (London: Verso, 1994); Steven Loza, *Barrio Rhythm: Mexican American Music in Los Angeles* (Urbana: University of Illinois Press, 1993); Jose D. Saldívar, *Border Matters: Remapping American Cultural Studies* (Berkeley: University of California Press, 1997); Frances Aparicio and Cándida F. Jáquez, eds., *Musical Migrations: Transnationalism and Cultural Hybridity in Latin/o America* (New York: Palgrave, 2003); and Curtis Marez, "Becoming Brown: The Politics of Chicana/o Popular Style," *Social Text* 48 (1996): 109–132.

5. The interviews I conducted are part of a longer, in-progress book manuscript tentatively titled *Punk Saints and Other Urban Goddesses,* which includes an analysis of interviews with Teresa Covarrubias, Alicia Armendariz Velasquez, and other Latinas involved with punk music in Los Angeles during the 1980s. In the interviews, the women discuss their artistic conditions of production, gender relations, and their relation to Chicana feminism, as well as the Chicana punk aesthetic that emerged in the 1980s.

6. Reyes and Waldman, *Land of a Thousand Dances,* 135.

7. Ibid.

8. For an excellent discussion of how Chicana artists "made do" with limited resources, see Laura Perez, "Spirit Glyphs: Reimagining Art and Artist in the Work of Chicana Tlamatinime," *Modern Fiction Studies* 44, no. 1 (1998): 36–76.

9. For an insightful essay on Chicana youth culture of the 1940s, see Catherine Ramírez, "Crimes of Fashion: The Pachuca and Chicana Style Politics," *Meridians: A Journal of Transnational Feminisms* 2, no. 2 (2002): 1–35; and Marie (Keta) Miranda's article on Chicana participation in the 1960s music scene, "'The East Side Revue, 40 Hits by East Los Angeles' Most Popular Groups!': The Boys in the Band and the Girls Who Were Their Fans," in *Beyond the Frame: Photography and Women of Color,* ed. Angela Y. Davis and Neferti Tadiar (New York: Palgrave, in press).

10. For discussions about the importance of Question Mark and the Mysterians in relation to the emergence of early punk, see Bernard Gendron, *Between Montmartre and the Mudd Club: Popular Music and the Avant-Garde* (Chicago: University of Chicago Press, 2002), 232, 233, 266; Dave Marsh, "Looney

Tunes," *Creem*, May 1971, 43. For the 1960s emergence of punk, see Greg Shaw, "Juke Box Jury," *Creem*, March 1971, 72–73.

11. Lester Bangs, *Psychotic Reactions and Carburetor Dung* (New York: Vintage, 1987), 38.

12. Gendron, *Between Montmartre and the Mudd Club*, 232.

13. For a discussion of the Farfisa organ and its connection to conjunto and punk "garage" bands, see Ed Morales, *The Latin Beat: The Rhythm and Roots of Latin Music from Bossa Nova to Salsa and Beyond* (Boston: Da Capo Press, 2003), 289–290.

14. Ibid., 290.

15. Gendron, *Between Montmartre and the Mudd Club*, 266.

16. Dave Marsh, *The Heart of Rock and Soul: The 1001 Greatest Singles Ever Made* (New York: Da Capo Press, 1999), 67, 68.

17. For a history of Chicanos in Los Angeles, see George Sánchez, *Becoming Mexican American: Ethnicity and Acculturation in Chicano Los Angeles, 1900–1945* (New York: Oxford University Press, 1993).

18. Reyes and Waldman, *Land of a Thousand Dances*, 135.

19. Ibid., 136.

20. Considering the importance of The Bags in the L.A. punk scene, it is curious that Alice Bag/Alicia Armendariz Velasquez is minimally quoted in the collected interview in Marc Spitz and Brendan Muller, *We Got the Neutron Bomb: The Untold Story of L.A. Punk* (New York: Three Rivers Press, 2001).

21. Pop music markets have undergone enormous change since the 1970s. Given the changes in the music industry and the "boom" in Latino pop music in the 1990s, a Latina performer like Shakira can become mainstream—although it must be taken into account too that Shakira is considered a rock singer, not a punk singer who pushes rock conventions. See Maria Elena Cepeda's insightful article, "Shakira as the Idealized, Transnational Citizen: A Case Study of Colombianidad in Transition," *Latino Studies* 1, no. 2 (July 2003): 211–357, to understand how and why Shakira translates to U.S. and Latin American audiences.

22. See José E. Muñoz, *Disidentifications: Queers of Color and the Politics of Performance* (Minneapolis: University of Minnesota Press, 1999), 93.

23. Ibid.

24. See Richard Durado's silkscreen poster for X's performance at the Punk Prom held at Self-Help Graphics in 1980, in the catalogue for Chon Noriega, ed., *Just Another Poster? Chicano Graphic Arts in California* (Santa Barbara: Regents of the University of California Art Museum, 2001), 59.

25. For photo, see Don Snowden and Gary Leonard, eds., *Make the Music Go Bang: The Early L.A. Punk Scene*, photographs by Gary Leonard (New York: St. Martin's Press, 1997), 76.

26. The ethnomusicologist Steven Loza speaks about the historical difficulty of marketing bicultural bands in the broadcast "Chicanas in Tune." "Chicanas

in Tune," produced by Ester Reyes for Life and Times Television, copyright Community Television of Southern California, broadcast on KCET, Los Angeles, 1994.

27. For pedagogical suggestions regarding Norte's spoken word, see Michelle Habell-Pallán, "Marisela Norte, *NORTE/word*," in *Reading U.S. Latina Writers: Remapping American Literature*, ed. Alvina E. Quintana (New York: Palgrave Macmillan, 2003), 163–172.

28. For a detailed analysis of Chicana cultural production and Chicana feminist discourses, see Sonia Saldivar-Hull, *Feminism on the Border: Chicana Gender Politics and Literature* (Berkeley: University of California Press, 2000).

29. The Official Alice Bag Website, "Biography," http://alicebag.com/bio.html, accessed July 17, 2004.

30. Angie Chabram-Dernersesian, "I Throw Punches for My Race, But I Don't Want to Be a Man—Writing Us Chica-nos (Girl, Us)/Chica*nas*—into the Movement Script," in *Cultural Studies,* ed. Lawrence Grossberg, Cary Nelson, and Paula Treichler (New York: Routledge, 1992), 81–95.

31. David Jones, "Destroy All Music: Punk Rock Pioneers of Southern California," forthcoming.

32. Kristine McKenna, "Female Rockers—A New Breed," *Los Angeles Times,* June 18, 1978, Calendar sec., 78–82.

33. Ibid., 78.

34. Ibid.

35. Ibid., 82.

36. Ibid., 78.

37. The Official Alice Bag Website, "Violence Girl," http://alicebag.com/violencegirl.html, accessed July 16, 2004.

38. Sincere thanks to Jim Fricke, former senior curator at the Experience Music Project, for allowing me to access the Yes L.A. compilation. For more on the rise of British punk, see Dave Laing's classic *One Chord Wonders: Power and Meaning in Punk Rock* (Philadelphia: Open University Press, 1985).

39. See Spitz and Mullen, *We Got the Neutron Bomb,* for varied testimonies of Canterbury's history.

40. A City of Los Angeles Cultural Affairs Department press release for the Gamboa 84 exhibition opening on April 15, 1984, at the Los Angeles Photography Center, documents that The Odd Squad, The Brat, and ASCO performed on the same program. Marisela Norte and Daniel Villarreal performed *Exito.* Harry Gamboa's *Shadow Solo* was performed by Sean Carrillo and Humberto Sandoval. Pseudoturquoiser was performed by Gronk. Diane Gamboa provided *Cold Blooded* paper fashions. See flyer held in the Tomás Ybarra-Frausto Research Material, 1965–1997, collection at the Archives of American Art, Smithsonian Institution.

41. Lysa Flores "starred in critically acclaimed indie-film, *Star Maps* (1997) by Miguel Arteta, and served as the film's musical director and soundtrack producer. She played the lead in *The Furthest Room* by Paul Saucido, a play based on her songs. She runs her own record label, Bring Your Love. She has been a member of legendary performance-artist El Vez's band since 1996." See Lysa Flores Official Website, "Biography," http://www.lysaflores.com/bio.html, accessed July 16, 2004.

42. I do not mean to suggest that Alice Bag and Teresa Covarrubias were the first Chicanas from East L.A. to participate in local music scenes. See Dionne Espinoza, "'Tanto Tiempo Disfrutamos . . .': Revisiting the Gender and Sexual Politics of Chicana/o Youth Culture in East Los Angeles in the 1960s," in *Velvet Barrios: Popular Culture and Chicana/o Sexualities,* ed. Alicia Gaspar de Alba (New York: Palgrave Macmillan, 2003), 89–106, for a discussion of Chicana participation in the East L.A. music scene in the 1950s and 1960s. In fact, in Reyes and Waldman, *Land of a Thousand Dances,* Covarrubias recalls refusing requests by her manager to rerecord a version of Rosie and the Originals' 1961 classic oldie "Angel Baby" because she wanted to create a new sound. Rosie and the Originals, although from San Diego, California, are often associated with the East L.A. sound.

43. Teresa Covarrubias, interview by author, East Los Angeles, August 8, 1998.

44. Covarrubias, interview by author.

45. "Chicanas in Tune," produced by Ester Reyes, broadcast on KCET, Los Angeles, 1994.

46. McKenna, "Female Rockers," 82.

47. Reyes and Waldman, *Land of a Thousand Dances,* 139.

48. "Chicanas in Tune."

49. Las Tres, *Live at the LATC,* Panocha Dulce-Black Rose-Bhima Music, 1993, audiocassette. "Happy Accident" was written by Alicia Armendariz Velasquez. Thanks to Antonia Garcia-Orozco for inventing the notion of Chicana Trova in relation to Nueva Trova; Chicana Trova is sung in English and lyrically calls for consciousness raising through a form of folk music that can be played on accessible instruments.

50. See Tiffany Lopez, *The Alchemy of Blood: Violence as Critical Discourse in U.S. Latina/o Literature* (Durham: Duke University Press, in press), and Angela Davis on incarceration and women of color in her recording *The Prison Industrial Complex,* AK Press, 2000, compact disk.

51. Reyes and Waldman, *Land of a Thousand Dances,* 136.

52. Ibid.

53. Teresa Covarrubias to M. Habell-Pallán, personal e-mail, February 24, 2003, bio for Chicana Punk Aesthetic Conference. According to a flyer announc-

ing a night of ASCO performances on June 24, 1982, Teresa Covarrubias was one of the participants in *Random Rumor* (her name was spelled as Therese Covarrbuias). Others performers in the piece included Humberto Sandoval, Lorraine Ordaz, Diane Gamboa, Daniel Villareal, Sean Carrillo, and Harry Gamboa. See flyer archived in the Tomás Ybarra-Frausto Research Material, 1965–1997, collection at the Archives of American Art, Smithsonian Institution.

54. Reyes and Waldman, *Land of a Thousand Dances,* 140.

55. Sean Carrillo, "East to Eden," in *Forming: The Early Days of L.A. Punk,* ed. Sean Carrillo, Christine McKenna, Claude Bessy, and Exene Cervenka (Santa Monica: Smart Art Press, 1999), 42. In addition to participating in the West Coast punk scene, Latinos were also part of New York's emerging hip-hop scene, which developed during the same time period. See Raquel Z. Rivera, *New York Ricans from the Hip Hop Zone* (New York: Palgrave, 2003).

56. See Keith Negus, *Popular Music in Theory: An Introduction* (Hanover, N.H.: University of New England Press, 1996), 183.

57. Ibid., 189.

58. Sonia Saldívar-Hull, "Feminism on the Border: From Gender Politics to Geopolitics," in *Criticism in the Borderlands: Studies in Chicano Literature, Culture, and Ideology,* ed. Hector Calderon and José D. Saldívar (Durham: Duke University Press, 1991), 204, 211.

59. Molly incorporates the great Tejano "punk" accordion player Steve Jordan into her conceptual map of Chicano culture. The scholar Rosa Linda Fregoso explained to me that Jordan has generally been left out in accounts of Tejano oppositional culture—unlike "Little Joe," a Tejano musician associated with the movement—because of his heroin addiction and his unconventional lifestyle. Molly also situates herself in dialogue with the music critic Greil Marcus. She fondly references Marcus's *Lipstick Traces.* See Greil Marcus, *Lipstick Traces: A Secret History of the Twentieth Century* (Cambridge, Mass.: Harvard University Press, 1989).

60. *Pretty Vacant,* dir. Jim Mendiola, 1996,

61. Ibid.

62. Norma Alarcón, "Cognitive Desires: An Allegory of/for Chicana Critics," in *Chicana (W)rites on Word and Film,* ed. María Herrera-Sobek and Helena María Viramontes (Oakland: Third Woman Press, 1996), 187.

63. *Pretty Vacant.*

64. Evey Chapa, "Mujeres por La Raza Unida," in *Chicana Feminist Thought,* ed. Alma Garcia (New York: Routledge, 1997), 179.

65. The limited black-and-white color spectrum of the photo image itself, because it cannot represent a visible brownness, lends itself to reproducing the problematic binary terms in which dominant debates about race and power relations are couched, terms that render invisible the bodies and concerns of women who are racialized as neither black nor white (such as *mestizas,* Native Ameri-

cans, and Asian Americans) but who are nevertheless positioned on the economic and/or political margins.

66. She is, in reality, the Tejana actress and performance artist Mariana Vasquez.

67. Mendiola, phone interview, 1999.

68. Mendiola, e-mail correspondence with author, December 18, 2003.

69. Mendiola, public lecture, University of California, Santa Barbara (UCSB), Center for Chicano Studies, January 22, 2003.

70. Ibid. For an exploration of black feminist punk aesthetics, see Daphne Brooks, "Burnt Sugar: Post-Soul Satire and Rock Memory," in *This Is Pop: In Search of the Elusive at Experience Music Project,* ed. Eric Weisbard (Cambridge, Mass.: Harvard University Press, 2004), 115.

71. Robert Young, *The Ballad of Gregorio Cortez* (1983); Luis Valdez, *Zoot Suit* (1981); Isaac Artenstein, *Break of Dawn* (1988); Cheech Marin, *Born in East L.A.* (1987); Luis Valdez, *La Bamba* (1987); Gregory Nava, *Mi Familia* (1995).

72. Sylvia Morales, *Chicana!* (1979); Lourdes Portillo, *Despues del Terremoto* (1995); Frances Salomé España, *Spitfire* (1991); Ela Troyano, *Carmelita Tropicana: Your Kunst Is Your Waffen* (1994); Frances Negrón-Mutaner, *Bricando el Charco* (1994).

73. See Rosa Linda Fregoso, "Chicana Film Practices: Confronting the Many-Headed Demon of Oppression," in *Chicana (W)rites on Word and Film,* ed. María Herrera-Sobek and Helena María Viramontes (Oakland: Third Woman Press, 1995), 259–276.

74. Outside the context of the film narrative, the image could be interpreted to suggest that she is turning the lens on the spectator—who could be the person on the other side of a second camera that is shooting her picture, or us, the viewer of the photo.

75. See Maylei Blackwell's groundbreaking essay "Contested Histories: Las Hijas de Chuauhtémoc, Chicana Feminisms, and Print Culture in the Chicano Movement, 1968–1973," on the function of print culture in the articulation of Chicana feminist thinking, in *Chicana Feminisms: A Critical Reader,* ed. Gabriela F. Arredondo, Aída Hurtado, Norma Klahn, Olga Nájera-Ramírez, and Patricia Zavella (Durham: Duke University Press, 2003), 59–89.

76. Mendiola, interview by author, January 25, 1999.

77. Ibid.

78. Ibid.

79. Mariana Vasquez, telephone interview by author, February 10, 1999.

80. Ibid.

81. See Deborah R. Vargas, "Cruzando Frontejas: Remapping Selena's Tejano Music 'Crossover,'" in *Chicana Traditions: Continuity and Change,* ed. Norma E. Cantú and Olga Najera-Ramirez (Urbana: University of Illinois Press, 2002).

82. Deborah Pacini Hernandez, Héctor Fernández L'Hoeste, and Eric Zolov, eds., *Rockin' Las Americas: The Global Politics of Rock in Latin/o America* (Pittsburgh: University of Pittsburgh Press, 2004).

NOTES TO CHAPTER 6

1. It has been my great pleasure to introduce the performance of El Vez to a community of serious scholars. This chapter, which "introduces" El Vez and was a natural outgrowth of my initial research conducted in 1994, has helped to widen the field of analysis of Chicana and Chicano studies. I am also pleased that this current research allows me to fulfill the charge of cultural studies to take seriously issues and objects "which critical work has excluded" (Lawrence Grossberg, *We Gotta Get Out of this Place: Popular Conservatism and Postmodern Culture* [New York: Routledge, 1992], 18). The power of a live performance I attended in January 1995 by El Vez and the Memphis Mariachis, while I was a graduate student at University of California, Santa Cruz, convinced me to continue this project. I presented an early version of this chapter at the 1996 Annual California Studies Association Meeting. I presented subsequent versions at the New Perspectives on Chicana and Chicano Culture Conference, Center for Chicano Studies, University of California, Los Angeles, May 1997; the Third International Conference on El Vez, Institute for the Living South, Memphis College of Art, Elvis Weep Week, August 1997; the Annual American Studies Association Meeting, Washington, D.C., December 1997; and the Shifting Boundaries: Place and Space in the Romance Cultures of North-America, Centro de Estudios Mexicanos, University of Groningen, The Netherlands, May 1998. Many thanks to those who commented on this chapter.

2. Jose D. Saldívar, *Border Matters: Remapping American Cultural Studies* (Berkeley: University of California Press, 1997), 95. Also see Claire Fox, *The Fence and the River: Culture and Politics at the U.S.-Mexico Border* (Minneapolis: University of Minnesota Press, 1999).

3. El Vez's transculturation of American mass culture is an analogue for the current transformation of the dominant culture engaged by Latinos. Diane Taylor, elaborating on the Cuban anthropologist Fernando Ortiz's definition of the term, explains that transculturation "suggests a shifting or circulation pattern of cultural transference" that is not necessarily based on equal power relations. She continues, "Transculturation affects the entire culture; it involves the shifting of socio-political, not just aesthetic borders; it modifies collective and individual identity; it changes discourse, both verbal and symbolic" (Diane Taylor, "Transculturating Transculturation," *Performing Arts Journal* 38 [1991]: 90).

4. See George Lipsitz, *Dangerous Crossroads: Popular Music, Postmodernism, and the Poetics of Place* (New York: Verso, 1994); Herman Gray, *Watching Race: Television and the Struggle for Blackness* (Minneapolis: Univer-

sity of Minnesota Press, 1995); and Grossberg, *We Gotta Get Out of This Place,* for compelling discussions of popular music and culture as a site where cultural struggles are staged.

5. See Marjorie Chodorov's documentary, *El Rey de Rock 'n' Roll,* Soap Box Films, 2000. Available at vlvtelvis1@aol.com.

6. Mary Pat Brady, *Extinct Lands, Temporal Geographies: Chicano Literature and the Urgency of Space* (Durham: Duke University Press, 2002), 53.

7. Jorge Mariscal, "Latinos on the Frontlines: Again," *Latino Studies* 1 (July 2003): 347. Mariscal also notes that Latinas and noncitizen Latina U.S. soldiers are often giving their live in Iraq; see Jorge Mariscal "Mexican American Women in Iraq: Las Adelitas 2003," *Counterpunch,* November 14, 2003, http://counterpunch.org/mariscal11142003.html. Also, see George Mariscal, ed., *Aztlán and Viet Nam: Chicano and Chicana Experiences of the War* (Berkeley: University of California Press, 1999). For more on the historical role of Chicanas in soldiering, see Elizabeth Salas, *Soldaderas in the Mexican Military: Myth and History* (Austin: University of Texas Press, 1990).

8. Gilbert B. Rodman, *Elvis after Elvis: The Posthumous Career of a Living Legend* (New York: Routledge, 1996), 40.

9. See the insert for *G.I. Ay, Ay! Blues* (Big Pop Records, 1996, compact disk) for a visual representation of Lopez's reappropriation of the signs of Latin American revolution, especially Che Guevara as revolutionary icon. Citing the folk singer Phil Ochs, the insert proclaims: "If there is any hope for America it lies in a Revolution. If there is any hope for a Revolution it lies in Elvis Presley becoming Ché Guevara." However, juxtaposing symbols of an anti-imperialist history of armed struggle (leaving Ché's torture and assassination unspoken) with the pleasures of rock 'n' roll history certainly does not alone advance social change and does leave Lopez open to criticism that he is diminishing and disrespecting the efforts of armed revolutionary struggle. Yet, by locating his aesthetic strategies between the multiracial punk rappers Rage Against the Machine and "just fun and parody," he uses his music and performance to wage a conscious negotiation between utter opposition and utter complacency. Through his negotiation, openings are formed that lead to the discourse of a different, progressive set of social possibilities, openings that can occur when people are not on the defensive.

10. El Vez, interview by author, Tucson, Arizona, September 27, 1996.

11. In this statement, El Vez employs the metaphor of the "blank Elvis" tongue-in-cheek, as he has chosen to embody the Chicano Elvis. Although his provocative statement around Elvis and sexuality needs to be teased out, space considerations prohibit me from addressing them further in this chapter. See Rodham, *Elvis after Elvis,* for an extended discussion of how fans come to see themselves reflected in the image of Elvis. While Rodham admits that the figure of Elvis engenders multiple interpretations, he argues that it is not "an 'empty

signifier' that can mean absolutely anything at all. On the contrary, . . . Elvis is an incredibly full signifier, one that is already intimately bound up with many of the most important cultural myths of our time. . . . Elvis is not (and never has been) merely a blank slate onto which fans and critics can write their own stories" (40). Vernon Chadwick's *In Search of Elvis: Music, Race, Art, Religion* (Boulder, Colo.: Westview Press, 1997) serves as a wonderful source for discussions of Elvis's many symbolic functions.

12. Inevitably, Lopez's style of blending Chicano and the dominant culture is a form of cultural politics that is not acceptable to those who still are heavily invested in Chicano ethnic nationalism. Chicano nationalist identity politics demands a rupture from the dominant culture, so the pleasures of "white" rock 'n' roll could never be openly indulged. Contrary to this nationalist position, El Vez's performance turns on the crossing of cultural and racial lines; more precisely, it is through the humorous reworking of the signifiers of the nation, both American and Chicano, that El Vez can speak to multiple marginalized communities affected by shifts in the global economy. El Vez's work suggests that cultural nationalism must always be surpassed by a *mestizo* politics of transformation in order to avoid imitating the trappings of the exclusionary model of nationalism of the dominant culture. Thus, in El Vez's work, both Chicano and mainstream national icons take on an international significance and become a site where the possibility for political alliance based on an identity, beyond the constraints of the nation-state, is imagined.

13. *Graciasland,* Sympathy for the Record Industry Records, 1994, compact disk.

14. "Immigration Time," *Graciasland,* Sympathy for the Record Industry Records, 1994, compact disk.

15. However, the introductory musical phrase of El Vez's version that superimposes the "who, who" soundings of both the Rolling Stones' and Jane's Addiction's versions of "Sympathy for the Devil" signals Lopez's general engagement with American popular music.

16. See Sam Howe Verhovek, "Border Patrol Is Criticized as Abusive; Human Rights Group Reports 'Cruel' Acts," *New York Times,* May 21, 1998, A12ff.

17. See Michael Fix and Jeffrey S. Passel, *Immigration and Immigrants: Setting the Record Straight* (Washington, D.C.: Urban Institute, 1994).

18. Lisa Lowe, *Immigrant Acts: On Asian American Cultural Politics* (Durham: Duke University Press, 1996), 174.

19. The graphic artist Lalo Alcaraz also employed his weekly comic, *L.A. Cucaracha,* as a public site for the counterhegemonic discussion of immigrant bashing in California.

20. El Vez, liner notes, *Graciasland.*

21. Aztlán is the mythical homeland—now called the American Southwest—

of the indigenous Mexican peoples that emerged from the Chicano Power Movement of the late 1960s.

22. The initials stand for "Movimiento Estudiantil Chicano de Aztlán" (Chicano Student Movement of Aztlán).

23. "Califas" means "California" in Chicano *caló*, an argot.

24. "Aztlán," *Graciasland*, Sympathy for the Record Industry Records, 1994, compact disk.

25. David Gutiérrez, *Walls and Mirrors: Mexican Americans, Mexican Immigrants, and the Politics of Ethnicity* (Berkeley: University of California Press, 1995), 17–18.

26. Even though this is not on the lyric sheet, he says it on the recorded version.

27. El Vez, interview by author.

28. See Gloria Anzaldúa, *Borderlands/La Frontera: The New Mestiza* (San Francisco: Spinsters/Aunt Lute, 1987).

29. See Kevin R. Johnson, "'Aliens' and the U.S. Immigration Laws: The Social and Legal Construction of Nonpersons," *Miami Inter-American Law Review* 28, no. 2 (1996): 263–287, for an in-depth analysis of rhetoric used against undocumented immigrant labor. For an extended, thorough analysis of how metaphors deployed in public discourse shape debate about Mexican immigrants in the United States, see Otto Santa Ana's *Brown Tide Rising: The Metaphors of Latinos in Contemporary American Public Discourse* (Austin: University of Texas Press, 2002).

30. "Taking Care of Business," *G.I. Ay, Ay! Blues*, Big Pop Records, 1996, compact disk.

31. Judith Halberstam, *Female Masculinities* (Durham: Duke University Press, 1998), 245. See also Eric Lott, "All the King's Men: Elvis Impersonators and White Working-Class Masculinity," in *Race and the Subject of Masculinities*, ed. Harry Stecopoulos and Michael Uebel (Durham: Duke University Press, 1997), 193.

32. Coco Fusco, "Introduction," in *Corpus Delecti: Performance Art of the Americas*, ed. Coco Fusco (New York: Routledge, 2000), 10.

33. Halberstam, *Female Masculinities*, 234.

34. Ibid., 238.

35. Ibid., 235.

36. Sergio de la Mora, "Fascinating Machismo: Toward an Unmasking of Heterosexual Masculinity in Arturo Ripstein's *El Lugar Sin Límites*," *Journal of Film and Video* 44, no. 3–4 (fall–winter 1992–1993): 83.

37. See Gayatri Gopinath, *Impossible Subjects: Queer Diasporas and South Asian Public Cultures* (Durham: Duke University Press, in press) for an excellent analysis of the way queer subjectivity is both out and hidden in South Asian diasporic cultural production.

38. De la Mora, "Fascinating Machismo," 83.

39. Ibid., 88.

40. Ibid., 86.

41. Ibid., 93.

42. Ibid., 92.

43. De la Mora acknowledges Laura Mulvey's classic feminist theory of the gaze.

44. Lowe, *Immigrant Acts,* 36.

45. El Vez, interview by author.

46. Ibid.

47. See Ayse S. Caglar, "The Prison House of Culture in the Study of Turks in Germany," in series *Sozialanthropologische Arbeitspapiere,* no. 31 (Berlin: Das Arabische Buch, 1990); Caglarä, "German Turks in Berlin: Social Exclusion and Strategies for Social Mobility," *New Community* 21, no. 3 (1995): 309–323; Andrew Phillips, "The Gates Slam Shut," *Maclean's,* June 14, 1993, 18–22; and Steven Vertovec, "Berlin Multikulti: Germany, 'Foreigners,' and World Openness," *New Community* 22, no. 3 (1996): 381–399.

48. Ruth Mandel, "Foreigners in the Fatherland: Turkish Immigrant Workers in Germany," in *The Politics of Immigrant Workers: Labor Activism and Migration in the World Economy since 1830,* ed. Camille Guerin-Gonzalez and Carl Strikwerda (New York: Holmes and Meier, 1993).

49. Erasmo Gamboa, *Mexican Labor and World War II: Braceros in the Pacific Northwest, 1942–1947* (Austin: University of Texas Press, 1990); and Pierrette Hondagneu-Sotelo, "The History of Mexican Undocumented Settlement in the United States," in *Challenging Fronteras: Structuring Latina and Latino Lives in the U.S.,* ed. Mary Romero et al. (New York: Routledge, 1996).

50. David M. Smith and Maurice Blanc, "Citizenship, Nationality, and Ethnic Minorities in Three European Nations," *International Journal of Urban and Regional Research* 20, no. 1 (1996): 66–81; and Thomas Faist and Hartmut Haubermann, "Immigration, Social Citizenship and Housing in Germany," *International Journal of Urban and Regional Research* 20, no. 1 (1996): 83–98. Only recently have changes in German citizenship requirements expanded the criteria by which noncitizens can become naturalized.

51. Public discourse about the place of working immigrants throughout Europe has intensified during the past ten years; for example, see Jolyon Jenkins, "Taken to the Cleaners: Germany has Its Turks, Kuwait Has the Filipinos, and the British Have Their Nigerians," *New Statesman and Society* (December 29, 1989): 10–11; and Phillips, "The Gates Slam Shut," 18–22.

52. Alan Cowell, "Turks Seek Acceptance of Culture in Germany," *New York Times* (international edition), December 14, 1995, A6.

53. Ayhan Kaya, "Construction of Diasporic Cultural Identity: Berlin Turks and Hip-Hop Youth Culture," unpublished manuscript, 1997.

NOTES TO THE EPILOGUE

An earlier version of this chapter was published, under the title "'Don't Call Us Hispanic': Latina/o Theater in Canada," in *Latina/o Popular Culture,* edited by Michelle Habell-Pallán and Mary Romero (New York: NYU Press, 2002). Reprinted by permission.

I wholeheartedly thank Carmen Aguirre for giving me an advance copy of *¿Qué Pasa con la Raza, eh?* (Winnipeg: Blizzard, 2000) and for granting me an interview. I also thank her for her valuable comments on this chapter. An early version of this essay was presented at the Nations, Pollinations, and Dislocations: Changing Imaginary Borders in the Americas International Symposium, Vancouver, Canada, October 31, 1999.

1. See Niko Price, "Border Crackdown Has Netted Snarls, But Not Terrorists," *Seattle Times,* November 3, 2003, p. A10.

2. See Jorge Mariscal, "Latinos on the Frontlines: Again," *Latino Studies* 1 (2003): 347.

3. See Jose D. Saldivar, *The Dialectics of Our América: Genealogy, Cultural Critique, and Literary History* (Durham: Duke University Press, 1991).

4. Marcelo Ballve, ed., "Mexican Guest Workers Allege Abuses in Canada" *El Norte Digest News Digest,* available at http://www.uslaboragainstwar.org/article.php?id=2309.

5. Aguirre's one-woman show *Chile con Carne* has toured Chile and Venezuela. She also plays the lead in *Sabor a Mi [Savor Me]* (1997), an independent film by the Canadian Latina filmmaker Claudia Morgado Escanilla. Aguirre is a graduate of the prestigious Studio 58 in Vancouver. This grass-roots project was funded, in part, by the City of Vancouver Cross-Cultural Initiatives Program.

6. For more on the theme of exile see Sylvie Perron, "Banished between Two Worlds: Exiles in Chilean Canadian Literature," in *The Reordering of Culture: Latin America, The Caribbean, and Canada in the Hood,* ed. Alvina Ruprecht and Cecilia Taima (Ottawa: Carleton University Press, 1995); and Lake Sagaris, "Countries like Drawbridges: Chilean-Canadian Writing Today," *Canadian Literature* 142–143 (1994): 12–24. *¿Qué Pasa con la Raza, eh?* has more in common with Guillermo Verdecchia's play *Fronteras Américas = American Borders* (Toronto: Coach House Press, 1993).

7. See Thomas Wright and Rody Oñate, eds., *Flight from Chile: Voices of Exile,* trans. Irene Hodgson (Albuquerque: University of New Mexico Press, 1998) for more detailed narratives about the repressive conditions that forced exiles to flee. Also see Gerald Volgenau, "Refugees from Latin America Are on Their Way to Canada," *Seattle Times,* February 22, 1987, A11.

8. Carmen Aguirre asserts that the Canadian government's statistics grossly undercount the population of Latin American descent in Vancouver. She esti-

mates that forty thousand people, including undocumented immigrants, of Latin American descent live in greater Vancouver. According to the Canada Statistics Census of 2001, the number of Latin Americans in the Visible Minority category equals 18,715. Canada statistics web page available at www.statcan.ca.

9. See Tanya Basok, *Tortillas and Tomatoes: Transmigrant Mexican Harvesters in Canada* (Montreal: McGill-Queen's University Press, 2003). Gloria Patricia Dias Barerro presented a insightful paper called "Migrant Latina Exotic Dancers and the Complicity of the Canadian State," which sheds light on the dangerous working conditions for these immigrant women, at the Annual American Studies Association Meeting, Hartford, Connecticut, 2003.

10. Due to recent immigration trends, Latin Americans and South Asians are far more likely to be manual laborers than other visible minorities. See Karen Kelly, "Visible Minorities: A Diverse Group," *Social Science Trends* (summer 95): 2–8, and Tanya Basok, "Migration of Mexican Seasonal Farm Workers to Canada and Development: Obstacles to Productive Investment," *International Migration Review* 34, no. 1 (spring 2000): 79–97.

11. The LTG member Angelo Moroni, quoted in Colin Thomas, "The Latino Quarter: Carmen Aguirre's Theatre Troupe Subverts Stereotypes and Confronts Traumatic Pasts," *Georgia Straight* (March 11–18, 1999): 69.

12. Carmen Aguirre, quoted in Thomas, "The Latino Quarter," 69.

13. Proper Dos, "Mexican Power," *Latin Lingo: Hip-Hop from La Raza* (WEA/Atlantic/Rhino Records, compact disc, 1995); El Vez, "Never Been to Spain," *How Great Thou Art* (Sympathy for the Record Industry, compact disk, n.d.).

14. For more on the cultural significance of El Vez, see Michelle Habell-Pallán, "El Vez Is Taking Care of Business," *Cultural Studies* 13, no. 2 (1999): 195–210. For an in-depth discussion of *Love and Rockets,* see William A. Nericcio, "A Decidedly 'Mexican' and 'American' Semi[er]otic Transference: Frida Kahlo in the Eyes of Gilbert Hernandez," in *Latino/a Popular Culture,* ed. Michelle Habell-Pallán and Mary Romero (New York: New York University Press, 2002).

15. The recently formed Vancouver arts organization, Americas on the Verge Society for the Advancement of Arts and Cultures, dedicates itself to promoting Latino-Canadian culture.

16. For an excellent collection that examines the effects of NAFTA on the most vulnerable of the labor force, see Isabella Bakker, ed., *Rethinking Restructuring: Gender and Change in Canada* (Toronto: University of Toronto Press, 1996).

17. "Coyote" is the vernacular name for those who, for a substantial fee, smuggle undocumented workers across the U.S.-Mexican border.

18. Augusto Boal, influenced by Paulo Freire, developed Theater of the Oppressed in Brazil during the 1960s as a response to military repression against theater companies and actors that did not support the dictatorship. Its goal is to

create a format that empowers those whose point of view has been silenced. See Augusto Boal, "Theater of the Oppressed," *Unesco Courier* 50, no. 1 (November 1997): 32–36, and Mady Schutzman and Jan Cohen-Cruz, eds., *Playing Boal: Theater, Therapy, and Activism* (New York: Routledge, 1994) for a more in-depth history.

19. Augusto Boal, *Legislative Theatre: Using Performance to Make Politics*, trans. Adrian Jackson (New York: Routledge, 1998), 9.

20. Angie Chabram-Dernersesian, "Introduction: Chicana/Latina Cultural Studies: Transnational and Transdisciplinary Movements," *Cultural Studies* 13, no. 2 (1999): 183.

21. See Néstor García-Canclini, "Latins or Americans: Narratives of the Border," *Canadian Journal of Latin American and Caribbean Studies* 23, no. 46 (1998): 117–131, for a discussion of the "polycentric" notion of frontier relations in the era globalization.

22. María de los Angeles Torres, "Transnational Political and Cultural Identities: Crossing Theoretical Borders," in *Borderless Borders: U.S. Latinos, Latin Americans, and the Paradox of Interdependence*, ed. Frank Bonilla et al. (Philadelphia: Temple University Press, 1998), 172.

23. Pedro Caban, "The New Synthesis of Latin American and Latino Studies," in *Borderless Borders: U.S. Latinos, Latin Americans, and the Paradox of Interdependence*, ed. Frank Bonilla et al. (Philadelphia: Temple University Press, 1998), 213.

24. See Mary Pat Brady, "The Fungibility of Borders," *Nepantla: Views from South* 1, no. 1 (2000): 181, 194.

25. Gregory Nava, producer. *El Norte* [*The North*] (Farmington Hills, Mich.: Independent Productions, 1984).

26. For an understanding of these tensions see Lina Y. Newton, "Why Some Latinos Supported Proposition 187: Testing Economic Threat and Cultural Identity Hypothesis," *Social Science Quarterly* 81, no. 1 (March 2000): 180–193. For a historical overview of these tensions, see David G. Gutiérrez, *Walls and Mirrors: Mexican Americans, Mexican Immigrants, and the Politics of Ethnicity* (Berkeley: University of California Press, 1995).

27. Manuel Pastor, Jr., "Interdependence, Inequality, and Identity: Linking Latinos and Latin Americans," in *Borderless Borders: U.S. Latinos, Latin Americans, and the Paradox of Interdependence*, ed. Frank Bonilla et al. (Philadelphia: Temple University Press, 1998), 18.

28. For specific details on the hate crimes Skin references, see Kim Bolan, "Phone Tip Led to Arrest of Racists in Temple Killing," *Vancouver Sun*, October 3, 1998, B5; Kim Bolan, "Security Tight as Five Face Hearing in Temple Killing," *Vancouver Sun*, October 6, 1998, A5; Kim Bolan, "Racists Attack Three Blacks at Bar," *Vancouver Sun*, June 6, 1998, B1; and Lori Culbert, "Squamish Youths Say They're Not Thugs," June 6, 1998, B1.

29. Border feminism recognizes the geopolitical interconnectedness of people of color in the Americas. For more on border feminism, see Sonia Saldívar-Hull, *Feminism on the Border: Chicana Gender Politics and Literature* (Berkeley: University of California Press, 2000). Of course, there is a long history of calls for cross-border solidarity. For an excellent revisiting of the notion of *Nuestra América*, see Jeffrey Belnap and Raúl Fernández, eds., *José Martí's "Our America": From National to Hemispheric Cultural Studies* (Durham: Duke University Press, 1998).

30. See Rosa Linda Fregoso, *The Bronze Screen: Chicana and Chicano Film Culture* (Minneapolis: University of Minnesota Press, 1993), for a discussion of cultural identity as process.

31. Guillermo Gómez-Peña, "Documented/Undocumented," in *The Graywolf Annual Five: Multicultural Literacy,* ed. Rick Simonson and Scott Walker (St. Paul, Minn.: Graywolf Press, 1998), 129.

32. Teresa McKenna, *Migrant Song: Politics and Process in Contemporary Chicano Literature* (Austin: University of Texas Press, 1997), 107.

33. See Michelle Habell-Pallán, "Family and Sexuality in Recent Chicano Performance: Luis Alfaro's Memory Plays," *Ollantáy Theater Journal* 4, no. 1 (1996): 33–42, for a discussion of Luis Alfaro's solo performance *Virgin Mary,* in which the narrator's doomed love affair with a young man who was "every Brady Bunch/Partridge Family episode rolled into one" forces him to examine rethink his ethnic identity.

34. Ricke Ouston and Marina Jimenez, "Latinos Still Haunted by Ghosts of War," *Vancouver Sun,* February 23, 1998, A1.

35. Peter Small, "Police Union Ad May Break Rules," *Toronto Star,* June 14, 1999, ed. 1, news section.

36. Bruce DeMara, "Subway Poster Spurs Call for Hate Crimes Probe," *Toronto Star,* June 16, 1999, ed. 1, news section. The poster was removed after the Canadian Hispanic Congress protested vigorously. Vannina Sztainbok and Magaly San Martin presented an insightful paper about the Latin American Coalition against Racism called "Making Space: Re-Constructing *latinoamericanidad* in Toronto" at the Annual American Studies Association Meeting, October 16, 2003, Hartford, Connecticut.

37. Rollo Triguero, quoted in Jennifer Van Evra, "Young Actors Put Human Face on Political Strife," *Vancouver Courier,* March 17, 1999, 24.

38. Carmen Aguirre, quoted in "The Latino Quarter: Carmen Aguirre's Theatre Troupe Subverts Stereotypes and Confronts Traumatic Pasts," *Georgia Straight,* March 11–18, 1999, 69.

39. Lighter Shade of Brown, "Homies"; Kid Frost, "La Raza"; Mellow Man, "Mentirosa"; and Proper Dos, "Mexican Power," all on *Latin Lingo: Hip-Hop from La Raza* (WEA/Atlantic/Rhino Records, compact disk, 1995). For the most

part, these songs speak back to racist practices enacted against U.S. Latinos; at the same time, they reproduce problematic notions of masculinity.

40. George Lipsitz, *Dangerous Crossroads: Popular Music, Postmodernism, and the Poetics of Place* (New York: Verso, 1994).

41. De los Angeles Torres, "Transnational Political and Cultural Identities," 178.

42. This sensibility was the subject of Chicano Cultural Production: The Third Wave, a symposium held at UC Irvine, April 15–19, 1999. Examples of third-wave production include *Pretty Vacant,* an independent film by Jim Mendiola, whose Tejana punkera feminista protagonista loves the *Love and Rockets* serial comics, the Sex Pistols, and rock en español; *Black Butterfly, Jaguar Girl, Piñata Woman, and Other Superhero Girls Like Me,* a spoken word/performance piece collaboratively written by Marisela Norte, Alma Cervantes, and Sandra D. Munoz and directed by Luis Alfaro, whose five protagonists, all under the age of sixteen, figure out how to survive as young women in East Los Angeles's bittersweet carnivalesque public culture; and *Graciasland* and *G.I. Ay Ay! Blues,* compact disks by the exceptional cabaret performance art of the Chicano Elvis, El Vez, and his Memphis Mariachis. In their own unique style, each of these addresses questions of citizenship, immigration, acculturation, nation, and gender. I argue in this work that each of these texts uses a playful sensibility to launch a serious critique of social issues; they are seriously playful.

43. For a general historical overview of Chicanos and Chicanas in the United States, see Richard Griswald del Castillo et al., eds., *North to Aztlán: Mexican Americans in the United States* (New York: Twayne, 1996).

44. Diane Taylor, "Transculturing Transculturation," *Performing Arts Journal* 38 (1991): 90–104.

45. Angie Chabram-Dernersesian, "Introduction."

46. See Carmen Rodriguez, *and a body to remember with* (Vancouver: Arsenal Pulp Press, 1997), for a collection of short stories that take place in Vancouver. In "a balanced diet," the narrator prepares for the next *peña*: "at the Ukrainian Hall and Pato and myself will speak . . . in Chile there are more than two thousand desaparecidos disappeared people captured by the secret agents of the dictatorship who never turned up again . . . at this very moment in Chile they are on an indefinite hunger strike until they get an explanation . . . we are showing our solidarity with them and from exile we join them until final victory" (161–162).

47. See David Román, "Latino Performance and Identity," *Aztlán* 22, no. 2 (fall 1997): 151–167; and Jose Muñoz, "No Es Facil: Notes on the Negotiation of Cubanidad and Exilic Memory in Carmelita's Milk of Amnesia," *Drama Review* 39, no. 3 (1997): 77, for more on the relationship among identity, theater, and performance.

Bibliography

Abrams, M. H. *A Glossary of Literary Terms*, 5th ed. San Diego: Harcourt Brace Jovanovich, 1988.

Aguirre, Carmen. *¿Qué Pasa con la Raza, eh?* In *Along Human Lines: Dramas from Refugee Lives*. Winnipeg: Blizzard, 2000.

Alarcón, Norma. "Chicana Feminism: In the Tracks of 'the' Native Woman." *Cultural Studies* 4, no. 3 (1990): 248–255.

———. "Cognitive Desires: An Allegory of/for Chicana Critics." In *Chicana (W)rites on Word and Film*. Ed. Maria Herrera-Sobek and Helena Maria Viramontes. Oakland: Third Woman Press, 1996.

Alfaro, Luis. "Pico-Union." In *Men on Men 4: Best New Gay Fiction*. Ed. George Stambolian. New York: Plume, 1992. 268–283.

———. "Virgin Mary." In *Men on Men 4: Best New Gay Fiction*. Ed. George Stambolian. New York: Plume, 1992. 271–275.

———. "Downtown." In *O Solo Homo: The New Queer Performance*. Ed. Holly Hughes and David Román. New York: Grove Press, 1998. 313–348.

Alfaro, Luis, Marisela Norte, and Chicano Secret Service. *Speaking Experiences: Emerging Chicano Performers*. San Diego: University of California, November 15, 1991.

Almaguer, Tomás. "Chicano Men: A Cartography of Homosexual Identity and Behavior." *Difference* 3, no. 2 (1991): 75–100.

———. *Racial Fault Lines: The Historical Origins of White Supremacy in California*. Berkeley: University of California Press, 1994.

Anaya, Rodolfo. *Bless Me, Ultima*. 1972; reprint, Berkeley, Calif.: Tonatiuh-Quinto Sol International, 1990.

Anzaldúa, Gloria. *Borderlands/La Frontera: The New Mestiza*. San Francisco: Spinsters/Aunt Lute, 1987.

Aparicio, Frances. Tropicalizing Language in the United States." In *Tropicalizations: Transcultural Representations of Latinidad*. Ed. Frances R. Aparicio and Susana Chávez-Silverman. Hanover, N.H.: University Press of New England, 1997. 1–17.

Aparicio, Frances, and Cándida F. Jáquez. *Musical Migrations: Transnationalism and Cultural Hybridity in Latin/o America*. New York: Palgrave, 2003.

Arana, Federico. *Guaraches de Ante Azul: Historia del Rock Mexicano 1.* Mexico City: Editorial Posada, S.A., 1985.

Arrizón, Alicia. "Contemporizing Performance: Mexican California and the Padua Hills Theatre." *Mester* 22, no. 2–23.1 (fall 1993–spring 1994): 5–30.

———. *Latina Performance: Traversing the Stage.* Bloomington: Indiana University Press, 1999.

Arrizon, Alicia, and Lilian Manzor, eds. *Latinas on Stage: In Practice and Theory.* Berkeley: Third Woman Press, 2000.

Bakker, Isabella, ed. *Rethinking Restructuring: Gender and Change in Canada.* Toronto: University of Toronto Press, 1996.

Balderrama, Francisco E., and Raymond Rodríguez. *Decade of Betrayal: Mexican Repatriation in the 1930s.* Albuquerque: University of New Mexico Press, 1995.

Ballve, Marcelo. "Mexican Guest Workers Allege Abuses in Canada." El Norte Digest News Digest. Available at http://www.uslaboragainstwar.org/article.php?id=2309.

Bangs, Lester. *Psychotic Reactions and Carburetor Dung.* New York: Vintage, 1987.

Basok, Tanya. "Migration of Mexican Seasonal Farm Workers to Canada and Development: Obstacles to Productive Investment." *International Migration Review* 34, no. 1 (spring 2000): 79–97.

———. *Tortillas and Tomatoes: Transmigrant Mexican Harvesters in Canada.* Montreal: McGill-Queen's University Press, 2003.

Bass, Holly. "More Ersatz Elvis, and More Royalties for the Newlyweds: El Rey of Rock and Roll Is a Mexican-American; Latest CD Is 'Graciasland.'" *Wall Street Journal Europe,* August 19–20, 1994, 1.

Behar, Ruth. *Translated Woman: Crossing the Border with Esperanza's Story.* Boston: Beacon Press, 1993.

Belnap, Jeffrey, and Raúl Fernández, eds. *José Martí's "Our America": From National to Hemispheric Cultural Studies.* Durham: Duke University Press, 1998.

Blackwell, Maylei. "Contested Histories: Las Hijas de Chuauhtémoc, Chicana Feminisms, and Print Culture in the Chicano Movement, 1968–1973." In *Chicana Feminisms: A Critical Reader.* Ed. Gabriela F. Arredondo, Aida Hurtado, Norma Klahn, Olga Najera-Ramirez, and Patricia Zavella. Durham: Duke University Press, 2003. 59–89.

Boal, Augusto. "Theater of the Oppressed." *Unesco Courier* 50, no. 1 (November 1997): 32–36.

———. *Legislative Theatre: Using Performance to Make Politics.* Trans. Adrian Jackson. New York: Routledge, 1998.

Bolan, Kim. "Phone Tip Led to Arrest of Racists in Temple Killing." *Vancouver Sun,* October 3, 1998, 85.

———. "Racists Attack Three Blacks at Bar." *Vancouver Sun,* June 6, 1998, B1.

———. "Security Tight as Five Face Hearing in Temple Killing." *Vancouver Sun,* October 6, 1998, A5.

Bolton, Herbert E. *The Spanish Borderlands: A Chronicle of Old Florida and the Southwest.* New Haven: Yale University Press, 1921.

Brady, Mary Pat. "The Fungibility of Borders." *Nepantla: Views from South* 1, no. 1 (2000): 181–194.

———. *Extinct Lands, Temporal Geographies: Chicana Culture and the Urgency of Space.* Durham: Duke University Press, 2002.

Breslauer, Jan. "Voice for a Silent Minority: Performance Artist Luis Alfaro Finds Stage Doors Opening for His Provocative Works Meshing Latino and Gay Experiences." *Los Angeles Times,* July 21, 1991, calendar section, 47.

———. "Pretty, Witty, and Mainstream: Lesbian Comedian Marga Gomez Says There Are Signs of Acceptance." *Los Angeles Times,* October 13, 1994, calendar section, 1ff.

———. "U.S., Mexican Artists Draw Connections in 'Danger Zone.'" *Los Angeles Times,* February 8, 1995, sec. F, 1, 8.

Brooks, Daphne. "Burnt Sugar: Post-Soul Satire and Rock Memory." in *This Is Pop: In Search of the Elusive at Experience Music Project.* Ed. Eric Weisbard. Cambridge, Mass.: Harvard University Press, 2004. 103–116.

Broyles-González, Yolanda. *El Teatro Campesino: Theater in the Chicano Movement.* Austin: University of Texas Press, 1994.

Buckley, Christopher, and Gary Young, eds. *The Geography of Home: California's Poetry of Place.* Berkeley: Heyday Books, 1999.

Burnham, Linda. "Viewpoint: Life: The ASCO Version." *High Performance* 8 (August 1985): 66–67.

———. "Marisela Norte." *High Performance* 35 (1986): 56.

Burton, Julianne. "Don (Juanito) Duck and the Imperial-Patriarchal Unconscious: Disney Studios, the Good Neighbor Policy, and the Packaging of Latin America." In *Nationalisms and Sexualities.* Ed. Andrew Parker, Mary Russo, Doris Sommer, and Patricia Yeager. New York: Routledge, 1992. 21–41.

Butler, Judith. "Imitation and Gender Insubordination." In *Inside/Out: Lesbian Theories, Gay Theories.* Ed. Diana Fuss. New York: Routledge, 1991. 13–31.

———. *Bodies That Matter: On the Discursive Limits of "Sex."* New York: Routledge, 1993.

Caban, Pedro. "The New Synthesis of Latin American and Latino Studies." In *U.S. Latinos/Latin American and the Paradox of Interdependence.* Ed. Frank Bonilla et al. Philadelphia: Temple University Press, 1998.

Caglar, Ayse S. "The Prison House of Culture in the Study of Turks in Germany." In series *Sozialanthropologische Arbeitspapiere,* no. 31. Berlin: Das Arabische Buch, 1990.

———. "German Turks in Berlin: Social Exclusion and Strategies for Social Mobility." *New Community* 21, no. 3 (1995): 309–323.

Calderón, Héctor, and José David Saldívar, eds. *Criticism in the Borderlands:*

Studies in Chicano Literature, Culture, and Ideology. Durham: Duke University Press, 1991.

Camacho, Alicia Schmidt. "The Violence of Citizenship: Border Crossing and Cultural Conflict in Marisela Norte's El Paso." In *Steel and Glass: Latin American Women Write the City.* Ed. Anne Lambright and Elisabeth Guerrero. Forthcoming.

Canada. Statistics Canada. *Ethnocultural Portrait of Canada, 2001 Census.* November 6, 2003.

Cantú. Lionel. "Entre Hombres/Between Men: Latino Masculinities and Homosexualities." In *Gay Masculinities.* Ed. Peter M. Nardi. Thousand Oaks: Sage, 2000.

———. "A Place Called Home: A Queer Political Economy of Mexican Immigrant Men's Family Experiences." In *Queer Families, Queer Politics: Challenging Culture and the State.* Ed. Mary Bernstein and Renate Reimann. New York: Columbia University Press, 2001.

———. "De Ambiente: Queer Tourism and the Shifting Boundaries of Mexican Male Sexualities." *GLQ: A Journal of Lesbian and Gay Studies* 8 (2002): 139–166.

Carrillo, Sean. "East to Eden." In *Forming: The Early Days of L.A. Punk.* Ed. Sean Carrillo, Christine McKenna, Claude Bessy, and Exene Cervenka. Santa Monica: Smart Art Press, 1999. 42.

Case, Sue-Ellen. *Performing Feminisms: Feminist Critical Theory and Theater.* Baltimore: Johns Hopkins University Press, 1990.

Case, Sue-Ellen, Philip Brett, and Susan Leigh Foster. *Cruising the Performative: Interventions into the Representation of Ethnicity, Nationality, and Sexuality.* Bloomington: Indiana University Press, 1995.

Cepeda, Maria Elena. "Shakira as the Idealized, Transnational Citizen: A Case Study of Colombianidad in Transition." *Latino Studies* 1, no. 2 (July 2003): 211–357.

Chabram-Dernersesian, Angie. "I Throw Punches for My Race, But I Don't Want to Be a Man: Writing Us—Chica-nos (Girl, Us)/Chicanas—into the Movement Script." In *Cultural Studies.* Ed. Lawrence Grossberg, Cary Nelson, and Paula Treichler. New York: Routledge, 1992. 81–95.

———. "'Chicana! Rican? No, Chicana-Riqueña!': Refashioning the Transnational Connection." In *Multiculturalism: A Critical Reader.* Ed. David Theo Goldberg. Cambridge, Mass.: Blackwell, 1995.

———. "Chicana/o Latina/o Cultural Studies: Transnational and Transdisciplinary Movements." *Cultural Studies* 13, no. 2 (1999): 183–194.

———. "Latina/o: Another Site of Struggle, Another Site of Accountability." In *Critical Latin American and Latino Studies.* Ed. Juan Poblete. Minneapolis: University of Minnesota, 2003. 105–137.

Chadwick, Vernon, ed. *In Search of Elvis: Music, Race, Art, Religion.* Boulder, Colo.: Westview Press, 1997.

Champane, Lenora, ed. *Out from Under: Texts by Women Performance Artists.* New York: Theater Communications Group, 1990.

Chapa, Evey. "Mujeres por La Raza Unida." In *Chicana Feminist Thought.* Ed. Alma Garcia. New York: Routledge, 1997.

Charles M. Tatum. *Chicano Popular Culture: Que Hable el Pueblo.* Tucson: University of Arizona Press, 2001.

Chavoya, Ondine C. "Pseudographic Cinema: ASCO's No-Movies." In *Performance Research*, special issue, "On America," edited by Nick Kaye, 3, no. 1 (1998): 1–14.

———. "Asco: Internal Exiles: The Interventionist Public and Performance Art of Asco." In *Space, Site, and Intervention: Situating Installation Art.* Ed. Erika Suderburg. Minneapolis: University of Minnesota Press, 2000. 189–208.

———. "Orphans of Modernism: The Performance Art of Asco." In *Corpus Delecti: Performance Art of the Americas.* Ed. Coco Fusco. New York: Routledge, 2000. 240–263.

Cisneros Morales, Jorge. "El Performance como Crónica Social." *El Nacional* [Mexico City], February 17, 1995, sec. Cultura, 32.

Covarrubias, Teresa. Personal e-mail to Michelle Habell-Pallán. February 24, 2003. Bio for Chicana Punk Aesthetic Conference.

Cowell, Alan. "Turks Seek Acceptance of Culture in Germany." *New York Times* (international edition), December 14, 1995, A6.

Cruz, Adam. "Latin Lookers." *Elle* (November 1988): 38–45.

Culbert, Lori. "Squamish Youths Say They're Not Thugs." *Vancouver Sun*, June 6, 1998, B1.

Damon, Maria. "Unmeaning Jargon." *South Atlantic Quarterly* (fall 1988): 708–709.

Dávila, Arlene. *Latinos, Inc.: The Marketing and Making of a People.* Berkeley: University of California Press, 2001.

Davis, Mike. *City of Quartz: Excavating the Future in Los Angeles.* New York: Vintage Books, 1992.

de la Mora, Sergio. "Fascinating Machismo: Toward an Unmasking of Heterosexual Masculinity in Arturo Ripstein's *El Lugar Sin Límites.*" *Journal of Film and Video* 44, no. 3–4 (fall–winter 1992–1993): 83–104.

———. *Virile Nationalism: Masculinity and Sexuality in Mexican Cinema.* Austin: University of Texas Press, in press.

De Lauretis, Teresa. *Feminist Studies/Critical Studies.* Bloomington: Indiana University Press, 1986.

———. *Technologies of Gender: Essays on Theory, Film, and Fiction.* Bloomington: Indiana University Press, 1987.

de los Angeles Torres, María. "Transnational Political and Cultural Identities: Crossing Theoretical Borders." In *U.S. Latinos/Latin American and the Paradox of Interdependence.* Ed. Frank Bonilla et al. Philadelphia: Temple University Press, 1998.

del Castillo, Richard Griswald, et al., eds. *North to Aztlán: Mexican Americans in the United States.* New York: Twayne, 1996.

DeMara, Bruce. "Subway Poster Spurs Call for Hate Crimes Probe." *Toronto Star,* June 16, 1999, ed. 1, news section.

Dent, Gina, ed. "Dialectically Down with the Critical Program." *Black Popular Culture.* Seattle: Bay Press, 1992. 48.

Deuel, Pauline B. *Mexican Serenade: The Story of the Mexican Players and the Padua Hills Theatre.* Claremont, Calif.: Padua Institute, 1961.

Dever, Susan. *Celluloid Nationalism and Other Melodramas: From Post-Revolutionary Mexico to Fin de Siglo Mexamerica.* Albany: State University of New York Press, 2003.

Dias Barerro, Gloria Patricia. "Migrant Latina Exotic Dancers and the Complicity of the Canadian State." Paper presented at the Annual American Studies Association Conference. Hartford, Conn., October 16, 2003.

Dolan, Jill. "Geographies of Learning: Theater Studies, Performance, and the 'Performative.'" *Theater Journal* 45 (1993): 417–441.

Durland, Steven, and Linda Burnham. "Art with a Chicano Accent: An Interview with Denise Lugo-Saavedra on the History of Chicano Art in Los Angeles." *High Performance* 35 (1986): 41ff.

Easthope, Anthony. *Literary into Cultural Studies.* New York: Routledge, 1991.

Ehrenberg, Felipe. "Territorios Harto Peligrosos." *La Opinion* [Los Angeles], February 3, 1995, sec. E, 9.

Espinoza, Dionne. "'Tanto Tiempo Disfrutamos . . .': Revisiting the Gender and Sexual Politics of Chicana/o Youth Culture in East Los Angeles in the 1960s." In *Velvet Barrios: Popular Culture and Chicana/o Sexualities.* Ed. Alicia Gaspar de Alba. New York: Palgrave Macmillan Press, 2003. 89–106.

Faist, Thomas. "From School to Work: Public Policy and Underclass Formation among Young Turks in Germany during the 1980s." *International Migration Review* 27, no. 2 (1993): 306–331.

Faist, Thomas, and Hartmut Haubermann. "Immigration, Social Citizenship and Housing in Germany." *International Journal of Urban and Regional Research* 20, no. 1 (1996): 83–98.

Fanon, Frantz. *The Wretched of the Earth.* 1961; reprint, New York: Grove Press, 1968.

Fix, Michael, and Jeffrey S. Passel. *Immigration and Immigrants: Setting the Record Straight.* Washington, D.C.: Urban Institute, 1994.

Flores, Juan. "The Latino Imaginary: Dimensions of Community and identity." In *Tropicalizations: Transcultural Representations of* Latinidad. Ed. Frances

Aparicio and Susana Chávez-Silverman. Hanover, N.H.: University Press of New England, 1997. 1–17.

Flores, Juan, and George Yúdice. "Living Borders/Buscando America: Languages of Latino Self-Formation." *Social Text* 8, no. 2 (1990): 57–84.

Flores, Lauro. "Introduction." In *The Floating Borderlands: Twenty-five Years of U.S. Hispanic Literature.* Ed. Lauro Flores. Seattle: University of Washington Press, 1998. 3–11.

Foley, Neil. Review of *The Spanish Redemption: Heritage, Power, and Loss on New Mexico's Upper Rio Grande,* by Charles Montgomery. In *American Historical Review* 108 (October 2003): 1156.

Foster, David William, ed. *Chicano/Latina Homoerotic Identities.* New York: Garland, 1999.

Foster, Sesshu. "From Logan to the Mission: North through Chicano Literary History with Juan Felipe Herrera." *Americas Review* 17 (fall/winter 1989): 68–87.

———. "The Spine of Califas." Latino L.A. web magazine, www.latinola.com/ story.phy?story=845, accessed March 20, 2003.

Foucault, Michel. "Of Other Places." *Diacritics* 16 (spring 1986): 22–27.

Fox, Claire F. *The Fence and the River: Culture and Politics at the U.S.-Mexico Border.* Minneapolis: University of Minnesota Press, 1999.

Franco, Jean. "*La Malinche*: From Gift to Sexual Contract." Chapter in *Critical Passions: Selected Essays.* Ed. and with an introduction by Mary Louise Pratt and Kathleen Newman. Durham: Duke University Press, 1999. 66–82.

Fregoso, Rosa Linda. *The Bronze Screen: Chicana and Chicano Film Culture.* Minneapolis: University of Minnesota Press, 1993.

———. "Chicano Film Practices: Confronting the 'Many-Headed Demon of Oppression.'" In *Chicana (W)rites on Word and Film.* Ed. Maria Herrera-Sobek and Helena Maria Viramontes. Oakland: Third Woman Press, 1996. 259–273.

Fusco, Coco. *English Is Broken Here: Notes on Cultural Fusion in the Americas.* New York: New Press, 1995.

———, ed. *Corpus Delecti: Performance Art of the Americas.* New York: Routledge, 2000.

Fuss, Diana, ed. "Imitation and Gender Insubordination." In *Inside/Out: Lesbian Theories, Gay Theories.* New York: Routledge, 1991.

Gamboa, Erasmo. *Mexican Labor and World War II: Braceros in the Pacific Northwest, 1942–1947.* Austin: University of Texas Press, 1990.

Gamboa, Harry, Jr. "Marisela Norte." *La Opinión* [Los Angeles], October 17, 1982, sec. La Comunidad, 10–11.

———. "ASCO." *Imagine: International Chicano Poets Journal* (summer/winter 1986): 64–66.

García, Mario. "A Chicano Perspective on San Diego History." *Journal of San Diego History* 18 (fall 1972): 14–21.

García, Matt. "'Just Put On That Padua Hills Smile': The Mexican Players and the Padua Hills Theatre, 1931–1974." *California History* 74 (fall 1995): 245–261.

———. *A World of Its Own: Race, Labor, and Citrus in the Making of Greater Los Angeles, 1900–1970.* Chapel Hill: University of North Carolina Press, 2001.

García-Canclini, Néstor. "Latins or Americans: Narratives of the Border." *Canadian Journal of Latin American and Caribbean Studies* 23, no. 46 (1998): 117–113.

Gaspar de Alba, Alicia. *Chicano Art Inside/Outside the Master's House: Cultural Politics and Cara Exhibition.* Austin: University of Texas, 1998.

Gendron, Bernard. *Between Montmartre and the Mudd Club: Popular Music and the Avant-Garde.* Chicago: University of Chicago Press, 2002.

George-Warren, Holly. "New Faces." *Rolling Stone,* May 13, 1993, 27.

Gilroy, Paul. *"There Ain't No Black in the Union Jack": The Cultural Politics of Race and Nation.* 1987; reprint, Chicago: University of Chicago Press, 1991.

———. *The Black Atlantic: Modernity and Double Consciousness.* Cambridge, Mass.: Harvard University Press, 1993.

———. "Diaspora Crossings: Intercultural and Transnational Identities in the Black Atlantic." In *Negotiating Identities: Essays on Immigration and Culture in Present-Day Europe.* Ed. Aleksandra Ålund and Raoul Granqvist. Amsterdam: Rodopi, 1995. 105–130.

Gledhill, Christine. "Klute 1: A Contemporary Film Noir and Feminist Criticism." In *Women in Film Noir.* Ed E. Ann Kaplan. London: BFI, 1994.

Goldberg, RoseLee. *Performance Art: From Futurism to the Present.* 1979; reprint, New York: Henry Abrams, 1988.

Goldman, Shifra. "Performances in the Danger Zones I." *Art Nexus.* April–June 1996, 62–66.

———. "Performances in the Danger Zones II." *Art Nexus.* July–September 1996, 52–56.

Gomez, Marga. "La Fabulosa." *Intercambios: A Publication of the National Network of Hispanic Women* 5, no. 1 (winter 1990): 14.

Gómez-Peña, Guillermo. "A New Artistic Continent." *High Performance* 35 (1986): 24ff.

———. "The Multicultural Paradigm: An Open Letter to the National Arts Community." *High Performance* (fall 1989): 18–27.

———. "Terreno Peligroso (Las Relaciones entre Chicanos y Chilangos)." *La Opinión,* February 3, 1995, sec. E, 7ff.

———. "Documented/Undocumented." In *The Graywolf Annual Five: Multicultural Literacy.* Ed. Rick Simonson and Scott Walker. St. Paul, Minn.: Graywolf Press, 1988. 129.

———. "Terreno Peligroso." *Reforma* [Mexico City], February 18, 1995, sec. Gente!, 12ff.

———. "1995—*Terreno peligroso*/Danger Zone: Cultural Relations between Chicanos and Mexicans at the End of the Century." In *Borderless Borders: U.S. Latinos, Latin Americans, and the Paradox of Interdependence*. Ed. Frank Bonilla, Edwin Meléndez, Rebecca Morales, and Maria de los Angeles Torres. Philadelphia: Temple University Press, 1998.

González, Jennifer, and Michelle Habell-Pallán. "Heterotopias: Navigating Social Spaces and Spaces of Identity." *Inscriptions* 7 (1994): 80–104.

Gopinath, Gayatri. *Impossible Desires: Queer Diasporas and South Asian Public Cultures*. Durham: Duke University Press, 2005.

Gray, Herman. *Watching Race: Television and the Struggle for Blackness*. Minneapolis: University of Minnesota Press, 1995.

Grossberg, Lawrence. *We Gotta Get Out of This Place: Popular Conservatism and Postmodern Culture*. New York: Routledge, 1992. 18.

Gutiérrez, David G. "*Sin Fronteras*? Chicanos, Mexican-Americans and the Emergence of the Contemporary Mexican Immigration Debate, 1968–1978." *Journal of American Ethnic History* 10, no. 4 (1991): 6–37.

———. *Walls and Mirrors: Mexican Americans, Mexican Immigrants, and the Politics of Ethnicity*. Berkeley: University of California Press, 1995.

Gutiérrez, Ramón A. "Community, Patriarchy, and Individualism: The Politics of Chicano History and the Dream of Equality." *American Quarterly* 45, no. 1 (1993): 44–72.

Gutiérrez-Jones, Carl. *Rethinking the Borderlands: Between Chicano Culture and Legal Discourse*. Berkeley: University of California Press, 1995.

———. "Humor, Literacy and Trauma in Chicano Culture." *Comparative Literature Studies* 40, no. 2 (2003): 112–126.

Haas, Lisbeth. *Conquests and Historical Identities in California, 1769–1936*. Berkeley: University of California Press, 1995.

Habell-Pallán, Michelle. "Family and Sexuality in Recent Chicano Performance: Luis Alfaro's Memory Plays." *Ollantáy Theater Journal* 4, no. 1 (January 1996): 33–42.

———. "El Vez Is Taking Care of Business." *Cultural Studies* 13, no. 2 (1999): 195–210.

———. "Marisela Norte, NORTE/word." In *Reading U.S. Latino Writers: Remapping American Literature*. Ed. Alivana E. Quintana. New York: Palgrave Macmillan, 2003. 163–172.

Halberstam, Judith. *Female Masculinity*. Durham: Duke University Press, 1998.

Hall, Stuart. "Notes on Deconstructing the 'Popular.'" In *People's History and Socialist Theory*. Ed. R. Samuel. New York: Routledge and Kegan Paul, 1981. 227–239.

———. "New Ethnicities." *ICA Documents* 7 (1989): 27–31.

Hammerman (no last name). "State of Language." In *Shattersheet*, no. 17 (February 1987): 9.

Haraway, Donna. *Simians, Cyborgs, and Women*. London: Free Association Books, 1991.

Hart, Lynda, ed. *Making a Spectacle: Feminist Essays on Contemporary Women's Theater*. Ann Arbor: University of Michigan Press, 1989.

Hart, Lynda, and Peggy Phelan, eds. *Acting Out: Feminist Performances*. Ann Arbor: University of Michigan Press, 1993.

Hebdige, Dick. *Subculture: The Meaning of Style*. New York: Routledge, 1979.

———. *Cut 'n' Mix: Culture, Identity and Caribbean Music*. New York: Methuen, 1987.

Hernandez, Deborah Pacini, Héctor Fernández L'Hoeste, and Eric Zolov, eds. *Rockin' Las Americas: The Global Politics of Rock in Latin/o America*. Pittsburgh: University of Pittsburgh Press, 2004.

Hernandez, Jaime, and Gilbert Hernandez. *Love and Rockets Sketchbook: Los Bros. Hernandez*. Seattle: Fantagraphic Books, 1989.

Herrera-Sobek, María. *The Mexican Corrido: A Feminist Analysis*. Bloomington: Indiana University Press, 1990.

Herrera-Sobek, Maria, and David Maciel, eds. *Culture across Borders: Mexican Immigration and Popular Culture*. Tucson: University of Arizona Press, 1998.

Heyd, Thomas. "Understanding Performance Art: Art beyond Art." *British Journal of Aesthetics* 31 (1991): 68–73.

Hicks, D. Emily. "The Artist as Citizen." *High Performance* 35 (1986): 34–38.

———. *Border Writing: The Multidimensional Text*. Minneapolis: University of Minnesota Press, 1991.

Hondagneu-Sotelo, Pierrette. "Women and Children First: New Directions in Anti-Immigrant Politics." *Socialist Review* 25 (1995): 169–190.

———. "The History of Mexican Undocumented Settlement in the United States." In *Challenging Fronteras: Structuring Latina and Latino Lives in the U.S.* Ed. Mary Romero et al. New York: Routledge, 1996.

hooks, bell. *Talking Back: Thinking Feminist, Thinking Black*. Boston: South End Press, 1989.

———. "Dialectically Down with the Critical Program." In *Black Popular Culture*. Ed. Gina Dent. Seattle: Bay Press, 1992. 48–55.

Huaco-Nuzum, Carmen. "(Re)constructing Chicana, Mestiza Representation: Frances Salomé España's *Spitfire*." In *The Ethnic Eye: Latino Media Arts*. Ed. Chon Noriega and Ana Lopez. Minneapolis: University of Minnesota Press, 1996.

Huerta, Jorge A. *Chicano Theater: Themes and Forms*. Ypsilanti, Mich.: Bilingual Press/Editorial Bilingüe, 1982.

———. *Chicano Drama: Performance, Society, Myth*. New York: Cambridge University Press, 2000.

Jackson, Helen Hunt. *Ramona: A Story.* 1884; reprint, New York: Avon, 1970.

James, David E. "Poetry/Punk/Production: Some Recent Writing in LA." In *Post-modernism and Its Discontents: Theories, Practices.* Ed. E. Ann Kaplan. London: Verso, 1988. 171.

Jenkins, Jolyon. "Taken to the Cleaners: Germany Has Its Turks, Kuwait Has the Filipinos, and the British Have Their Nigerians." *New Statesman and Society* (29 December 1989): 10–11.

Johnson, Kevin R. "'Aliens' and the U.S. Immigration Laws: The Social and Legal Construction of Nonpersons." *Miami Inter-American Law Review,* 28, no. 2 (1996–1997): 263–287.

Jones, David. *Destroy All Music: Pioneers of Punk Rock in Southern California.* Berkeley: University of California Press, in press.

Jordon, Glenn, and Chris Weedon. *Cultural Politics: Class, Gender, Race, and the Postmodern World.* Cambridge: Blackwell, 1995.

Kanellos, Nicolás, ed. *Hispanic Theater in the United States.* Houston, Texas: Arte Publico Press, 1984.

———. *Mexican American Theater: Legacy and Reality.* Pittsburg: Latin American Literary Review Press, 1987.

———. *A History of Hispanic Theater in the United States: Origins to 1940.* Austin: University of Texas Press, 1990.

———. *The Hispanic Almanac: From Columbus to Corporate America.* Detroit: Visible Ink Press, 1994.

Kaplan, Caren. *Questions of Travel: Postmodern Discourses of Displacement.* Durham: Duke University Press, 1996.

Kaya, Ayhan. "Construction of Diasporic Cultural Identity: Berlin Turks and Hip-Hop Youth Culture." Unpublished manuscript, 1997.

Kelly, Karen. "Visible Minorities: A Diverse Group." *Social Science Trends* (summer 1995): 2–8.

Kosiba-Vargas, S. Zaneta. *Harry Gamboa and ASCO: The Emergence and Development of a Chicano Art Group.* Ph.D. diss., University of Michigan, 1988.

Laing, Dave. *One Chord Wonders: Power and Meaning in Punk Rock.* Philadelphia: Open University Press, 1985.

la Torre, Adela de, and Beatríz M. Pesquera, eds. *Building with Our Hands: New Directions in Chicana Studies.* Berkeley: University of California Press, 1993.

Limerick, Patricia Nelson. *The Legacy of Conquest: The Unbroken Past of the American West.* New York: Norton, 1987.

Limón, José. *Dancing with the Devil: Society and Cultural Poetics in Mexican-American South Texas.* Madison: University of Wisconsin Press, 1994.

Lipsitz, George. *Time Passages: Collective Memory and American Popular Culture.* Minneapolis: University of Minnesota Press, 1990.

———. "*Con Safos*: Can Cultural Studies Read the Writing on the Wall?" Unpublished essay, December 1991.

———. *Dangerous Crossroads: Popular Music, Postmodernism, and the Poetics of Place*. New York: Verso, 1994.

———. "We Know What Time It Is: Race, Class, and Youth Culture in the Nineties." In *Microphone Fiends: Youth Music and Youth Culture*. Ed. Andrew Ross and Tricia Rose. New York: Routledge, 1994. 17–28.

———. *American Studies in a Moment of Danger*. Minneapolis: University of Minnesota Press, 2001.

Lopez, Tiffany. *The Alchemy of Blood: Violence as Critical Discourse in U.S. Latina/o Literature*. Durham: Duke University Press, in press.

Lott, Eric. "All the King's Men: Elvis Impersonators and White Working-Class Masculinity." In *Race and the Subject of Masculinities*. Ed. Harry Stecopoulos and Michael Uebel. Durham: Duke University press, 1997. 192–227.

Lowe, Lisa. *Immigrant Acts: On Asian American Cultural Politics*. Durham: Duke University Press, 1996.

Loza, Steven. *Barrio Rhythm: Mexican American Music in Los Angeles*. Urbana: University of Illinois Press, 1993.

Lysa Flores Official Website. "Biography." http://www.lysaflorres.com/bio.html (accessed July 16, 2004).

Maceda, Elda. "Artistas Mexicanos y Chicanos Pisan 'Terrenos Peligroso.'" *El Universal* (Mexico City), January 28, 1995, n.p.

MacKenzie, Arch. "Central Americans Pour into Canada Seeking New Homes. *Toronto Star*, January 15, 1987, A1.

———. "U.S. Crackdown Boosts Exodus to Canada." *Toronto Star*, January 15, 1987, A1, CP.

Mandel, Ruth. "Foreigners in the Fatherland: Turkish Immigrant Workers in Germany." In *The Politics of Immigrant Workers: Labor Activism and Migration in the World Economy Since 1830*. Ed. Camille Guerin-Gonzalez and Carl Strikwerda. New York: Holmes and Meier, 1993.

Marcus, Greil. *Lipstick Traces: A Secret History of the Twentieth Century*. Cambridge, Mass.: Harvard University Press, 1989.

Marez, Curtis. "Becoming Brown: The Politics of Chicana/o Popular Style." *Social Text* 48 (1996): 109–132.

Mariscal, George, ed., *Aztlán and Viet Nam: Chicano and Chicana Experiences of the War*. Berkeley: University of California Press, 1999.

Mariscal, Jorge. "Can Cultural Studies Speak Spanish?" In *English Studies, Cultural Studies: Institutionalizing Dissent*. Ed. Isaiah Smithson. Urbana: University of Illinois Press, 1994. 1–24.

———. "Latinos on the Frontlines: Again." *Latino Studies* 1 (July 2003): 347–351.

———. "Mexican-American Women in Iraq: Las Adelitas 2003." *Counterpunch*, November 14, 2003. http://www.counterpunch.org/mariscal111420 03.html.

Marranca, Bonnie, Marc Robinson, and Una Chaudhuri. "Criticism, Culture, and Performance: An Interview with Edward Said." *Performing Arts Journal* 37 (1991): 21–42.

Marrero, M. Teresa. "Out of the Fringe: Desire and Homosexuality in the '90s Latino Theatre." In *Velvet Barrios: Popular Culture and Chicana/o Sexualities.* Ed. Alicia Gaspar de Alba. New York: Palgrave Macmillan, 2003. 283–294.

Marsh, Dave. "Looney Tunes." *Creem,* May 1971, 42–43.

———. *The Heart of Rock and Soul: The 1001 Greatest Singles Ever Made.* New York: Da Capo Press, 1999.

Martínez, Elizabeth. "A Call for *Chicanisma.*" *CrossRoads* (29 March 1993): 6.

Martínez, Rubén. "East Side, West Side: Taking the Best from a Childhood of Spanish, Prayers, and Rock 'n' Roll." *Los Angeles Times Sunday Magazine,* May 3, 1992, 12.

———. *The Other Side: Notes from the New L.A., Mexico City, and Beyond.* New York: Vintage Books, 1993.

———. *Diva L.A.: A Salute to L.A.'s Latinas in the Tanda Style.* Program notes. Los Angeles. July 2, 1995.

———. "El Terreno Peligroso en Que Vivimos." *La Opinión* [Los Angeles], February 3, 1995, sec. E, p. 15.

———. "El Evangelio Según San Lucas." *Reforma* [Mexico City], February 18, 1995, sec. Gente!, 12ff.

McConachie, Bruce, and Daniel Friedman, eds. *Theater for Working-Class Audiences in the United States, 1830–1980.* Westport, Conn.: Greenwood Press, 1985.

McDowell, Linda. *Gender, Identity, and Place: Understanding Feminist Geographies.* Minneapolis: University of Minnesota Press, 1999.

McKenna, Kristine. "Female Rockers—A New Breed." *Los Angeles Times,* June 18, 1978, calendar section, 78–82.

McKenna, Teresa. *Migrant Song: Politics and Process in Contemporary Chicano Literature.* Austin: University of Texas Press, 1997.

McKenna, Teresa, Richard Griswold del Castillo, Richard Chabram, and Yvonne Yarbro-Bejarano, eds. *Chicano Art: Resistance and Affirmation, 1965–1985.* Los Angeles: Wight Gallery, University of California, Los Angeles, 1991.

McRobbie, Angela, ed. *Zoot Suits and Second-Hand Dresses: An Anthology of Fashion and Music.* Boston: Unwin Hyman, 1988.

McWilliams, Carey. *North from Mexico: The Spanish-Speaking People of the United States.* 1948. New York: Greenwood Press, 1968.

———. *Southern California: An Island on the Land.* 1946; reprint, Salt Lake City: Peregrine Smith Books, 1973.

Meier, Ellen Bick, and Birgit Jeng, prod. Program notes. "L.A.'s Metropolitanas."

By Marisela Norte. Perf. Marisela Norte. *Hispanics in the USA*. Udgvet al Danmarks Radio for Undervisnings-ministenet, Denmark. 1984, p. 17.

Mendiola, Jim. Public lecture, University of California at Santa Barbara, January 22, 2003.

———. E-mail correspondence with author, December 18, 2003.

Miflin, Margot. "Performance Art: What Is It and Where Is It Going?" *Artnews* (April 1992): 84–89.

Millet, Kate. *Sexual Politics*. 1970; reprint, New York: Simon and Schuster, 1990.

Miranda, Marie (Keta). "'The East Side Revue, 40 Hits by East Los Angeles' Most Popular Groups!': The Boys in the Band and the Girls Who Were Their Fans." In *Beyond the Frame: Photography and Women of Color*. Ed. Angela Y. Davis and Neferti Tadiar. New York: Palgrave, in press.

Mitchell, Tony. "Performance and the Postmodern in Pop Music." *Theater Journal* 41 (October 1989): 273–293.

Monroy, Douglas. *Thrown among Strangers: The Making of Mexican Culture in Frontier California*. Berkeley: University of California Press, 1990.

———. "The New Face of America." *Time* (special issue) (fall 1993): 56ff.

Morales, Ed. *The Latin Beat: The Rhythms and Roots of Latin Music from Bossa Nova to Salsa and Beyond*. Boston: Da Capo Press, 2003.

Muñoz, Jose. "No Es Facil: Notes on the Negotiation of Cubanidad and Exilic Memory in Carmelita's Milk of Amnesia." *Drama Review* 39, no. 3 (1997): 77–90.

———. *Disidentifications: Queers of Color and the Performance of Politics*. Minneapolis: University of Minnesota Press, 1999.

Negrón-Muntaner, Frances. *Boricua Pop: Puerto Ricans and American Culture from West Side Story to Jennifer Lopez*. New York: New York University Press, 2004.

Negus, Keith. *Popular Music in Theory: An Introduction*. Hanover, N.H.: University Press of New England, 1997.

Nericcio, William A. "A Decidedly 'Mexican' and 'American' Semi[er]otic Transference: Frida Kahlo in the Eyes of Gilbert Hernandez." In *Latino/a Popular Culture*. Ed. Michelle Habell-Pallán and Mary Romero. New York: New York University Press, 2002.

Newton, Lina Y. "Why Some Latinos Supported Proposition 187: Testing Economic Threat and Cultural Identity Hypothesis." *Social Science Quarterly* 81, no. 1 (March 2000): 180–193.

Noriega, Chon A. *The Future of Latino Independent Media: A NALIP Sourcebook*. Los Angeles: UCLA Chicano Studies Research Center Publications, 2000.

———. *Just Another Poster? Chicano Graphic Arts in California*. Santa Barbara: Regents of the University of California Art Museum, 2001.

Noriega, Chon, and Ana M. Lopez, eds. *The Ethnic Eye: Latino Media Arts.* Minneapolis: University of Minnesota, 1996.

Norte, Marisela. "Pictures." *Milestone Magazine* (1978): 31.

———. "june 24th." *Milestone Magazine* (1978): 21.

———. "Each Street/Each Story." In *201: Homenaje a la Ciudad de Los Angeles: Latino Experience in Literature and Art.* Ed. Helena Viramontes Velóz. Los Angeles: Los Angeles Writers Association/Self Help Graphics and Art, 1982. 57.

———. "Salmo Para: Ella." *Corazón de Aztlán* (March–April 1982): 8–9.

———. "Harry Gamboa Jr.: No-Movie Maker." *Revista El Tecolote Literaria/El Tecolote Literary Magazine* 4.2 (1983): 3, 12.

———. "La Bruja y La Señorita." *Electrum* (summer 1983): 30–32.

———. "L.A.'s Metropolitanas." *Revista El Tecolote Literaria/El Tecolote Literary Magazine* 4.2 (1983): 7.

———. "Peeping Tom Tom Girl." *Revista El Tecolote Literaria/El Tecolote Literary Magazine* 4.2 (1983): 9. Available in the Harry Gamboa, Jr., Papers, 1965–1995, Department of Special Collections and University Archives, Stanford University.

———. "Se habla inglés." *Raras Avis: Southern California Women Writers* 6–7 (1983): 89–93.

———. *Exito,* in *Spectacle: A Field Journal from Los Angeles,* no. 1 (1984): 18–21.

———. "El Club Sufrimiento 2000." *Rattler: American Poetry and Art* (1987): 37–42.

———. "Soy: la que nunca nació." In *Akrilica.* Ed. Juan Felipe Herrera. Santa Cruz: Alcatraz Editions, 1989. 65.

———. "Dolores Fuertes." *Alchemy* 1 (1992): 14–16.

———. "Wind cries mari." *Alchemy* 1 (1992): 32–33.

———. "Misfortune in Woman's Eyes." *untitled: a literary art journal* 2, no. 1 (1993): 29–32.

———. "Shelf Life." *Caffeine* 1, no. 2 (1993): 23–26.

———. "976-LOCA." In *Recent Chicano Poetry/Neueste Chicano-Lyrick.* Ed. Heiner Bus and Ana Castillo. Bamberg, Germany: Bamberger Editionen, 1994. 15–30.

———. Public lecture, Arte y Cultura Lecture Series and Exhibit, Carnegie Art Museum, Oxnard, California, October 17, 2002.

The Official Alice Bag Website. "Biography." http://alicebag.com/bio.html (accessed July 16, 2004).

———. "Violence Girl." http://alicebag.com/violencegirl.html (accessed July 16, 2004).

Omi, Michael, and Howard Winant. *Racial Formation in the United States: From the 1960s to the 1980s.* New York: Routledge, 1986.

Ouston, Ricke, and Marina Jimenez. "Latinos Still Haunted by Ghosts of War." *Vancouver Sun,* February 23, 1998, A1.

Pacini Hernandez, Deborah, Héctor Fernández L'Hoeste, and Eric Zolov, eds. *Rockin' Las Americas: The Global Politics of Rock in Latin/o America.* Pittsburgh: University of Pittsburgh Press, 2004.

Padilla, Genáro. *"My History, Not Yours": The Formation of Mexican American Autobiography.* Madison: University of Wisconsin, 1993.

Paredes, Américo. *"With His Pistol in His Hand": A Border Ballad and Its Hero.* Austin: University of Texas Press, 1958.

———. *Folklore and Culture on the Texas-Mexican Border.* Ed. Richard Bauman. Austin: Center for Mexican American Studies, University of Texas at Austin, 1993.

Paredes, Raymond. "The Origins of Anti-Mexican Sentiment in the United States." *New Scholar* 6 (1974): 139–165.

Parker, C. "Spoken Word: Hollywood Babylon." *Wire* 121 (March 1994): 24.

Pastor, Manuel, Jr. "Interdependence, Inequality, and Identity: Linking Latinos and Latin Americans." In *U.S. Latinos/Latin American and the Paradox of Interdependence.* Ed. Frank Bonilla et al. Philadelphia: Temple University Press, 1998. 18.

Peña, Manuel. *The Texas-Mexican Conjunto: History of a Working-Class Music.* Austin: University of Texas Press, 1985.

Pérez, Laura. "Spirit Glyphs: Reimagining Art and Artist in the Work of Chicana Tlamatinime." In *Modern Fiction Studies* 44, no. 1 (1998): 36–76.

Pérez-Torres, Rafael. *Movements in Chicano Poetry: Against Myths, Against Margins.* New York: Cambridge University Press, 1995.

Perkins, Kathy A., and Roberta Uno, eds. *Contemporary Plays by Women of Color: An Anthology.* New York: Routledge, 1996.

Perron, Sylvie. "Banished between Two Worlds: Exiles in Canadian Literature." In *The Reordering of Culture: Latin America, The Caribbean, and Canada in the Hood.* Ed. Alvina Ruprecht and Cecilia Taiana. Ottawa: Carleton University Press, 1995.

Pettit, A. C. *The Image of Mexican-Americans in Fiction and Film.* College Station: Texas A and M University Press, 1980.

Phillips, Andrew. "The Gates Slam Shut." *Maclean's,* June 14, 1993, 18–22.

Pitt, Leonard. *The Decline of the Californios: A Social History of the Spanish-Speaking Californians, 1846–1890.* Berkeley: University of California Press, 1966.

Price, Niko. "Border Crackdown Has Netted Snarls, But Not Terrorists." *Seattle Times,* November 3, 2003, A10.

Prieto, Antonio. "Incorporated Identities: The Subversion of Stigma in the Performance Art of Luis Alfaro." In *Chicano/Latino Homoerotic Identities.* Ed. David William Foster. New York: Garland, 1999. 147–157.

Prieto-Stambaugh, Antonio. "La Actuación de la Identidad a Traves del Performance Chicano Gay." *Debate Feminista* 7, no. 13 (1996): 285–315.

Pritchard, Démian. "Policing the Border: Politics and Place in the Work of Miguel Méndez, Marisela Norte, and Leslie Marmon Silko." Ph.D. diss., University of California, San Diego, 2003.

Rabinowitz, Paula. *Black and White and Noir: America's Pulp Modernism.* New York: Columbia University Press, 2002.

Ramírez, Catherine. "Crimes of Fashion: The Pachuca and Chicana Style Politics." *Meridians: A Journal of Transnational Feminisms* 2, no. 2 (2002): 1–35.

Ramírez, Josephine. "Nuestros Performances Vivieron una Traducción Cultural." *El Universal* [Mexico City], February 23, 1995, sec. Cultural, 2.

Redhead, Steve. *The End-of-the-Century Party: Youth and Pop toward 2000.* New York: St. Martin's Press, 1990.

Reinelt, Janelle, and Joseph Roach, eds. *Critical Theory and Performance.* Ann Arbor: University of Michigan Press, 1992.

Reyes, David, and Tom Waldman. *Land of a Thousand Dances: Chicano Rock 'n' Roll from Southern California.* Albuquerque: University of New Mexico Press, 1998.

Ríos Alfaro, Lorena. "Terreno Peligroso/Danger Zone, Arte Acción en el Foro X'Teresa." *Uno Más Uno* [Mexico City], February 23, 1995, sec. Ciencia, Cultura y Espectaculos, 20.

Rivera, Edward. *Family Installments.* New York: Morrow Press, 1982.

Rivera, Raquel Z. *New York Ricans from the Hip Hop Zone.* New York: Palgrave, 2003.

Rodman, Gilbert B. *Elvis after Elvis.* New York: Routledge, 1996.

Rodríguez, Ana Patricia. *Dividing the Isthmus: Central American Transnational Literatures and Cultures.* Austin: University of Texas Press, in press.

Rodríguez, Carmen. *and a body to remember with.* Vancouver: Arsenal Pulp Press, 1997.

Rodríguez, Juana Maria. *Queer Latinidad: Identity Practices, Discursive Spaces.* New York: New York University Press, 2003.

Román, David. "Teatro Viva! Latino Performance and the Politics of AIDS in Los Angeles." In *¿Entiendes? Queer Readings, Hispanic Writings.* Ed. Emilie Bergmann and P. Julian Smith. Durham: Duke University Press, 1995. 346–369.

———. "Latino Performance and Identity." *Aztlán* 22, no. 2 (fall 1997): 151–167.

———. *Acts of Intervention: Performance, Gay Culture, and AIDS.* Bloomington: Indiana University Press, 1998.

Romero, Mary. *Maid in the U.S.A.* New York: Routledge, 2002.

———. "Nanny Diaries and Other Stories: Imagining Women's Labor in the Social Reproduction of American Families." In *Beyond Belonging: Challenging the Boundaries of Nationality. DePaul Law Review* 52, no. 3 (2003): 809–847.

Romero, Mary, and Michelle Habell-Pallán, eds. *Latino/a Popular Culture*. New York: New York University, 2001.

Rosado, Wilfredo. "Our Latin Thang." *Interview* (February 1988): 101.

Rose, Cynthia. "Word UP!" *Face* (December 1991): 23.

Ruiz, Blanca. "X Teresa, Un 'Terreno Peligroso.'" *Reforma* [Mexico City], December 27, 1994, sec. Cultura, 1.

———. "Van a 'Terreno Peligroso.'" *Reforma* [Mexico City], January 28, 1995, sec. Cultura, 14.

Ruprecht, Alvina, and Cecilia Taima, eds. *The Reordering of Culture: Latin America, The Caribbean, and Canada in the Hood*. Ottawa: Carleton University Press, 1995.

Sagaris, Lake. "Countries like Drawbridges: Chilean-Canadian Writing Today." *Canadian Literature* 142–143 (1994): 12–24.

Salas, Elizabeth. *Soldaderas in the Mexican Military: Myth and History*. Austin: University of Texas Press, 1990.

Saldívar, José D. *The Dialectics of Our America: Genealogy, Cultural Critique, and Literary History*. Durham: Duke University Press, 1991.

———. "Postmodern Realism." In *The Columbia History of the American Novel*. Ed. Emory Elliott. New York: Columbia University Press, 1991.

———. *Border Matters: Remapping American Cultural Studies*. Berkeley: University of California Press, 1997.

Saldívar-Hull, Sonia. "Feminism on the Border: From Gender Politics to Geopolitics." In *Criticism in the Borderlands: Studies in Chicano Literature, Culture, and Ideology*. Ed. Héctor Calderón and José David Saldívar. Durham: Duke University Press, 1991.

———. *Feminism on the Border: Chicana Gender Politics and Literature*. Berkeley: University of California Press, 2000.

Sánchez, George J. *Becoming Mexican American: Ethnicity, Culture, and Identity in Chicano Los Angeles, 1900–1945*. New York: Oxford University Press, 1993.

Sánchez, Rosaura. "Postmodernism and Chicano Literature." *Aztlán* 18, no. 2 (1987): 1–14.

———. "The History of Chicanas: Proposal for a Materialist Perspective." In *Between Borders: Essays on Mexicans/Chicana History*. Ed. Adelaida R. Del Castillo. Encino, Calif.: Floricanto Press, 1990.

———. *Telling Identities: The Californio Testimonios*. Minneapolis: University of Minnesota Press, 1995.

Sandoval, Chela. "U.S. Third World Feminism: The Theory and Method of Oppositional Consciousness in the Postmodern World." *Genders* 10 (1991): 1–24.

———. *Methodology of the Oppressed*. Minneapolis: University of Minnesota Press, 2000.

Sandoval-Sanchez, Alberto. *Jose, Can You See? Latinos On and Off Broadway.* Madison: University of Wisconsin Press, 1999.

Santa Ana, Otto. *Brown Tide Rising: The Metaphors of Latinos in Contemporary American Public Discourse.* Austin: University of Texas Press, 2002.

Schutzman, Mady, and Jan Cohen-Cruz, eds. *Playing Boal: Theater, Therapy, and Activism.* New York: Routledge, 1994.

Senelick, Laurence, ed. *Gender in Performance: The Presentation of Difference in the Performing Arts.* Hanover, N.H.: University Press of New England, 1992.

Shaw, Greg. "Juke Box Jury." *Creem,* March 1971, 72–73.

Shohat, Ella, and Robert Stam. *Unthinking Eurocentrism: Multiculturalism and the Media.* New York: Routledge, 1994.

Small, Peter. "Police Union Ad May Break Rules." *Toronto Star,* June 14, 1999, ed. 1, news section.

Smith, Anna Deavere. *Twilight: Los Angeles, 1992, on the Road.* New York: Anchor Books, 1994.

Smith, David M., and Maurice Blanc. "Citizenship, Nationality, and Ethnic Minorities in Three European Nations." *International Journal of Urban and Regional Research* 20, no. 1 (1996): 66–81.

Snowden, Don. "A New Spin on Words and Music. *Los Angeles Times,* December 3, 1991, F6.

Snowden, Don, and Gary Leonard, ed. *Make the Music Go Bang: The Early L.A. Punk Scene.* New York: St. Martin's Press, 1997.

Soja, Edward. *Postmodern Geographies: The Reassertion of Space in Critical Theory.* New York: Verso, 1989.

Spitz, Marc, and Brendan Mullen. *We Got the Neutron Bomb: The Untold Story of L.A. Punk.* New York: Three Rivers Press, 2001.

Stecopoulos, Harry, and Michael Uebel, eds. *Race and the Subject of Masculinities.* Durham: Duke University Press, 1997.

Svich, Caridad, and Maria Teresa Marrero, eds. *Out of the Fringe: Contemporary Latina/Latino Theatre and Performance.* New York: Theatre Communications Group, 2000.

Swiss, Thomas. "Essay Reviews: Sweet Nothings: An Anthology of Rock and Roll in American Poetry and Aloud: Voices from the Nuyorican Poets Café," *Popular Music* 15, no. 2 (May 1996): 233–240.

Taylor, Diana. "Transculturating Transculturation." *Performing Arts Journal* 38 (1991): 90–104.

Taylor, Diana, and Roselyn Costantino, eds. *Holy Terrors: Latin American Women Perform.* Durham: Duke University Press, 2003.

Taylor, Diana, and Juan Villegas, eds. *Negotiating Performance: Gender, Sexuality, and Theatricality in Latin/o America.* Durham: Duke University Press, 1994.

"Terreno Peligroso, Performance Sobre México y LA." *La Jornada* [Mexico City], February 23, 1995, sec. Cultura, 25. No author.

Thomas, Colin. "The Latino Quarter: Carmen Aguirre's Theatre Troupe Subverts Stereotypes and Confronts Traumatic Pasts." *Georgia Straight,* March 11–18, 1999, 69.

Torres, Edén. *Chicana without Apology: The New Chicana Cultural Studies.* New York: Routledge, 2003.

Troyano, Alina. *I, Carmelita Tropicana.* Ed. Chon A. Noriega. Boston: Beacon Press, 2000.

Ugwu, Catherine, ed. *Let's Get It On: The Politics of Black Performance.* Seattle: Bay Press, 1995.

Ulin, David. "The Ballad of Luis Alfaro." *Los Angeles Times Magazine,* November 15, 1998, 14ff.

Valdez, Luis, and El Teatro Campesino. *Luis Valdez-Early Works: Actos, Bernabé and Pensamiento Serpentino.* 1971; reprint, Houston: Arte Publico Press, 1990.

Valdivia, Angharad N. *A Latina in the Land of Hollywood and Other Essays on Media Culture.* Tucson: University of Arizona Press, 2000.

Van Erven, Eugéne. *Radical People's Theater.* Bloomington: Indiana University Press, 1988.

Van Evra, Jennifer. "Young Actors Put Human Face on Political Strife." *Vancouver Courier,* March 17, 1999, 24.

Vargas, Deborah R. "Cruzando Frontejas: Remapping Selena's Tejano Music 'Crossover.'" In *Chicana Traditions: Continuity and Change,* ed. Norma Cantú and Olga Najera-Ramirez. Urbana: University of Illinois Press, 2002.

Varney, Ginger. "Faces in the Crowd." *L.A. Style* (November 1985): 77.

Velasquez, Alicia Armendariz. Conference Program. Popular Music Studies Annual Conference. Experience Music Project, Seattle, 2004.

Verdecchia, Guillermo. *Fronteras Americas = American Borders.* Toronto: Coach House Press, 1993.

Verhovek, Sam Howe. "Border Patrol Is Criticized as Abusive; Human Rights Group Reports 'Cruel' Acts." *New York Times,* May 21, 1998, A12ff.

Vertovec, Steven. "Berlin Multikulti: Germany, 'Foreigners,' and World Openness." *New Community* 22, no. 3 (1996): 381–399.

Villa, Raúl Homero. *Barrio-Logos: Space and Place in Urban Chicano Literature and Culture.* Austin: University of Texas Press, 2000.

Volgenau, Gerald. "Refugees from Latin America Are on Their Way to Canada." *Seattle Times,* February 22, 1987, A11.

Weber, David J. "John Francis Bannon and the Historiography of the Spanish Borderlands: Retrospect and Prospect." Chapter in *Myth and the History of the Hispanic Southwest.* Albuquerque: University of New Mexico Press, 1988. 55–88.

———. "The Idea of the Spanish Borderlands." In *Columbian Consequences: The Spanish Borderlands in Pan-American Perspective.* Ed. David Thomas. Washington, D.C.: Smithsonian Institution Press, 1991. 3–20.

Weizman, Alan. "Born in East L.A." *Los Angeles Times Sunday Magazine,* March 27, 1988, 11ff.

Williams, Raymond. *Marxism and Literature.* New York: Oxford University Press, 1977.

Winer, Laurie. "A Usually Reliable Company Disappoints Its 'Neighbors.'" *Los Angeles Times,* December 16, 1997, F1.

Woffler, Lorena. "Atajos Para un Encuentro en Terreno Peligroso: ¡En Sus Marcas, Listos! . . . El Diálogo Comienza." *La Opinión* [Los Angeles], February 3, 1995, sec. E, 8, 13.

Woll, Allen. *The Latin Image in American Film,* rev. ed. Los Angeles: UCLA Latin American Center Publications, 1980.

Wright, Thomas, and Rody Oñate, eds. *Flight from Chile: Voices of Exile.* Trans. Irene Hodgson. Albuquerque: University of New Mexico Press, 1998.

Yarbro-Bejarano, Yvonne. "The Image of the Chicana in Teatro." In *Gathering Ground: New Writing by Northwest Women of Color.* Ed. Northwest Women of Color Collective. Seattle: Seal Press, 1984.

———. "The Female Subject in Chicano Theater: Sexuality, 'Race,' and Class." *Theater Journal* 38, no. 4 (1986): 389–407.

———. "Gloria Anzaldúa's *Borderlands/La Frontera*: Cultural Studies, 'Difference,' and the Non-Unitary Subject." *Cultural Critique* 28 (fall 1994): 5–28.

———. "The Lesbian Body in Latina Cultural Production." In *¿Entiendes? Queer Readings, Hispanic Writings.* Ed. Emilie Bergmann and P. Julian Smith. Durham: Duke University Press, 1995. 81–197.

———. *The Wounded Heart: Writing on Cherríe Moraga.* Austin: University of Texas Press, 2001.

Ybarra-Frausto, Tomás. "Rasquachismo: A Chicano Sensibility" *Chicano Art: Resistance and Affirmation.* Ed. Teresa McKenna, Richard Griswold del Castillo, and Yvonne Yarbro-Bejarano. Los Angeles: Wight Gallery, University of California, Los Angeles, 1992. 155–162.

Yúdice, George. *The Expediency of Culture: Uses of Culture in the Global Era.* Durham: Duke University Press, 2003.

———. "Rethinking Area and Ethnic Studies in the Context of Economic and Political Restructuring." In *Critical Latin American and Latino Studies.* Ed. Juan Poblete. Minneapolis: University of Minnesota, 2003. 76–102.

Zavella, Patricia. "Feminist Insider Dilemmas: Constructing Identity with 'Chicana' Informants." *Frontiers: A Journal of Women's Studies* 13 (1992): 21–40.

AUDIO RECORDINGS

Act of Faith. Time Bomb Music Company. 1991.

Alfaro, Luis. *Downtown.* Marisela Norte, associate producer. New Alliance Records, 1993, compact disk.

The Bags. "We Don't Need the English." On compilation *Yes, L.A.* Dangerhouse Records, 1979.

The Brat. *Attitudes.* Fatima Records, 1980.

Davis, Angela. *The Prison Industrial Complex.* AK Press, 2000, compact disk.

El Vez. *Boxing with God.* Sympathy for the Record Industry Records, 2001, compact disk.

———. *G.I. Ay, Ay! Blues.* Big Pop Records, 1996, compact disk.

———. *Graciasland.* Sympathy for the Record Industry Records, 1994, compact disk.

———. *How Great Thou Art.* Sympathy for the Record Industry, n.d., compact disk.

Kid Frost. *Hispanic Causing Panic.* Virgin Records, 1990. Virgin 86169.

Las Tres. *Las Tres Live at the LATC.* Panocha Dulce-Black Rose-Bhima Music, 1993.

Lighter Shade of Brown. *Hip Hop Locos.* Polygram Records, 1992. Polygram 522268.

Mellow Man Ace. *Escape from Havana.* Capitol Records, 1989. CDP 7912952.

Norte, Marisela. "Lost in Los." *Black and Tan Club.* New Alliance Records, 1991, compact disk.

———. *NORTE/word.* New Alliance Records, 1991, compact disk.

———. "Three Little Words." *DisClosure: Voice of Women.* New Alliance Records, 1992, compact disk.

Proper Dos. *Latin Lingo: Hip-Hop from La Raza.* WEA/Atlantic/Rhino Records, 1995, compact disk.

Velasquez, Alicia Armendariz. "Happy Accident," recorded on Las Tres, *Live at the LATC.* Panocha Dulce-Black Rose-Bhima Music, 1993, audiocassette.

VIDEOGRAPHY AND FILMOGRAPHY

"Angel." Marisela Norte. *L.A. Photo Journal.* Videodisc. Voyager, 1992.

The Ballad of Gregorio Cortez. Directed by Robert Young. MGM/United Artists Studios, 1982.

Born in East L.A. Directed by Cheech Marin. Universal Studios, 1987.

Break of Dawn. Directed by Isaac Artenstein. Vanguard Cinema, 1988.

Brincando el Charco. Directed by Frances Negrón-Muntaner. Women Make Movies Productions, 1994.

Carmelita Tropicana: Your Kunst Is Your Waffen. Directed by Ela Troyano. First Run Features, 1996.

Chicana! Directed by Sylvia Morales. Sylvia Morales Productions, 1979.

"Chicanas in Tune." Produced by Ester Reyes. Community Television of Southern California, 1994.

Despues del Terremoto [*After the Earthquake*]. Directed by Lourdes Portillo. Portillo Productions, 1979.

Dirty Laundry: A Homemade Telenovela. Directed by Cristina Ibarra. Cristina Ibarra, 2000.

Electronic Bodies. Directed by Rita Gonzalez. Rita Gonzalez, 1996.

El Norte. Produced by Gregory Nava. Farmington Hills: Independent Productions, 1984.

El Rey de Rock 'n' Roll. Produced by Marjorie Chodorov. Video. Soap Box Films, 2000.

El Vez: The Mexican Elvis. Video. El Vez Productions, 1994.

Exito. Screenplay by Marisela Norte. Directed by Harry Gamboa, Jr. ASCO productions, 1985, videocassette.

La Bamba. Directed by Luis Valdez. Columbia/Tristar Studios, 1987.

Mi Familia [My Family]. Directed by Gregory Nava. New Line Studios, 1997.

Pretty Vacant. Directed by Jim Mendiola. Mero Mero Productions, 1996.

Sabor a Mi/Savor Me. Claudia Morgado Escanilla, 1997.

Spitfire. Directed and produced by Frances Salomé España. FSE Productions, 1991.

Star Maps. Directed by Miguel Arteta. Twentieth-Century-Fox, 1997.

The Three Caballeros. Walt Disney Studios, 1945.

Zoot Suit. Directed by Luis Valdez. Universal Studios, 1982.

PERFORMANCES

Chile con Carne. Written and performed by Carmen Aguirre. Firehall Arts Centre, Vancouver, Canada, January 14, 1999.

La Condición Feminina. Performed and written by Marisela Norte and María Elena Gaitán. Directed by Marisela Norte and María Elena Gaitán. Self Help Graphics, Los Angeles, August 7, 1982.

Exito. By Marisela Norte. Directed by Marisela Norte. Galería de la Raza, San Francisco, July 1983.

Deep in the Crotch of My Latino Psyche. Written and performed by Luis Alfaro, Monica Palacios, and Albert Antonio Araiza. Highways Performance Space, Santa Monica, California, December 11, 1993.

Ladybird: The Life and Times of a Roller Derby Queen. By Luis Alfaro. La Jolla

Playhouse. Toured San Diego, Imperial County, and Tijuana schools, community centers, and libraries, January 2002–March 2002.

A Line around the Block. Written and performed by Marga Gomez. John Anson Ford Theater, Los Angeles, California, April 14, 1995.

Los Vecinos: A Play for Neighbors. Co-written by Luis Alfaro and Diane Rodriguez. Cornerstone Theater's Community Collaborations, December 4–21, 1997.

¿Qué Pasa con la Raza, eh? Performed by the Latino Theater Group. Directed by Carmen Aguirre. The Fire Arts Center, Vancouver, B.C., March 27, 1999.

Speaking Experiences: Emerging Chicago Performers. By Luis Alfaro, Marisela Norte, and Chicago Secret Service. University of California, San Diego, November 15, 1991.

Terreno Peligroso/Danger Zone: A Mexico–U.S. Latino Performance Exchange. University of California, Los Angeles, February 9–12, 1995, and El Foro X'Teresa, Mexico City, February 23–26, 1995.

[Untitled]. By Marisela Norte. Centro Cultural de La Raza, Balboa Park, San Diego, California, May 15, 1992.

"Untitled." *Diva L.A.: A Salute to L.A.'s Latinas in the Tanda Style.* By Marisela Norte. Mainstage, Mark Taper Forum, Los Angeles, California, July 2, 1995.

INTERVIEWS AND CORRESPONDENCE

Alfaro, Luis. Personal correspondence with author. 1991.

———. Luis. Personal interview with author. August 1996.

———. Personal interview with author. December 2002.

Carillo, Sean. E-mail correspondence with author. 8 November 2003.

Covarrubias, Teresa. Personal interview with author. 8 August 1998.

Garza, Ray. Letter to the author with author. 25 September 1995.

Gomez, Marga. Personal interview with author. 28 February 1994.

Lopez, Robert. Personal interview with author. 27 September 1996.

Mendiola, Jim. Personal interview with author. 25 January 1999.

Norte, Marisela. Personal interview with author. 3 July 1995.

Rodríguez, Diane. Personal interview with author. 15 August 1996.

Valle, Victor. E-mail correspondence with author. 12 February 2002.

Vasquez, Mariana. Personal interview with author. 10 February 1999.

Velasquez, Alicia Armendariz. Personal interview with author. 12 August 1998.

Index

Italicized page numbers refer to an illustration or its caption.

About the Author

Michelle Habell-Pallán is Assistant Professor of American Ethnic Studies at the University of Washington. A former fellow of the Andrew Mellon and Rockefeller Foundations, she co-edited *Latino/a Popular Culture* (2002).